THE CIVIL WAR BATTLES
OF THE
WESTERN THEATRE

Bryan S. Bush

Technical Advisors

John C. Harrison III and D. Steve Munson

TURNER PUBLISHING COMPANY

Turner Publishing Company Staff:
Publishing Consultant: Douglas W. Sikes
Project Coordinator: John Mark Jackson
Designer: Ina F. Morse

Copyright © 1998, 2000 Bryan S. Bush, All rights reserved.
Publishing Rights: Turner Publishing Company
Additional copies may be purchased directly from
Turner Publishing Company.

This book or any part thereof may not be reproduced without the
written consent of Bryan S. Bush and Turner Publishing Company.

Library of Congress Catalog Card Number: 98-60774
ISBN: 978-1-68162-420-4
Limited Edition: Printed in the U.S.A.
First printing: 1998
Second printing: 2000

Photo Credits: Elvin Smith, Jr.

Special Thanks must be given to the following:
Steve Munson, Jack Harrison, Ernest Spencer, Lyle Sloan, Ralph
Handy, John Bersoe, Ken Hamilton, Tom Fugate, Judy Haviland,
Gay Reading, Susan Harger and The Board of Directors of the Old
Bardstown Village Civil War Museum: The Battles of the Western
Theatre, in particular: Hank and Rita Hermann, Dr. Harry Spalding,
Joe Masterson, the Hunt-Morgan House, and the Kentucky Mili-
tary History Museum.

The Civil War Museum of Bardstown, Kentucky- The Civil War
Museum of Bardstown, Kentucky features the "War of the West."
The Civil War Museum was opened in 1988 in the old water works
building in Bardstown, Kentucky and between 1988-1992 it served
over 250,000 visitors. Between 1992 and 1996 the museum was
totally renovated and was incorporated into the Kentucky State
Parks system. It officially reopened on June 28, 1996 to the pleasure of Civil War buffs from around the world. The Civil War
Museum is now in the process of opening a 1800s village adjacent to the Civil War Museum featuring several original log cabins to depict life during these times. It was our pleasure to be
included in this great undertaking and to be a part of the "War in
the Western Theatre" book, published by Turner Publishing and
written by Mr. Bryan Bush.

Respectfully,

Hank and Rita Herrmann
1-800-638-4877

**Hunt-Morgan House and the Blue Grass Trust for Historic
Preservation,** The Blue Grass Trust for Historic Preservation is a
not for profit association of concerned citizens, working together
to preserve, and revitalize the historic houses in the Lexington,
Kentucky area. They have worked to preserve the Hunt Morgan
House, the Dudley House, Shakertown at Pleasant Hill, the Adam
Rankin House, Belle Breezing's Row Houses, the Mary Todd Lincoln House and the Stilfield Log House. Their latest acquisition
has been the Senator John and Eliza Pope Villa. In 1955, the Blue
Grass Trust bought the Hunt-Morgan House. It is also known as
the "Hopemont," and was built for John Wesley Hunt in 1814. As
the home of the Hunt's daughter, Henrietta, it is known as the family seat of General John Hunt Morgan, "Thunderbolt of the Confederacy" and was the birthplace of the Nobel Prize winner Dr.
Thomas Hunt Morgan, "Father of Modern Genetics." The Alexander
T. Hunt Civil War Museum displays relics and exhibits of the time
of Morgan's men.

The Kentucky Military History Museum-The Kentucky Military Museum is located on East Main Street in downtown Frankfort, Kentucky. The museum is open to the public, at no charge,
Monday through Saturday from 9:00 a.m. to 4:00 p.m. and Sunday
12:00 noon till 4:00 p.m.. The Kentucky Military Museum is operated by the Kentucky National Guard and the Kentucky Historical
Society, the Kentucky Militia, State Guard, and other volunteer military organizations, from the Revolution through the Gulf War. Displays include an impressive array of firearms, edged weapons, artillery, uniforms, flags, photographs, personal items, and other equipment that illustrates the Commonwealth's martial heritage and
strives to preserve all of Kentucky's Military history. Special thanks
must go to Tom Fugate.

The Waveland State Park-The Waveland State Historic Site is
located on 225 Hibee Mill Road, Lexington, Kentucky. The
Waveland site is a pillar in Bluegrass history and tradition: Daniel
Boone and the Bryan family, Bryan's Station, the Civil War, trotting horses and racing in the Bluegrass. Waveland exemplifies plantation life in Kentucky in the 19th century; from the acres of grain
and hemp waving in the breeze, to the raising and racing of blooded
trotting horses. In 1847, Joseph Bryan inherited his father's
homeplace, and built Waveland. The outbuildings of Waveland,
such as the slave quarters, smokehouse, and icehouse, are important reminders of the social and economic climate of the time.
The mansion is a Greek revival architectural style, and features
grand symmetry and a graceful Ionic-columned portico. The house
is lavishly furnished with Sheraton and Empire style furniture,
and many family heirlooms. There is an admission charge. It is
open from March 1-mid December, Monday through Saturday,
10:00 a.m. till 5:00 p.m., and Sunday 1:00 p.m. till 5:00 p.m.

Susan Harger

**The Hall of Valor Civil War Museum-New Market Battlefield
Historical Park-Judy Haviland-**The Hall of Valor, established in
1970, is a monument to those V.M.I. Cadets and the American Civil
War soldiers who forged a heritage of courage and discipline in
one of the war's most poignant episodes, the Battle of New Market. The museum has two award winning films on the battle and
one on "Stonewall" Jackson's famed 1862 Shenandoah Valley Campaign, which are presented on laser disk in the 125 seat theater.
Colorful dioramas emphasize the incredible acts of endurance and
resilience demonstrated by soldiers, North and South. The Jacob
and Sarah Bushong farm can also be visited. The farm became a
battlefield and their house became a hospital. The farm is equipped
with a wheelwright shop, blacksmith shop, loom house, and summer kitchen depicting the 19th century. The museum is located in
New Market, Virginia.

**The Perryville Battlefield Preservation Association, Inc. and
Chaplin Hills Historic Properties, Inc.** The Perryville Battlefield Preservation Association, Inc. is multi faceted economic development, education, land conservation and heritage tourism
project that relies on the support and interest of people throughout
the Commonwealth and nation. Their mission is to protect the land,
interpret the battle of Perryville and the historic village of Perryville
while stimulating the economy of the region. The Perryville village on Merchant's Row and the Battlefield are open to the public.
Special Thanks must go to Mary Breeding and Alan Hoeweler.

(From the original front cover flap)

Bryan Bush was born in 1966 in Louisville, Kentucky and has been a native of that city ever since. He graduated with honors from Murray State University with a degree in History and Psychology. Bryan has always had a passion for history, especially the Civil War. He has been a member of many different Civil War historical preservation societies, has consulted for movie companies, coordinated with other museums on displays of various museum articles and artifacts, has written for magazines, such as *Kentucky Civil War Magazine*, and worked for many different historical sites, and has always fought hard to maintain and preserve Civil War history in the Western Theatre.

Bryan has been a Civil War reenactor for five years, portraying a Confederate Artillerist, and later a Lt. Colonel in the Confederate Medical Corps. He has also been a member of the Sons of Confederate Veterans since 1994. For the last year, Bryan has been the assistant curator of the Old Bardstown Civil War Museum and Village: The Battles of the Western Theatre Museum in Bardstown, Kentucky.

Foreword

Walter Crutcher

Some 137 years have passed since the great drama of the Civil War erupted on American soil. Never in recorded history have so many lives and families been affected by the horrors of civil conflict. Nowhere was it more prevalent than in the Western Theater, where brother fighting against brother and family verses family were played out. This unparalleled effort to document this history of the war in the Western theater is long over due.

Much has been written about the war in the Eastern Theater of operations with little reference to operations in the West. With this epic undertaking the unsung heroes of the Western Theater speak to us through their individual deeds of valor.

We are taken back in time to the conflict through the thoughts and deeds of these unsung heroes by this publication. Each artifact speaks to us through time and reminds us that although in the throughs of war, we were all Americans and were linked by a common bond of patriotism.

With this scholarly endeavor we are transported back in time and through the voices of our dead heroes, the war again erupts to fill our emotions with valiant deeds and actions of common men made heroes by their actions. All Americans whether Northern or Southern should take pride in the convictions of our forefathers.

Through the cooperation of Bryan S. Bush, Steve Munson and John C. Harrison, III of the Bardstown Civil War Museum, Tom Fugate of the Kentucky Military History Museum, Ken Hamilton, of the Hunt-Morgan House, Allen Hoeweler and Mary Breeding of the Perryville Enhancement Committee and Chaplin Hills Properties, Inc., Sarah Harger of the Waveland State Historic Site, and Lt. Col. Gibson of the New Market Battlefield, they have helped make this publication a reality. We dedicate this publication to the past and future generations interested in the Civil War history.

Walter Crutcher
- ★ Collector of Kentucky Made Arms and
    Sharp's Percussion Arms
- ★ Sons of Colonial War
- ★ American Society of Arms Collectors
- ★ Filson Club
- ★ Life Member of Kentuckiana Arms
    Collectors Association
- ★ Life Member of Ohio Gun
    Collectors Association
- ★ Life Member N.R.A.

Table of Contents

3rd Kentucky Mounted Infantry, C.S.

39th Kentucky Mounted Infantry, U.S.

Second National,
1st Kentucky Cavalry, C.S.

"Battle flag" 1st Kentucky Cavalry, C.S.

13th Kentucky Infantry, U.S.

Table of Contents

Reverse of First National 2nd Kentucky Infantry, C.S.

First National 2nd Kentucky Infantry, C.S.

National 6th Kentucky Infantry, U.S.

Glassies Battery, U.S.

Regimental 1st Kentucky Infantry, U.S.

DARK CLOUDS GATHER

Slave Trade — A Tradition of Human Misery

Starting in 1619, slavery was a part of the life and growth of North America for 246 years before it was finally abolished in the United States in 1865. During the American Revolution, more than 150 years after the first slaves were imported, slavery was practiced in all but one of the colonies.

Within ten years of discovering the New World, Spain began transporting African slaves to work in its new possessions, and other European nations quickly followed suit. Great Britain became the leader; within 250 years it had transported twice as many slaves as all of the other countries combined. For twenty years starting in 1713, England brought 15,000 slaves annually to America. In 1786 the English brought more than 97,000 slaves to America and had more than 800 slave ships operating out of Liverpool alone. Most of these Africans went to the West Indies to work in the sugarcane fields. There the slave ships would load up with molasses and continue on to New England where that cargo would be exchanged for rum, which in 1750 was New England's chief product. The ships would carry the rum back to the Old World and exchange it for slaves; thus the profitable "triangle trade" in human misery continued for generations.

Massachusetts joined the slave trade in 1638, followed by Rhode Island, where the chief slave port in the American colonies was located, rivaling Liverpool in England. Slave trading and the export of rum became the basis of New England's economy. The Southern colonies were not a part of the trade, having neither ships nor molasses. In 1774, the importation of slaves was forbidden by the people of North and South Carolina. On October 5, 1778, Virginians outlawed the slave trade in their state. In 1787, the new U.S. Constitution forbade Congress from banning the importation of slaves for another 20 years. This allowed the North to slowly liquidate the slaves they already had. After the American Revolution, slavery was done away with gradually in the North, because it was not profitable. The system of gradual emancipation allowed the Northern slave owners to remove their property to the South, sell the slaves, and make a profit.

By the 1820s, the South was becoming an agrarian economy based on cotton, tobacco, and indigo crops, which were very labor intensive, and hence the need for slaves. The Southern economy was based on selling the raw products to the North. The North would use the raw material to make clothes, textiles and other products, and then ship them to England and France, all the while growing in the areas of manufacturing and export, and with an established European trade route, the North was rapidly becoming an industrialized center. In order to manufacture and ship these products, the North began to build better railroads, canals, and iron foundries. Before the outbreak of the Civil War, the South was a very rural area, and it had a population of about 9,103,332 people, 3,521,110 of which were slaves. The North was more urbanized, and it had a population of about 19,034,434 people. These statistics do

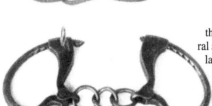

Top: Slave ball and chain/shackle. Bottom: Slave handcuffs and key. (BCWM)

not include the border states of Delaware, District of Columbia, Maryland, Missouri, and the New Mexico Territory, which would add another 3,305,557 people. The South did not have the manpower or the proper resources to fight a protracted war against the North. The South had to strike quickly, before the North could bring it's manufacturing might and manpower to bear.

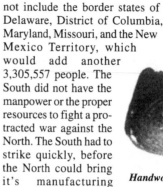

Handwoven slave straw hat. (BCWM)

Missouri Compromise of 1820

When the Missouri territorial assembly petitioned Congress for admission to the Union in 1818, the United States had 22 states: 11 slave, 11 free. At that time, legislators admitted states by alternating between slave and free. Missouri Territory had 3,000 slaves and to admit Missouri into the Union as a slave state would have upset the balance of power in favor of the South in the Senate, although not in the House, where the difference in population gave the Northerners 105 votes to the South's 81.

On February 13, 1819, New York Representative James Talladge proposed an amendment to exclude slavery from the territory, which passed in the House but was blocked by Southerners in the senate. Through the efforts of Henry Clay, the stalemate was broken when Maine broke from Massachusetts on March 3, 1820 and petitioned for admission into the Union as a free state. Illinois Senator Jesse Thomas proposed admitting Missouri as a slave state but restricting slavery thereafter in the Louisiana Purchase to land below latitude 36 degrees latitude 30 degrees longitude.

Compromise of 1850

Kentucky Senator Henry Clay placed before Congress several provisions that he hoped would placate sectional antagonisms. The bill was written by Stephen Douglas, and called for California to be admitted as a free state; for the passage of the Fugitive Slave Law; for new territories in the Southwest to be allowed to organize without restrictions on slavery; for protecting slavery in the District of Columbia while abolishing domestic slave trade there; and for a settlement of 10 million dollars to Texas if the state would relinquish certain lands in New Mexico Territory. Senator Calhoun reiterated the Southern position; if the South couldn't be made secure on the slavery issue, it would never remain in the Union. Clay's compromise passed in September 1850. The people and their representatives were lulled into believing the nation's problems had been solved, but the statesman had bought a fragile peace that lasted scarcely a decade.

Kansas-Nebraska Act of 1854

Written by Stephen Douglas, after the acquisition of Oregon and California called into question the status of the Great Plains, the act divided into two territories, along the 40th parallel, the unorganized land of the Louisiana Purchase. It conformed to the Compromise of 1850 for Utah and New Mexico, giving the inhabitants territorial discretion over slavery without repealing the Missouri Compromise. Southern Congressmen protested, arguing that unless the 36 degrees latitude, 30 degrees longitude line was nullified, slaveholders would be excluded from settling in a large block of land open to free soilers who would then vote against slavery. The 36 degrees latitude 30 degrees longitude line was repealed. Congress passed the act on May 30, 1854. The Kansas-Nebraska Act angered the free soil North and cost Douglas his popularity in the South. Free soil advocates polarized against pro slavery factions, leading to the formation of the Republican party.

"Bleeding Kansas"

With the passage of the Kansas-Nebraska Act of 1854, Kansas moved toward civil war. Northern abolitionists encouraged settlers to populate the territory in anticipation of a struggle for statehood between pro slavery and free soil advocates. With the repeal of the Missouri Compromise, pro slavery factions attacked Lawrence, Kansas on May 21, 1856, and two days later, the massacre at Pottawatomie of five pro slavery men by John Brown occurred. President Franklin Pierce sent in Federal troops to calm the insurrection. Five constitutions were drafted before the Kansas territory was admitted to the Union as a free state in 1861. At least fifty men were killed over the slavery issue.

John Brown

John Brown's Raid

October 16-18, 1859. John Brown was a fanatical abolitionist, and he believed that God appointed him to rid the country of slavery. After murdering five pro slavery settlers in Pottawatomie, Kansas, John Brown spent three years forming a band of raiders in the mountains of Virginia. He gathered slaves and armed them, established a freemen's republic, and incited slave insurrections. In the summer of 1859, Brown rented a farm in Maryland across the Potomac from Harper's Ferry, where a Federal arsenal was located. On October 16, Brown and 21 recruits seized the United States Arsenal, and the nearby Hall's Rifle Works. Brown's mission was to capture the weapons and arm the slaves in Virginia, and to march throughout the South with his army of freed slaves, inciting other slaves to join him in a great uprising that would put an end to American slavery once and for all. He captured leading citizens of Harper's Ferry and kept them as hostages, including the great grandnephew of George Washington.

On the 17th, militia and armed citizens surrounded the arsenal. The men in the arsenal were driven out and into a firehouse. Three locals were killed, as were John Brown's two sons. During the night, Lt. Col. Robert E. Lee arrived with a detachment of United States Marines from Washington, DC On the 18th, Lee sent a white flag to demand Brown's surrender. When Brown refused, Lt. J.E.B. Stuart leading the Marines, charged the firehouse and quickly battered down the door. The Marines holding their fire to protect the hostages, stormed into the engine house, bayoneted two of the raiders, and captured Brown and his four remaining men. On December 2, 1859 in Charlestown, Western Virginia, Brown was found guilty of treason and was hanged. Southerners blamed the Republicans in this attempt at slave insurrection and warned that if a Republican was elected president in 1860, they would secede. Brown predicted that the sin of slavery "will never be purged away; but with blood.

The Lincoln-Douglas Debates

In 1856, Abraham Lincoln switched his allegiance from the Whig Party to the new Republican party. Lincoln ran for the United States Senate against the "Little Giant" Stephen A. Douglas. Though Lincoln lost, the race attracted national attention because of the candidates' widely reported debates over the slavery issue in the territories. Lincoln's standing was further enhanced on February 1860, when, in New York City, before an influential audience, he delivered his brilliant Cooper Union speech, in which he argued the Federal government's power to limit slavery in the territories.

1860 Election

As the nation prepared for the 1860 election, divisions among the major political parties placed four presidential candidates before the public, three of the tickets represented desperate attempts to placate sectional antagonisms that Southerners insisted would lead to disunion if Abraham Lincoln won the election. On the Republican ticket with Lincoln was Hannibal Hamlin of Maine, and they ran on a platform that down played the slavery issue, while endorsing government homesteads, free land and citizenship for German immigrants, and protection for American industries. The Constitutional Union party, a pro-compromise coalition of Whigs and Unionists, nominated Tennessee's John Bell for president and Edward Everett of Massachusetts as his running mate. The Democratic party split over the slavery issue, the Northern contingent nominating the Popular Sovereignty champion Stephen Douglas of Illinois and Georgia's Herschel Johnson ; the Southerners states-rights and proslavery men, but not the radical secessionists, put forward Kentucky's John C. Breckinridge and Joseph Lane of Oregon. Each party made devotion to the Union the focal point of its campaign.

Voting split along sectional lines. Lincoln carried the North with a sweeping majority of 180 electoral votes. Southerners divided, giving Breckinridge 72 electoral votes, Bell 39. The Northern Democrats hoped that Douglas would appeal to moderates in both sections, but he took only 12 electoral votes from Missouri and New Jersey. The popular vote, however, was much closer. Lincoln polled 1,866,452 votes, but not one was cast for him in 10 of the Southern states. Douglas came in a surprisingly close second with 1,376,957. Breckinridge trailed with 849,781, Bell with 588,879.

Had the unsuccessful contenders consolidated their popular votes into a majority, the election's outcome would not have changed. With his victories in the densely populated North, and in California and Oregon, Lincoln's electoral votes outnumbered those of his three opponents combined. Unquestionably, the United States had elected in valid contest a minority president who owed no part of his victory to the division of his political adversaries.

Secession

With Lincoln winning the election, the Southerners felt that they had no choice but to follow up on their threat that if a Republican was made president of the United States, they would break away from the Union. To the surprise of Lincoln, who thought the threat to be a bluff, the South began to make plans for secession. On November 10, 1860, four days after the election, the Legislature in South Carolina became the first of the Southern congresses to call for a convention to consider secession. South Carolina seceded on December 20, 1860 at a convention in Charleston. The first state to secede, South Carolina was soon joined by others, and early in 1861, eleven states formed the Confederate States of America, with hopes that their independence might be maintained peaceably. Jefferson Davis, who was a senator in the Congress of the United States, was elected president of the Confederate States of America on February 22, 1862, and his vice president would be Alexander Stevens.

Colonel Robert E. Lee

THE WAR BEGINS

Ft. Sumter, South Carolina

April 12-14, 1861
Campaign: Operations in Charleston Harbor (April 1861)
Principal Commanders: Maj. Gen. Robert Anderson (US);
Brig. Gen. P.G.T. Beauregard (CS)
Forces Engaged: Regiments: 580 (US 80, CS Est. 500)

Now both sides waited to see who was going to be the one to fire the first shots to start this Civil War. The time came on April 12, 1861. On March 5, 1861, the day after Lincoln's inauguration as President, Union Maj. Robert Anderson sent a message telling Lincoln that his men only had six weeks of food left in the fort. Believing a conflict to be inevitable, Lincoln ingeniously devised a plan that would cause the Confederates to fire the first shot and thus, he hoped, inspire the states that had not yet seceded to unite in the effort to restore the Union.

On April 8th, Lincoln notified Gov. Francis Pickens of South Carolina that he would attempt to resupply the fort. The Confederate commander at Charleston, General Pierre G. Beauregard, was ordered to demand the evacuation of the fort and if refused, to force its evacuation. Capt. Stephen D. Lee sent a message to Anderson demanding his surrender. The Confederates said they would hold their fire if Anderson gave them the exact time when he could evacuate his fort. Anderson told Lee that he would leave by the 15th. The ships coming to supply him would have arrived by that time. Lee reported back to Beauregard and Beauregard was told by the Confederate government that this was unacceptable. Beauregard sent Lee with a message to Anderson saying that he would fire on the fort in one hour.

On April 11, 1861, at 4:30 a.m., a 34 hour duel began. Union Major General Robert Anderson and 127 men held Ft. Sumter in the Charleston harbor. Capt. Abner Doubleday was Anderson's second in command. P.G.T. Beauregard had put batteries on Ft. Moultrie and Ft. Johnson on the harbor's north and south shores. Ft. Sumter mounted 66 cannons, and Beauregard's harbor batteries were comprised of 43 cannons. The supply ships that Anderson was hoping for were kept at bay by the Confederate batteries. By dawn, April 13, three fires had broken out at Ft. Sumter, threatening to blow up the powder magazines. On April 14, Anderson surrendered, and was allowed to give a 100 gun salute to the American flag before he took it down. The 50th gun exploded killing one man who was the only casualty of the battle. The Civil War had begun.

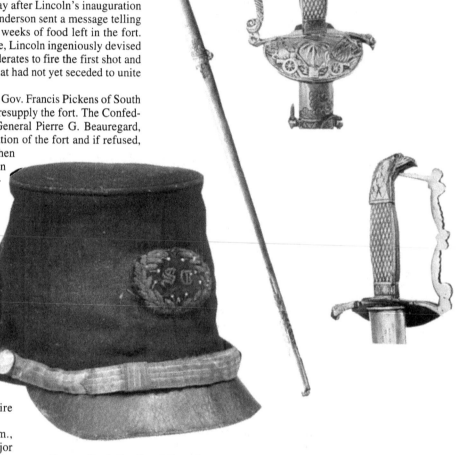

South Carolina collage. Model 1840 South Carolina Artillery Officer's Sword manufactured by Ames Manufacturing Company Chicopee, Massachusetts. (BCWM)

Pre-war South Carolina Officers forage cap featuring South Carolina "S.C." within the embroidery wreath insignia. (BCWM)

South Carolina sword belt (BCWM)

1850s South Carolina Chapeau made by Bird & Company, Charleston, South Carolina. Note inset: The gold embroidered palmetto tree. (BWCM)

Oil Rendering of Brig. Gen. Frederick West Lander. (BCWM)

Left sword: Lander's Line sword is a Non Regulation Model 1850 Staff Officer's Sword, manufactured by Emons & Marshall, Philadelphia. This sword was worn by Lander's when he was shot in battle. (BCWM)
Sword hilt at right: Lander's Presentation sword is a model 1850 Staff and Field Officer's sword, manufactured by Shelby & Fisher. These type swords were used only on dress occasions. (BCWM)

Battle of First Manassas or Bull Run

July 21, 1861
Campaign: Manassas Campaign (July 1861)
Principal Commanders: Brig. Gen. Irvin McDowell (US); Brig. Gen. Joseph E. Johnston and Brig. Gen. P.G.T. Beauregard (C.S.)
Forces Engaged: 60,680 (US 28,450; CS 32,230)

On July 16th, Lincoln ordered Brig. Gen. Irvin McDowell's 35,000 men to crush the rebellion in the South once and for all. McDowell left Washington, DC and advanced across northern Virginia. Major General Robert Patterson, with 18,000 men, was directed to prevent Confederates in the Shenandoah Valley from reinforcing the army facing McDowell. Opposing Patterson were 12,000 Confederates under Brig. Gen. Joseph E. Johnston. Johnston abandoned his lines in front of Patterson and boarded trains for Manassas Junction. This was the first time in history that a railroad was used to achieve strategic mobility.

By 2 a.m., July 21st, McDowell had his 12,000 man flanking column marching down the Warrenton Pike from Centreville where they had been camped since the 18th. His plan was to attack Beauregard near a small stream called Bull Run. It was sound strategy, but it was too much for the new Federal recruits to execute and McDowell was unaware that spies had reported his advance, giving Gen. Joseph Johnston time to reinforce Beauregard.

A little after 5 o'clock, the Federal artillery opened fire, while Federal infantry feinted against the eight mile long line. The flanking column forded the stream at Sudley Springs and deployed three hours behind schedule. Confederate signalmen had already detected the movement and Confederate troops were rushed north to meet the threat.

Confederate Col. Nathan Evans led six companies of the 4th South Carolina and a battalion of Louisiana Tigers, a total of 1,000 men to oppose the Union attack force. Col. Evans did not know that the entire Union force under Irvin McDowell was facing him. McDowell had launched a surprise attack on the Confederate flank. Evans quickly placed his command in defensive positions under cover of woods on Matthews Hill, overlooking the road the blue clad soldiers would take from Sudley Springs Ford as they crossed Bull Run.

The Confederates were outnumbered and raced back across Young's Branch and the Warrenton Road. McDowell bolstered his attack force by funneling other units across Bull Run. Col. Ambrose Burnside and two Rhode Island regiments charged up Matthew's Hill. The Rebel volleys stopped the Federal advance and Burnside brought up more reinforcements. Suddenly 500 Louisiana Tigers screamed down the hill toward the Federals. The charge was beaten back, but Evans and his hard fighting soldiers had stalled the Union force long enough for reinforcements to begin to arrive.

Beauregard and Johnston sent the fresh troops scrambling to their crumbling left flank. Brig Gen. Thomas Jackson and his Virginia units took a position on Henry's Hill, down whose slope the remnants of Evan's and Bee's troops were streaming. Bee, trying to rally his shattered brigade, pointed to Jackson's line and shouted, "Look! There is Jackson standing like a stone wall. Rally behind the Virginians!" Bee soon fell mortally wounded.

About 2 p.m., the Federals regrouped and attacked Stonewalls' position. Beauregard and Johnston arrived to direct the defense personally. For two hours, the battle blazed up and down the hillside. There were no standard uniforms, so confusion reigned. At one point, two Union batteries were captured when the Federal commander of the battery thought that a Confederate infantry regiment was one of his own. He assumed the blue uniforms that the Confederates were wearing indicated they were friendly troops. The Confederates opened up with a point blank volley into the battery and it was captured immediately.

The Confederate commanders continued to bring up reinforcements, and at 4 p.m., the Rebels ripped into McDowell's right flank and rolled up the Yankee line. The exhausted Federals retreated, and soon the retreat turned into a rout. Southern losses were 1,982, Yankees 2,896.

Frederick W. Lander
Forgotten Martyr of the Civil War

The story of Frederick W. Lander is the story of one of the forgotten, great figures of the Civil War. Lander was not only a Civil War General, but he was also a transcontinental explorer, and poet. Lander was a visionary to the great contributions that the railroad would make in helping to expand our country. He also helped stop the Baltimore & Ohio Railroad's destruction by Confederate General Thomas "Stonewall" Jackson's troops during the Civil War. His story is one of courage, bravery, and undying devotion to his country.

Frederick W. Lander was born in Salem, Massachusetts on December 17, 1822. He was the son of Captain Edward and Eliza (West) Lander. His sister, Louisa would become a sculptress. He also had a brother named Edward, who later became a judge. He

was educated at Franklin and Dummer Academies and studied Civil Engineering at South Andover. He was first employed on the Eastern Railroad and then on other railroads, rising to the position of a Chief Engineer. In 1842-43, he took charge of the first icehouse cutting enterprise established at Wehham Lake, and under his supervision a group of icehouses were built, with a spur railroad track to connect them with the Eastern Railroad, a dwelling house and extensive stables.

In 1853, he became the Chief Engineer of the Northern Pacific Survey. Landers thought that a railroad line from Puget Sound by way of the Colombia and Snake Rivers to the Mississippi River, connecting with a railroad to California might be a good idea for a transcontinental route. In early 1854, he raised funds to equip a party to examine the feasibility of building this line. He made his journey in only a matter of weeks.

Lander acted for one year as Chief Engineer of the Overland Railroad wagon road, and for three years as Superintendent of the Pacific Railroad. In laying out these rails over vast tracts of land, he was also exposed to Indian attacks. In 1858, Lander's party was attacked by Piute Indians, but the Indians were repulsed. The railroad cut-off, north of Salt Lake on the Pacific Railroad, bore his name, and was of great benefit to the immigrants crossing the plains. A town is named after Lander in Arizona and also a mountain peak. During his career as a railroad engineer and surveyor, he led or participated in no less than five transcontinental surveys.

Just before the outbreak of the Civil War, Lander married Margaret Davenport, an actress from England, who had come to this country in 1838. Upon the outbreak of the Civil War, Lincoln entrusted Lander with a secret and confidential mission to Gov. Sam Houston of Texas, with full authority to order Federal troops then in Texas to support Houston if he thought it advisable. Sam Houston told Lander that he declined all military assistance from the United States, and he protested against any concentration of troops, or the construction of fortifications, within the border of Texas. Houston also requested that all Federal troops be removed from Texas.

Major General Irvin McDowell and his nephew Malcolm McDowell's shoulder straps worn at the Battle of Bull Run. On the back of Irwin McDowell's epaulettes, the original tag has inscribed "Used by Uncle Irwin at the Battle of Bull Run." Malcolm McDowell was in the Paymaster's Department. (BCWM)

Gen. Beauregard   *Brig. Gen McDowell*

Maj. Gen. George B. McClellan   *Gen. Anderson*

His mission a failure, Lander returned to Washington, which was under the threat of attack. Lander was sent across the James River alone, in order to reconnoiter the opposite shore, and scout Rebel movements in the vicinity of that city.

He then voluntarily served as a colonel on Gen. George B. McClellan's staff in Western Virginia. On May 17, 1861, Lander received a commission as brigadier general. While with Gen. McClellan he was involved in the battles of Philippi, and Rich Mountain. In June1861, Confederate General Robert Garnett's 7,000 men occupied Laurel Hill, about 13 miles south of Philippi. Union General George B. McClellan was at Beverly, and his plan was to hit Garnett's flank and rear. Gen. T. A. Morris advanced to Philippi, and faced the Confederate earthworks. McClellan ordered Gen. William Rosecrans to attack Garnett's rear. Rosecrans reached Hart's farm and forced his way up the side of Rich mountain and reached the summit at 1 p.m., June 3, 1861. The Federals drove the Confederates from their positions and caused them to fall back to their entrenchments at the base of the mountain. With McClellan at Beverly, Garnett realized that his retreat was cut off and he abandoned his earthworks at Laurel Hill and retreated to Saint George. During the battle, Col. Lander, on orders of Gen. William Rosecrans, led his column over the difficult country to get in the rear of Gen. Garnett's troops, which were entrenched around the base of Rich Mountain. McClellan said that Lander "displayed extraordinary activity and courage in the battle." He escaped unhurt when his horse was disabled by a canister shot. After Col. Lander's horse was shot out from under him, he then fought on foot and attacked a Rebel cannon. He shot three men of the crew of six serving the gun. The remainder fled, leaving a lieutenant to work the gun alone. Lander ordered him to surrender, but the lieutenant refused and continued to fire. Gen. Lander turned away and exclaimed to his men: " I cannot shoot so brave a man, you must do it!" The lieutenant fell, pierced by four bullets. After the battle, Lander ordered the body to be conveyed under escort across the mountain to a point near the enemy's camp, and delivered to his late companions in arms. The Confederates lost 135 killed, including Gen. Garnett and 800 wounded or captured. Union losses at the battle of Rich Mountain and Philippi were 12 killed and 59 wounded, including Col. Benjamin Kelley.

In July, Lander was in command of a brigade in General C. P. Stone's division on the upper Potomac. In September, by Special Order No. 145, Brig. Gen. Lander was assigned the command of a brigade consisting of the 19th, and 20th Massachusetts Volunteers, and Berdan's Sharpshooters. After the fatal disaster at Ball's Bluff (October 21, 1861), Gen. George B. McClellan called Gen. Lander from Washington to help support the Union troops under Gen. Charles Stone at Ball's Bluff. On October 22, 1861, Lander arrived in time for the skirmish at Edward's Ferry, Maryland. The 16th Indiana, and 13th Pennsylvania regiments were ordered across

Edward's Ferry. Encamped near the ferry on the crest of a hill were the 1st Minnesota, 2nd New York, the 34th New York, and 7th Michigan. Lander's sharpshooters were on the right, near a farm occupied by the 19th Massachusetts Tiger Zouaves. At 4 p.m. on the 22nd, the Confederates began their advance. The artillery and sharpshooters fired on the Rebels, and they fell back to Leesburg. At 9 p.m., the Federals were ordered to recross the bridge to Virginia. During the skirmish, Gen. Lander received a wound from which he never recovered, a flesh wound to his leg. After the skirmish, Gen. Lander couldn't mount his own horse without severe pain. Gen. Lander asked Gen. McClellan to relieve him of command because of his wound. McClellan told Lander to take as much time as he needed to rest, but not to resign.

During the months of January and February, Lander was keeping Confederate General Thomas "Stonewall" Jackson from destroying the Baltimore & Ohio Railroad. On February 6th, Lander pushed Jackson out of Romney, and was moving on Winchester.

On February 14, 1862, with only 2,600 men, Lander surprised the 4,000 Confederate troops led by Gen. Carson. Lander ordered 500 cavalry attached to his brigade to take the advance, and to construct a bridge for the passage of his infantry over the Cacapon River. The bridge was completed in four hours at night, and it was 180 feet long! The Rebels had pulled back, expecting an attack, and Gen. Lander immediately took up the pursuit, overtaking the fleeing Rebels two miles from Bloomington Gap. The Rebels fired on Lander's cavalry who quickly retreated. Lander ordered an advance and charge, but no one moved. In desperation, Lander exclaimed, "Follow Me!" One private, John Gannon, followed Lander. Accompanied by Maj. Armstrong, Maj. Bannister, and Fitz James O'Brien, Lander rode forward to a group of Rebel officers, several hundred yards in the distant, and ordered them to surrender, which they promptly agreed to do. Gen. Lander then ordered his cavalry to attack the Rebel infantry. After repeated orders, the cavalry reluctantly advanced and charged the enemy. The Rebels retreated, and an eight mile chase ensued, the Rebels leaving for parts unknown. Lander's troops captured 18 commissioned officers and 45 non commissioned officers and privates. Five of them were captured by Lander himself. They also captured 15 baggage wagons. The Confederates lost 20 killed and 75 captured. Lander received a special letter of commendation from the Secretary of War, Edwin Stanton.

After Bloomington Gap, Gen. Lander was totally exhausted, and was still suffering from his wound, but he stayed with his command. On February 27th, Gen. Lander was ordered to Martinsburg, where he finally made camp at Paw Paw, Camp Chase. On March 2, 1862, S. F. Barstow, Assistant Adjutant General reported to McClellan that Lander was very ill and had "been sleeping under morphine for 24 hours." Even though Lander was ill and dying, he still gave directions for a new movement, and a silent march. During the previous night, roused for a few minutes from his sleep, his quick ear caught the sound of mustering troops. Instantly he was fully awake and gave the command to hush the bugle, or the Rebel forces might hear their approach. This would be the last time that Gen. Lander would awaken. He laid down to his last, long sleep, on March 2, 1862, at 5 o'clock in the afternoon.

Gen.McClellan was devastated to hear that his friend had died, and on March 3rd, issued an order announcing Lander's death. In his order he said these words about Lander: "tall of stature, and of great strength and activity, with a countenance expressive of intelligence, courage, and sensibility, Gen. Lander's presence was commanding and attractive. As a military leader, he combined a spirit of the most daring enterprise with clearness of judgment in the adaptation of means to results. As a man, his devotion to his country, his loyalty to affection and friendship, his sympathy with suffering, and his indignation at cruelty and wrong, constituted him a representative of true chivalry. He has died in the flower of his manly prime, and in full bloom of his heroic virtues; but history will preserve the record of his life and character, and romance will

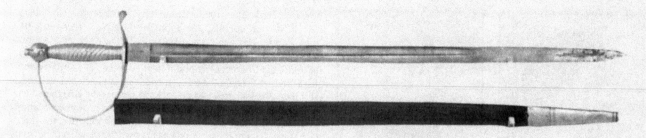

Artillery style militia short sword with brass mounted leather scabbard. The pommel has a rooster cast into it. This sword came out of a barn in Perryville, Kentucky. (BCWM)

Above: Regulation issue artillery shell jacket with red piping on collar, cuffs, and seam. It has the twelve button front, is fully lined, and has the maker and inspector marks in the sleeve. (BCWM)

At left: Pennsylvania Zouave uniform jacket. (BCWM)

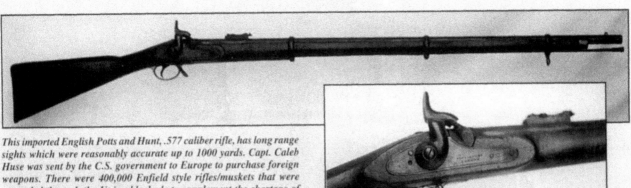

This imported English Potts and Hunt, .577 caliber rifle, has long range sights which were reasonably accurate up to 1000 yards. Capt. Caleb Huse was sent by the C.S. government to Europe to purchase foreign weapons. There were 400,000 Enfield style rifles/muskets that were smuggled through the Union blockade to supplement the shortage of Confederate arms. The Enfield style musket was a favorite of the C.S. infantrymen because of it's high quality. (BCWM)

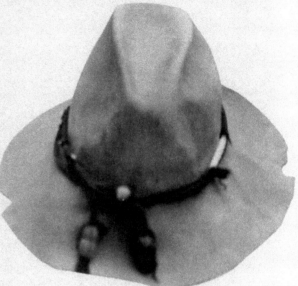

Above: Non-bound Confederate tan infantry officer's slouch hat, belonging to W. D. Hardy, Adjutant of the 5th South Carolina Infantry. Hat also has the standard hat cord that is bound around the wooden acorns. (BCWM)

At left: South Carolina officer's shell jacket. This early war shell jacket has the South Carolina state seal buttons, the early war shoulder straps and the braided gold bullion piping on the collar, sleeves and the front of the coat. It also has the imported English two piece snake belt buckle, which was smuggled through the Union blockade. (BCWM)

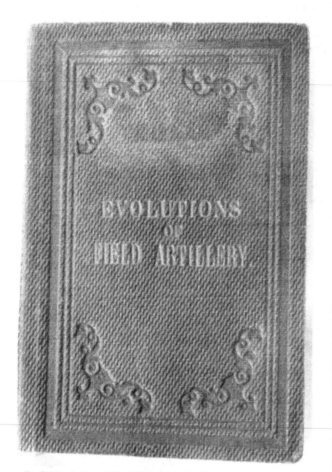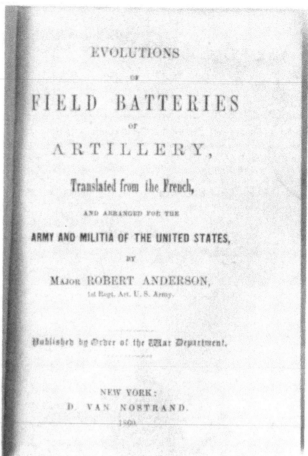

Book "Evolutions of Field Batteries of Artillery" by Major Robert Anderson in 1860. Anderson translated the book from French for the Army and Militia of the United States, and the book was then published by the War Department. BCWM

delight in portraying a figure so striking, a nature so noble, and a career so gallant. While paying public tribute of respect, the General Commander feels most deeply that, in the death of this brave and distinguished soldier, he has personally lost one of the truest and dearest friends."

Gen. Lander's body was taken to New York by special train from Washington, DC, and then to Boston, Massachusetts. The body was then escorted by a Guard of Honor consisting of twenty sharpshooters under Capt. John Saunders of Salem, and also by Capt. S. F. Barstow, Assistant Adjutant General of the staff. When the body arrived at the depot of the Worchester Road in Boston, the 2nd Battalion of Infantry, numbering 100 men, was drawn up to escort the body through the city, and then to the Eastern Railroad depot where a special train, draped in black, took it to Salem.

When the body arrived in Salem, the coffin was taken off the train by the sharpshooters, who then transported the coffin to City Hall, where it was put on display. Frederick Lander was laid out in the full dress uniform of a Brigadier General. Thousands of people came to City Hall to pay their last respects. His body was then escorted to South Church by the Salem Cadets, the Boston Independent Cadets, Gov. Andrew of Massachusetts, and the Mayor of Salem. After the church ceremony, he was taken to Broad Street cemetery and given a military salute with three volleys over the grave, then the Salem Artillery fired their cannons in salute. A National Mourning Card was made for Brig. Gen. Frederick W. Lander. On the card was a poem, written by Thomas Bailey Aldrich. The poem reads:

Close his black eyes-they shall no more
Flash victory where the cannon roar;
And lay the battered sabre at his side,

(His to the last, for so he would have died!)
Though he no more may pluck from out it's sheath.
Lead the worn war-horse by the plumed bier-
Even his horse, now he is dead, is dear!

Take him, New England, now his work is done.
He fought the Good Fight valiantly-and won.
Speak of his daring. This man held his blood
Cheaper than water for the nation's good.
Rich Mountain, Fairfax, Romney-he was there.
Speak of him gently, of his mien, his air;
How true he was, how his strong heart could bend
With sorrow, like a woman's, for a friend:
Intolerant of every base desire:
Ice where he liked not; where he loved, all fire.

Take him, New-England, gently. Other days,
Peaceful and prosperous, shall give him praise.
How will our children's children breathe his name,
Bright on the shadowy muster roll of fame!
Take him, New-England, gently; you can fold
No purer patriot in your soft brown mould.

So, on New-England's bosom, let him lie,
Sleeping awhile-as if Good could die!

Brig. Gen. Frederick W. Lander was laid to rest on March 8, 1862. Gen. Lander was brave, chivalrous, and devoted to his country. Lander is truly one of the forgotten heroes of the Civil War.

EARLY MISSOURI

Battle of Wilson's Creek

August 10, 1861

Campaign: Operations to Control Missouri (1861)

Principal Commanders: Brig. Gen. Nathaniel Lyon & Maj. Gen. Samuel D. Sturgis (US); Maj. Gen. Sterling Price, Missouri State Guard, and Brig. Gen. Ben McCulloch (CS)

Forces Engaged: Army of the West (US); Missouri State Guard and McCulloch's Brigade (CS)

Order of Battle
Union Forces
Gen. Nathaniel Lyon
Maj. Samuel Sturgis

1st Brigade
Major Sturgis
1st Battalion Infantry (Plummer)
2nd Missouri Infantry Battalion
2nd U.S. Artillery, Battery F
2nd Kansas Mounted Volunteers (one company)
1st U.S. Cavalry Regulars, Company B (Canfield's)

2nd Brigade
Lt.Col. Andrews
1st Missouri Infantry
Du Bois Light Battery
Regular Battalion

3rd Brigade
Col. G. Deitzler
1st Kansas
2nd Kansas

Missouri Volunteers
2nd Brigade
Col. F. Sigel
3rd Missouri
5th Missouri
1st U.S. Cavalry, Company I
2nd U.S. Dragoons, Company C
Backof's Missouri Artillery

Unattached
1st Iowa Infantry
Wright's Missouri Home Guard Cavalry
Switzler's Missouri Home Guard
1st U.S. Cavalry, Company D
Missouri Pioneers

Confederate Forces
Brig. Gen. Benjamin McCulloch
Missouri State Home Guard
Maj. Gen. Sterling Price

Rain's Division
Brig. Gen. James Rains

1st Brigade
Col. Weightman
Col. J. Graves
1st Infantry
3rd Infantry
4th Infantry
5th Infantry
Graves Infantry
Bledsoe's Battery

2nd Brigade
Col. Cawthon
Unknown

Parsons' Brigade
Brig. Gen. M. Parsons
Kelley's Infantry
Brown's Cavalry
Guibor's Battery

Clark's Division-Brig. Gen. John Clark
Burbridge's Infantry
1st Cavalry Battalion

Slack's Division-Brig. Gen. W. Y. Slack
Hughes's Infantry
Thornton's Infantry
Rives's Cavalry

McBride's Division-Brig. Gen. James McBride
Wingo's Infantry
Foster's Infantry
Campbell's Cavalry

Arkansas Forces-Brig. Gen. N. B. Pearce
1st Cavalry
Carroll's Company (Cavalry)
3rd Infantry
4th Infantry
5th Infantry
Woodruff's Battery
Reid's Battery

McCulloch's Brigade
1st Arkansas Mounted Riflemen
2nd Arkansas Mounted Riflemen
Arkansas Infantry Battalion
South Kansas-Texas Mounted Regiment
3rd Louisiana Infantry

Brig. Gen. Nathaniel Lyon's Army of the West was camped at Springfield, Missouri, as Confederate troops under the command of Brig. Gen. Ben McCulloch approached. On August 9th, both sides formulated their plans of attack. Union troops were to form two columns of attack. Sigel was to take a column to the south and come in on the Confederate right flank and rear, while Lyon, with his main force of 4,200 men, was to come from the north against the Confederate left. Lyon's opponents were Governor Jackson, McCulloch, and Price's 11,000 men. About 5:00 a.m. on the 10th, Franz Sigel, with about 1,200 men and a battery of artillery, attacked the Confederates. Lyon hit the Confederates on Wilson's Creek about 12 miles southwest of Springfield. Rebel cavalry received the first blow and fell back from Bloody Hill. Confederate forces soon rushed up and stabilized their positions. The Confederates attacked the Union forces three times that day but failed to break through the Union line. The battle raged on for

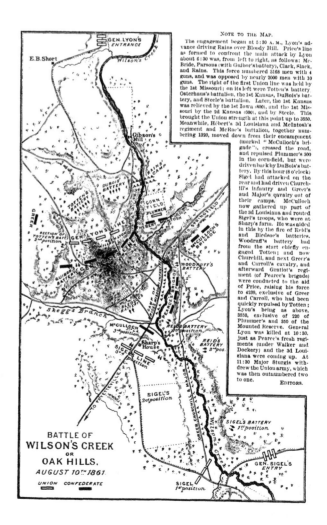

NOTE TO THE MAP.

The engagement began at 5:30 A. M., Lyon's advance driving Rains over Bloody Hill. Price's line as formed to confront the main attack by Lyon about 6:30 was, from left to right, as follows: McBride, Parsons (with Guibor's battery), Clark, Slack, and Rains. This force numbered 5168 men with 4 guns, and was opposed by nearly 2000 men with 10 guns. The right of the first Union line was held by the 1st Missouri; on its left were Totten's battery Osterhaus's battalion, the 1st Kansas, DuBois's battery, and Steele's battalion. Later, the 1st Kansas was relieved by the 1st Iowa (800), and the 1st Missouri by the 2d Kansas (500), and by Steele. This brought the Union strength at this point up to 3550. Meanwhile, Hébert's 3d Louisiana and McIntosh's regiment and McRae's battalion, together numbering 1320, moved down from their encampment (marked "McCulloch's brigade"), crossed the road, and repulsed Plummer's 300 in the corn-field, but were driven back by DuBois's battery. By this hour (8 o'clock) Sigel had attacked on the rear and had driven Churchill's infantry and Greer's and Major's cavalry out of their camps. McCulloch now gathered up part of the 3d Louisiana and routed Sigel's troops, who were at Sharp's farm. He was aided in this by the fire of Reid's and Bledsoe's batteries. Woodruff's battery had from the start chiefly engaged Totten; and now Churchill, and next Greer's and Carroll's cavalry, and afterward Gratiot's regiment (of Pearce's brigade) were conducted to the aid of Price, raising his force to 4299, exclusive of Greer and Carroll, who had been quickly repulsed by Totten; Lyon's being as above, 3550, exclusive of 220 of Plummer's and 350 of the Mounted Reserve. General Lyon was killed at 10:30, just as Pearce's fresh regiments (under Walker and Dockery) and the 3d Louisiana were coming up. At 11:30 Major Sturgis withdrew the Union army, which was then outnumbered two to one.

EDITORS.

BATTLE OF
WILSON'S CREEK
OR
OAK HILLS.
AUGUST 10TH 1861

UNION   CONFEDERATE

Major General Sterling Price, C.S.A.

Brigadier General Nathaniel Lyon

Confederate modified Grimsley officer's saddle, with silver inlaid Trans-Mississippi Medallions (inset photo), with white buff officer's gauntlets. (BCWM)

five hours. Lyon was killed during the battle and Maj. Samuel D. Sturgis replaced him. Meanwhile, the Confederates had routed Sigel's column south of Skegg's Branch. Following the third Confederate attack, which ended at 11:00 a.m., the Confederates withdrew. Sturgis, however, realized that his men were exhausted and his ammunition was low so he ordered a retreat to Springfield. The Confederates were too disorganized and ill equipped to pursue. Wilson's Creek was a Confederate victory. This victory buoyed southern sympathizers in Missouri and served as a springboard for a bold thrust north that carried Price and his Missouri State Guard as far as Lexington. In late October, a rump convention, convened by Gov. Claiborne Jackson, met in

Neosho and passed an ordinance of secession. Wilson's Creek, the most significant 1861 battle in Missouri, gave the Confederates control of southwestern Missouri.

Casualties: 2,330 total (US 1,235; CS 1,095)

Siege of Lexington

September 12-20,1861

On August 10th, Maj. Gen. Sterling Price, fresh from his victory at Wilson's Creek, started a new offensive in Missouri. He decided to attack Lexington, located on the Missouri River about

General Leonidas Polk, Bishop of Louisiana (Killed near Kenesaw, June, 1864).

Major General Ben. McCulloch, C.S.A.

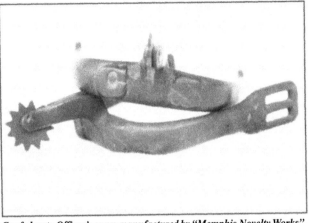

Confederate Officer's spurs manufactured by "Memphis Novelty Works". They are brass with iron rowels and have an embossed "CS" on the heel and a star on the side rails. These two spurs were found in Resaca, Georgia. (BCWM)

125 miles northwest of Springfield. Price was determined to take back Missouri with his 7,000 men of the Missouri State Guard. Lexington was defended by 2,800 men, under Col. James A. Mulligan. His men were inside an earthworks surrounding the Masonic College. On September 13th, Price's men encountered the Union pickets at Lexington. After a sharp skirmish, the pickets fell back to the earthworks, where the Yankees were under siege for nine days. Price had more and more reinforcements come by train, and soon the entire campus was surrounded. Outnumbered and completely out of food and water, the Union troops surrendered at 2:00 p.m. on September 20th. Price captured a full commissary of supplies, 215 horses, 100 wagons, five pieces of artillery and 3,000 muskets. Union losses were 159 casualties. Even though Price had won a great victory, he could not hold on to Missouri. Fremont's army of 38,000 men forced Price to flee the state.

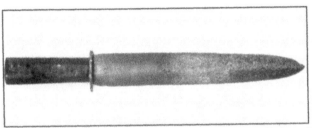

Massive 1840's period "Arkansas toothpick" with spear point blade, and hexagonal tiger striped maple handle. A favorite weapon of the Confederate foot soldier. (BCWM)

Battle of Columbus/Belmont
Principal commanders: Brig. Gen. Ulysses S. Grant (US); Maj. Gen. Leonidas Polk & Brig. Gen. Gideon Pillow (CS)

Order of Battle: Belmont
Union Forces
Ulysses S. Grant
First Brigade
Brig. Gen. John McClernand
27th Illinois
30th Illinois
31st Illinois

Second Brigade
Col. Henry H. E. Dougherty
22nd Illinois
7th Iowa

Dollin's Company Illinois Cavalry
Delano's Company Illinois Cavalry
Battery B, 1st Illinois Light Artillery

Gunboats
Tyler
Lexington

Confederate Forces
Maj. Gen. Leonidas Polk
Brig. Gen. G. J. Pillow
Brig. Gen. B. F. Cheatham

Marks Brigade
Col. S. F. Marks
13th Arkansas
11th Louisiana
Blythe's Mississippi

Walker's Brigade
Col. J. K. Walker
2nd Tennessee

Russell's Brigade
Col. R.M. Russell
12th Tennessee
13th Tennessee
21st Tennessee
22nd Tennessee

Smith's Brigade
Col. P. Smith
154th Senior Tennessee

Watson's Louisiana Battery
Mississippi Cavalry- Lt. Col. John Walker
Tennessee Cavalry- Lt. Col. T. H. Logwood
15th Tennessee

Kentucky Side of River:
Brig. Gen. John McGown
Point Coupe Louisiana Battery
Mississippi Battery- Capt. Melancthon Smith
Seige Battery- Capt. S.H. D. Hamilton
Fort Artillery -Maj. A.P. Stewart

On November 6th, Grant with 3,114 men, made ready to attack Belmont, a key Confederate stronghold, defended by heavy guns and a huge garrison. Grant and his men left their camp at Cairo, Illinois and boarded transport boats for the trip to Missouri. Grant landed his men just north of the hamlet of Belmont, and found himself facing a Confederate force of 5,000 men, 2,330 manning the garrison and Gideon Pillow's 2,300 men. Grant's men attacked Belmont at 8:30 a.m., November 7, 1861. After four hours of fighting, the Union troops under Grant drove the Confederates to the river banks. Grant's men stopped at the Confederate camp in Belmont and began looting. Across the river, General Leonidas Polk expected an attack on his main line in Columbus, but none came, so he fired his cannon on the Union troops in Belmont and sent several regiments across the river, 2,700 Confederate soldiers in all, to land both upstream, and downstream of the Union forces and get between Grant's men and their boats. The Union troops were surrounded, and had to fight their way back to the river. The Federals were driven away and the Confederates counted Belmont as their victory. Grant said that Belmont was a victory for the Union. In fact, neither side won or lost. There were 607 Union casualties and 641 casualties for the Confederates. The Battle of Belmont was Gen. Ulysses Grant's first Civil War Battle, and would not be his last.

EARLY KENTUCKY

Battle of Middle Creek

January 10, 1862

Campaign: Offensive in Eastern Kentucky (1862)

Principal Commanders: Col. James Garfield (US); Brig. Gen. Humphrey Marshall (CS)

Forces Engaged: 18th Brigade (US); Brigade (CS)

More than a month after Confederate Col. John S. Williams left Kentucky, following the fight at Ivy Mountain, Brig. Gen. Humphrey Marshall led another force into southeast Kentucky to continue recruiting activities. From his headquarters in Paintsville, Marshall recruited volunteers and had a force of more than 2,000 men by early January, but could only partially equip them. Union Brigadier General Don Carlos Buell directed Col. James Garfield to force Gen. Marshall to retreat back into Virginia. Leaving Louisa on December 23rd, Garfield took command of the 18th Brigade and began his march south on Paintsville. He compelled the Confederates to

Confederate shell jacket utilizing "Kentucky Military Institute" buttons. (BCWM)

abandon Paintsville and retreat to the vicinity of Prestonburg. Garfield slowly headed south, but swampy areas and numerous streams slowed his movements, and he arrived in the vicinity of Marshall on the 9th. Heading out at 4:00 a.m. on January 10th, Garfield marched a mile south to the mouth of Middle Creek. At 8:00 a.m., Garfield fought off some Rebel cavalry and turned west to attack Marshall. At noon they confronted Marshall's force. Marshall had his battle line set up at a hillside west of the creek,

Uniform of Capt. Thomas Elkin, Aide de camp to Generals Thomas and Rousseau, Commander of the 5th Kentucky Cavalry, U.S.

Thomas Allen Elkin was born in Shelby County, KY and spent his boyhood days in Lincoln and Garrard counties. He was described as 5'9", with brown eyes, red hair, and a ruddy complexion. When the Civil War started, he was one of the first to enlist at Camp Nelson, in September 1861. On Oct. 15, 1861, he enlisted with Company H, 19th Kentucky Volunteer Infantry, and was commissioned a Lieutenant on Dec. 12, 1861 at Harrodsburg, KY. He fought at the Battle of Mill Springs. He was later detailed to command 14 men to escort the body of Confederate General Zollicoffer overland to Lebanon, KY where it was put on a train for transport to Nashville, TN. Because of bad weather seven of the men died of exposure and Lt. Elkin was "sent home on a stretcher" with pneumonia.

After his recovery from illness, Elkin served as aide de camp to Gen. George Thomas and Gen. Rousseau. He was promoted to Captain, Company A, 5th Kentucky Volunteer Cavalry on Dec. 20, 1863. He was promoted after the Battle of Chickamauga. He also fought in the Atlanta campaign.

He resigned from the army on Jan. 20, 1865, and returned to his home in Lancaster, KY. He spent the rest of his life as a farmer.

Capt. Thomas Elkin was one of the oldest Civil War Veterans in Central Kentucky, when he died at the age of 91. He was survived by his five children: Sally Elkin, T.F. Martin, E.P. Halley, W.S. Elkin, Jr., and T.C. Elkin. He was buried in the Lancaster Cemetery. [Reference: Kentucky Military History Museum] (Kentucky Military History Museum original photograph of Capt. Elkin is the property of Mary Estill Rose.)

C.D.V. of Confederate General Simon Bolivar Buckner wearing his personally designed Confederate uniform. (BCWM)

C.D.V. of the famous Confederate General "Cavalier" John H. Morgan, "the Marion of the South", published in New York in his pre-war U.S. uniform. (BCWM)

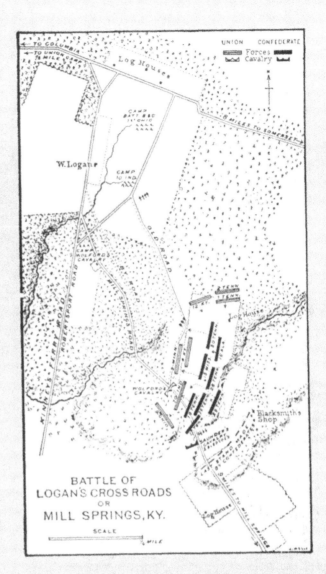

BATTLE OF
LOGAN'S CROSS ROADS
OR
MILL SPRINGS, KY.

Map of Big Sandy River and Middle Creek Battlefield, January 10, 1862.

just north of its juncture with Lost Fork. Cols. John S. Williams & Alfred C. Moore's men were on the hillside east of the stream, and Marshall's four cannons were on a hill on his own left. Garfield attacked shortly after noon. He sent a portion of his men to cross Middle Creek and slammed into the Confederate right. The fighting continued for most of the afternoon until 700 Union reinforcements arrived at 4:00 p.m., just in time to dissuade the Confederates from assailing the Federal left. The Confederates decided not to continue the battle and retired south, and were ordered back to Virginia on the 24th. Both sides claimed a victory. Garfield lost one dead & 20 wounded, and Marshall lost 10 killed, 15 wounded, and 25 captured. Garfield's force moved to Prestonburg after the fight and then retired to Paintsville.

Battle of Mill Springs

January 19, 1862
Campaign: Offensive in Eastern Kentucky
Principal Commanders: Brig. Gen. George H. Thomas (US);
Maj. Gen. George Crittenden (CS)
Forces Engaged: 1st Division, Army of the Ohio, and Brig. Gen. A. Schoepf's Brigade (total of four brigades) (US); Division of two brigades (CS)

Order of Battle
Union Forces
Brig. Gen. George Thomas

2nd Brigade	3rd Brigade	12th Brigade
Col. M. D. Manson	Col. R. L. McCook	Col. S. Carter

Major General Gideon J. Pillow, C.S.A. *Major General J.S. Bowen, C.S.A.*

Zollicoffer being shot by Col. Speed Fry at the Battle of Mill Springs.

10th Indiana Infantry	9th Ohio Infantry	12th Kentucky Infantry
10th Kentucky Infantry	2nd Minnesota Infantry	1st Tennessee
14th Ohio Infantry		2nd Tennessee
4th Kentucky Infantry		1st Kentucky Cavalry
1st Ohio, Battery B		
1st Ohio, Battery C		
9th Ohio Battery		
Wetmore's Battery		

Schoepf's Brigade
17th Ohio Infantry
31st Ohio Infantry
38th Ohio Infantry, Company A

18th U.S. Infantry
Battalion of Michigan Engineers

Confederate Forces
Maj. Gen. George Crittenden

1st Brigade	2nd Brigade
Brig. Gen. Zollicofer	Brig. Gen. W. Carroll
15th Mississippi	17th Tennessee
19th Tennessee	28th Tennessee
20th Tennessee	29th Tennessee
25th Tennessee	McClung's Battery
Rutledge's Battery	16th Alabama
Saunder's Cavalry Battalion	Branner's Cavalry Battalion
Bledsoe's Cavalry Battalion	McClellan's Cavalry Battalion

Although Brig. Gen. Felix K. Zollicoffer's main responsibility was to guard the Cumberland Gap, in November 1861 he advanced west into Kentucky with 4,000 men, to strengthen control in the area around Somerset. He found a strong defensive position at Mill Springs and decided to make this his winter quarters. He fortified the area, especially both sides of the Cumberland River. Union Brigadier General George Thomas received orders to drive the Rebels across the Cumberland River and break up Maj. Gen. George B. Crittenden's army. Thomas left Lebanon and slowly marched through rain soaked country, arriving at Logan's Cross-roads on January 17th, where he waited for Brig. Gen. A. Schoeph's troops from Somerset to join him. Maj. Gen. George Crittenden, Zollicoffer's superior, had arrived at Mill Springs and taken command of the Confederate troops. He knew that Thomas was in the vicinity and decided that his best defense was to hit the Federals first. The Rebels attacked Thomas at Logan's Crossroads at dawn on January 19th. Unbeknownst to the Confederates, some of Schoeph's troops had arrived and reinforced the Union troops which now numbered around 4,000 men. Initially, the Rebel attack forced the 10th Indiana to retire but during this battle Gen. Zollicoffer was killed. Zollicoffer was nearsighted and rode up to a Union officer. The officer, Col. Speed Fry, shot Zollicoffer dead. After Zollicoffer was killed, Crittenden took over and rallied his men to attack. Crittenden's men were armed with flintlock rifles that didn't shoot well in the rain, and his men began to retreat. The Federals were equipped with percussion capped rifles. Union counterattacks on the Confederate right, led by Col. Samuel P. Carter's brigade, and the left, led by the 9th Ohio Infantry, were successful, forcing the Confederates from the field. Crittenden had to abandon 12 cannons and large quantities of stores in Beech Grove, and then crossed the Cumberland River headed toward Knoxville. Crittenden lost 439 men, Federal losses were 232. The Battle of Mill Springs, along with one at Middle Creek, broke whatever Confederate strength there was in eastern Kentucky.

Lieutenant General W.J. Hardee, C.S.A.

BATTLES OF FORT HENRY & FORT DONELSON

"The Gate To Nashville"

February 6-16, 1862

Campaign: Federal Penetration up the Cumberland and Tennessee Rivers.

Principal Commanders at Fort Henry: Brig. Gen. Ulysses S. Grant and Flag Officer A.H. Foote (U.S.); Brig. Gen. Lloyd Tilghman (CS)

Principal commanders at Fort Donelson: Brig. Gen. Ulysses S. Grant and Flag-Officer A.H. Foote (US); Brig. Gen. John B. Floyd, Brig. Gen. Gideon Pillow, and Brig. Gen. Simon Buckner (CS)

Forces engaged at Fort Henry: District of Cairo (US); Fort Henry Garrison (CS)

Forces engaged at Fort Donelson: Army in the Field (US), Fort Donelson Garrison (CS)

Order of Battle: Fort Henry & Fort Donelson
Union Forces

District of Cairo
Brig. Gen. Ulysses S. Grant
First Division: Brig. Gen. John McClernand

1st Brigade	2nd Brigade	3rd Brigade
Col. R. Oglesby	Col. W. Wallace	Col. W. Morrison
8th Illinois	11th Illinois	Col. L. Ross
18th Illinois	20th Illinois	17th Illinois
29th Illinois	45th Illinois	49th Illinois
30th Illinois	48th Illinois	
31st Illinois	1st Light Artillery,	
Illinois Light Artillery,	Battery B	
Battery A	1st Illinois Light Artillery, Battery D	
2nd Illinois Light Artillery, 4th Illinois Cavalry		
Battery E		

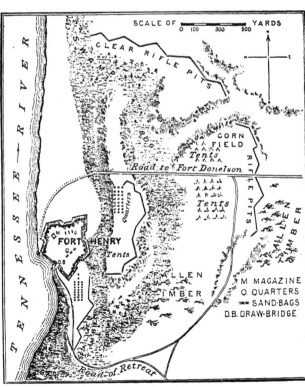

Map of Fort Henry, Feb. 6, 1862.

2nd Illinois Cavalry,
   Company A & B
2nd U.S. Cavalry, Company C
4th U.S. Cavalry, Company I
Carmichael's Illinois Cavalry
O'Harnett's Illinois Cavalry
Dollins Illinois Cavalry
Stewart's Illinois. Cavalry

Second Division: Brig. Gen. Charles Smith

1st Brigade	3rd Brigade	4th Brigade	5th Brigade
Col. J. McArthur	Col. J. Cook	Col. J. Lauman	Col. M. Smith
9th Illinois	7th Illinois	25th Indiana	8th Missouri
12th Illinois	50th Illinois	2nd Iowa	11th Indiana
41st Illinois	52nd Indiana	7th Iowa	
	12th Iowa	14th Iowa	
	13th Missouri	Birge's Sharpshooters	
	1st Missouri Light Artillery, Battery D		
	1st Missouri Light Artillery, Battery H		
	1st Missouri Light Artillery, Battery K		

Third Division: Brig. Gen. Lew Wallace

1st Brigade	2nd Brigade	3rd Brigade	Not Brigaded
Col. C. Cruft	46th Illinois	Col. J. Thayer	1st Illinois Light
31st Indiana	57th Illinois	1st Nebraska	Artillery, Battery A
44th Indiana	58th Illinois	58th Ohio	32nd Illinois,
17th Kentucky		68th Ohio	Company A
25th Kentucky		76th Ohio	

Union Ironclads and Gunboats
Flag Officer Andrew Foote
St. Louis, Carondelet, Louisville, Pittsburg, Tyler, Conestoga

Confederate Forces at Fort Donelson
Brig. General Gideon Pillow, Brig. General John B. Floyd, and Simon B. Buckner
Buckner's Division

Second Brigade	Third Brigade	Artillery
Col. Wm. Baldwin	Col. J. Brown	Kentucky Battery (Capt. Graves)
2nd Kentucky	3rd Tennessee	Porter's Tennessee Battery
14th Mississippi	18th Tennessee	Jackson's Virginia Battery
20th Mississippi	32nd Tennessee	
26th Tennessee		
41st Tennessee		

Johnson's Command: Brig. General Bushrod Johnson

Heiman's Brigade	Davidson's Brigade	Drake's Brigade
Col. A. Heiman	Col. T. J. Davidson	Col. J. Drake
27th Alabama	8 Kentucky	Alabama Battalion
10th Tennessee	1st Mississippi	15th Arkansas
42nd Tennessee	3rd Mississippi	4th Mississippi
48th Tennessee	7th Texas	Browder's Tennessee
53rd Tennessee		Battalion

Floyd's Division:

First Brigade	Second Brigade	Artillery
Col. G. C. Wharton	Col. J. McCausland	Guy's Virginia Battery
51st Virginia	36th Virginia	French's Virginia Battery
56th Virginia	50th Virginia	Green's Kentucky Battery

Garrison's Forces
30th Tennessee
49th Tennessee
50th Tennessee

Fort Batteries at Fort Donelson
30th Tennessee, Battery A
50th Tennessee, Battery A
Maury's Tennessee Battery

Cavalry
Col. Nathan Bedford Forrest's Tennessee Regiment
9th Tennessee Battalion
Milton's Company Tennessee Cavalry

Confederate General Simon Bolivar Buckner's Bear Skin Shawl. Simon Buckner was born on April 1st, 1823 in Hart City, KY. He attended the U.S. Military Academy at West Point and graduated 11th in the class of 1844. He served under Gen. Winfield Scott's army in the Mexican War, winning two brevets and suffering a wound at Churubusco. After the war, he returned to teaching at his alma mater. Feeling that the mandatory presence at Sunday chapel was a violation of his rights, he quit that post and returned to infantry service in 1849. In 1852 he transferred to the commissary branch. In 1855, he resigned from the army and returned to his business interests. Between 1855 till 1860, he was adjutant general of the Illinois militia and directed the reorganization of his native state's armed forces. In 1860, he formed the Kentucky State Guard and became the Major General and inspector general, Kentucky State Guard. In 1861, he refused a commission in the Union army. In July he resigned from the Kentucky State Guard and fled south to avoid arrest as a suspected traitor. He was appointed Brigadier General in the Confederacy on Sept. 14, 1861 and occupied Bowling Green at the center of Albert Sidney Johnston's line. On Feb. 16, 1862, Buckner surrendered to Grant at Fort Donelson. He was exchanged during the summer of 1862, and participated in Confederate General Braxton Bragg's invasion of Kentucky in August 1862. He led the Third Division under Maj. Gen. William Hardee and fought at the Battle of Perryville, losing heavily before taking the Union line. In December 1862, he was sent to improve coastal defenses on the Gulf, and in April 1863, he was transferred back to Bragg's army and commanded the left wing corps at Chickamauga, but did not play a major role. When President Jefferson Davis visited the Confederate Army of Tennessee to try and solve the dispute between Bragg and his Generals, Buckner was one of the Generals to try and have Bragg relieved of command. Bragg and Jefferson Davis were good friends and Bragg was left in command of the army. Bragg took revenge on all the Generals who were against him. Bragg sent Buckner with Confederate General Longstreet to Knoxville. On Sept. 20, 1864, Buckner was appointed Lieutenant General and was transferred to the Trans-Mississippi Department, where he served as chief of staff to General Edmund Kirby Smith.

After the war, Buckner was not allowed to return to Kentucky for three years, during that time he lived in New Orleans and recovered his fortune. In 1867, he returned to Kentucky. In 1887, he ran for Governor, winning the election. During his term as Governor, he brought Kentucky honest and efficient government. In 1896, he ran for the vice presidency on John M. Palmer's God Democrats ticket. On Jan. 8, 1914, Buckner died at his home near Munfordsville, KY and was the last survivor of the top three Confederate Generals ranks. Buckner is currently buried in Frankfort, KY. [Reference: Who Was Who In the Confederacy, Historical Times Illustrated Encyclopedia of the Civil War.] (Kentucky Military History Museum)

Unattached:
Major S. H. Colms Tennessee Battalion Infantry

Ft. Henry and Ft. Donelson were in the middle of the South's defense line stretching from Columbus, Kentucky to Bowling Green, Kentucky, then southward to the Cumberland Gap. Loss of the forts would allow the North invasion routes by land and by water. In November 1861, the forts were commanded by Rebel General Lloyd Tilghman. Ft. Henry, located above a bend in the Tennessee River, commanded a stretch of river three miles long but had obvious weaknesses: on low ground and subject to flooding, it was also overshadowed by hills on both sides of the river. Though he had 11 of Ft. Henry's 17 guns facing the river, Tilghman still felt that the fort couldn't stand an attack. He sent most of his men to Ft. Donelson, only 10 miles away, keeping 100 artillerymen with him to serve the guns.

On January 30, 1862, Henry Halleck, commander of the Department of Missouri, gave Grant permission to seize Ft. Henry. Grant commanded 17,000 infantry on board transport boats and Flag Officer Andrew Foote commanded seven gunboats. On February 3rd, Grant unloaded his infantry from the transports onto land just outside the range of the guns at Fort Henry. On February 6th, Brig. Gen. Charles Smith seized the heights above the fort and Brig. Gen. John McClernand advanced to cut off the escape route. The gunboat Cincinnati attacked Ft. Henry and knocked out two of Capt. Jesse Taylor's most important guns, a six inch rifled cannon, and a 128 pound cannon. Taylor then lost two more guns, both 32 pounders. With only four guns still serviceable at Fort Henry, Gen. Lloyd Tilghman and Capt. Taylor surrendered to Andrew Foote. By the time Grant's infantry arrived, The Battle of Fort Henry was over.

Grant now focused his attention on Fort Donelson. Halleck sent Grant 10,000 reinforcements.

Gen. Albert Sidney Johnston, at Bowling Green, decided to give up his position there and retire to Nashville. Johnston left 5,000 men at Fort Donelson and placed Brigadier Generals John Floyd, Gideon Pillow, and Simon Buckner in command. He also sent 12,000 men to take on Grant's 15,000 men. On February 12th, Grant's force of 15,000 men were approaching Ft. Donelson. On the 14th, Foote's gunboats arrived and 12 army transports with 10,000 men on board hove into view. Gen. Wallace arrived with troops from Fort Henry. Three divisions were formed under Lew Wallace, McClernand, and Gen. Smith. At 3:30 p.m., Foote's gunboats attacked, but were repulsed by the shore batteries. Foote was wounded in the battle, and the St. Louis, the Pittsburg, Carondelet, and the Louisville were severely damaged.

The Confederates decided to attack the Federals the next day and then make their escape from Fort Donelson. Gideon Pillow was to attack McClernand, Buckner was to leave the 13th Tennessee Infantry in the trenches to the right, facing Gen. Smith's division, and move the bulk of his men to the center. Once Pillow rolled the Federal troops back, Buckner would strike the hinge and hold the door open while Pillow's division marched out safely. Buckner would follow, fighting a rear guard action to make sure the army escaped. The attack began at daylight, and the battle went well for the Confederates at first, and they were close to a victory. Their escape route was open, and they had managed to drive off McClernand and Wallace's divisions. By 1:00 p.m., Grant had arrived on the scene and realized what the Confederates were trying to do, and immediately ordered Wallace and McClernand to counterattack. Grant also ordered Foote's gunboats to fire, and Smith to take the fort by attacking the Confederate right. The troops under Capt. Jack Slaymaker rushed the Confederate earthworks and Buckner's 30th Tennessee fell back. The Federals brought guns to bear on the entrenchments. Pillow ordered a retreat back into the fort. At 1:00 a.m., the generals left Buckner to surrender the garrison, while Floyd and Pillow would escape with Nathan Bedford Forrest's cavalry. On February 16th, Buckner surrendered to Grant. Grant took 12,000 to 15,000 prisoners, 2,000 to 4,000 horses, 48 cannons, 17 heavy guns, and large quantities of commissary stores.

Map of Fort Donelson, as invested by General Grant; based on the official map by General J.B. McPherson.

of Paducah, Kentucky, adopting the state as his own in 1852. Tilghman tried to remain neutral, but on July 5, 1861, Tilghman and his 3rd Kentucky Infantry Regiment joined the Confederacy. Tilghman was made colonel of the Third Kentucky, and A.P. Thompson was made Lieutenant Colonel.

On September 6, 1861, Brig. Gen. Ulysses S. Grant entered the city of Paducah. Grant says that when he entered the city Tilghman had left with his "Rebel Army". Grant took over the city without firing a gun. Grant goes on to say that "Before I landed, the secession flags had disappeared, and I ordered our flags to replace them. I found at the railroad depot a large number of complete rations and about two tons of leather, marked for the Confederate Army. Took possession of these; took possession of the telegraph office; I took possession of the railroad; I left two gunboats and one of the steamboats at Paducah, placed the post under command of Gen. E.A. Paine, last night I ordered the Eighth Missouri Volunteers to reinforce Gen. Paine at Paducah tonight."

Col. Tilghman went to Camp Boone, near Clarksville, Tennessee, where he was promoted to Brigadier General on October 18, 1861. A.P. Thompson was promoted to colonel of the Third Kentucky Regiment on the same day. Tilghman was then sent to Hopkinsville, Kentucky where he trained 3,000 men, although getting arms for these men was a massive undertaking. Tilghman

The victories at Fort Henry and Fort Donelson brought Grant to national prominence. The capture of the forts forced the Confederates to evacuate Nashville and Columbus. They lost their grip on Southern Kentucky and lost virtually all of Middle and Western Tennessee. Fort Donelson will go down as the tenth most costly battle of the Civil War.

Casualties at Fort Henry: 119 (U.S. 40; C.S. 79)

Casualties at Fort Donelson: 16,550 (U.S. 500 men killed, 2,100 wounded; C.S. 450 killed, 1,500 wounded, 12,000 prisoners)

Lloyd Tilghman

Lloyd Tilghman was born on January 26, 1816, near Claiborne, Maryland, and was the only son of James and Ann Caroline Shoemaker. Tilghman entered the United States Military Academy at West Point, on July 1, 1831, at the age of fifteen. He graduated 46th in the class of 1836. Three months after graduation, Lloyd Tilghman decided that he did not want to be a military career man, so he quit his position as a second lieutenant in the 1st Dragoons on September 30, 1836, and instead accepted the position of civil engineer on the Baltimore & Susquehanna Railroad, which he held until 1837. In 1837, he became an engineer of the Norfolk and Wilmington Canal for the Eastern Shore Railroad, resigning to later work for the Baltimore & Ohio Railroad, until 1840. He superintended public improvements for the city of Baltimore afterward.

When the Mexican War broke out in 1846, Tilghman rejoined the army. He became the aide-de-camp to Gen. David E. Twiggs. He fought in the battle of Palo Alto on May 8, 1846, and the Battle of Resaca de la Palma the next day. On August 14, 1847, Tilghman became captain of the Maryland and District of Columbia Volunteer Artillery and served in this capacity until his unit was disbanded on July 13, 1848.

After the Mexican War, he returned to civilian life and was a civil engineer for the railroad until the Civil War. He was a resident

Confederate General Lloyd Tilghman.

Ft. Anderson, Marine Hospital, Paducah, KY.

Confederate General Simon Bolivar Buckner

wrote to Gen. Albert Sidney Johnston on September 23, 1861, that "not a single gun can be procured, of any sort, under any circumstances. The brigade numbers near 3,000 men, about one sixth badly armed. The brigade is in advance, and the want of arms has a most demoralizing effect on the men. A failure to arm us promptly will act ruinously on our friends in Kentucky." The lack of arms was not the only problem he faced, as uniforms for the men were in short supply. On October 27, 1861, he wrote a letter to Gen. Albert Sidney Johnston that stated "a vast deal of suffering exists, owing to the condition of the men. I have made arrangements for 200 women to work on clothing, and hope for a better contribution of blankets and clothing from the society at this place." He also mentions that "I am sorry to hear about the inefficient condition of things at Fort Donelson." He also made a plea for "artillery, wagons, mules, harness, forage, and horses for artillery commands."

Once Gen. Tilghman had his army ready for marching, he was ordered to Forts Henry and Donelson, and was made commander of both forts. Gen. Tilghman pointed out to Lt. Gen. Leonidas Polk, district commander, that both forts where in horrible shape and were not ready for battle. He begged Polk to send him the manpower to complete the forts, but none came.

Tilghman did the best job he could to prepare for the upcoming battle, taking personal command of Fort Henry. When Gen. Grant finally arrived with his 16,000 Federals against Gen. Tilghman's 2,600 poorly armed troops, Tilghman decided to send all but eighty men to Fort Donelson. For two hours, Tilghman made a brave stand against the Union gunboats, finally surrendering after his main guns were knocked out. He was taken prisoner and after spending six months in Yankee prisons he was exchanged on August 27, 1862, for Union General John Reynolds. Tilghman and Simon Buckner and 10,000 exchanged men were then ordered to Jackson, Mississippi. In a few months, Gen. Tilghman equipped,

clothed, and armed these men and formed them into artillery, cavalry, and infantry units.

Gen. Tilghman was then transferred to Mississippi where on December 5, 1862, Maj. Gen. Ulysses S. Grant was making his first march to Vicksburg and was following the Mississippi Central Railroad. This path would lead him directly to Tilghman's forces at Coffeeville, Mississippi. At 2:30 p.m., fighting began in the town of Coffeeville, where Grant's forces had pushed a mile into town. Gen. Lovell, commander of the First Corps, had sent a division of Tilghman's to check the advance. Lovell rode with Tilghman to the front and sent the First Brigade, under Brig. Gen. Baldwin on the right of the main road leading into Water Valley, and Col. A. P. Thompson and the 3rd Kentucky were sent on the road leading out of Coffeeville to the west of the main road, to watch the left flank. Artillery was brought up, and soon an artillery duel broke out. Tilghman's rifled guns soon silenced the Yankee cannon.

Gen. Tilghman then asked permission to advance on the enemy. Permission was given and Tilghman ordered the 14th Mississippi, under Gen. Ross, which had been in reserve, to take position on the extreme right of his line. The cavalry under Col. W. H. Jackson was also made ready, and moved to the rear of the main line. Gen. Rust, with two brigades on Tilghman's right, was also made ready. Tilghman then ordered Col. Thompson, Gen. Rust, and Gen. Ross to advance. As soon as they got within 200 yards, the Yankees opened up on the Confederates. Col. A. P. Thompson ordered the 9th Arkansas, and the 8th Kentucky to return fire, and press the enemy. Even though the Yankees made two stands, they were quickly driven off. The Yankees were then pushed to the edge of an open field, where the Blue Coats mounted their horses and retreated. When they reached the edge of a wooded area, they dismounted and began to fire at the exposed Confederates who were pursuing them across the open field.

Gen. Tilghman feared that Gen. Rust had not moved far enough to cover his right flank and he immediately ordered Lt. Barbour, commanding his bodyguard, to move to the extreme right. As soon as Lt. Barbour moved into position he was immediately fired upon by the Yankees, who by this time, had been pushed almost three miles from Coffeeville, and commanded the high ground outside of town. The heaviest fire was now directed down upon the 8th Kentucky and 9th Arkansas, but the Confederates pushed on, and soon overran the Yankee position.

Their objective of pushing back the enemy was complete, and Gen. Tilghman ordered his men to halt and cease fire. The Confederates killed 34 Union soldiers, including Lt. Col. William McCullough, and 2nd Lt. Thomas Woodburn. They captured 17 prisoners. The Confederates lost seven killed, and 43 wounded. The besting of Grant at the Battle of Coffeeville was in a small measure, Gen. Tilghman's pay back for the defeat he suffered at Grant's hands at Fort Henry.

During his military career, Gen. Tilghman also led a brigade at the Battle of Corinth, Mississippi, and was the rear guard after the Battle of Holly Springs. In the defense of Vicksburg, he was in charge of the camp of paroled and exchanged prisoners. When Grant crossed the river south of the city, Tilghman's brigade served as a part of John C. Pemberton's field force. On May 16, 1863, at Champion Hill, Mississippi, Tilghman had only 1,550 men and was being forced back by 6,000 to 8,000 of Grant's troops. Tilghman dismounted and took command of a section of field artillery of the 1st Mississippi Light Artillery, and was in the act of sighting a howitzer when he was struck in the hip by a cannonball from the Chicago Mercantile Battery's number two gun. He lived about three hours after he was wounded and was carried to a peach tree where he died while in the arms of Gen. Powhattan Ellis.

Tilghman was survived by his wife Augusta Murray Boyd, and his three sons; Lt. Lloyd Tilghman, Jr., Frederick and Sidell. Col. A. E. Reynolds, who replaced Tilghman as commander, said in his report of Gen. Tilghman, after the battle of Champion's Hill: "I cannot refrain from paying a slight tribute to the memory of my late commander. As a man, a soldier and a general, he had few if any superiors, and was always at his post. He devoted himself day and night to his command. Upon the battlefield he was cool, collected and observant. He commanded the entire respect and confidence of every officer and soldier under him, and the only censure ever cast upon him was that he always exposed himself too recklessly. The tears by his men on the occasion and the grief felt by his entire brigade are the proudest tribute that can be given to the gallant dead." Two months later, young Lt. Lloyd Tilghman, Jr. was thrown from his horse, and like his father, gave up his life for the cause they both held so dear.

A. P. Thompson

Albert (Bert) P. Thompson was born March 4, 1829, eight miles northwest of Murray, Kentucky in Calloway County. He was a lawyer by trade. He was married to Mary Jane Bowman, who died a year after their marriage. He later married Harriet Harding, who also died. He then married the daughter of Attorney Mayer of Mayfield, and settled down in Paducah to practice law. He lived on the southeast corner of Seventh and Monroe Street. When the Union Forces entered Paducah and raised the American flag over the state capitol, Thompson entered the Confederate army and joined the 3rd Kentucky Infantry Regiment. He became commander of the 3rd Kentucky Regiment on October 18, 1861.

In July, 1862, A.P. Thompson was serving in Breckinridge's Division, Army of the Missssippi, and participated in the attack on Baton Rouge, Louisiana. Confederate Major General John C. Breckinridge and 5,000 men were sent to Camp Moore to join with troops under Brig. Gen. Daniel Ruggles, raising the force to 6,000 men. The Confederates believed that Brig. Gen. Thomas William's force at Baton Rouge numbered about 3,500 men, but in reality only 800 were fit enough to fight, because sickness, malaria, and scurvy had taken a terrible toll on his men. Breckinridge organized his force in two divisions, the first was commanded by Brig. Gen. Ben Hardin Helm, and Col. T.B. Smith, 20th Tennessee; the second division under Brig. Gen. Daniel Ruggles, was composed of the brigades of Col. A. P. Thompson, 3rd Kentucky and Col. H. W. Allen, 4th Louisiana. To these were attached three batteries of artillery, two mounted companies and 250 Partisan rangers.

On August 5, 1862, Breckinridge moved to the attack, with Ruggles deployed on the left of the road from Greenwell Springs to Baton Rouge, and Clark on its right. William's stood to receive the attack, his troops deployed in a single line, with reserves covering the rear of the town. No entrenchments had been dug and the line was open to attack from any direction except the river. From left to right, the Union forces were posted: 4th Wisconsin beyond Baton Grosse; 9th Connecticut next; 14th Maine at the crossing of the Bayou Sara and Greenwell Springs roads on the left of the latter; 21st Indiana on its right; 6th Michigan across the Perkins and Clay Cut roads near the fork; 7th Vermont and the 30th Massachusetts in reserve supporting the center and right.

Ruggles engaged first, then Clark joined the attack. The battle went well at first for the Confederates, but then the Union troops advanced and drove back the Confederates. By 10 o'clock the battle was over and the Union defenders held the city of Baton Rouge. Union losses were 84 killed, 200 wounded, and 33 missing, including Brig. Gen. Thomas Williams. Confederate losses were 84 killed, 315 wounded, and 57 missing. Confederate Brigadier General Charles Clark was severely wounded and was captured, along with three other brigade commanders; Col. Thomas Hunt, Col. H. W. Allen, and Col. A. P. Thompson.

Col. Thompson was later exchanged and given his old command back. Col. Thompson and the 3rd Kentucky infantry were then attached to Buford's Brigade at Jackson, Mississippi and Port Hudson, Louisiana. They were then ordered to Middle Tennessee, but the brigade had its orders changed so that it could face Grierson's raid through Mississippi in April 1863. With Grant's army threatening Vicksburg, Thompson and the brigade fought at Champion Hill where, with the rest of Loring's Division, they were cut off

from Pemberton's army and subsequently joined Confederate Gen. Joseph Johnston's army. During this campaign, Thompson was detached with six of his companies to serve as mounted infantry. With the fall of Vicksburg, Thompson continued to serve in the Mississippi area until March 1864 when his regiment was mounted and he was given command of a brigade of cavalry under Forrest. He was assigned to the Third Brigade, Second Division, Forrest's Cavalry Corps, Army of the Mississippi.

In March 1864, Forrest prepared to attack Paducah, Kentucky. His main objective was to seize the supply depots at Fort Anderson, named after Robert Anderson, Louisville native and commander of Fort Sumter. Fort Anderson was located on the east side of Fourth street and extended from Clay through Trimble Street in downtown Paducah. It was over 400 feet in length, and 160 feet wide, from Fourth Street to the river. It also had a fifty foot trench, with abatis, and 8 mounted cannons, with an array of artillery.

Forrest left Mobile, Alabama and came through Tennessee to western Kentucky, reaching Mayfield, after nightfall on March 24th. He spent the night there, then on the next morning Forrest and his 1,500 cavalrymen rode at double quick pace on the old Mayfield road and arrived at the picket line at Eden's Hill at 2:10 on March 25, 1864. Forrest quickly drove back the Federal pickets. General Abraham Buford joined Forrest's division on the way into the city. Several squads of Federal infantry were captured on Broadway. Col. Thompson reached 15th and Broadway at 3 o'clock, and could see the Federals rushing into the Fort, and wanted to pursue them, but was told to halt because their main objective was ammunition and medical supplies, not prisoners. Col. Thompson was about a mile from the Fort when he ordered his men to dismount. Forrest rode up, and stated that since Col. Thompson and his men were from Paducah, they should be the ones to deliver a message to the Fort. Four men were chosen and they delivered it under a flag of truce to Col. Stephen G. Hicks, of the 40th Illinois, who was commander of Fort Anderson. The message from Forrest ordered Hicks to surrender. Hicks wrote back, saying that he would not surrender. While Forrest was reading the message, shells from the gunboats Peosta and Paw Paw began falling on the city.

Forrest ordered Gen. Buford to cease firing at the parapet, as three unsuccessful attempts had already been made by Buford. Col. Thompson was seated on his horse and surrounded by his staff officers near the alley of Trimble Street between Fifth & Sixth Streets. The sun had gone down by this point. The raid was successful, and the Federal supply depots had been looted. The Confederates who were attacking the Fort, soon fell back about 500 feet. The ditch was impassible around the Fort, and shell and grape shot from the ships and the Fort were inflicting heavy losses.

Gen. Buford ordered Col. Thompson to fall back under cover of a line of houses, where the men could be protected from further Federal fire. Before the order could reach Col. Thompson, a cannonball, which was fired from one of the gunboats, came directly up Trimble Street and hit Col. Thompson. The cannonball hit the pommel of Col. Thompson's saddle and he was literally torn to pieces. The men then fell back to their horses around 8 o'clock. The Federals in the Fort saw them falling back and changed the sights on their cannons to fire on the horses. The Confederates finally were able to leave Paducah at 11 o'clock. Federal losses were 14 killed and 46 wounded. Confederate losses were 11 killed and 39 wounded.

After his death, Thompson was promoted to brigadier general. His monument reads: "Gen. Albert P. Thompson, 3rd Ky. Brigade, C.S.A. Fell at Paducah, March 25, 1864, age 35 years, 22 days." It also says: "In view of home, in the midst of his neighbors, he laid down his life." Also written: "No country ever had a truer son,
"No cause a nobler champion,
"No people a bolder defender,
"No principle a purer victim."
The final words are: "While God keeps his soul, the people for whom he died will cherish and defend his memory."

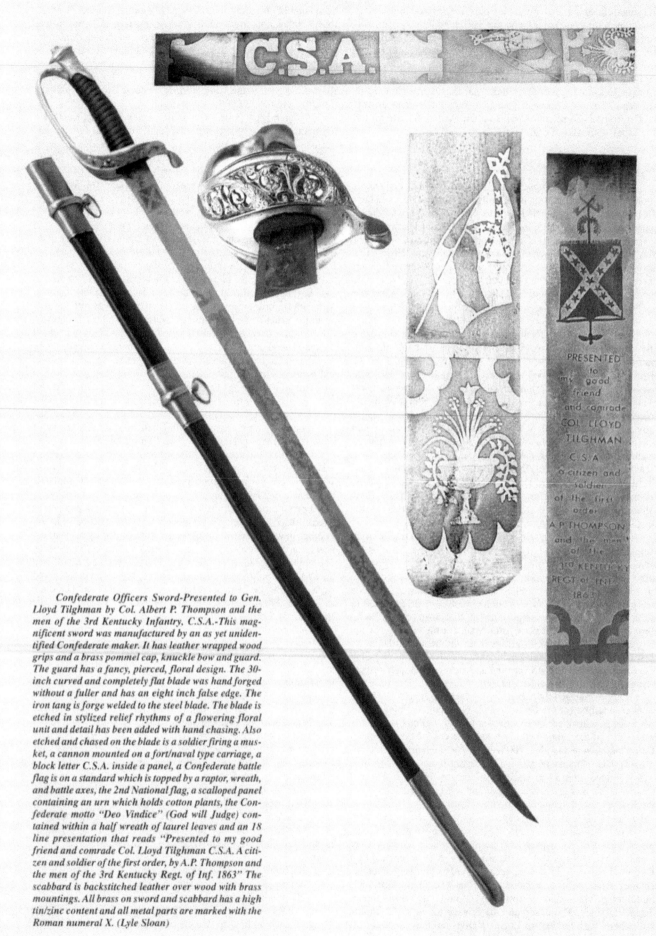

Confederate Officers Sword-Presented to Gen. Lloyd Tilghman by Col. Albert P. Thompson and the men of the 3rd Kentucky Infantry, C.S.A.-This magnificent sword was manufactured by an as yet unidentified Confederate maker. It has leather wrapped wood grips and a brass pommel cap, knuckle bow and guard. The guard has a fancy, pierced, floral design. The 30-inch curved and completely flat blade was hand forged without a fuller and has an eight inch false edge. The iron tang is forge welded to the steel blade. The blade is etched in stylized relief rhythms of a flowering floral unit and detail has been added with hand chasing. Also etched and chased on the blade is a soldier firing a musket, a cannon mounted on a fort/naval type carriage, a block letter C.S.A. inside a panel, a Confederate battle flag is on a standard which is topped by a raptor, wreath, and battle axes, the 2nd National flag, a scalloped panel containing an urn which holds cotton plants, the Confederate motto "Deo Vindice" (God will Judge) contained within a half wreath of laurel leaves and an 18 line presentation that reads "Presented to my good friend and comrade Col. Lloyd Tilghman C.S.A. A citizen and soldier of the first order, by A.P. Thompson and the men of the 3rd Kentucky Regt. of Inf. 1863" The scabbard is backstitched leather over wood with brass mountings. All brass on sword and scabbard has a high tin/zinc content and all metal parts are marked with the Roman numeral X. (Lyle Sloan)

Battle of Shiloh
(Pittsburg Landing)

April 6-7, 1862

"The South never smiled again after Shiloh."-George Washington Cable

Campaign: Federal Penetration up the Cumberland and Tennessee Rivers(1862)

Principal Commanders: Maj. Gen. Ulysses S. Grant and Maj. Gen. Don Carlos Buell (US): Gen. Albert Sidney Johnston and Gen. P.G. T. Beauregard (CS)

Forces Engaged: Army of the Tennessee and Army of the Ohio (65, 900) (U.S.): Army of Mississippi (44,968) (CS)

Order of Battle
Union Forces
Army of the Tennessee
Maj. Gen. Ulysses S. Grant
48,000

First Division: Maj. Gen. John A. McClernand

1st Brigade	2nd Brigade	3rd Brigade
Col. Abraham Hare	Col. C. Marsh	Col. Julius Raith
8th Illinois	11th Illinois	17th Illinois
18th Illinois	20th Illinois	29th Illinois
11th Iowa	45th Illinois	43rd Illinois
13th Iowa	48th Illinois	49th Illinois

Attached

1st Battalion Illinois Cavalry
Stewart's Illinois Cavalry
Battery D, 1st Illinois Artillery
Battery E, 2nd Illinois Artillery
14th Ohio Battery
Battery D, 2nd Illinois Artillery

Second Division: Maj. Gen. W.H. L. Wallace

1st Brigade	2nd Brigade	3rd Brigade
Col. J. Tuttle	Brig. Gen. J. McArthur	Col. T. Sweeny
2nd Iowa	9th Illinois	8th Iowa
7th Iowa	12th Illinois	7th Illinois
12th Iowa	81st Ohio	50th Illinois
14th Iowa	13th Missouri	52nd Illinois
	14th Missouri	57th Illinois
		58th Illinois

Attached

Battery A, 1st Illinois Artillery
Battery D, 1st Missouri Artillery
Battery H, 1st Missouri Artillery
Battery K, 1st Missouri Artillery
2 Companies, U.S. Batttery

Cavalry

2 Companies, 2nd Illinois Cavalry

Third Division: Maj. Gen. L. Wallace

1st Brigade	2nd Brigade	3rd Brigade	Attached
Col. M. Smith	Col. J. Thayer	Col. C. Whittlesey	Bat. I, 1st
11th Indiana	68th Ohio	20th Ohio	Missouri
24th Indiana	23rd Indiana	56th Ohio	9th Indiana Bat.
8th Missouri	1st Nebraska	78th Ohio	5th Ohio Cav.
	58th Ohio	76th Ohio	11th Illinois Cav.

Fourth Division: Maj. Gen. Stephen Hurlbut

1st Brigade	2nd Brigade	3rd Brigade	Attached
Col. N. Williams	Col. J. Veatch	Brig. Gen. J. Lauman	2nd Michigan Bat.
28th Illinois	14th Illinois	31st Indiana	Bat. C, 1st
32nd Illinois	15th Illinois	44th Indiana	Missouri Art.
41st Illinois	46th Illinois	17th Kentucky	13th Ohio Battery
3rd Iowa	25th Indiana	25th Kentucky	5th Ohio Cavalry

Fifth Division: Brig. Gen. William T. Sherman

1st Brigade	2nd Brigade	3rd Brigade	4th Brigade
Col. J. McDowell	Col. D. Stuart	Col. J. Hildebrand	Col. R. Buckland
40th Illinois	55th Illinois	53rd Ohio	48th Ohio
6th Iowa	54th Ohio	57th Ohio	70th Ohio
46th Ohio	71st Ohio	77th Ohio	72nd Ohio

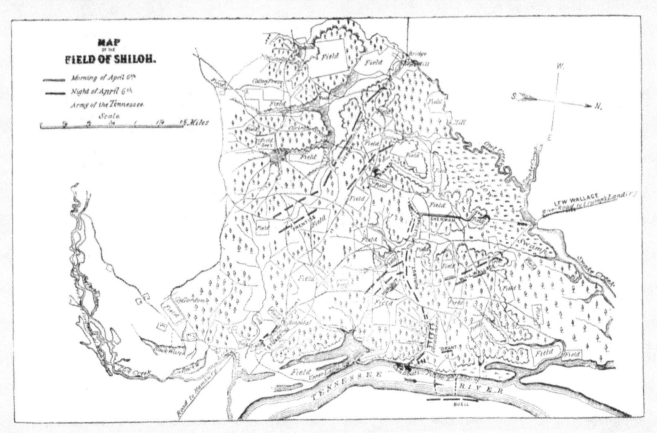

MAP of the FIELD OF SHILOH.

Morning of April 6th
Night of April 6th
Army of the Tennessee.
Scale

General Albert Sidney Johnston   *Gen. P.G.T. Beauregard*

Attached
Battery B, 1st Illinois Artillery
Battery E, 1st Illinois Artillery
6th Indiana Battery
4th Illinois Cavalry
Thielemann's Cavalry

Sixth Division: Brig. Gen. Benjamin Prentiss

1st Brigade	2nd Brigade	Attached
Col. E. Peabody	Col. M. Miller	11th Illinois Cavalry
12th Michigan	61st Illinois	5th Ohio Battery
21st Missouri	18th Missouri	23rd Missouri
25th Missouri	18th Wisconsin	15th Iowa
16th Wisconsin	16th Iowa	1st Minnesota Battery

Unassigned Troops
15th Michigan
14th Wisconsin
8th Ohio Battery
Battery H, 1st Illinois Artillery
Battery I, 1st Illinois Artillery
Battery B, 2nd Illinois Artillery
Battery F, 2nd Illinois Artillery

Army of the Ohio
Maj. Gen. Don Carlos Buell
17,900 men

Second Division: Brig. Gen. Alexander McCook

4th Brigade	5th Brigade	6th Brigade	Artillery
Brig. Gen. L. Rousseau	Col. E. Kirk	Col. W. Gibson	Battery H, 5th
6th Indiana	34th Illinois	32nd Indiana	U.S. Artillery
5th Kentucky	29th Indiana	39th Indiana	
15th U.S.	30th Indiana	15th Ohio	
16th U.S.	77th Pennsylvania	49th Ohio	
19th U.S.			
1st Ohio			

Fourth Division: Brig. Gen. William Nelson

10th Brigade	19th Brigade	22nd Brigade	Attached
Col. J. Ammen	Col. W. Hazen	Col. S. Bruce	2nd Indiana Cav.
36th Indiana	9th Indiana	1st Kentucky	
6th Ohio	6th Kentucky	2nd Kentucky	
24th Ohio	41st Ohio	20th Kentucky	

Fifth Division: Brig. Gen. Thomas Crittenden

11th Brigade	14th Brigade	Artillery
Brig. Gen. J. Boyle	Col. W. Smith	Bat. G, 1st Ohio Art.
9th Kentucky	11th Kentucky	Bat. H, M, 4th U.S. Art.
13th Kentucky	26th Kentucky	(Mendenhall)
19th Ohio	13th Ohio	
59th Ohio		

Sixth Division: Brig. Gen. T. Wood

20th Brigade	21st Brigade
Brig. Gen. J. Garfield	Col. G. Wagner
13th Michigan	15th Indiana

64th Ohio
65th Ohio
40th Indiana
57th Indiana
24th Kentucky

Confederate Forces
Army of Mississippi
Gen. Albert Johnston/Gen. P. G. T. Beauregard
44,968
I Corps: Maj. Gen. Leonidas Polk

First Division: Brig. Gen. Charles Clark

1st Brigade	2nd Brigade
Col. R. Russell	Brig. Gen. A. Stewart
12th Tennessee	13th Arkansas
13th Tennessee	4th Tennessee
22nd Tennessee	5th Tennessee
Bankhead's Tennessee Battery	33rd Tennessee
11th Louisiana	Stanford's Mississippi Battery

Second Division: Brig. Gen. Benjamin Cheatham

1st Brigade	2nd Brigade	Attached
Brig. Gen. B. Johnson	Col. W. Stephens	1st Mississippi Cav.
Blythe's Mississippi Regt.	7th Kentucky	Brewer's Cav. Battalion
2nd Tennessee	1st Tennessee Battalion	
15th Tennessee	6th Tennessee	
154th Tennessee	9th Tennessee	
Polk's Tennessee Battery	Smith's Mississippi Battery	

II Corps: Maj. Gen. Braxton Bragg
First Division: Brig. Gen. Daniel Ruggles

1st Brigade	2nd Brigade	3rd Brigade
Col. R. L. Gibson	Brig. Gen. P. Anderson	Col. P. Pond, Jr.
1st Arkansas	1st Florida Battalion	16th Louisiana
4th Louisiana	17th Louisiana	18th Louisiana
13th Louisiana	20th Louisiana	Crescent Louisiana
19th Louisiana	9th Texas	Regiment
2 Companies,	Confederate Guards	Orleans Guard
Alabama Cav.	Response Battalion	Louisiana Battalion
	Hodgson's Louisiana	38th Tennessee
	Battery	Ketchum's Alabama
		Battery

Second Division: Brig. Gen. Jones M. Withers

1st Brigade	2nd Brigade	3rd Brigade
Brig. Gen. A. H. Gladden	Brig. Gen. J. Chalmers	Brig. Gen. J. Jackson
21st Alabama	5th Mississippi	17th Alabama
22nd Alabama	7th Mississippi	18th Alabama
25th Alabama	9th Mississippi	19th Alabama
26th Alabama	10th Mississippi	2nd Texas
1st Louisiana	51st Tennessee	Girardey's Georgia
Robertson's Florida Bat.	52nd Tennessee	Bat.
	Gage's Alabama Bat.	47th Tennessee
		1st Corps Cavalry,
		Clanton's
		Alabama Regiment

III Corps: Maj. Gen. William Hardee

1st Brigade	2nd Brigade	3rd Brigade
Brig. Gen. T. Hindman	Brig. Gen. P. Cleburne	Brig. Gen. S. Wood
2nd Arkansas	15th Arkansas	16th Alabama
6th Arkansas	6th Mississippi	8th Arkansas
7th Arkansas	2nd Tennessee	9th Arkansas
3rd Confederate	5th Tennessee	3rd Mississippi Battn.
Swett's Mississippi Battery	23rd Tennessee	27th Tennessee
Miller's Tennessee Battery	24th Tennessee	44th Tennessee
Trigg's Arkansas Battery	Hubbard's Arkansas	Calvert's Arkansas
Harper's Mississippi Battery	Battery	Battery
		55th Tennessee
		Georgia Dragoons
		7th Alabama

Reserve Corps: Brig. Gen. John C. Breckinridge

1st (Orphan) Brigade	2nd Brigade	3rd Brigade
Col. R. Trabue	Brig. Gen. J. Bowen	Col. W. Statham
31st Alabama	9th Arkansas	15th Mississippi
3rd Kentucky	10th Arkansas	22nd Mississippi

4th Kentucky	2nd Confederate	19th Tennessee
5th Kentucky	1st Missouri	20th Tennessee
6th Kentucky	Hudson's Mississippi Bat.	28th Tennessee
Crew's Tennessee Batn.	Beltzhoover's Louisiana Bat.	45th Tennessee
Cobb's Kentucky Bat.	Thompson's Kentucky Cav.	Rutledge's Tennessee Bat.
Byrne's Bat.		Forrest's Tennessee Cav.
4th Alabama Bat.		
Morgan's Kentucky Cavalry		

Unassigned Troops
Wharton's Texas Cavalry Regiment
Adam's Mississippi Regiment
McClung's Tennessee Battery
Robert's Arkansas Battery
Clanton's 1st Alabama Cavalry

Lieutenant General Alex P. Stewart   *Lieutenant General B. F. Cheatham*

Once Fort Henry and Fort Donelson had been taken, Grant was free to move into Tennessee. Grant arrived at Pittsburgh Landing in March. Henry Halleck, Commander of all forces in the West, ordered Don Carlos Buell's army at Nashville to join Grant at Pittsburg Landing, and then to attack Corinth, Mississippi. Confederate Gen. Albert Sidney Johnston concentrated his forces at Corinth to oppose Grant. By the end of March, he had 44,000 men, commanded by Lt. Gen. Leondias Polk, Maj. Gen. John Breckinridge, Gen. Braxton Bragg and Maj. Gen. William Hardee. They would be facing Ulysses Grant's 39,000 men. Johnston knew that he must attack Grant before Buell's 36,000 men reached Pittsburg Landing. Grant was not expecting an attack, so no defensive plans were formulated and no trenches or earthworks were dug. Sherman set up his headquarters at a place called Shiloh Church. Since Grant assumed that there would be no attack, he placed Sherman's raw recruits in the advance position. Because of rain, and a lost division under Bragg, Johnston was not able to reach Pittsburg Landing until April 6th.

Johnston's troops were now less than two miles from the Federal camps. At 5:00 a.m. on Sunday morning, April 6, 1862, Union Maj. James Powell of the 25th Missouri and 300 men scouted the area, and collided with Confederate Maj. Aaron Hardcastle's 3rd Mississippi Infantry Battalion, the advance guard of Wood's brigade, Hardee's Corps. The Confederates began to fire, and the Federals under Powell stood their ground as reinforcements were brought up. Jesse Appler of the 53rd Ohio, deployed his men, but soon fell back before the massive Confederate onslaught. Cleburne now began to advance, his goal being to seize the crossroads at Shiloh Church. Braxton Bragg moved up to support William Hardee. Grant now called for Buell's troops, who had arrived in Savannah the day before, and were on the east

War log from a farm near Shiloh with an unexploded six pound Bormann shell embedded in the heart of the log with several mini balls surrounding it. For a century, the lumber industry in the South was plagued by shells embedded in logs, and many saw blades were ruined by cutting into them. War logs are becoming extremely scarce. (BCWM)

bank of the river. Grant also called for Lew Wallace to get his men ready to move out. At 9:00 a.m., Grant rode from his headquarters to the front. By 10:00 a.m., the Confederates had driven through the camps of three Union divisions, sending the surprised blue-clad soldiers reeling back toward the river. Union General Benjamin M. Prentiss' division was pushed back almost a mile. The Confederates now stopped at Prentiss' camp and began to eat the food that Prentiss' men had been cooking for their breakfast. This gave Prentiss time to take up a good defensive position on high ground along a sunken road. About 1,000 men formed along the road, which was about a mile behind their original position. Other units formed on either side of Prentiss: Hurlbut sent two brigades on his left, and W.H. L. Wallace aligned three brigades on Prentiss' flanks, two on Prentiss' right and one to his far left, beyond Hurlbut. To the right of Wallace were two brigades of McClernand's division and then Sherman's division. These troops made a desperate attempt to slow the Confederate advance. Union General Ulysses Grant looked over the new line and ordered Prentiss to "maintain that position at all hazards."

Cheatham's division now advanced upon the new Federal line, and when they came within 150 yards, the Federals unleashed their artillery. At 30 yards, Union Col. William Shaw and his 14th Iowa, fired at the oncoming Confederates. The Confederate line fell back. On Cheatham's extreme right, Union Brigadier General Jacob Lauman's brigade of Hurlbut's division, took on the Confederates. His men opened fire on the Rebels at 100 yards, but the Confederates approached until they were within 10 yards of the 31st Indiana before they were stopped. The Rebel troops under Braxton Bragg continued crashing and screaming through the woods, toward the Federal position. Bragg ordered the 4th, 13th, and the 19th Louisiana and the 1st Arkansas to attack the Federals on the sunken road. Charge after charge, twelve in all, were made against Prentiss' position, and each was repulsed with great slaughter. "It's a hornet's nest in there!" cried the Rebels, recoiling from the blasts of canister and case shot and the fire from the 8th Iowa's eight hundred rifles. By 2:30 p.m., after two hours of fighting, the Confederates were no closer to taking the Federal lines at the Hornet's Nest than they were at the Sunken Road, and the Confederate onslaught began to grind to a halt. There were massive problems on the field. There was no overall Confederate commander, and no coherent plan of attack. The Confederates had 17,000 men against Grant's 4,000 men under Prentiss, but the Confederate troops were sent in piecemeal. Orders were given and then countermanded by different generals. At some points along the line Confederate companies halted because there were no further orders for them. Beauregard was in the rear and did not know what was going on at the front and only sent men where he heard fighting. Corps commanders reduced themselves to small unit commanders.

A Confederate attack led by Gen. Albert Sidney Johnston broke through Union troops in the Peach Orchard on Prentiss' left, led by the Kentucky troops under Gen. John C. Breckinridge, and the Rebels pushed back the troops on his right, leaving what was left of Prentiss's division without support. Johnston led the Kentucky Confederate troops toward the Peach Orchard, but about halfway there he was struck in the leg by a bullet that severed a major artery and the blood was flowing into his boot. Johnston soon became disoriented and dismounted. Johnston had a field tourniquet in his pocket, but his officer's didn't know how to use it, and earlier in the battle he had sent his personal surgeon, Dr. Yandell away to tend to the wounded soldiers. Gen. Johnston soon bled to death.

After Albert Sidney Johnston's death, Gen. P.G.T. Beauregard took command of the Rebel forces. Beauregard now was obsessed with the Hornet's Nest also. He could have gone to the flanks, and driven the Federals right into the river at Pittsburg Landing, but he chose not to. Beauregard soon massed the largest assembly of cannons in the War up to that point, 62 in all, and he aimed them at point blank range at the Hornet's Nest and the Sunken Road. At about 4:00 p.m., he began a bombardment with shell and canister that was like "a mighty hurricane sweeping everything before it." The Hornet's Nest exploded under the fire, but still Prentiss and his men held on, their lines bending back into a horseshoe shape as more and more pressure was applied to their flanks. By 5:30 they were completely surrounded and being attacked on all sides. Unable to do any more to obey Grant's order to hold his position, Prentiss ordered cease-fire and surrendered his remaining 2,200 men at 6:00 p.m. However, his gallant defense had given Grant the time he needed to construct a new line to the rear. Grant's new line ran inland at a right angle from the river above Pittsburgh Landing northwest toward Owl Creek. The line was three miles long and strongly defended. Col. J.D. Webster grouped cannons on the left of the line while Sherman and McClernand protected a road that ran north parallel to the Tennessee River. Lew Wallace arrived at 7:00 p.m. and set up at the far right of the new line. Col. Jacob Ammen's brigade, from Buell's corps arrived. The division commander, Brig. Gen. William Nelson and his men followed Ammen's brigade across the river and took their positions on Grant's new line.

The Confederates had been fighting for 12 hours and were exhausted and hungry, having not eaten since 3:00 a.m. that morning. Many of the Confederates refused to go on and sat down in the abandoned Federal camps and began to eat. Most of the Confederates believed they had won a great victory and thought they had beaten most of the Union forces. Bragg and Polk tried to rally the men for one more attack before darkness set in. Bragg, on the left, could only gather Chalmers troops and John Jackson's men, who were already out of ammunition. Bragg's two divisions tried to rush the new line, but Federal artillery ripped Bragg's men to pieces. Polk and Hardee, on the right, fought with Sherman's and McClernand's troops, but were not successful in capturing any of them. As twilight settled, Beauregard suspended the assault on the Federals, and recalled Polk and Bragg.

During the night, Nathan Bedford Forrest's cavalry scouted the Federal lines. Forrest reported to Hardee that Grant now had about 45,000 men, against their 20,000 Confederates. Grant decided that he would attack the Confederates the next day.

On April 7th, the Union forces rolled forward at about 7:30 a.m. and the outnumbered Confederates were pushed back. Grant took back most of the ground he had lost the previous day. Cleburne

put up some resistance around Shiloh Church leading an attack on Sherman's men, but his soldiers became entangled in the thick undergrowth, and soon his lines were decimated by the Federals. Confederate Brigadier General Sterling A. M. Wood tried to hold Shiloh Church, but his left was crumbling and as his flanks became exposed to Federal fire, he pulled back. At 2:30 p.m., Beauregard ordered a withdrawal to Corinth. An hour later, the Confederates began to withdraw. The Union troops were just as exhausted as the Confederates and did not pursue them. On April 8th, Nathan Bedford Forrest's cavalry, the rear guard for the Confederates, was overtaken by Sherman's skirmishers. Forrest led a charge against them, but outdistanced his men in the process and soon realized that he was alone against 2,000 Federals, all aiming their rifles at him. Forrest was shot in the side by a Federal soldier. The bullet lodged against Forrest's spine, but somehow he managed to pick up a Federal soldier and use him as a shield and ride back to his own lines. Forrest was the last man to be injured in the Battle of Shiloh, the first great bloody battle of the war. Union losses were 13,047. Confederate losses were 10,694. Halleck arrived at Pittsburgh Landing on April 11th, and removed Grant from field command. Halleck personally organized the army into a 100,000 man force, with 200 cannons, and arrived on the outskirts of Corinth on May 28th. Beauregard, outnumbered two to one, tried to trick Halleck into thinking that Confederates had more men than they actually had, by sending trains in and out of Corinth. Each time the train arrived the townspeople and soldiers would give a great cheer as if a new train load of soldiers had arrived. The ruse worked well and bought Beauregard enough time to safely escort his men out of town. On May 30th, the Federals entered a deserted Corinth and seized the Memphis & Charleston Railroad. Confederate President Jefferson Davis said "this railroad was the vertebra of the West," and now it was in Federal hands. The Battle of Shiloh will go down as the ninth most costly battle of the Civil War.

The jacket has ball buttons attached and the crimson red color is indicative of many of the pre-war and militia units. The belt is a early 1840 style militia belt. This coat was found in Northern Florida and probably saw use in the Western theater. (BCWM)

BATTLE OF CORINTH, MISSISSIPPI

October 3-4, 1862
"The enemy was finally driven back in great slaughter." Gen. Ulysses S. Grant

Campaign: Iuka and Corinth Operations (1862)
Principal commanders: Maj. Gen. William S. Rosecrans (US); Maj. Gen. Earl Van Dorn (CS)
Forces Engaged: Army of the Mississippi (US); Army of West Tennessee (CS)

Order of Battle
Union Forces
Army of the Mississippi

Maj. Gen. William Rosecrans
Second Division: Brig. Gen. David Stanley

1st Brigade	2nd Brigade
Col. J. Fuller	**Col. J. Mower**
27th Ohio	26th Illinois
39th Ohio	47th Illinois
43rd Ohio	5th Minnesota
63rd Illinois	11th Missouri
Illinois Cavalry, Jenk's Company	8th Wisconsin
Michigan Light Artillery, 3rd Battery	Iowa Light Artillery, 2nd Battery
Wisconsin Light Artillery, 8th Battalion	
2nd U.S. Artillery, Battery F	

Third Division: Brig. Gen. Charles Hamilton

1st Brigade	2nd Brigade	Cavalry Division
Brig. Gen. N. Buford	**Brig. Gen. J. Sullivan**	**Col. J. Mizner**
48th Indiana	Col. S. Holmes	7th Illinois
59th Indiana	56th Illinois	11th Illinois

White Confederate linen shell jacket with single pocket and coin buttons. These coats were used during the summer campaigns and were used extensively in the Western Theater. The clip cornered 1840 militia belt was found with the uniform and belonged to J. Prentice. Pvt. J. Prentice, Co. K, 1st Ark. Vols. He enlisted on 7-21-1862 at Evening Shade, Arkansas and served in Co. F, 38th Ark., Trans-Mississippi Department. He was captured on Sept. 18, 1863 at Benton, Ark. and sent to prison at Alton, Ill. on Sept. 29, 1864. While in prison he enlisted in the 5th U.S. Vol. Infantry becoming a "Galvanized Yankee".

At right: Prentice wearing white linen shell jacket. (BCWM)

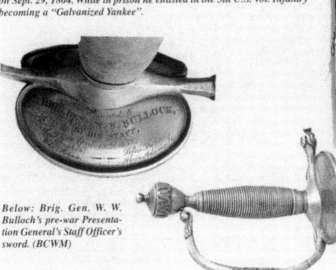

Below: Brig. Gen. W. W. Bulloch's pre-war Presentation General's Staff Officer's sword. (BCWM)

5th Iowa	10th Iowa	2nd Iowa
4th Minnesota	17th Iowa	7th Kansas
26th Missouri	10th Missouri	3rd Michigan
1st Missouri Light	24th Missouri, Company F	5th Ohio,
Artillery, Battery M	80th Ohio	Company E, H, I, K
Ohio Light Artillery,	Wisconsin Light Artillery, 6th Battery	
11th Battery	Wisconsin Light Artillery, 12th Battery	

Unattached
64th Illinois (Yate's Sharpshooters)
1st U.S. Artillery, Batteries A, B, C, D, H, and I (Siege Artillery)

Army of West Tennessee
Second Division
Brig. Gen. Thomas Davies

1st Brigade	2nd Brigade	3rd Brigade
Brig. Gen. P. Hackelman	Brig. Gen. R. Oglesby	Col. S. Baldwin
Col. T. Sweeny	Col. A. Mersy	Col. J. V. Du Bois
52nd Illinois	9th Illinois	7th Illinois
58th Illinois (detachment)	12th Illinois	50th Illinois
2nd Iowa	22nd Ohio	57th Illinois
7th Iowa	81st Ohio	
8th Iowa (detachment)		
12th Iowa (detachment)		
14th Iowa (detachment)		

Artillery
Maj. G. Stone
1st Missouri Light Artillery, Battery D
1st Missouri Light Artillery, Battery H
1st Missouri Light Artillery, Battery I
1st Missouri Light Artillery, Battery K

Unattached
14th Missouri (Western Sharpshooters)

Sixth Division: Brig. Gen. Thomas McKean

1st Brigade	2nd Brigade	3rd Brigade
Col. B. Allen	Col. J. Oliver	Col. M. Crocker
Brig. Gen. J. McArthur	Illinois Cav., Ford's Co.	11th Iowa
21st Missouri	15th Michigan	13th Iowa
16th Wisconsin	18th Missouri, Companies	15th Iowa
17th Wisconsin	A, B , C, E	16th Iowa
	14 Wisconsin	
	18th Wisconsin	

Artillery
Capt. Hickenlooper
2nd Illinois Light Artillery, Battery F
Minnesota Light Artillery, 1st Battery
Ohio Light Artillery, 3rd Battery
Ohio Light Artillery, 5th Battery
Ohio Light Artillery, 10th Battery

Confederate Forces
Army Of West Tennessee
Maj. Gen. Earl Van Dorn
Price's Corps: Maj. Gen. Sterling Price

Herbert's Division

1st (Gate's) Brigade	2nd Brigade	3rd (Green's) Brigade
1st Missouri Cavalry	Col. B. Colbert	Brig. Gen. Green
2nd Missouri Inf.	3rd Louisiana Inf.	4th Missouri Inf.
3rd Missouri Inf.	3rd Texas Cavalry	6th Missouri Inf.
5th Missouri Inf.	1st Texas Legion	3rd Missouri Cavalry
16th Arkansas Inf.	14th Arkansas Regt.	7th Mississippi Batn.
Wade's Battery	17th Arkansas Regt.	Landis Battery
	40th Mississippi Regt.	43rd Mississippi Regt.
	Saint Louis Battery	Guibor's Battery
	Clark Battery	

4th Brigade
Col. R. McLain
36th Mississippi Regiment
37th Mississippi Regiment
38th Mississippi Regiment
37th Alabama Regiment
Luca's Battery

Maury's Division

Moore's Brigade	Cabell's Brigade	Phifer's Brigade
42nd Alabama	18th Arkansas Regt.	6th Texas Cav.
Lyle's (Arkansas) Regt.	19th Arkansas Regt.	9th Texas Cav.
35th Mississippi Regt.	20th Arkansas Regt.	3rd Arkansas Cav.
Boone's (Arkansas) Regt.	21st Arkansas Regt.	Stirman's S.S.*
2nd Texas Regiment	Rapley's Battalion S.S.*	McNally's Battery
Bledsoe's Battery	Appeal Battery	
	Jones (Arkansas) Battalion	

Action at Hatchie or Davis Bridge	Cavalry Brigade	Reserve Batteries
6th Texas Cavalry	Adam's Cavalry	Sengstak's Battery
9th Texas Cavalry	Slemon's Cavalry	Hoxton's Battery
3rd Arkansas Cavalry		
Stirman's S.S.*		
McNally's Battery		

District of the Mississippi
First Division: Maj. Gen. Mansfield Lovell

1st Brigade	2nd Brigade	3rd Brigade	Cavalry Brigade
Brig. Gen. Rust	Brig. Gen. J. Villepigue	Brig. Gen. J.Bowen	Col. Jackson
4th Alabama Batn.	33rd Mississippi	6th Mississippi	1st Mississippi
31st Alabama	39th Mississippi	15th Mississippi	7th Tennessee
35th Alabama	(*) Not all units	22nd Mississippi	
9th Arkansas	reported in from this	Mississippi Battalion	
3rd Kentucky	brigade	1st Missouri	
7th Kentucky		Watson's Louisiana Battery	
Hudson's Mississippi Battery			

Battalion of Louisiana Zouvaes
Maj. Dupiere

*sharpshooter

There were two sizeable Confederate forces moving in on Corinth, Mississippi. The first was at Holly Springs, Mississippi about 50 miles west of Corinth and the other was at Tupelo, about the same distance to the south. The force at Tupelo, led by Sterling Price, seized Iuka on September 14th. Iuka was a supply depot for the Federals. Grant immediately ordered Rosecrans and Ord to march on Iuka; if they could trap Price, they could destroy his 17,000 man army before it could link up with 10,000 Confederates under Maj. Gen. Earl Van Dorn. Ord came in from the north at Iuka, Rosecrans came from the south. Ord was to engage only when he heard Rosecrans troops engaging the Confederates from the south. Rosecrans assaulted the Confederates on September 19th. Grant was with Ord's men. Because of an odd atmospheric occurrence called acoustic shadow, Grant and Ord never heard Rosecrans battling the Confederates. At 2:30 p.m., Price sent Brig. Gen. Henry Little to charge Rosecrans position. Little seized the Federal guns of the 11th Ohio Battery, and overwhelmed and put to flight the 80th Ohio Infantry. Price then ordered Little to send forward his entire division, but Little was killed by a Yankee bullet before he could give the order. The confusion caused by Little's death allowed Rosecrans to deploy the bulk of his men. The Federals recaptured the guns of the 11th Ohio Battery but were again driven off. Darkness ended the battle. The Federals lost 825 men, 141 killed. The Confederates lost 693, with 86 dead. Price slipped away during the night and linked up with Van Dorn.

Corinth was defended by two sets of earthworks that guarded the northern approach to town. Confederate Maj. Gen. Earl Van Dorn's 22,000 men left Chewalla, Tennessee, at dawn, on Oct. 3, 1862. Marching 10 miles south to Corinth, Mississippi, they assaulted Maj. Gen. William Rosecrans, 23,000 Federals in these works. The Confederates, a combined command of Van Dorn's and Maj. Gen. Sterling Price's troops, intended to take the town, regain control of the Mobile and Ohio and Memphis and Charleston Railroads, and organize an invasion of Tennessee. At the least, the Federals would be diverted from Gen. Braxton Bragg's preparations to invade Kentucky.

Van Dorn believed Rosecrans thought that the Confederates were moving against Northern railroad lines. Rosecrans, unsure of Confederate intent, recalled all his troops within the Corinth lines. Van Dorn's attack, calculated as a surprise, depended on three divisions, under Brig. Gen. Dabney Maury, Brig. Gen. Louis Hebert and Maj. Gen.

Major General Earl Van Dorn

Mansfield Lovell, rushing the town's western works on a broad front and carrying them by shock.

Driving in Union pickets, Confederates lines were formed with Lovell's division on the right and Maury's and Hebert's on the left. As the Federals approached the pickets, three earthquake tremors occurred, frightening the troops. Van Dorn, conscious of his men's morale, urged commanders to show firmness in the assault.

Federals manned a chain of field forts on Corinth's western perimeter. A four hundred yard expanse of felled timber surrounded them. Corinth sat over a half mile to the rear, surrounded by a second fortified line. Rosecrans posted only half his troops in the works. When a brigade of skirmishers rushed into the lines on October 3rd, crying that Confederates were about to attack, the defenders were ill prepared for the massive attack that ensued. Lovell's three divisions of Confederates crashed into the Union works, manned by Brig. Gen. Thomas Davies Federal division.

Confederates dressed ranks in the fallen timber, rushed forward, carried the works, and drove the Federals toward their interior lines. All three of Davies brigade commanders were wounded, Brig. Gen. Pleasant Hackelman would later die of his wounds. Van Dorn's troops pursued, but 90 degree heat, fatigue, and water shortages slowed them. An hour's halt was called for rest, allowing the Federals to reinforce a second line outside the interior fortifications. A renewed Confederate assault failed. Rosecrans men, holding a compact front, gave stiffer resistance. As daylight faded, Van Dorn consulted with Price, and the battle was stopped. Lovell had performed poorly in the October 3rd fighting. Price claimed that a reliable performance from him might have made a last assault successful.

At 10:00 a.m., the battle would resume, with Hebert attacking and flanking the Union right and, at the same time Maury was to rush on the Union center, and Lovell would advance from the southwest to roll up the Union left. Three artillery batteries on high ground west of town would soften up the yankees. But at 4 a.m., the Confederate cannons were smothered by heavier Union guns. Hebert reported sick after his advance was delayed, and his replacement, Brig. Gen. Martin E. Green, lost an hour fumbling with instructions. Maury's unsupported troops escalated their skirmishing with the Federals to pitched proportions, bringing enemy artillery fire down on Confederate positions. The Southerner's center advanced and Green's division followed.

At 9:30 Lovell's troops skirmished but did not move forward. He never appeared at the front or ordered an attack. Maury's and Green's men fought into the Federal lines, Maury's piercing them

and charging into Corinth itself. Without Lovell's support on the south, the breakthrough was thrown back by the Union troops. Confederates in Col. W. H. Moore's brigade managed to break through the Federal line, capture a redoubt and overrun a battery. The 20th Arkansas fought in the streets of Corinth until their colonel was killed. They were soon cut off, and caught in a crossfire by Union troops. Rosecrans soon regained his lost ground, and by 11:30 a.m., the fighting was over.

On the Con-federate's right-center, Confederate Brigadier General John Moore led five regiments against Battery Robinett. Col. William P. Rogers, commander of the 2nd Texas, was in the vanguard of the assault. The Southern troops briefly took possession of the work. Rogers was killed, and three of Moore's regimental commanders had fallen. A counterattack by four Federal regiments recaptured the battery, and the Confederates fled to the rear.

By noon, the Confederates had withdrawn toward the road north to Chewalla. Nearly a third of those engaged in the October 4th fighting were casualties. Lovell's division reported few. Rosecran's troops, badly shaken, did not pursue. A two day Confederate retreat took Van Dorn's troops to Ripley.

Rosecrans lost nearly 2,500 killed and wounded in the two day fight. Confederates lost 2,470 dead and wounded, and another 1,763 missing in battle or deserted during the retreat to Ripley, both Hebert and Lovell were relieved of command weeks later.

Lt. Col. W. W. Bullock's Sword, Commander of the 30th Massachusetts Infantry.

Inscription on sword reads: "Presented to Brig. Gen. W.W. Bullock by his staff, April 29, 1858. Axil Dearborn-Solon Fisher-John Moran-Alvin Adams, Jr.

Lt. Col. William Bullock fought in some of the less familiar battles that took place in the West. His Regiment's movements were in large part in conjunction with the Vicksburg Campaign, under Gen. Ulysses S. Grant. The battles in which Bullock was involved played an important part in securing the waterways and the roads leading into Louisiana, allowing the Union forces to deeply penetrate the heartland of the Confederacy. Bullock and the 30th Massachusetts played a vital role in securing Louisiana for the Federal troops, and helped to divert Confederate forces away from Vicksburg.

William W. Bullock was born in 1819. He was 5' 5", and weighed about 150 pounds. He served during the Mexican War as a brigadier general commanding a Massachusetts Militia unit. On March 7, 1862, at the age of 43, William Bullock became a lieutenant colonel and was made commander of the 30th Massachusetts Infantry by Gov. Andrew of Massachusetts. Bullock signed up for three years, and was mustered in Boston, Massachusetts. He was assigned to command Fort Macomb, Department of the Gulf. Fort Macomb was located on the south or west bank of the Chef Menteur Pass, a winding water connection between Lake Pontchartrain on the north, to Lake Borgen and the Gulf of Mexico on the south. Fort Macomb was occupied by the Federals on April 25th, 1862, when Confederate Col. C. A. Fuller commanding the 1st Regiment of Regular Artillery of Louisiana ordered Capt. Capers to destroy the guns and evacuate Fort Macomb. Bullock was not in command of the fort for very long. On April 15th, his regiment was immediately sent to participate in the operations against Forts St. Phillip and Jackson on the Mississippi River. He stayed in the area until April 28, 1862. The 30th Massachusetts then moved to New Orleans on April 29-30. On May 1st, they occupied New Orleans, and on May 9-10, made an expedition on the New Orleans & Jackson Railroad. Bullock and his men then moved to Baton Rouge on May 30-31, and led an expedition from Baton Rouge between June 7-9. They then joined Brig. Gen. Thomas Williams expedition to Vicksburg, Mississippi, and operations in that vicinity, on June 18th through July 23rd., Ellis Cliff on June 22nd and Hamilton Plantation, near Grand Gulf, on June 24th. Returning to Baton Rouge on July 23-26, they performed duties there until August 21st, when they were involved in the Battle of Baton Rouge on August 5, 1862.

The Confederate forces under Maj. Gen. John C. Breckinridge attacked Baton Rouge with 5,000 men. He picked up another 1,000 men when Brig. Gen. Daniel Ruggles joined his force. The Rebel force at Baton Rouge was about 2,500 men under Brig. Gen. Thomas Williams. Shortly after daylight, Breckinridge moved to the attack, as Ruggles deployed on the left of the road from Greenwell Springs to Baton Rouge, Brig. Gen. Charles Clark deployed on its right. Williams' troops were strung out in a single line, with reserves covering the rear of the town. No attempt had been made to entrench. Because of the lay of the land, their line of battle was open to attack from any direction except the river. Williams' troops were deployed from left to right: 4th Wisconsin beyond Bayou Grosse; 9th Connecticut next; 14th Maine at the crossing of the Bayou Sara and Greenwell Springs roads on the left of the latter; 21st Indiana on its right; 6th Michigan across the Perkins and Clay Cut Roads near the fork; 7th Vermont and 30th Massachusetts in reserve supporting the center and right; the batteries from left to right, Manning, Everett, Nims, with Brown in reserve.

Ruggles soon was engaged and Clark quickly followed. They managed to push back the Union troops and took Brown's two guns, which were captured by the 4th Louisiana, but were retaken by the 6th Michigan. Williams reformed his lines. The 21st Indiana and the 6th Michigan were moved onto the line of battle. The 9th Connecticut moved to the flank to support the left. The 30th Massachusetts covered the interval on the left of the 6th Michigan, and the 4th Wisconsin went to assist the 14th Maine, which was currently engaging Clark's Confederate forces. The Union troops advanced, the Confederates were driven back, and by 10 o'clock the battle was over. Union forces lost 84 killed, 200 wounded, 33 missing, in all 317. Among the Union killed was Col. George Roberts, 7th Vermont, and Brig. Gen. Thomas Williams, who was hit in the chest by a minie ball, just after giving the final order to attack. The Confederates lost 84 killed, 315 wounded, 57 missing for a total of 456. Brig. Gen. Charles Clark was severely wounded and taken prisoner. Also wounded and captured were Col. Thomas Hunt, Col. A.P. Thompson, and Col. H.W. Allen.

By August 20th, the Union troops, including Bullock and the 30th Massachusetts, evacuated Baton Rouge and proceeded to Carrolton, just above New Orleans, where Bullock's men and other units set to work to extend and strengthen the Confederates old line and put everything in good condition for defense. On November 4th, Bullock's men did garrison duty at New Orleans until January 13, 1863. On January 13-14, the regiment moved to Baton Rouge, Louisiana. While on his expedition to Port Hudson on March 7-27, Lt. Col. Bullock was taken ill and was laid up for some time in Baton Rouge, Louisiana. During his sickness, Bullock formed an obstruction in his nasal passage which made his right eye water, and his right nostril was very inflamed and painful. Bullock and his men were exposed to severe hardships in the camps and bivouacs. His condition worsened when he was further exposed to the elements while marching with his men. He rejoined the regiment and made operations against Port Hudson, on May 12-24. On May 13, 1863, the 30th Massachusetts was involved in a fairly large skirmish at Merritt's Plantation. The 30th Massachusetts commanded by Lt. Col. W. W. Bullock; Col. Benjamin Grierson, commanding the 6th and 7th Illinois Cavalry; the 2nd Louisiana Volunteers; four pieces of artillery of Arnold's Battery, Col. Paine commanding; 161st New York Volunteers, commanded by Col. Harrower; six companies of the 174th New York Volunteers, commanded by Lt. Col. Gott, and Capt. Godfrey's Cavalry were marching on the Bayou Sara road leading to Newport. The column proceeded unmolested until they reached the road running from Clinton plank road to Port Hudson. A skirmish broke out with Grierson's cavalry and the enemy's pickets. Capt. Pierce of the 60th Illinois Cavalry, Company A, was ordered to destroy

the railroad tracks along the road. He managed to destroy 300 yards of track and the telegraph wires. Col. Grierson then found 200 cattle under Confederate guard. Grierson charged the Confederates and seized the cattle. Later that evening Grierson destroyed a Confederate cavalry camp. Another skirmish was fought on the Port Hudson road and the 30th Massachusetts was ordered to cover the roads and hold them.

On May 19, 1863, Bullock was awakened at night when an alarm went up on the picket line at Merritt's Plantation. He immediately formed his men and began to advance. He injured his groin when he strained himself by jumping a ditch during the advance. Bullock was unable to do much for several days, and complained that the pain in his groin intensified on long marches and he would fatigue easily. It was more than obvious that Bullock had ruptured a groin muscle. Bullock's problem with his right eye continued, and it would water profusely, but he remained with his regiment.

On May 23, 1863, the 30th Massachusetts encountered Confederate forces at Plain's Store. The 30th Massachusetts along with other units, proceed up the Bayou Sara Road to the opening of the first plain, where the advance came upon a large Confederate picket force which was quickly dispersed by Godfrey's Cavalry. The column continued to march until they were near the clearing on the west side of the plains, about three-fourths of a mile from the Plains Store, when a brisk skirmish was opened by Capt. Fiske's and Lt. Johnston's companies of the 30th Massachusetts Volunteers, which were thrown out onto the edge of the woods in front of the enemy's battery position. One section of Light Battery G was placed on the Bayou Sara road and engaged the Rebel batteries for a full half hour. The 18th New York battery was brought up, but could not silence the Rebel battery. Other batteries were placed on the left and right of the road. The 2nd Louisiana Volunteers, with the 161st New York Volunteers moved through the woods on the right towards the Confederate battery. The skirmish fire of these regiments along with three companies of the 30th Massachusetts, drove the Rebels from their position. The rest of the 30th Massachusetts was ordered to move to the front and position near the Plains Store, where they were then ordered to the right flank to support Holcomb's Battery. Holcomb's Battery drove the enemy in their front. The 30th Massachusetts took position on the field, and camped that night on the field they had just taken hours before. During the battle, Lt. Col. Charles Everett of the 2nd Louisiana, and 1st Lt. Norcross of the 30th Massachusetts, were severely wounded.

Bullock's regiment was engaged at the siege of Port Hudson on May 24-July 9. His troops then assaulted Port Hudson on May 27th and June 14th. Port Hudson finally surrendering on July 9th. The regiment then moved to Cox's Plantation, and Donaldsonville on July 12-13. His troops returned to Baton Rouge and stayed in camp from August 1st until September 2nd. Their next assignment was the Sabine Pass Expedition, which was from September 4th through 11th. The 30th moved from Algiers to Brashear City on September 16th, and then to Berwick and to Camp Bisland on September 26th. Bullock's men then participated in the Western Louisiana (Teche) Campaign on October 3rd through November 30th. By this time, Bullock had totally ruptured his right groin muscle and he could hardly stand or march without severe pain. Bullock was finally discharged on November 25, 1863. He returned to his home on 382 Main Street, Charlestown, Middlesex, Massachusetts.

Bullock and the 30th Massachusetts must be commended for their bravery and fortitude. They faced not only the Confederates, but the harsh elements, disease, and malaria that plagued the armies of the Gulf. His unit played a vital role in securing the waterways along the Mississippi, which in turn opened the heart of the Confederacy to Union troops. Bullock not only contributed to this country's history during the Civil War, but also during the Mexican War, and must be included in our history books as one of the unsung heroes of the Western Theatre.

BATTLE OF PERRYVILLE

October 7-8, 1862
"Shiloh Was Nothing Compared To Perryville"-Union Gen. Lovell Rousseau.
Campaign: Confederate Heartland Offensive
Principal Commanders: Maj. Gen. Don Carlos Buell (US); Gen. Braxton Bragg (CS)
Forces engaged: Army of the Ohio (US); Army of Mississippi (CS)

Order of Battle
Union Forces
Army of the Ohio
Maj. Gen. Don Carlos Buell & Maj. Gen. George Thomas
60,000 Men

First Army Corps
Maj. Gen. Alexander McCook
Third Division
Brig. Gen. Lovell Harrison Rousseau

9th Brigade	17th Brigade	28th Brigade
Col. Leonard A. Harris	Col. William H. Lytle	Col. John Starkweather
38th Indiana	42nd Indiana	24th Illinois
2nd Ohio	88th Indiana	79th Pennsylvania
33rd Ohio	15th Kentucky	1st Wisconsin
94th Ohio	3rd Ohio	21st Wisconsin
10th Wisconsin	10th Ohio	Indiana Light Artillery, 4th Battery

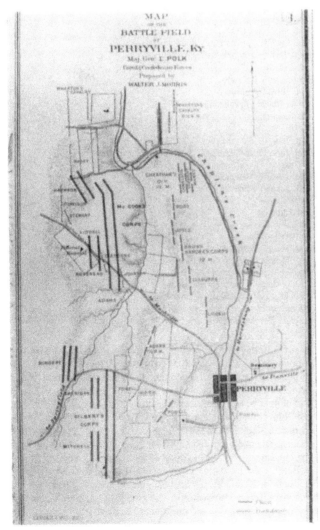

Indiana Light Artillery, 5th Battery	Michigan Light Artillery. 1st Battery	Kentucky Light Artillery, Battery A

Unattached
Col. Buckner Board
2nd Kentucky Cavalry
1st Michigan Engineer & Mechanic

10th Division
Brig. Gen. James S. Jackson

33rd Brigade	34th Brigade
Brig. Gen. William Terrill	Col. George Webster
80th Illinois	80th Indiana
123rd Illinois	50th Ohio
105th Ohio	98th Ohio
Parson' Battery	121st Ohio
	Indiana Light Artillery, 19th Battery

Second Army Corps
Maj. Gen. Thomas Leonidas Crittenden

Fourth Division
Brig. Gen. William Smith

10th Brigade	19th Brigade	22nd Brigade
Col. William Grose	Col. William Hazen	Brig. Gen. Charles Cruft
84th Illinois	110th Illinois	31st Indiana
36th Indiana	9th Indiana	1st Kentucky
23rd Kentucky	6th Kentucky	2nd Kentucky
6th Ohio	27th Kentucky	20th Kentucky
24th Ohio	41st Ohio	90th Ohio
4th U.S. Artillery, Battery H	1st Ohio Light Artillery, Battery F	1st Ohio Light Artillery, Battery B
4th U.S. Artillery, Battery M		2nd Kentucky Cavalry (4 companies)

Fifth Division
Brig. Gen. Horatio P. Van Cleve

11th Brigade	14th Brigade	23rd Brigade
Col. Samuel Beatty	Col. Pierce Hawkins	Col. Stanley Matthews
79th Indiana	44th Indiana	35th Indiana
9th Kentucky	86th Indiana	8th Kentucky
13th Kentucky	11th Kentucky	21st Kentucky
19th Ohio	26th Kentucky	51st Ohio
59th Ohio	13th Ohio	99th Ohio
		Indiana Light Artillery, 7th Battery Pennsylvania Light Artillery, Battery B Wisconsin Light Artillery, 3rd Battery

Sixth Division
Brig. Gen. Thomas Wood

15th Brigade	20th Brigade	21st Brigade
Brig. Gen. Milo Hascall	Col. Charles Harker	Col. George Wagner
100th Illinois	51st Indiana	15th Indiana
17th Indiana	73rd Indiana	40th Indiana
58th Indiana	13th Michigan	57th Indiana
3rd Kentucky	64th Ohio	24th Kentucky
26th Ohio	65th Ohio	97th Ohio (4 Companies)
Indiana Artillery, 8th Batt.	Ohio Artillery, 6th Batt.	Indiana Artillery, 10th Batt.

Col. Edward McCook's Cavalry	Unattached
2nd Indiana	1st Michigan Engineers & Mechanics (4 companies)
1st Kentucky	1st Ohio Cavalry (4 companies)
3rd Kentucky	3rd Ohio Cavalry (4 companies)
7th Pennsylvania	

Third Army Corps
Maj. Gen. Charles Gilbert
First Division
Brig. Gen. Albin Schoepf

1st Brigade	2nd Brigade	3rd Brigade
Col. Moses Walker	Brig. Gen. Speed Fry	Brig. Gen. James Steedman
82nd Indiana	10th Indiana	87th Indiana

12th Kentucky
17th Ohio
31st Ohio
38th Ohio

74th Indiana
4th Kentucky
10th Kentucky
14th Ohio

2nd Minnesota
9th Ohio
35th Ohio
18th U.S.
Michigan Light Artillery, 4th Battery
1st Ohio Light Artillery, Battery C
4th U.S. Battery, Company I

Ninth Division
Brig. Gen. Robert Mitchell

30th Brigade	31st Brigade	32nd Brigade
Col. Michael Gooding	Col. William Carlin	Col. William Caldwell
59th Illinois	21st Illinois	25th Illinois
75th Illinois	38th Illinois	35th Illinois
22nd Indiana	101st Ohio	81st Indiana
Wisconsin Light Artillery, 5th Battery	15th Wisconsin	8th Kansas
	Minnesota Artillery, 2nd Battery	Wisconsin Artillery, 8th Battery
		36th Illinois Cavalry

Eleventh Division
Brig. Gen. Philip Sheridan

35th Brigade	36th Brigade	37th Brigade
Lt. Col. Bernard Laibolt	Col. Daniel McCook	Col. Nicholas Greusel
44th Illinois	85th Illinois	36th Illinois
73rd Illinois	86th Illinois	88th Illinois
2nd Missouri	125th Illinois	21st Michigan
15th Missouri	52nd Ohio	24th Wisconsin
		2nd Illinois Light Artillery, Battery I
		1st Missouri Light Artillery, Battery G

Capt. Ebenezer Gay's Cavalry Brigade
9th Kentucky
2nd Michigan
9th Pennsylvania

Confederate Forces
Army of Mississippi

Gen. Braxton Bragg
15,000 Men
Right Wing
Maj. Gen. Leonidas Polk
First Division
Maj. Gen. Benjamin F. Cheatham

1st Brigade	2nd Brigade	3rd Brigade
Brig. Gen. Daniel S. Donelson	Brig. Gen. Alexander P. Stewart	Brig. Gen. George Maney
8th Tennessee	4th Tennessee	41st Georgia
15th Tennessee	5th Tennessee	1st Tennessee
16th Tennessee	24th Tennessee	6th Tennessee
38th Tennessee	31st Tennessee	9th Tennessee
51st Tennessee	33rd Tennessee	27th Tennessee
Carnes Tennessee Battery	Standford's Mississippi Battery	Turner's Mississippi Battery

4th Brigade
Col. Preston Smith
Escort: 3rd Tennessee Cavalry
12th Tennessee
13th Tennessee
47th Tennessee
154th Tennessee
9th Texas
Capt. J.M. Martin's Florida Light Artillery

Left Wing
Maj. Gen. William Hardee
Second Division
Brig. Gen. James Patton Anderson

1st Brigade	2nd Brigade	3rd Brigade
Brig. Gen. John Calvin Brown	Brig. Gen. Daniel Adams	Col. Samuel Powell

1st Florida
3rd Florida
41st Mississippi
Palmers 14th Georgia Battalion, Battery A

14th Battalion Louisiana Sharpshooters
13th Louisiana
16th Louisiana
20th Louisiana
25th Louisiana
Slocomb's 5th Battery, Company of the Washington Artillery

45th Alabama
1st Arkansas
24th Mississippi
29th Tennessee
Barret's Missouri Battery

4th Brigade
Brig. Gen. Thomas Marshall Jones
27th Mississippi
30th Mississippi
34th Mississippi
Capt. Charles Lumsden's Alabama Battery

Third Division
Maj. Gen. Simon Buckner

1st Brigade	2nd Brigade	3rd Brigade
Brig. Gen. Saint John Liddell	Brig. Gen. Patrick Cleburne	Brig. Gen Bushrod Johnson
2nd Arkansas	2nd Tennessee	5th Confederate
5th Arkansas	35th Tennessee	17th Tennessee
6th Arkansas	48th Tennessee	23rd Tennessee
7th Arkansas	13th/15th Arkansas Consolidated	25th Tennessee
8th Arkansas	Carlton's Texas Sharpshooters	37th Tennessee
Swett's Mississippi Battery	Calvert's Arkansas Battery	44th Tennessee
		Capt. Putnam Darden's Mississippi Battery

4th Brigade
Brig. Gen. Sterling Wood
16th Alabama
32nd Mississippi
33rd Alabama
45th Mississippi
15th Mississippi Battalion Sharpshooters
Capt. Henry Semple's Alabama Battery

1st Cavalry Brigade
Col. John Wharton
1st Kentucky (3 companies)
4th Tennessee
8th Texas
2nd Georgia (5 companies)
Maj. John Davis Tennessee Battalion (4 Companies)

2nd Cavalry Brigade
Col. Joseph Wheeler
1st Alabama
3rd Alabama
6th Confederate
8th Confederate
2nd Georgia Battalion
3rd Georgia (2 or three companies)
1st Kentucky (6 companies)
Lt. Col. James Bennett's Battalion
12th Tennessee Battalion (4 companies)
6th Kentucky (2 or 3 companies)
Georgia Cavalry Battalion (Sumner Smith's Legion)

Confederate General Braxton Bragg and Major General Edmund Kirby Smith met in Chattanooga, Tennessee, July 31, 1862 to plan their invasion of Kentucky. Both Generals were hoping to bring Kentucky into the fold of the Confederacy. Braxton Bragg had high hopes for Kentucky. Kentucky Confederate Calvary General John Hunt Morgan promised that Braxton Bragg would be able to pick up 100,000 men if he entered this state. Bragg was also looking for badly needed supplies. Edmund Kirby Smith was the first to enter the state in August 1862, and was very much supported by the locals, as large crowds came out to greet him. At Lexington, Kentucky, Smith was greeted with Confederate flags waving as he entered the town. The greeting would not be the same for Bragg. Bragg entered the state in areas where Union support was very high. He was hoping to link up with Smith, and then both armies were to march on Louisville. They were trying to get to Louisville before Union General Don Carlos Buell's Ohio Army arrived from Knoxville, Tennessee. Bragg was never able to link up with Smith, and ended up fighting a battle at Munfordville, Kentucky, in September. The battle delayed Bragg long enough to allow Don Carlos Buell to arrive in Louisville first. While in Louisville, Buell picked up recruits and brought his

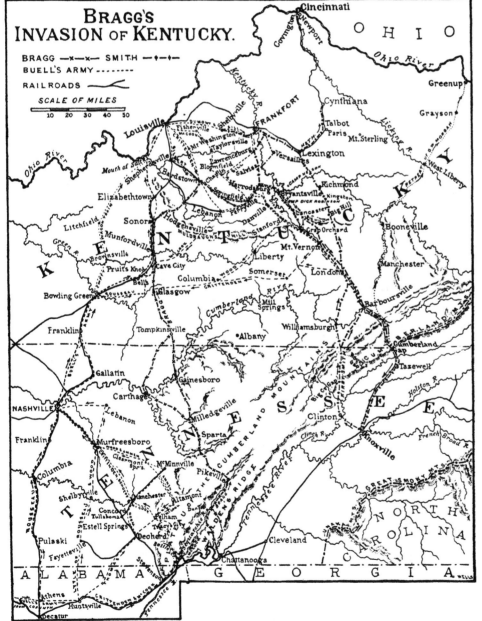

General Braxton Bragg

army to 58,000 men. Bragg had about 15,000 men and Smith had the main army of about 25,000. Buell now secured Louisville and was awaiting Bragg. Buell's job was on the line, and he knew that he had to win a victory, or else. Buell originally did not want the job of commanding the Ohio Army, but the commanding officer before him, Gen. Bull Nelson was killed in the lobby of the Galt House in Louisville by Union General Jeff Davis. Buell got the job by default and was unaware of the true size of Bragg's army.

During the summer of 1862, Kentucky was going through one of its worst droughts ever. Both armies were looking for water sources. Bragg had heard that there was water at the Chaplin River, Doctor's Creek, Bull Run, and Wilson Creek in Perryville, Kentucky. Bragg arrived in Perryville first. William Hardee, along with Simeon Buckner's Division came in from the west along the Springfield road on October 6th. They were falling back from Bardstown, Kentucky and were hoping to settle in at Harrodsburg, Kentucky. Hardee stopped for water in Perryville, thinking that the Union army under Buell was to the north, and was confused when he saw heavy numbers of Union troops traveling along the Springfield Pike. Hardee asked for support and was given two division's from Leonidas Polk's Corps, Patrick Cleburne's and Anderson's. At 3:00 a.m. on October 7th, Anderson moved out with Patrick Cleburne following. Polk commented that the Union force approaching Hardee was not large. He was very wrong.

The Yankee force converging at Perryville was three corps strong, a total of 60,000 men. Gen. Buell's plan had been to keep the Rebels guessing as to where his force was, hoping to prevent Bragg and Smith from linking up. The strategy worked.

Buell moved northeast from Louisville with his main force, while launching a feint toward Frankfort, with McCook's Corps led by Joshua Sill and supported by Dumont. These 20,000 men were to confuse Bragg as to the real direction of Buell's army. Bragg swallowed the bait and was sure that Buell was going to attack Harrodsburg.

The Union army approached Perryville on three roads. On the Federal left, moving by the Mackville road, was the three division corps of Maj. Gen. Alexander McCook. On the Federal right flank, advancing on Perryville via the Lebanon road, was the corps of Maj. Gen. Thomas Crittenden, also comprised of three divisions. Occupying the center was the corps of Maj. Gen. Charles Gilbert, moving towards Perryville on the Springfield road. Gilbert arrived before McCook and Crittenden.

The Federals now would have to fight the Rebels to get the water since the Rebels already had the water sources secured.

Hardee deployed his forces, and after positioning two of Buckner's three brigades be-

Six Pound Smoothbore Field Gun "Greenwood Number 20"-This cannon was cast in 1861 by the Eagle Foundry of Cincinnati, Ohio, and was one of twelve sold to the State of Indiana. Serial numbers 20 and 21, both six pounder smoothbores, were issued to Peter Simonson's Fifth Battery, Indiana Mounted Light Artillery. Simonson's Battery was also equipped with two, six pounder rifled guns, and two twelve pounder field howitzers for a total of six cannons. This particular cannon was involved in the capture of Huntsville, Alabama, in December 1861. On August 31, 1863, it fought in a seven hour artillery action at Stevenson, Alabama that killed one of the battery horses. The battery then moved into Kentucky and fought at the Battle of Perryville. During the Battle of Perryville, Simonson's battery arrived on the field at about 11:00 a.m. they went into action at about 1:00 p.m. in support of Harris' Brigade, and were soon involved in a long range duel against the Confederate Batteries of Lumsden, Darden, and Stanford. They then had to contend with the Washington Artillery which arrived later on Simonson's right front. Having fired most of their ammunition by about 3:30 p.m. they retired to their second position, where one of Simonson's Limbers was exploded by a shell from Lumsden's Alabama Battery. The Battery returned again and fired all its remaining ammunition. The battery fired 755 shots. The battery also lost two men killed and 14 wounded. During that battle, the battery lost one caisson and a limber, as well as 21 horses. This cannon was also heavily engaged at Stone's River at Murfreesboro, Tennessee. After Stone's River, the six pounder section of Simonson's Battery was exchanged for a section of 3 inch rifles. Numbers 20 and 21 spent the rest of the war in Fortress Rosecrans in Murfreesboro, Tennessee, and were used in the defense of the city when it was attacked in late 1864. The cannon currently resides in the Perryville Battlefield State Historic Site. (Alan Hoeweller, Chaplin Hills Historic Properties, Inc.)

tween the Harrodsburg Pike and the Chaplin river, sent St. John Liddell to occupy Peter's Hill, where the Turpin House was located.

On October 7th, Buell was less than five miles from Perryville. McCook was eight miles outside of Perryville, and Crittenden was to the south much farther away looking for water. Gilbert was moving forward on the Springfield Road, which was heavily patrolled by Confederate Joseph Wheeler's cavalry. Six miles outside the city, Robert Mitchell's division was halted, and Union Brigadier General Phil Sheridan was brought up and formed on the front and right of Mitchell. At midnight, Lt. Col. Carroll sent Companies A and E in advance of the skirmishers. They soon found Rebels across Peter's Hill and fell back when fighting broke out.

At two o'clock, Sheridan sent the brigade of Col. Daniel McCook and Barnett's battery to occupy the heights in front of Doctor's Creek. McCook moved forward, and chased the Confederates from Doctor's Creek and seized the heights beyond. Before sunrise, McCook reported to Sheridan that he held the high ground.

St. John Liddell ordered a counter attack with Sweet's Mississippi Battery concentrating their fire on the wood's of Peter's Hill. Capt. Charles Barnett's Battery returned fire as Liddell's troops moved forward. McCook then ordered his men to open fire and received a galling fire in return. Sheridan and McCook watched as Gilbert ordered his men not to bring on an engagement.

Sheridan wanted the water at Doctor's Creek and ordered Col. Bernard Talbott's brigade to attack Liddell. Two Illinois regiments and a Missouri regiment attacked and drove Liddell back. Sheridan deployed his line way beyond the Federal main line and his flanks were dangerously exposed. Sheridan's victory misled Buell into thinking the enemy was in complete disarray. Buell put off the battle until the next day. The Federal command was relaxed when Bragg launched his major attack against McCook's corps.

Buell thought that the main Rebel force was in front of him, having received no reports from George Thomas regarding the size of the Confederate force, Buell grossly overestimated the number of Confederates facing him. Bragg assumed incorrectly that only a

Confederate side knife with wooden scabbard, inscribed "Perryville", the blade is made from an old metal file. (BCWM)

General William Rousseau's framed buttons with handwritten letter. Inscription reads: "Buttons from the coat of General Rousseau of the U.S. Army, Uncle of Miss Georgia Rousseau of the 17th and Madison Street School," Louisville, Kentucky. (BCWM)

small Union force was in front of him. Buell knew his job was on the line, and wanted to make sure that all his corps were ready before he launched his attack. A fatal mistake. Buell was at the Dorsey House, which was five miles outside of town, nursing an injured leg. He was thrown off his horse on October 7th. The only corps that was in position was McCook's. Buell had no idea where George Thomas, his second in command was. Thomas was moving with Gen. Crittenden's corps. The terrain was also a problem for Buell because he never heard heavy rifle fire. Buell was not even aware that a battle was being fought on the 8th, until it was too late.

Union General James Jackson marched his division in behind Rousseau's division as Starkweather's unit came up from the rear. McCook halted his men west of the Benton road and set his corps headquarters at the Russell House, located on the Mackville Road, just east of it's intersection with the Benton Road. Rousseau was on the Benton (White) road, on Gilbert's left flank. Jackson placed his command on Rousseau's left.

Rousseau ordered Lytle to advance and allow his men to fill their canteens. On the left of Jackson was Gen. William Terrill, whose brigade was closest to the Chaplin River.

Meanwhile, Wharton's Confederate cavalry was joined by the 8th Texas Cavalry Regiment, the 4th Tennessee and the 1st Kentucky. They passed Cheatham's lines to the far right,

This Confederate Shell Jacket is made according to the typical pattern as specified by the CS regulations. The exceptions to the regulations are simple practical changes made by many Confederate manufacturers. Total cotton construction with vegetable dyes for color, wooden buttons to save the brass, and liner of cheap cotton weave. Pvt. Andrew Jackson Duncan of the 21st Mississippi wore this jacket, in the western war.(Alan Hoeweller Collection, Chaplin Hills Historic Properties, Inc.)

Private Andrew Jackson Duncan of the 21st Mississippi used this western made Frock Coat in the first days of the War. Duncan was a member of the "New Albany Grays," a militia organization out of New Albany, Mississippi which fought in the Army of the Mississippi. (Alan Hoeweller Collection, Chaplin Hills Historic Properties, Inc.)

Don Carlos Buell   *Lieutenant General E. Kirby Smith*

crossing the Chaplin River and moved into attack formation behind the hills, free from Federal observation. The charging cavalry surprised the 33rd Ohio Infantry Regiment on the bluff above the river, and the Yankee pickets fled. Rousseau then halted the Confederate pursuit. The Federals assumed that the enemy was giving ground, and that there would be no further Rebel attacks. The 42nd Indiana were cooking and eating when the Rebel attack wave broke upon them.

At 2:00 p.m., Cheatham gave the order to advance, and the first line moved across the river. Jackson's and Rousseau's divisions were shocked to see the gray clad lines almost on top of them. Polk and Cheatham yelled out "Give it to 'em boys."

Daniel Donelson's brigade advanced, followed closely by Alexander Stewart's command. Donelson's men were not prepared for the scene unfolding in front of them. In order to reach the Federals, they had to cross a depression in the terrain which paralleled the enemy line. The 80th Illinois, 123rd Illinois, and the 105th Ohio were still taking their positions to form the Federal left. The Confederate attack was striking straight toward the Federal line. Donelson's brigade was facing Rousseau's division. The 2nd and 33rd Ohio and the 24th Illinois, were sent from John Starkweathers brigade, along with Jackson's units, to their right front.

Parson's Federal battery, located beyond the line where Terrill's infantry was forming, soon fired on the right flank of Donelson's brigade, while the battery of Samuel Harris opened up on his left flank.

Donelson's brigade was shattered, losing a third of its strength. Alexander Stewart's brigade rushed to Donelson's aid, along with the 5th Tennessee Regiment.

Cheatham assigned George Maney's brigade the task of silencing the Yankee guns. Maney moved to the right, ascending the bluff and was able to go into attack formation while concealed from the Yankees, both by a wooded area and a slight depression of the ground. From the left to right were the regiments of the 9th Tennessee and 6th Tennessee, and the 41st Georgia. In reserve were the 1st and 27th Tennessee.

Maney's brigade plunged forward until the troops were only 300 yards apart. The Yankees said the Rebels came out of nowhere. Left of the Union position, Gen. James Jackson was with Parson's Battery as he moved his cannon and blasted into Maney's gray ranks. The 123rd Illinois also opened fire on the approaching Confederate troops.

Maney's columns confronted a fence, and their advance came to a halt. Maney realized if he stayed at the fence, his troops would be massacred, so he urged his men onward.

Jackson remarked, "Well, I'll be damned, if this is not getting rather particular." Right after he said these words, he was struck down and killed instantly. The 123rd Illinois fell back in panic. Gen. Terrill ordered the regiment of 700 men forward when Maney's Rebels began their advance. Once Maney's men got past the fence, they raked the 123rd Illinois, and the Yankees fled in fear.

Maney's fierce attack overran the Yankee position on their extreme left. Parson's battery lost half of its officers and men and most of its horses. Parson stood and drew his sword as if at parade rest, expecting to be killed. Parson's men finally pulled him away before he was captured. The Rebels next moved up Slocomb's battery alongside Parson's Battery. The hold on McCook's line collapsed. The Union troops had stopped the Confederate onslaught at the Benton Road.

On Cheatham's left, Simeon Buckner was driving Yankees before him. Buckner's men were opposed by Leonard Harris and William Lytle, of Rousseau's division. Brig. Gen. Thomas Jones made first contact with the Yankees and along with three Mississippi regiments pounded them down a steep hill just north of Mackville Road and across the dry bed of Doctor's Creek. There the Union troops hit them with a volley of musket and artillery fire. The Mississippi troops returned fire. The 10th Wisconsin, which was on the left and the 42nd Indiana, which was on the right, along with Peter Simonson's Indiana Battery, raked the Mississippians. The Confederate advance was brought to a halt, and the Mississippians retreated.

On Jones' left, Maj. Gen. Simeon Buckner's Rebel command was about to go in against Brig. Gen. Rousseau. Brig. Gen. Bushrod Johnson, with his six regiments was to spearhead the assault, while Brig. Gen. Daniel Adams, of Brig. Gen. J. Pattons Anderson's division, positioned himself on Johnson's left. His brigade was comprised of the 7th, 23rd, 25th, 37th, and 44th Tennessee, and the 5th Confederate.

Johnson's brigade approached Doctor's Creek at the Mackville Road, near Squire Bottoms house. Confusion prevailed when an oblique wheel to the left was attempted. Adams' brigade marched to join Johnson left flank. Johnson's Tennesseans lurched forward in disjointed fashion. The most intense fighting broke out. The Confederate advance drove back the Federal skirmishers, then quickly came to a halt. Several stone fences were south of the Mackville road and both sides took advantage of them. Confederates began firing from the stone walls on the west bank of Doctor's Creek, while Federals of the 3rd Ohio and 15th Kentucky crouched behind fences on the hillside west of the Bottoms house. Slocomb's battery blasted the Yankee troops. There were two hundred dead from the 500 man Ohio regiment alone.

Maj. Gen. Philip H. Sheridan

Green River Bridge, Munfordville.

Gen. Rousseau said: "Shiloh was nothing" compared to Perryville.

Adams' brigade was now on the flank held by the 3rd Ohio and the 15th Kentucky, who were being tormented by Slocomb's battery. Bushrod continued pressure on the front of the Federal line.

On Johnson's right, Brig. Gen. John Calvin Brown from Anderson's division, moved up to where Brig. Gen. Thomas Jones had been repulsed, applying pressure on the left flank. Brig. Gen. Patrick Cleburne was moving in front of Johnson and Brown. At double quick, Cleburne's men crossed the creek. A barn that was on fire forced the Yankees of the 3rd Ohio and the 15th Kentucky back up the hill and soon the entire Federal line followed them up the hill in full retreat. But the advance faltered when the Confederates were fired upon by their own artillery. Cleburne renewed the attack once the artillery was stopped.

The Confederates on the Benton Road continued their advance through a cornfield, firing into the rear of the retreating Yankees. Gilbert's men saw from Peter's Hill the collapse of McCook's corps and Sheridan tried to help McCook by firing his artillery at the Confederate forces in the valley below him.

Buell ordered Gilbert to send a message to order Sheridan to stop firing his cannon and wasting ammunition. Sheridan and Gilbert were not engaged for the entire battle, because Gilbert remained at Army Headquarters to eat with Buell. Sheridan quieted his artillery, but he did not notify his corps commanders nor the army commander that a battle was fought off to his left.

The Rebels were placing two batteries on Sheridan's flank and massing troops behind them. Sheridan was on high ground and the Confederates tried four times to throw him off the hill but failed each time.

The ridge along the Benton Road was held by Starkweather. He occupied the high ground and was responsible for saving the Union army from total defeat. As Terrill's brigade broke, they fled up the hill to Starkweather's position. Maney's brigade topped the ridge in front of Starkweather and began streaming down the western slope. Federal artillery on Starkweather's main line along Benton road opened on these Confederates. Stone's Battery A, Kentucky Light Artillery was at the point where Benton Road turns west. Bush's Battery, the 4th Indiana Light Artillery was on Stone's left. The 21st Wisconsin managed to hold off the Confederates approaching from the cornfield long enough to allow the regiments under Terrill to rally. The Union troops stood their ground, supported by Bush and Stone's Battery.

Confederate General A.P. Stewart marched to support Maney's men as they moved forward and the Union line laid down a heavy fire as Maney's troops struggled to the top of the ridge and grappled hand to hand with the Union troops. Maney's whole brigade became confused and disorientated and retreated back down the slope, where they rallied and once again charged back up the slope. The ground was slippery with blood around the cannons and on the hillside. The Rebels could not make it back up the bloody hill. Stewart and Maney called their men back. Maney's brigade lost half its men and Starkweather lost a third of his command. Gen. Terrill was killed when an artillery shell exploded directly in front of him.

The battle was ending on the Yankee's extreme far left flank. Starkweather held firm, but later that night he would pull back along the Benton road to the west to lick his wounds.

At the Union center, Gen. Rousseau learned that the brigades of Lytle and Harris had been driven to the Russell House where Lytle had been captured. The 15th Kentucky fell back from the stone wall and was now at the Russell House. Rousseau saw a heavy force on his right, and ordered Loomis' battery to open fire on them, and took a salvo from the Rebel guns in return. The Rebels made their attack at 2 o'clock and steadily advanced. Gen. William Hardee ordered Sam Wood across Doctor's Creek to strengthen the attack. Wood's men formed on Cleburne's right flank as Cleburne and Adams assaulted the Russell House. Neither side gained an advantage. An artillery duel broke out when the main Confederate effort shifted to Cleburne's right, where Union General Webster was killed. At 3:30 p.m., the Union troops received help from Gilbert in support of McCook. Col. Michael Gooding's brigade was sent to help. Gooding's brigade included the 59th Illinois, the 75th Illinois, and the 22nd Indiana. Gooding was opposed by Wood's brigade. Confederate artillery at the Bottoms house and Rebel infantry badly outnumbered Gooding's 1,550 men, so Liddell's Arkansas troops were thrown into the mix. It was now 5 o'clock, and the visibility so poor it was difficult to tell friend from foe. Polk advanced too far and soon realized he was among Yankees and quickly galloped back to his own lines. Gooding's line collapsed and his men retreated northwest of the intersection of the Mackville and Benton roads, while Liddell stopped his advance at the intersection. The Battle of Perryville was over. It was a tactical victory for Bragg, but it was a strategic victory for the Union, because Bragg would pull out that night from Perryville, and move towards Harrodsburg. Once Bragg linked up with Edmund Kirby Smith, Bragg made for the Cumberland Gap and crossed back into Tennessee, never to return to Kentucky again.

Casualties: 7,407 total (US 4,211: CS 3,196)

Brig. Gen. Thomas Harrison (C.S.)
8th Texas Cavalry
"Terry's Texas Rangers"

Thomas Harrison was born on May 1, 1823, in Jefferson, City, Alabama. His brother was James E. Harrison, who would later become a brigadier general in the Confederate Army. Harrison would later move to Monroe City, Mississippi, and then to Texas. While in Texas, he became a lawyer in 1843. He briefly returned to Mississippi, and was a member of Jefferson Davis' 1st Mississippi Rifles during the Mexican War. After the war he returned to Texas, and lived in Houston, and later Waco, serving a term in the state legislature.

When the Civil War broke out, Harrison was a captain in the state militia and was assigned to the West Texas Frontier. Early in 1862, following an epidemic of measles that seriously reduced the ranks of the 8th Texas Cavalry in Tennessee, he and his company were enlisted in the regiment as replacements. Harrison became a major of the 8th Texas Cavalry. On November 8, 1862, Harrison was promoted to colonel of the 8th Texas Cavalry, better known as Terry's Texas Rangers.

Terry's Texas Rangers were formed by Benjamin Franklin Terry and Thomas Lubbock. The two Texans received commissions after the battle of Bull Run and were ordered to form a cavalry company. Operating out of Houston, Terry and Lubbock recruited ten companies, mustering them into service on September 9, 1861. The command proceeded to Bowling Green, Kentucky, where it received horses and was formally organized into the 8th Texas Cavalry. In November, Terry was made colonel, and Lubbock a lieutenant colonel. On December 17, 1861, at Woodsville, Kentucky, Terry was killed during a charge against a Federal force. Lubbock succeeded Terry, and it was then that they adopted the name Terry's Texas Rangers.

Harrison served with Terry's Texas Rangers throughout the war. He was a field officer at Shiloh, and he fought at Corinth, and Perryville. He commanded the regiment at Murfreesboro and during the Tullahoma campaign. He lead a brigade at Chickamauga, Knoxville, and during the Atlanta, and Savannah campaigns. Following the fall of Savannah, Harrison was made a brigadier general, and was given the command of the 8th and 11th Texas, 4th Tennessee, 3rd Arkansas, and 1st Kentucky Cavalry. His command was absorbed into Lt. Gen. Wade Hampton's cavalry for the final campaign in the Carolina's.

After the war, Harrison returned to Texas and served as a district judge and a politician, serving as an anti-Reconstruction Democrat. He died in Waco, Texas on July 14, 1891.

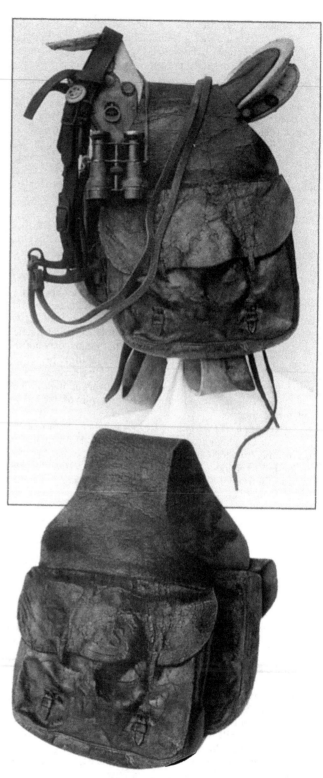

Above: "The Perryville Cannon" — This six pound iron tube is thought to be one brought to Frankfort following the Battle of Perryville in October 1862. At that time it was apparently claimed to have been captured from the Confederates during the battle. In fact, however, no Confederate artillery pieces were captured there. One Union artillery unit, Parson's battery, was overrun by the Confederates. It seems likely that a Confederate unit, Turner's Battery, occupied the site originally held by Patton's Battery and exchanged this rather outdated gun for a more modern gun abandoned by the Union gunners. Union troops returning to the site after the battle found this gun left there by the Confederates and thus "Captured" it. (Kentucky Military History Museum)

Below, left: Gen. Harrison's First Production Model 1859 Sharp's Carbine inscribed with "Lt. Col. T. Harrison, 8th Texas Cavalry", and inlaid into the stock is the Texas Star motif. Below, right: General Tom Harrison's Officer's sword. The sword is of French origin, the tin scabbard is of Confederate manufacture.

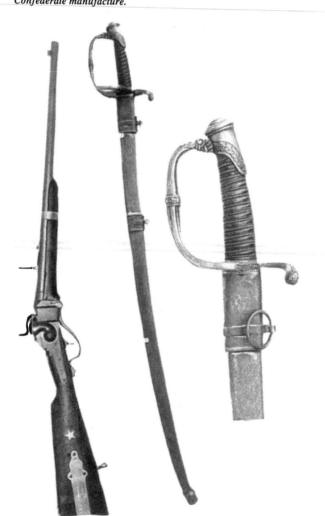

General Tom Harrison, of the 8th Texas Cavalry "Terry's Texas Rangers", Texas Hope saddle, binoculars, C.S. marked saddle bags, bridle with Texas star rosettes, and a Georgia hand foraged bit. (BCWM)

BATTLE OF STONE'S RIVER (MURFREESBORO, TN.)

December 31, 1862-January 2, 1863.

"They had opened the door of Hell, and the devil himself was there to greet them." — Federal observer witnessing the opening Federal cannonade upon Confederate General John C. Breckinridge's men, on January 2, 1863.

Campaign: Stone's River Campaign

Principal Commanders: Maj. Gen. William Rosecrans (US); Gen. Braxton Bragg (CS)

Forces Engaged: Army of the Cumberland (US); Army of Tennessee (CS)

Order of Battle
Union Forces
Army of the Cumberland
Maj. Gen. William S. Rosecrans
41,400 men

Right Wing
Maj. Gen. Alexander McCook

General W. E. Woodruff's Brig. General's double breasted frock coat. The Brig. Gen. rank is denoted by the spacing of the buttons on the front of the coat, having the regulation 16 buttons overall. It also has the single star shoulder straps. The frock coat has the velvet cuffs and collar with three buttons on each cuff. These general staff buttons are back marked "Extra-Quality." (BCWM)

First Division: Brig. Gen. Jefferson Davis

1st Brigade	2nd Brigade	3rd Brigade	Divisional Artillery
Col. Post	Col. Carlin	Col. Woodruff	
59th Illinois	21st Illinois	25th Illinois	3rd Minnesota Batt.
74th Illinois	38th Illinois	35th Illinois	5th Wisconsin Batt.
75th Illinois	101st Ohio	81st Indiana	8th Wisconsin Batt.
22nd Indiana	15th Wisconsin		

Second Division: Brig. Gen. Richard Johnson

1st Brigade	2nd Brigade	3rd Brigade	Divisional Artillery
Brig. Gen. Willich	Brig. Gen. Kirk	Col. Baldwin	
89th Illinois	34th Illinois	6th Indiana	5th Indiana Battery
32nd Indiana	79th Illinois	5th Kentucky	Battery A, 1st Ohio
39th Indiana	29th Indiana	1st Ohio	Artillery
15th Ohio	30th Indiana	93rd Ohio	Battery E, 1st Ohio
49th Ohio	77th Pennsylvania		Artillery

Cavalry
3rd Indiana
Companies G,H,I,K

Third Division: Brig. Gen. Philip Sheridan

1st Brigade	2nd Brigade	3rd Brigade	Divisional Artillery
Brig. Gen. Sill	Col. Schaefer	Col. Roberts	Capt. Hescock
36th Illinois	44th Illinois	22nd Illinois	Battery C, 1st Illinois
88th Illinois	73rd Illinois	27th Illinois	Artillery
21st Michigan	2nd Missouri	42nd Illinois	4th Indiana Artillery
24th Wisconsin	15th Missouri	51st Illinois	Battery G, Missouri
			Artillery

Center
Maj. Gen. George Thomas
First Division: Maj. Gen. Lovell Rousseau

1st Brigade	2nd Brigade	3rd Brigade	4th Brigade
Col. Scribner	Col. Beatty	Col. Starkweather	Lt. Col. Shepherd
38th Indiana	42nd Indiana	24th Illinois	1st Battalion/15th US
2nd Ohio	88th Indiana	79th Pennsylvania	2nd Battalion/16th US
33rd Ohio	15th Kentucky	1st Wisconsin	3rd Battalion/18th US
94th Ohio	3rd Ohio	21st Wisconsin	1st Battalion/19th US
10th Wisconsin			

Divisional Artillery
Capt. Loomis, Battery A, Kentucky
Battery A, 1st Michigan Artillery
Battery H, 5th US Artillery

Cavalry
2nd Kentucky (six companies) Maj. Nicholas
Second Division: Brig. Gen. James Negley

1st Brigade	2nd Brigade	3rd Brigade	Divisional Artillery
Brig. Gen. Spears	Col. Stanley	Col. Miller	
1st Tennessee	19th Illinois	37th Indiana	Battery B, Kentucky
2nd Tennessee	11th Michigan	21st Ohio	Artillery
3rd Tennessee	18th Ohio	74th Ohio	Battery G, 1st Ohio
5th Tennessee	69th Ohio	78th Pennsylvania	Artillery
			Battery M, 1st Ohio
			Artillery

Third Division: Brig. Gen. Speed Fry

1st Brigade	Divisional Artillery
Col. Walker	
82nd Indiana	Battery D, Michigan Artillery
17th Ohio	
31st Ohio	
38th Ohio	

Fourth Division: Brig. Gen. Mitchell
(Only regiments engaged at Stones River listed)
60th Illinois (eight companies)
10th Michigan (two companies)
52nd Ohio (five companies)
85th Illinois (detached under Brig. Gen. Spears with the 1st Brigade, 2nd Division)
3rd Tennessee (detachments with Gen. Spears and Col. McCook)
10th Wisconsin (two sections with Gen. Spears)

Left Wing
Maj. Gen. Thomas Crittenden
First Division: Brig. Gen. Thomas Wood

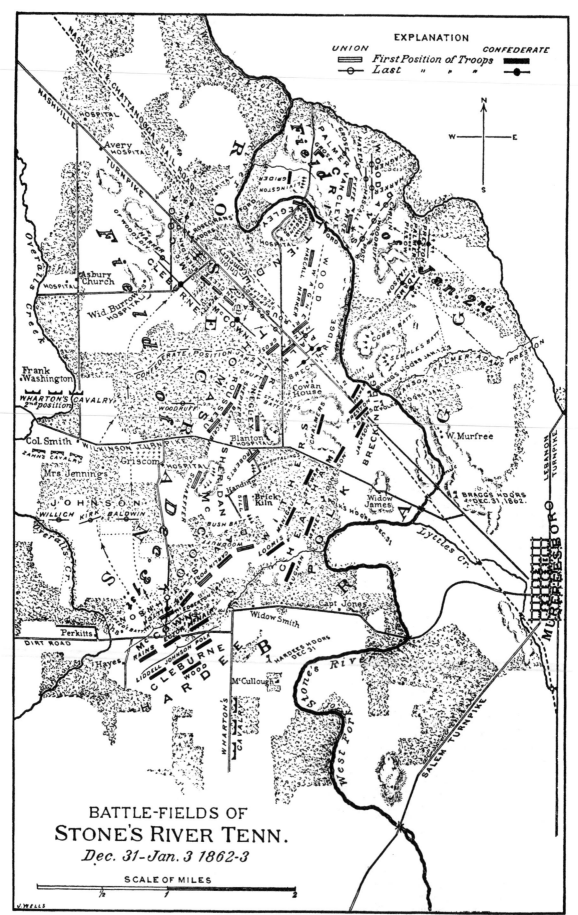

BATTLE-FIELDS OF STONE'S RIVER TENN.

Dec. 31–Jan. 3 1862-3

SCALE OF MILES

The Round Forest mentioned in the text included the right of Harker's first position and all of Hazen's position, field of December 31st.

1st Brigade	2nd Brigade	3rd Brigade	Divisional Artillery
Col. G. Buell	Col. Wagner	Col. Harker	Maj. Seymour Race
100th Illinois	15th Indiana	51st Indiana	8th Indiana Battery
58th Indiana	40th Indiana	73rd Indiana	10th Indiana Battery
3rd Kentucky	57th Indiana	13th Michigan	6th Ohio Battery
26th Ohio	97th Ohio	64th Ohio	
		65th Ohio	

Second Division: Brig. Gen. John Palmer

1st Brigade	2nd Brigade	3rd Brigade	Division Artillery
Brig. Gen. Cruft	Col. Hazen	Col. Grose	Capt. William Standart
31st Indiana	110th Illinois	84th Illinois	Battery D, 1st Ohio Artillery
1st Kentucky	9th Indiana	36th Indiana	Battery F, 1st Ohio Artillery
2nd Kentucky	6th Kentucky	23rd Kentucky	Battery H, 4th U.S. Artillery
90th Ohio	41st Ohio	6th Ohio	Battery M, 4th U.S. Artillery
		24th Ohio	

Third Division: Brig. Gen. Horatio Van Cleve's

1st Brigade	2nd Brigade	3rd Brigade	Divisional Artillery
Col. Beatty	Col. Fyffe	Col. Price	Capt. George Swallow
79th Indiana	44th Indiana	35th Indiana	7th Indiana Battery
9th Kentucky	86th Indiana	8th Kentucky	Battery B (26th), Pennsylvania Battery
11th Kentucky	13th Ohio	21st Kentucky	3rd Wisconsin Battery
19th Ohio	59th Ohio	51st Ohio	
		99th Ohio	

Cavalry Division
Col. John Kennett

1st Brigade	2nd Brigade	Reserve Cavalry
Col. Minty	Col. Zahm	15th Pennsylvania
2nd Indiana	1st Ohio	1st Middle Tennessee (5th)
3rd Kentucky	4th Ohio	2nd Tennessee
4th Michigan	Battery D, 1st Ohio Artillery	4th U.S. Cavalry (unattached)
7th Pennsylvania		

Pioneer Brigade: Capt. James Morton
1st Battalion
2nd Battalion
3rd Battalion
Illinois Light Artillery, Stokes Battery
Engineers & Mechanics
1st Michigan

Provost Guard
10th Ohio Infantry: Lt. Col. Joseph Burke
Commanding Artillery Officer
Col. James Barnett
General Escort
Anderson Troops-Pennsylvania Cavalry: Lt. Thomas Maple

Brig. Gen. William Wards' Brigade
102nd Illinois
100th Illinois
70th Indiana
79th Ohio
Indiana Light Artillery, 13th Battery: (Capt. Nicklin)

Cavalry:
1st Kentucky
7th Kentucky
11th Kentucky

Confederate Forces
Army of Tennessee
Gen. Braxton Bragg
34,739 men

Polk's Corps
Lt. Gen. Leonidas Polk
First Division: Maj. Gen. Franklin Cheatham

1st Brigade	2nd Brigade	3rd Brigade
Brig. Gen. Donelson	Brig. Gen. Alexander Stewart	Brig. Gen. Maney
8th Tennessee	4th Tennessee	1st Tennessee
16th Tennessee	5th Tennessee	27th Tennessee
38th Tennessee	19th Tennessee	4th Tennessee
51st Tennessee	24th Tennessee	6th Tennessee
84th Tennessee	31st Tennessee	9th Tennessee
(Carnes) Tennessee Batt.	33rd Tennessee	Tennessee Sharpshooters
	Mississippi Battery	Smith's Battery

4th Brigade (Preston Smith's)
Col. Vaughan, Jr.
12th Tennessee
13th Tennessee
29th Tennessee
47th Tennessee
154th Tennessee
9th Texas
Allin's (Tennessee) Sharpshooters
Tennessee Battery (Capt. Scott)

Second Division: Maj. Gen. Jones Withers

1st Brigade	2nd Brigade	3rd Brigade
Col. Loomis	Brig. Gen. Chalmers	Brig. Gen. Anderson
19th Alabama	7th Mississippi	45th Alabama
22nd Alabama	9th Mississippi	24th Mississippi
25th Alabama	10th Mississippi	27th Mississippi
26th Alabama	41st Mississippi	29th Mississippi
39th Alabama	9th Battalion Mississippi S.S.*	30th Mississippi
17th Alabama S.S.*	Blythe's Alabama Regiment	39th North Carolina
1st Louisiana	Garrity's (Alabama) Battery	Missouri Battery
Robertson's Battery		

4th Brigade
Col. Manigault
28th Alabama
24th Alabama
10th South Carolina
19th South Carolina
Alabama Battery

Hardee's Corps
Lt. Gen. William Hardee
First Division: Maj. Gen. John C. Breckinridge

1st Brigade	2nd Brigade	3rd Brigade
Col. Adams	Col. Palmer	Brig. Gen. Preston
32nd Alabama	18th Tennessee	1st Florida
13th Louisiana	26th Tennessee	3rd Florida
16th Louisiana	28th Tennessee	4th Florida
20th Louisiana	32nd Tennessee	60th North Carolina
25th Louisiana	45th Tennessee	20th Tennessee
14th Louisiana Battalion	Moses Georgia Battery	Tennessee Battery
Washington (5th Co.) Battery		

4th Brigade
Brig. Gen. Hanson
41st Alabama
2nd Kentucky
4th Kentucky
6th Kentucky
9th Kentucky
Cobb's Kentucky Battery

Jackson's Brigade
Brig. Gen. Jackson
5th Mississippi
8th Mississippi
5th Georgia
2nd Georgia Sharpshooters Battalion
Lumsden's (Alabama) Battery
Pritchard (Georgia) Battery

Second Division: Maj. Gen. Patrick Cleburne

1st Brigade	2nd Brigade	3rd Brigade
Brig. Gen. L.E. Polk,	Brig. Gen. Liddell	Brig. Gen. Johnson
1st Arkansas	2nd Arkansas	17th Tennessee
13th Arkansas	5th Arkansas	23rd Tennessee

Woodruff's Presentation sword is a Model 1850 Staff and Field highly ornate Presentation Grade Officer's Sword, manufactured by Schuyler, Hartley & Graham. Inscribed on the scabbard is "Presented to Col. Wm. E. Woodruff by his friends of Louisville-April 23rd, 1862." Woodruff's Line sword is a Model 1850 Staff and Field Officer's sword, inscribed with "Presented to Col. Wm. E. Woodruff by his friends in Louisville- April 23rd, 1862." This is the sword General Woodruff carried into battle. (BCWM)

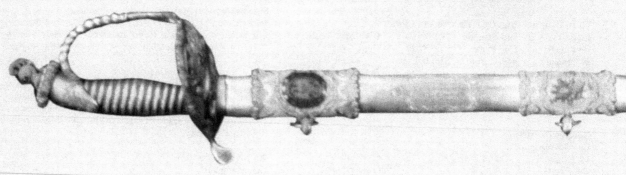

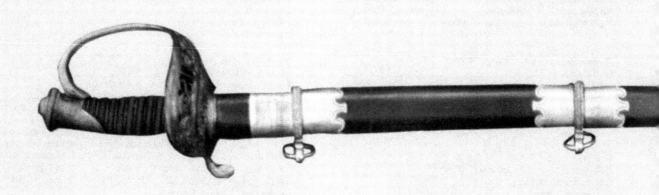

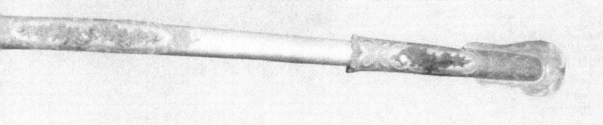

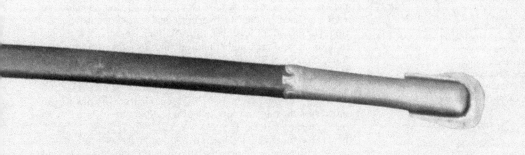

15th Arkansas	6th Arkansas	25th Tennessee
5th C.S.A.	7th Arkansas	37th Tennessee
2nd Tennessee	8th Arkansas	44th Tennessee
5th Tennessee		Warren (Mississippi) Artillery

Jefferson Flying (Mississippi) Artillery
Helena (Arkansas) Artillery

4th Brigade
Brig. Gen. Wood
16th Alabama
33rd Alabama
3rd C.S.A.
45th Mississippi
15th Mississippi Battalion Sharpshooters
(Semple) Alabama Battery

Maj. Gen. J. P. McCown's Division

1st Brigade	**2nd Brigade**
Brig. Gen. Ector	**Brig. Gen. Rains**
10th Texas Cavalry (dismounted)	3rd Georgia Battalion
11th Texas Cavalry (dismounted)	9th Georgia Battalion
14th Texas Cavalry (dismounted)	22nd North Carolina
15th Texas Cavalry (dismounted)	11th Tennessee
Texas Battery	Eufaula (Alabama) Light Artillery

3rd Brigade
Brig. Gen. McNair
1st Arkansas Mounted Rifles (dismounted)
2nd Arkansas Mounted Rifles (dismounted)
4th Arkansas
30th Arkansas
4th Arkansas Battalion
Arkansas Battery (Humphrey's)

Cavalry
Brig. Gen. Joseph Wheeler's Division

Wheeler's Brigade	**Wharton's Brigade**	**Buford's Brigade**
1st Alabama Cavalry	14th Alabama	3rd Kentucky Cavalry
3rd Alabama Cavalry	1st C.S.A. Cavalry	5th Kentucky Cavalry
51st Alabama Cavalry	3rd C.S.A. Cavalry	6th Kentucky
8th C.S.A. Cavalry	2nd Georgia Cavalry	
1st Tennessee Cavalry	3rd Georgia Cavalry (detached)	
Tennessee Batn. (Douglas)	2nd Tennessee Cavalry	
Tennessee Batn. (Holman)	4th Tennessee Cavalry	
Arkansas Battery	Tennessee Battalion (Davis)	
	8th Texas Cavalry	
	Murray's Tennessee Regiment	
	Escort Company (Capt. Anderson)	

Pegram's Brigade
1st Georgia Cavalry
1st Louisiana Cavalry

Divisional Artillery
Tennessee Battery
Louisiana Battery (dismounted)
Georgia Battery (dismounted)

Brigadier General R.W. Hanson

Rosecrans was feeling pressure from Washington to launch an offensive campaign against Bragg. Washington was afraid that Bragg might attack Nashville, reinforce Lee, or possibly outflank the Capitol and move against Grant. Instead, Bragg decided to wait for Rosecrans at Murfreesboro, and take a defensive position. The day after Christmas, 1862, William Rosecrans, with over half his army of the Cumberland, advanced southeast from Nashville, Tennessee. Rosecrans attempted to fool Bragg by moving in three different directions. Thomas Crittenden came from the Murfreesboro Pike, Maj. Gen. Alexander McCook parallel to and 15 miles west of Bragg, and Maj. Gen. George Thomas was to move straight south on McCook's right, then turn east and strike the Confederate flank. The ruse worked and Bragg was confused. From December 26th to December 30th, the Yankee army moved ahead in separate columns the 30 miles to Confederate General Braxton Bragg's position in front of Murfreesboro. With 38,000 men from his Army of Tennessee, Bragg was deployed along a four mile front arching inward. About one and a half miles west and northwest of Murfreesboro, his lines covered the Nashville Pike and the winding Stone's River, which passed behind his men, under the pike, and then meandered northwest along the east of the pike. Recent heavy rains had raised the level of the river. Bragg put Patrick Cleburne's division on the far left resting on the westward bend of the river, with a brigade of cavalry extending south. In the wood's to Cleburne's right was Leonidas Polk's corps, extending a mile and a half across the open side of a wide eastward bend of the river, then resting on the stream. Breckinridge's division was on the east side. His

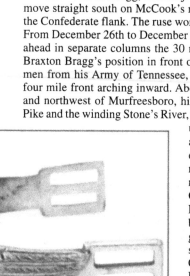

Elegant gold washed eagle spurs used by Gen. Woodruff. The other spur was lost in the Battle of Stone's River.

left meeting with Polk's right across the river, and extending at right angles east across the northern approach to Murfreesboro. Breckinridge was in a good position to cross the river and reinforce Polk's center, but several hundred yards to his front was a commanding position called Wayne's Hill.

Rosecrans troops skirmished daily with Bragg's cavalry and advance infantry until arriving before Bragg's main line on December 30th. Rosecrans was only a few hundred yards from Bragg's army. The Federal commander believed that if he could push Bragg from Murfreesboro, he could secure Nashville's supply lines and eliminate threats from the Army of Tennessee until spring. Bragg hoped to do the opposite, and used the days of Rosecrans' slow advance to plan the coming battle. By late on December 30th, facing the Confederates from right to left, he had deployed Maj. Gen. John C. Breckinridge's division (east of the pike and the river), Lt. Gen. Leonidas Polk's corps (from the pike river crossing to a point about one and one fourth mile west) and Lt. Gen. William Hardee's corps (from Polk's left, west about one and three-fourths mile). He planned on assaulting

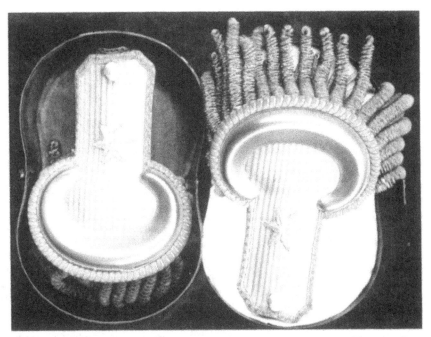

Brig. General Woodruff's epaulettes. Epaulettes were used on dress occasions. These epaulettes were given to Woodruff by the Eighth Wisconsin Battery in gratitude for saving their battery from annihilation by the Confederates on the first day at the Battle of Stone's River. (BCWM)

Rosecrans right with Hardee's corps and turning the entire Union force, putting its back to the river, and ideally, cutting off its northwest line of retreat on the Nashville Pike. A second road, the Wilkinson Pike, traveling west-northwest, cut the intervening ground between the Confederate left and the Nashville Pike, and intersected and ended at the Nashville Pike about a quarter of a mile behind the Southern lines. Bragg established headquarters at the intersection and ordered an attack for daylight December 31st.

Rosecrans plan of battle was for McCook to hold the right, for Thomas' center troops to begin with skirmishing, and Crittenden's left wing to maneuver to Stones River and cross two divisions, and then assail Bragg's right. Rosecrans intelligence revealed that Breckinridge's lone division held the Confederate line east of the river. With two divisions to Breckinridge's one, he would thrust the Confederates back, attain Bragg's rear and flank, and with the Union line wheeling to its left, push the Confederates west and southwest, out and away from Murfreesboro. To ensure an overextension of the Confederate lines, he ordered McCook to send detachments farther to the left after dark on December 30th, and to build campfires to give the illusion of a longer Union line. He then ordered an attack for 7:00 a.m. on December 31st.

Deceived by the false extension of Rosecrans lines, Bragg pulled his lone reserve division, commanded by Maj. Gen. John McCown, and a second line division of Hardee's, led by Maj. Gen. Patrick Cleburne, and threw them out on his left against McCook's phantom troops. Bragg attacked at 6:00 a.m., before Rosecrans had a chance to attack and his assault caught the Federals unprepared. McCown moved forward as Cleburne put his division 500 yards behind the first line to attack Rosecrans right flank. Willich's brigade saw the Rebels coming and fired when they got within 200 yards of the Federals. Union Brigadier General Edward Kirk was wounded. Willich, who had been away, rode up only to be captured by the Rebels. Rosecrans right totally collapsed. McCown was pulled off course in his wheel movement, and Cleburne had to fill in where McCown's position was. Cleburne now faced Union Jefferson Davis' 1st brigade under Col. Sidney Post. Post couldn't handle the assault and gave way. At 7:30 a.m., the Federals reformed with fresh regiments and held until Confederate assaults broke their lines. All of Rosecrans five brigades collapsed and

Rosecrans line was pushed a mile back on the right flank. The Rebel assault now hammering against McCook's left wing pushed McCook's troops back on George Thomas. Polk forged ahead, startling the Federals. Polk sent Cheatham's division to attack Sheridan's division, under Brig. Gen. Joshua Sill, and Brig. Gen. Jefferson Davis Division, under Col. William P. Carlin and Col. William Woodruff. Woodruff was on the edge of woods on the south side of a rise. Brig. Gen. Sill was on Woodruff's left, facing east and making a sharp angle with Woodruff's line at the top of the wooded slope. Woodruff's infantry, the 25th Illinois, 30th Illinois, and 81st Indiana with the help of the 8th Wisconsin Battery, managed to fight back attacks from Confederate infantry under Col. Loomis, comprised of the 26th, 39th, and 25th Alabama. His right three regiments, the 1st Louisiana, 19th Alabama, and 22nd Alabama hit Sill's line. Col. Loomis was injured in the heavy fighting and his men retreated. Confederate Col. Vaughan sent in his infantry after Loomis' men fell back. Woodruff's line had taken back lost ground and fell in on their old line at Sill's right. Vaughn attacked Woodruff's battered regiments, but Woodruff held, and Vaughn retreated. On Loomis' right, Col. A.M. Manigault attacked Sill. Sill was killed when he was riding over to Bush's guns to aid in the advance and his men fell back on Woodruff. Woodruff was now flanked on both sides and Woodruff had no choice but to retreat. Sheridan ordered a fighting retreat.

Sheridan's men reformed their position on the Wilkinson Pike, west of a farm. Brig. Gen. James Negley's division, of George Thomas' center corps, was linked on Sheridan's left and extended northeast toward the Nashville Pike. Sheridan's position was a cedar forest that was so dense no one could see where his men were hidden. Sheridan supplied his men with ammunition, and under the cover of the forest, he massed 57 pieces of artillery. Sheridan's strong position now provided Rosecrans with an anchor for his right.

As the Federals fell back on the Nashville Pike, the first Union division sent across Stone's River to assault Breckinridge was recalled. Rosecrans moved the line of George Thomas to form another division in front of the massed artillery that Sheridan had assembled on the Nashville Pike. The Chattanooga and Nashville Railroad ran parallel to the pike on the east, and around it grew a four acre wood called the Round Forest, dubbed by soldiers "Hell's

Half Acre." Rosecran pulled his artillery to an elevation behind these woods. Now protected from attacks from the south by Union Maj. James Negley's division, Sheridan's division held the Federal center. The Union line resembled a narrow V, its right and left being pressed back on one another. By 11:00 a.m., Sheridan's troops had fallen back, with Negley's men following quickly behind him, and the new line was created with the Round Forest forming a sharp salient. The forest itself was held by five brigades, under Col. William Hazen, Brig. Gen. Charles Cruft, Col. William Grose, Brig. Gen. Milo Hascall, and Col. George Wagner. Supported by the massed artillery in their rear, they withstood repeated Confederate attacks by Polk's men. Chalmers was wounded during the attack on the Round Forest and was replaced by Donelson, who was immediately attacked, but Col. William Hazen stood firm. Two brigades under Breckinridge were sent in, but the attacks were piecemeal, and were not successful in dislodging the Federals from the Round Forest. Darkness ended the assaults by the Confederates. At nightfall, a thin line of Union divisions held the road to Nashville, and additional troops stretched around to the east of the Round Forest, facing Stone's River and Breckinridge's Confederates.

On January 1, 1863, neither side renewed the battle. Rosecrans had pulled his troops from the Round Forest salient during the night, establishing a new line to the north. Still retaining some of its V shape, it covered both the Nashville Pike and the river. Bragg expected Rosecrans to retreat north on the pike and had his cavalry ready to disrupt any attempts at re-supply. After dark, January 1, 1863, Union Col. Samuel Beatty led Crittenden's 3rd Division across Stone's River and established it on a ridge facing Breckinridge.

On January 2nd, Confederate General John C. Breckinridge scouted the Federal lines and noticed that reinforcements and artillery were being brought up. While he was scouting, he was recalled to Bragg's Headquarters. Bragg ordered John Breckinridge to drive the Federals out of his front and back across the river. The assault would be sheer suicide and everyone knew it. Breckinridge drew on the ground with a stick and tried to explain to Bragg that the Federals were on higher ground and could sweep his men with fire from cannons and rifles. Polk and Hardee also argued against the attack. Bragg was punishing Breckinridge for not arriving in time to help out in his Kentucky Campaign in 1862. Poor railroads and politics in Knoxville kept Breckinridge in Tennessee and he was too late for the battle of Perryville. Bragg ordered Breckinridge to assault Beatty's position and Breckinridge massed 4,500 men for the assault. He was to move in two lines-Hanson on the left in the first line with Gideon Pillow's brigade on the right, Col. Randall Gibson's brigade on the left in the second line and Preston's brigade to his right. The second line formed 150 yards behind the first and served as a reserve. Each line was two regiments wide and six miles deep. Breckinridge crashed into Price's men and overran their position as Price fell back. Breckinridge now went up against the 35th, 44th, and 86th Indiana and the 30th Ohio. Breckinridge then turned off to face the 99th Ohio, 21st Kentucky, and the 19th Ohio. Fyffe fell back to the low ford on the river. Grider and Price fell back before Breckinridge's powerful onslaught. The 23rd Kentucky (US) and the 24th Ohio were routed, but Grose's final line tried to stop the Confederates. The battle was being observed by Union General Thomas Crittenden from a distance. Crittenden ordered his artillery chief, Maj. John Mendenhall, to mass his guns at the ford where Beatty had crossed. Breckinridge now advanced up the hill. Hanson advanced and chased Beatty across the river. The Confederate attack was supposed to stop at the heights, and then Breckinridge was to bring up his guns, but his men wanted to get the battle over with and advanced further. Hanson was struck in the leg by a bullet, and later died of his wounds. At 4:45 p.m., Mendenhall opened on Breckinridge with the concentrated fire of 57 cannons. The Confederates were ripped to pieces. Breckinridge pressed on and reached a cornfield, behind a hill. Union Col. Miller,

of Negley's division, was on the other side of the hill and surprised Breckinridge's men when they climbed the hill and fired a thousand rounds into Breckinridge's troops. Miller's troops then charged across the ford and by nightfall had driven Breckinridge back to his original position. On the left, the 2nd and 6th Kentucky (C.S.) followed the retreating Federals across the river. The Union brigades counterattacked across the river and Fyffe led his brigade forward. Beatty now rallied his men as Gibson retreated and the Federals took back the ridge. Soon it began to rain, and darkness ended the fighting. Breckinridge soon discovered that he had lost over twenty five percent of his division, and was heard to say, "My poor orphans! They have cut them to pieces."

Confederate Major General Benjamin Cheatham and Maj. Gen. Withers, commanders of divisions that had suffered greatly on December 31st, wrote a memorandum to Bragg the night of January 2nd, asking to be allowed to retreat. Endorsed by Polk, the memorandum first angered Bragg, who rejected the idea. He reconsidered at 10 a.m., January 3rd and ordered a retreat that evening, believing falsely that Rosecrans had been reinforced. Left in possession of the field, Rosecrans declared Stone's River a Union victory. The stalemate cost him 1,730 dead, 7,803 wounded, and 3,717 missing. Bragg had 1,294 dead, 7,945 wounded, and 1,027 missing. Bragg withdrew to Shelbyville, Tennessee, while Rosecrans declined to pursue and occupied Murfreesboro instead. The Battle of Stone's River is counted as the eighth most costly battle of the Civil War.

Brig. Gen. William Woodruff (U.S.)
2nd Kentucky Infantry

William Woodruff was a 34 year old from Louisville, Kentucky, who signed up for three years in 1861. He was made a major on May 6, 1861, and transferred by election to colonel of the 2nd Kentucky Infantry on June 10, 1861. He arrived with his new rank at Camp Dennison on June 28, 1861. He was captured at Scarey Creek (Charlestown), Virginia, while reconnoitering on July 17, 1861 and was held as a prisoner of war in Richmond, Virginia. His career could have been cut short because of an incident that occurred while he was a prisoner. J. P. Benjamin, Acting Secretary of War for the Confederacy, wrote to Brig. Gen. John Winder in Richmond, Virginia and asked him to select 13 prisoners to be treated as infamous criminals. The reason for the harsh treatment of Union prisoners of war was because 13 Confederate Navy men were being treated as pirates in New York, and they were going to be executed for piracy. In retaliation, Brig. Gen. Winder vowed to execute as many men as the North did. Lots were chosen and Woodruff happened to be one of the men selected to be executed, along with Capts. Bowman, Keffer, and J.W. Rockwood; Cols. Lee, Cogswell, Wilcox, Wood, Cochran; Lt. Cols. Bowman, Neff; and Majs. Potter, Revere, and Vogdes. Fortunately the sentences were never carried out. Woodruff remained a prisoner of war and was later moved to Columbia, South Carolina. Woodruff sent numerous letters to the Governor of Kentucky asking to be paroled. Woodruff stated that he and Capt. Austin, and Lt. Col. Neff were still prisoners and should be the first to be exchanged. By this time he had been a prisoner for nine months. Finally, Maj. Gen. George B. McClellan set the wheels in motion and Woodruff was exchanged for Confederate Col. W. J. Willey on April 4, 1862. In January 1862, he was transferred to a skeleton Regiment by the War Department. On October 15, 1862, Brig. Gen. Robert Mitchell assigned Woodruff the command of the 32nd Brigade of the 2nd Division, by Special Order No. 10. On November 25, 1862, by Special Order No. 285, Woodruff was made a brigadier general by Maj. Gen. Wright. Wright put Woodruff on special duty and sent him to Louisville, where he was given command of the 3rd Brigade, 2nd Division, Army of Kentucky. On September 11, 1862, Woodruff wrote a letter to the War Department confirming his appointment to brigadier general. The War Department replied, telling Woodruff that his appointment as brigadier general "was premature, the appointment never having been made." On November 25, 1862, Woodruff was assigned to Maj. Gen. Wright, who was commanding the Department of the Ohio, for special duty. On December 12, 1862, Maj. Gen. William Rosecrans, at Nashville, made Woodruff the brigade commander of the 10th Ohio, and the 3rd, and 6th Tennessee Regiments. He was later made a colonel of the 3rd Brigade, 1st Division (under Jefferson Davis), Right Wing, 14th Army Corps, Department of the Cumberland, at Stone's River.

At Stone's River he injured his ankle and joints of his right foot and requested a leave of absence from the army while in the hospital on the Nashville Turnpike. On January 26, 1863, the surgeon agreed that Brig. Gen. Woodruff (Woodruff was still wearing his brigadier general epaulets) was unable to perform his duties because of his injuries and his sickness from the weather. The surgeons report, along with Woodruff's request for leave, were sent to headquarters. Woodruff seems to have been very upset that his promotion to brigadier general was overturned, and for good reason. While in the hospital, Woodruff sent his resignation letter to Rosecrans. The letter as written, follows:

"Nashville, Tennessee, Jan. 19, 1863
To Maj. Gen.. W.S. Rosecrans
Commanding Department of the Cumberland

Sir,

Having been mustered into the service of the United States as colonel of the 2nd Regt. Kentucky Vol. Infantry June 9, 1861, and while in the performance of duty was captured by the Rebels and remained a prisoner in their hands for nine months suffering all manner of indignities.

The War Department during that imprisonment by order deprived me of the command of my Regiment and another colonel was placed in my stead. On my return I remonstrated with the Department in the injustice done me and protested in person against the assumed right to supply a vacancy that did not in reality exist, and claimed the right to command my Regiment but could not prevail on the Department to restore me to the actual command while it admitted one as the colonel of said regiment, thereby having and permitting said Regiment to have two colonels which continues to the present time.

Hoping that the evil might by remedied I have waited long and patiently.

The President of the United States, however, in June 1862 appointed me a brigadier general of Vols. and I was ordered home to remain "until ordered to a station." During this time not desiring to be idle, and as Brig. Gen. Gilbert was there organizing the Army of Kentucky I tendered my services to him and was immediately placed in command of a brigade. While thus engaged I was ordered to duty by the War Department as a brigadier general and was advised and did assume the strap and insignia of that rank of the acceptance of which I duly notified the Department. Shortly after my letter was returned stating that I had been "prematurely assigned to duty as a brigadier general as the appointment had never been made." This was indeed mortifying to me and I wrote the Department on the subject and respectfully asked that the matter might be adjusted and that I be placed in my proper position. While awaiting a reply I went into the field at the request and by the special order of Brig. Gen. Gilbert, although I had no orders so to do from the Department, so anxious was I to be on duty, and remained in command of brigade and divisions until we reached here. On the night, and while at Bowling Green I was ordered by the Department to join my Regiment, but by your order remained in my then command, and with a brigade of

that command participated in the late Battle of Murfreesboro, when I endeavored to do my duty. As my report will fully verify, until sick of fever, exhausted and injured I was sent by order of the surgeon to this place, where I now lie sick and unable to take the field.

I have had the recommendations of yourself as well as those of several other general officers forwarded to the Department in my behalf, as yet accomplishing nothing, though a Sufficient time has now elapsed, fully satisfying me that nothing will be done unless I can visit Washington myself, which as an officer of the U.S. Government I cannot do unless ordered there by the Department.

Jealousies do and will exist because I as colonel am assigned to the command of brigades over colonels who have and justly the right as seniors to command the brigades in which their Regiments are serving, in the absence of superior officers. I have done my duty and more than my duty in the field at all times; for I have gave on duty when on leave of absence, and on the march when sick and unable I have done all a man can in honor do for my country without apparently a recognition of that position to which I am entitled by my country.

The greater part of all these circumstances, as well as others not herein mentioned are already known to you, and while I thank you for your interest always manifested in me I deem that I have waited sufficiently for justice to be done me. I have borne these injuries patiently until I am at last compelled in honor to vindicate myself and ask to be relieved from the false position I have been forced to occupy by the Department. Therefore I cannot in justice to the service or myself continue in this quasi state amidst the uncertainties and jealousies it engendered, nor can I humbly go back to the Regiment even if it was it in as good condition now as where I left it, but now decimated, but a handful as it were remaining, and these undisciplined and demoralized beyond redemption, it is not such a command as I ought to assume if I would. Hence in view of all these facts which you well know, and to justify myself which I am compelled in honor to do, although with much regret I do so, I hereby tenure this my resignation as colonel of the 2nd Regiment of Kentucky Vol. Infantry to be immediate and unconditional, and earnestly pray its acceptance.

I am not indebted to the Government of the United States and have no property belonging to said Government in my possession.

I have never been absent without leave and have had leave of absence except by order of the War Department and then not at my solicitation.

Will you please give this immediate attention and oblige-

Your very Respectfuland obedient servant
W.E. Woodruff
Col. 2nd. Ky. Vol. Inf."

On January 28, 1863, his resignation was approved, and Woodruff went home to Louisville, Kentucky. On June 4, 1888, when Woodruff was 61 years of age, he was finally given justice when a special act of Congress and the House of Representatives gave him the commission of General for his meritorious service. He was entitled to a $50.00 a month pension. Woodruff died on July 5, 1915, in Louisville, Kentucky. He was survived by his wife, Francis, and his three children; E. Belle Woodruff, Charles Woodruff, and Edith M. Woodruff. Woodruff must be counted as one of the unsung heroes of the Civil War and be given a proper place among the great Union Generals.

BATTLE OF VICKSBURG

From Mid-Oct, 1862 & April 1-July 4, 1863

"All was now ready for the pick and spade." — Ulysses S. Grant

Campaign: Grant's Operations against Vicksburg (1862-63)

Principal Commanders: Maj. Gen. Ulysses Grant (US); Lt. Gen. John Pemberton (CS)

Forces engaged: Army of the Tennessee (US); Army of Vicksburg (CS)

Order of Battle
Union Forces
Army of the Tennessee (U.S.)
Maj. Gen. Ulysses S. Grant
75,000 Men

Ninth Army Corps: Maj. Gen. John Parke
First Division: Brig. Gen. Thomas Welsh

1st Brigade	3rd Brigade	Artillery
Col. Bowman	**Col. D. Leasure**	Pennsylvania Light
36th Massachusetts	2nd Michigan	Artillery, Battery D
17th Massachusetts	8th Michigan	
27th Massachusetts	20th Michigan	
45th Pennsylvania	79th New York	
	100th Pennsylvania	

Second Division: Brig. Gen. Robert Potter

1st Brigade	2nd Brigade	3rd Brigade
Col. S. Griffin	**Brig. Gen. E. Ferrero**	**Col. B. Christ**
6th New Hampshire.	35th Massachusetts	29th Massachusetts

9th New Hampshire	11th New Hampshire	46th New York
7th Rhode Island	51st New York	50th Pennsylvania
	51st Pennsylvania	

Artillery
2nd New York Light Artillery, Battery L

Artillery Reserve
2nd U.S. Artillery, Battery E

Thirteenth Corps: Maj. Gen. John McClernand; Maj. Gen. Ord
Pioneers- Independent Company Kentucky Infantry
Ninth Division- Brig. Gen. Peter Osterhaus; Brig. Gen. Albert Lee

1st Brigade	2nd Brigade	Cavalry	Artillery
Brig. Gen. T. Garrard	**Col. L. Sheldon**	2nd Illinois	**Capt. J. Foster**
Brig. Gen. A. Lee	**Col. D. Lindsey**	(5 companies)	7th Michigan
Col. J. Keigwin	54th Indiana	3rd Illinois	1st Wisconsin
118th Illinois	22nd Kentucky	(3 companies)	
49th Indiana	16th Ohio	6th Missouri	
69th Indiana	42nd Ohio	(7 companies)	
7th Kentucky	114th Ohio		
120th Ohio			

Tenth Division: Brig. Gen. Andrew Smith

1st Brigade	2nd Brigade	Artillery
Brig. Gen. S. Burbridge	Col. W. Landram	Illinois Battery
16th Indiana	77th Illinois	(Mercantile)
60th Indiana	97th Illinois	17th Ohio Battery
67th Indiana	130th Illinois	
83rd Ohio	19th Kentucky	
96th Ohio	48th Ohio	
23rd Wisconsin		

Twelfth Division: Brig. Gen. Alvin Hovey

1st Brigade	2nd Brigade	Artillery

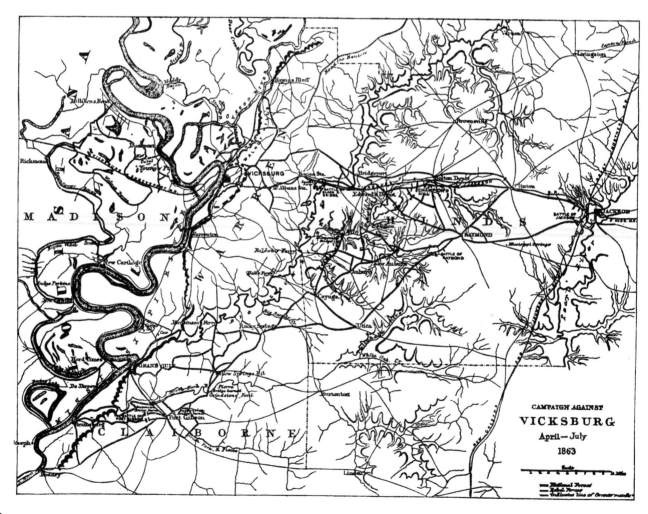

CAMPAIGN AGAINST
VICKSBURG
April — July
1863

Brig. Gen. G. McGinnis	Col. J. Slack	1st Missouri Light
11th Indiana	87th Illinois	Artillery, Battery A
24th Indiana	47th Indiana	2nd Ohio Light Artillery
34th Indiana	24th Iowa	16th Ohio Light Artillery
46th Indiana	28th Iowa	
29th Wisconsin	56th Ohio	

Fourteenth Division: Brig. Gen. Eugene Carr

1st Brigade	2nd Brigade	Artillery
Brig. Gen. W. Benton	**Col. C. Harris**	2nd Illinois Light Artillery,
Col. H. Washburn	**Col. W. Stone**	Battery A
Col. D. Shunk	**Brig. Gen. M. Lawler**	1st Indiana Light Artillery
33rd Illinois	21st Iowa	
99th Illinois	22nd Iowa	
8th Indiana	23rd Iowa	
18th Indiana	11th Wisconsin	
1st U.S. Siege Guns		

Fifthteenth Corps: Maj. Gen. William T. Sherman
First Division: Maj. Gen. Frederick Steele

1st Brigade	2nd Brigade	3rd Brigade	Artillery
Col. F. Manter	**Col. T. Woods**	**Brig. Gen. J. Thayer**	1st Iowa
Col. B. Farrar	25th Iowa	4th Iowa	2nd Missouri
13th Illinois	31st Iowa	9th Iowa	Light Artillery,
27th Missouri	3rd Missouri	26th Iowa	Batt. F
29th Missouri	12th Missouri	30th Iowa	4th Ohio Light
30th Missouri	17th Missouri		Artillery
31st Missouri	76th Ohio		
32nd Missouri			

Cavalry
Kane's Illinois Company
3rd Illinois, Company D

Second Division: Maj. Gen. Frank Blair, Jr.

1st Brigade	2nd Brigade	Artillery
Col. G. Smith	**Col. T. Smith**	1st Illinois Light Artillery, Batt. A
113th Illinois	Brig. Gen. J. Lightburn	1st Illinois Light Artillery, Batt. B
116th Illinois	55th Illinois	1st Illinois Light Artillery, Batt. H
6th Missouri	127th Illinois	8th Ohio Light Artillery
8th Missouri	83rd Indiana	
13th U.S.	54th Ohio	
	57th Ohio	

Cavalry
Thielemann's Battalion (Illinois) Companies A, B
10th Missouri Cavalry, Company C

Third Division: Brig. Gen. James Tuttle

1st Brigade	2nd Brigade	3rd Brigade
Brig. Gen. R. Buckland	**Brig. Gen. J. Mower**	**Brig. Gen. Matthies**
Col. W. McMillen	47th Illinois	Col. J. Woods
114th Illinois	5th Minnesota	8th Iowa
93rd Indiana	11th Maryland	12th Iowa
72nd Ohio	8th Wisconsin	35th Iowa
95th Ohio		

Cavalry	Artillery
4th Iowa Cavalry	1st Illinois Light Artillery, Battery E
	2nd Iowa Light Artillery

Sixteenth Corps: Maj. Gen. Cadwallader Washburn
First Division: Brig. Gen. William Smith

1st Brigade	2nd Brigade	3rd Brigade	4th Brigade
Col. Loomis	**Col. S. Hicks**	**Col. J. Cockrell**	**Col. W. Sanford**
26th Illinois	40th Illinois	97th Indiana	48th Illinois
90th Illinois	103rd Illinois	99th Indiana	6th Iowa
12th Indiana	15th Michigan	53rd Ohio	
100th Indiana	46th Ohio	70th Ohio	

Artillery
Capt. Cogswell
1st Illinois, Company F
1st Illinois, Company I
Cogswell Illinois Battery
6th Indiana Light Artillery

Fourth Division: Brig. Gen. Jacob Lauman

1st Brigade	2nd Brigade	3rd Brigade	Cavalry
Col. I. Pugh	**Col. C. Hall**	**Col. G. Bryant**	15th Illinois Light
41st Illinois	14th Illinois	Col. H. Johnson	Artillery, Batt. F, I
53rd Illinois	15th Illinois	26th Illinois	
3rd Iowa	46th Illinois	32nd Illinois	
33rd Wisconsin	76th Illinois		
	53rd Indiana		

Artillery
Capt. George Gumbart
2nd Illinois Light Artillery, Batt. E
2nd Illinois Light Artillery, Batt. K
5th Ohio Light Artillery
7th Ohio Light Artillery
15th Ohio Light Artiller

Provisional Division: Brig. Gen. Nathan Kimball

Engelmann's Brigade	Montgomery's Brigade	Richmond's Brigade
43rd Illinois	**Col. M. Montgomery**	**Col. J. Richmond**
61st Illinois	40th Iowa	18th Illinois
106th Illinois	3rd Minnesota	45th Illinois
12th Michigan	25th Wisconsin	126th Illinois
	27th Wisconsin	22nd Ohio

Seventeenth Corps: Maj. Gen. James McPherson
Third Division: Maj. Gen. John Logan

1st Brigade	2nd Brigade	3rd Brigade
Brig. Gen. J. Smith	**Brig. Gen. E. Dennis**	**Brig. Gen. J. Stevenson**
Brig. Gen. M. Leggett	Brig. Gen. M. Leggett	8th Illinois
20th Illinois	Col. M. Force	17th Illinois
31st Illinois	Capt. F. Shaklee	81st Illinois
45th Illinois	68th Ohio	7th Missouri
124th Illinois	78th Ohio	32nd Ohio
23rd Indiana		

Artillery
Maj. Charles Stolbrand
1st Illinois Light Artillery, Battery D
2nd Illinois Light Artillery, Battery G
2nd Illinois Light Artillery, Battery L
8th Michigan Light Artillery
3rd Ohio Light Artillery

Sixth Division: Brig. Gen. John McArthur

1st Brigade	2nd Brigade	3rd Brigade
Brig. Gen. H. Reed	**Brig. Gen. T. Ransom**	**Col. W. Hall**
1st Kansas	11th Illinois	Col. A. Chambers
16th Wisconsin	72nd Illinois	11th Iowa
	95th Illinois	13th Iowa
	14th Wisconsin	15th Iowa
	17th Wisconsin	16th Iowa

Artillery
2nd Illinois Light Artillery, Battery F
1st Minnesota Light Artillery
1st Missouri Light Artillery, Battery C
10th Ohio

Seventh Division: Brig. Gen. Marcellus Crocker: Brig. Gen. Isaac Quimby: Brig. Gen. John Smith

1st Brigade	2nd Brigade	3rd Brigade	Artillery
Col. J. Sanborn	Col. S. Holmes	**Col. G. Boomer**	Capt. Frank Sands
48th Indiana	Col. G. Raum	Col. H. Putnam	Capt. Henry Dillon
59th Indiana	56th Illinois	Brig. Gen. C. Matthies	1st Missouri Light
4th Minnesota	17th Iowa	93rd Illinois	Artillery, Batt. M
18th Wisconsin	10th Missouri	5th Iowa	11th Ohio Light
	24th Missouri,	10th Iowa	Artillery
	Company E	26th Missouri	6th Wisconsin Light
	80th Ohio		Artillery
			12th Wisconsin
			Light Artillery

Herron's Division: Maj. Gen. Francis Herron

1st Brigade	2nd Brigade	Unattached Cavalry
Brig. Gen. W. Vandever	**Brig. Gen. W. Orme**	5th Illinois Cavalry

37th Illinois	94th Illinois	3rd Iowa Cavalry
26th Indiana	19th Iowa	2nd Wisconsin Cavalry
20th Iowa	20th Wisconsin	
34th Iowa	1st Missouri, Company B	
38th Iowa		
1st Missouri, Company E		
1st Missouri, Company F		

District of North East Louisiana- Brig. Gen. Elias Dennis
Detached Brigade
Col. G. Neely
63rd Illinois
108th Illinois
120th Illinois
131st Illinois
10th Illinois Cavalry (4 companies)

Colored Brigade- Col. Isaac Shepard
Post of Milliken's Bend-Col. H. Schofield
8th Louisiana
11th Louisiana
13th Louisiana
1st Mississippi
3rd Mississippi

Post of Goodrich's Landing-Col. William Wood
1st Arkansas
10th Louisiana

Confederate Forces
Lt. Gen. John Pemberton
28,000 men
First Division: Maj. Gen. W.W. Loring

1st Brigade	2nd Brigade	3rd Brigade
Brig. Gen. Lloyd Tilghman	**Brig. Gen. W. Featherstone**	**Brig. Gen. A. Buford**
Col. Reynolds	3rd Mississippi	27th Alabama
1st Conf. Battalion	22nd Mississippi	35th Alabama
6th Mississippi	31st Mississippi	54th Alabama
15th Mississippi	33rd Mississippi	55th Alabama
20th Mississippi	1st Mississippi Battalion S.S.*	9th Arkansas
23rd Mississippi		3rd Kentucky
26th Mississippi		(4 companies)
Mississippi Battery (Culbertson's)		7th Kentucky
		12th Louisiana
		Pointe Coupee
		(Louisiana)-Artillery
		(Bouanchaud)

Stevenson's Division: Maj. Gen. Carter Stevenson

1st Brigade	2nd Brigade (Moore's)
Brig. Gen. S. Barton	**Brig. Gen. J. Moore**
40th Georgia	37th Alabama
41st Georgia	40th Alabama
42nd Georgia	42nd Alabama
43rd Georgia	1st Mississippi Light Artillery
52nd Georgia	35th Mississippi
Hudson's Mississippi Batt.	40th Mississippi
Pointe Coupee (Louisiana) Batt. Section A	2nd Texas
Pointe Coupee (Louisiana) Batt. Section C	Alabama Batt. Sengstak
	Pointe Coupee (Louisiana)
	Artillery

Smith's Division: Maj. Gen. Martin Smith

1st Brigade	Vaughan's Brigade	Third Brigade
Brig. Gen. W. Baldwin	**Brig. Gen. Vaughan**	**Brig. Gen. E. Shoup**
17th Louisiana	60th Tennessee	26th Louisiana
31st Louisiana	61st Tennessee	27th Louisiana
4th Mississippi	62nd Tennessee	28th Louisiana
46th Mississippi		McNally's Batt.
Tennessee Batt. (Tobin)		(Arkansas)

Mississippi State Guards / **Attached**

Mississippi State Guards	Attached
Brig. Gen. John Harris	4th Mississippi Battalion
5th Regiment	Mississippi Partisan Rangers (Smyth)
3rd Battalion	

Bowen's Division: Maj. Gen. John Bowen

1st Missouri Brigade	2nd Brigade
Col. F. Cockrell	**Brig. Gen. Martin Green (K)**
1st Missouri	Col. Dockery
2nd Missouri	Col. C. Davis
3rd Missouri	15th Arkansas
4th Missouri	19th Arkansas
5th Missouri	20th Arkansas
6th Missouri	21st Arkansas
Missouri Battery (Guibor's)	1st Arkansas Cavalry Batn. (dismounted)
Missouri Battery (Landis)	12th Arkansas Batn. Sharpshooters
Missouri Battery (Wade's)	1st Missouri Cavalry (dismounted)
	3rd Missouri Cavalry (dismounted)
	3rd Missouri Battery (Dawson)
	Lowe's Missouri Battery
	Stirman's Battalion

River Batteries- Col. Edward Higgins
1st Louisiana Artillery-Lt. Col. Beltzhoover
8th Louisiana Artillery Battalion-Maj. F. N. Ogden
23rd Louisiana Artillery.-Capt. Samuel Jones
1st Tennessee Artillery-Col. A. Jackson, Jr..
Tennessee Battery-Capt. J. B. Caruthers
Tennessee Battery-Capt. T.N. Johnston
Tennessee Battery-Capt. J.P. Lynch
Vaiden (Mississippi) Battery- Capt. S.C. Bains

Misc. Units
54th Alabama Detachment
City Guards-Capt. E. B. Martin
Mississippi Cavalry-Col. Wirt Adams

Johnston's Forces-Maj. Gen. Joseph Johnston

Gregg's Brigade	Gist's Brigade	Walker's Brigade
Brig. Gen. J. Gregg	Col. P. Colquitt	Brig. Gen. W.H.T. Walker
1st Tennessee Battalion	46th Georgia	1st Battalion Sharpshooters
3rd Tennessee	14th Mississippi	Georgia Battery (Martin)
10th Tennessee	24th South Carolina	
30th Tennessee	Mississippi Battery (Hoskins)	
41st Tennessee		
50th Tennessee		
7th Texas		
Missouri Battery (Bledsoe)		

Unattached
3rd Kentucky Mounted Infantry
8th Kentucky Mounted Infantry
Reinforcements
Rust's Brigade
Maxey's Brigade
Ector's Brigade
McNair's Brigade
Breckinridge's Brigade
W. H. Jackson's Division
Evans' Brigade
Loring's Division
  (Pemberton's Command)

Reinforcements arriving after Grant's withdrawal from Jackson to Vicksburg
1st Mississippi Light Artillery consists of Batteries A, C, D, E, G, I

*Sharpshooters

Major General C.L. Stevenson

In late 1862, Grant began to set his sights on Vicksburg, Mississippi. Vicksburg was a strategic location because it controlled the center of the Mississippi River, and it was a transfer point for both rail and river traffic headed east toward the heart of the Confederacy. It was also one of the few rail links to the west. Vicksburg was not going to be easy to take, situated, as it was, on a series of frowning bluffs above the river. The fortifications were 300 feet above the river and protected the city from any attack from that

Brass flag holder used with a over the shoulder leather harness, featuring the "C.S.A." engraved shield. The flag holder was dug near Vicksburg. (BCWM)

12 vessels south past the Vicksburg batteries, losing one to Confederate fire. On the 17th Grierson's Raid began. Led by Brig. Gen. Benjamin Grierson, Federal cavalry left for Louisiana from Grange, Tennessee. For sixteen days Grierson rode through central Mississippi to Baton Rouge, Louisiana, pulling away large units from Vicksburg's defense to pursue them. Porter, encouraged by light losses on his first try, ran a large supply flotilla past the Vicksburg batteries the night of April 22nd. Sherman's troops, many at work on the canal project at Duckport, abandoned this work and joined in a last action along the Yazoo River, northeast of Vicksburg, and on April 29th-30th made a demonstration against Confederate works at Haynes Bluff and Drumgould's Bluffs, diverting more of Pemberton's force. Also on April 29th, as McClernand's and McPherson's troops gathered near Hard Times, Porter's fleet assailed Confederate batteries at Grand Gulf, 33 miles southwest of Vicksburg, testing the Grand Gulf area as a landing site for Union troops. Though Porter found the guns there too strong, he had succeeded in further diverting Pemberton from Vicksburg.

Grant had originally determined that Rodney, Mississippi, would be the starting point of his invasion, but took the advice of a local slave and picked Bruinsburg instead. McClernand's and McPherson's corps were ferried east across the Mississippi from Hard Times on April 30th. That day Grant sent word north for Sherman to follow McPherson's route and join him.

On May 1st the Federal invasion force engaged the Confederates in the battle of Port Gibson. Pemberton had just over 40,000 men assigned to the Vicksburg region. Since they were scattered throughout the area, chasing Grierson and wary of Sherman, few of them could be brought to bear against Grant on short notice. Defeated at Port Gibson, Pemberton's troops moved north. Grant, to Pemberton's confusion, pushed northeast. Sherman's corps joined him on May 8th, and on May 12th the engagement at Raymond was fought. Johnston sent Brig. Gen. John Gregg to move up through Jackson and then march west for 15 miles to Raymond. Gregg was to attack Grant's flank and rear. Pemberton didn't know that Grant was also marching on Jackson. McPherson's XVII Corps, 10,000 men strong, was in the lead, and Gregg's brigade was in it's path. Gregg attacked thinking McPherson's force was small. Gregg sent the 7th Texas and 3rd Tennessee south across 14 mile Creek to pin down the Federals, while four other regiments forded the creek to the east and hit McPherson's right flank. The Texans and Tennesseans launched a furious attack, slamming into the 23rd Indiana. Panic spread among the Federals because the dense woods wouldn't allow them to form up or fix bayonets. Maj. Gen. John Logan, commander of the 3rd Division, rallied the men and launched an attack, and the Confederates were driven back across the creek. By the time Gregg launched his attack on the flank, Logan was in command along the creek. Decimated by fire in front and flank, the Confederates faltered, then fell back. By 2 p.m., Gregg had retreated toward Raymond. The Federals lost 442 men. The Confederates lost 514. Gregg abandoned Raymond and headed for Jackson.

Johnston took personal command of the Confederates at Jackson, 15 miles northeast of Raymond, on May 13th. Johnston was cut off from Pemberton's forces, so he left Brig. Gen. W.H.T. Wallace and Col. Peyton Colquitt astride the Clinton Road and assigned the 3rd Kentucky Mounted Infantry and some sharpshooters to guard the southwest approach to Jackson. On May 14 Federals, under Brig. Gen. Marcellus Crocker and Brig. Gen. William Tecumsheh Sherman, with four regiments under Col. Samuel Holme's brigade, attacked, and quickly won an engagement at Jackson. Federal losses were 300, Gregg lost 200 men. Sherman and Crocker had cut off Johnston from Pemberton, and ensured the latter's isolation for the rest of the campaign. In two weeks, Grant's force had come well over 130 miles northeast from their Bruinsburg landing site.

Ordering Sherman to destroy Jackson's heavy industry and

direction. The surrounding areas were swamps and bogs. East of the city, the line of bluffs fell away to a plain, and hillsides commanded the eastern approaches. Gen. Grant made several attempts to take Vicksburg. Following failures in the First Vicksburg Campaign, the battle of Chickasaw Bluffs, the Yazoo Pass Expedition, and Steel's Bayou Expedition, in the Spring of 1863, he prepared to cross his troops from the west bank of the Mississippi River to a point south of Vicksburg and drive against the city from the south and east. Commanding Confederate batteries at Port Hudson, Louisiana., farther south prevented the transportation of waterborne supply and any communication from Union forces in Baton Rouge and New Orleans. Naval support for his campaign would have to come from Rear Adm. David Porter's fleet north of Vicksburg. Running past the powerful Vicksburg Batteries, Porter's vessels, once south of the city, could ferry Federals to the east bank. There the infantry would face two Confederate forces, one under Lt. Gen. John C. Pemberton at Vicksburg and another around Jackson, Mississippi, soon to be commanded by Joseph Johnston.

In January 1863, Grant organized his force into the XIII Corps under Maj. Gen. John McClernand, the XV Corps under William Tecumsheh Sherman, the XVI Corps under Maj. Gen. Stephen Hurlbut, and the XVII Corps under Maj. Gen. James McPherson. Simultaneous with Grant's Vicksburg offensive Maj. Gen. Nathaniel Banks began his maneuvering along the Red River in Louisiana. Hurlbut's Corps was subsequently transferred to New Orleans. With his remaining corps, Grant began operations late in March. On the 29th and 30th McClernand's and McPherson's men, at Miliken's Bend and Lake Providence, northwest of Vicksburg, began working their way south, building a military road to New Carthage, Louisiana, preparatory to a move south to Hard Times, Louisiana, a village opposite Bruinsburg, Mississippi.

On the night of April 16th, at Grant's request, Porter took

Very unusual C.S. rectangular two piece sword belt plate. (BCWM)

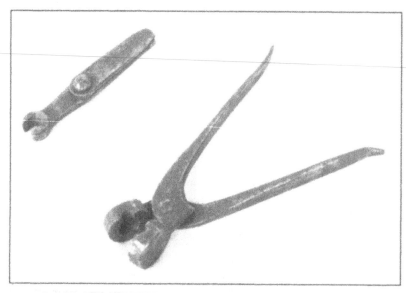

Dug .69 caliber bullet mold and nipple wrench from Vicksburg area. (BCWM)

ing was to the north, where McClernand's XIII Corps was to strike the angle of Pemberton's line at Champion Hill from the east, while Logan's division of McPherson corps attacked from the north. Only one of McClernand's divisions came into action, Brig. Gen. Alvin Hovey's. At 10:30 a.m., Hovey sent his two brigades to charge up Champion Hill. Holding the Confederate left was Gen. Stevenson. Some of his regiments were spread out over 300 yards. Before Stevenson was the Federal brigade of Brig. Gen. McGinnis. During the battle, Capt. Samuel Ridley's Mississippi Battery was captured and Ridley was hit six times. By 1:00 p.m., The Confederate left was falling apart. At 1:30 p.m., Bowen began to move towards Pemberton. Bowen launched a counterattack against Hovey's troops, with Col. Francis Cockrell's Missouri brigade on the left and Brig. Gen. Martin Green's Arkansas brigade on the right. Hovey retreated under the Confederate assault. Grant now ordered two brigades from the XVII Corps under Col. George Boomer, and Col. Samuel Holmes to help Hovey. On the right flank atop Champion Hill, the 34th Indiana was rallied by Gen. Logan, who then led his men forward. At 2:30 p.m., McClernand ordered the division of Brig. Gen. Peter Osterhaus forward. Hovey had driven Pemberton's left back until the Confederate line faced almost due north; now, Osterhaus advancing from the east threatened Bowen's right flank. Champion Hill's defense line collapsed for the Confederates and Loring's men were rushing in with no order. Pemberton called a retreat, and ordered Brig. Gen. Lloyd Tilghman to hold his opposition one mile east of the crossing. One of the last casualties was Tilghman himself, killed when solid shot from a Federal cannon ripped through his hip. Pemberton made it across the Raymond Road bridge, Loring's 6,550 men were cut off, and he abandoned his artillery and supplies. Three days later he joined Johnston's army at Jackson. Union losses at Champion Hill were 2,441, Pemberton lost 3,839. Pemberton took a beating there and pulled his army into the defense of Vicksburg.

Pemberton set up entrenchments along the Big Black River and sent Bowen and Brig. Gen. John Vaughn to protect the earthworks. On May 17th, the Federals under Brig. Gen. Michael Lawler, attacked the Confederates at Big Black River Bridge, fighting their way across the Big Black. The Confederates destroyed their river crossings behind them: undeterred, the Federals threw up their own bridges and continued the pursuit the next day. Federal losses at Big Black Creek were 39 killed and 237 wounded, including Col. William Kinsman of the 23rd Ohio. The Confederate losses were 200 men, with 1,751 being captured.

Approaching from the east and northeast, McClernand's, McPherson's, and Sherman's corps neared the Vicksburg defenses May 18th. Sherman veered north to take the hills overlooking the Yazoo River. Possession of these heights assured Grant reinforcement and supply lines from the North. On May 19th, Grant made

rail facilities, Grant turned west, roughly following the Southern Mississippi Railroad to Bolton. On May 14th, Pemberton called for the first council of war and asked his generals what to do. The generals decided for Johnston to move north of Jackson, calling for Pemberton to move toward him. Pemberton told his men to march south then north and rendezvous with Johnston's force at Clinton. They were halfway there when the Federals intercepted them. On May 16th, Grant fought the last battle of his field campaign, at Champion Hill, Mississippi. Pemberton had 23,000 men against McPherson's and McClernand's 32,000. Pemberton deployed three divisions a mile east of Baker's Creek to cover the bridges on the Jackson and Raymond roads. His line extended four miles northeast to the crest of Champion Hill, then curved back two miles west to where the Jackson road crossed Baker's Creek. Maj. Gen. Carter Stevenson commanded Pemberton's left, Maj. Gen. John Bowen the center, and Maj. Gen. William Loring the right. The battle began in the south, where Maj. Gen. Andrew Jackson Smith's Federal division, marching west on Raymond Road, came under fire from Loring's artillery. The heaviest fight-

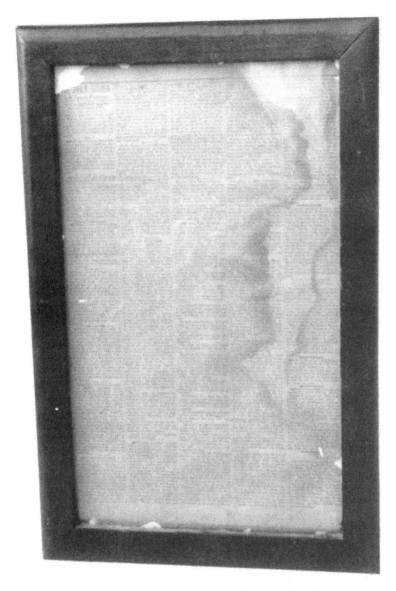

Newspaper printed in Vicksburg on July 3, 1863, utilizing old floral design wall paper due to the shortage of printing paper with in the city. (BCWM)

ality, McClernand had already lost his hold on the forts. Sherman's and McPherson renewed their attacks based on McClernand's information. The Federals under their command took heavy losses, and could not break through the forts. The Federals lost 3,199 men, the Confederates 500. The attack showed the strength of the miles of Confederate works arching east around the city, and convinced Grant that Pemberton could only be defeated in a protracted siege.

The siege of Vicksburg began with the repulse of the May 22nd assault and lasted until July 4, 1863. As the siege progressed, Pemberton's 20,000 man garrison was reduced by disease and starvation and the city's residents were forced to seek the refuge of caves and bombproofs in the surrounding hillsides, where they sometimes ate rats to satisfy their great hunger. Grant was now being reinforced, and he would soon have 70,000 men along a 12 mile front. By mid June, Grant had assembled 200 pieces of artillery. Grant tried several times to gain access to the fort by tunneling under it and trying to blow a hole to allow the infantry to charge into the city's earthworks. On June 23rd, Capt. Andrew Hickenlooper, Chief Engineer for the XVII Corps, dug a gallery 45 feet long in two days, and the tunnel was filled with 2,200 pounds of black powder. The Confederates heard the digging, so they began to dig a counter tunnel but just before it was completed, the Federals exploded their tunnel, killing six Confederates. Brig. Gen. Mortimer Leggett's Federal brigade charged into the crater left by the explosion, but they did not bring ladders with them, and could not get out to the front. The Confederates began firing right down on top of the Federals. At 5:00 p.m., the Yankees retreated from the crater and returned to their trenches. The Federals lost 200, the Confederates lost 200. On July 1st, Grant tried one more time to blow a hole under the same Confederate earthworks. Twelve Confederates were killed, and 108 wounded in the blast. The Federals once again failed to take the earthworks. Grant opted for an all out assault on July 6th. It just so happened that on this same day, Johnston, who was in Jackson, was to attack Grant and help Pemberton. He had massed 30,000 men, but he was too late. Hunger and daily bombardments by Grant's forces and Porters gunboats compelled Pemberton to ask for surrender terms on July 3rd. Grant offered none, and asked for unconditional surrender. Grant later changed his mind and decided to parole all of Pemberton's men if Pemberton would surrender the fort. Pemberton surrendered the city on July 4, 1863, thus ending the Second Vicksburg Campaign. On July 4th, thousands of Confederates were being paroled, so Sherman moved his force to oppose this new threat. Sherman's march would result in the siege of Jackson. On this same date, at a place called Gettysburg, Pennsylvania, Confederate General Robert E. Lee and the Army of Northern Virginia suffered a humiliating blow to their forces. On July 9th, Port Hudson surrendered to the Federals. The Mississippi River was now open to Union shipping along it's entire length.

his first attack on the city's seven mile long entrenchments. McClernand attacked on the east, and McPherson and Sherman on the north. Sherman's XV Corps made the initial assault. Col. Stiles Smith, of the 1st Brigade, in Maj. Gen. Frank Blair Jr.'s, 2nd Division, led his five regiments, the 113th, and the 116th Illinois, the 6th, and the 8th Missouri, and the 13th U.S., toward Stockade Redan. Capt. Charles Ewin, of the 13th U.S. Inf., managed to gain only a foothold on a ditch north of the stockade, but the stockade itself was not captured. Grant lost 942 men, Pemberton only lost 250. The second assault on May 22nd, was a disaster for Union forces. For four hours, the Federals attacked Railroad Redoubt and Col. Ashbel Smith's 2nd Texas, just to the north. The Federals were bogged down. Grant ordered another assault in mid-afternoon, based on McClernand's report that he had two forts on the Railroad Redoubt and that he needed Grant to send McPherson and Sherman to help him hold them. In actu-

Battle of Chickamauga, Georgia

"Bloody River"

September 19-20, 1863
Campaign: Chickamauga Campaign
Principal Commanders: Maj. Gen. William Rosecrans and Maj. Gen. George Thomas (US); Gen. Braxton Bragg and Lt. Gen. James Longstreet (CS)
Forces Engaged: The Army of the Cumberland (US); Army of Tennessee (CS)

Order of Battle

Army of the Cumberland
Maj. Gen. William Rosecrans
58,200 men

XIV Corps
Maj. Gen. George Thomas
First Division
Brig. Gen. Absalom Baird

First Brigade Col. B. Scribner	Second Brigade Brig. Gen. J. Starkweather	Third Brigade Brig. Gen. J.H. King
38th Indiana	1st Wisconsin	15th U.S., 1st Battalion
94th Ohio	21st Wisconsin	16th U.S., 1st Battalion
2nd Ohio	24th Illinois	18th U.S., 1st Battalion
33rd Ohio	79th Pennsylvania	18th U.S., 2nd Battalion
10th Wisconsin		19th U.S., 1st Battalion

Artillery
1st Michigan Light, Battery A
4th Indiana Light Battery
5th U.S., Battery H

Second Division
Maj. Gen. James Negley

1st Brigade Brig. Gen. J. Beatty	2nd Brigade Col. T. Stanley	3rd Brigade Col. W. Sirwell
42nd Indiana	Col. W. Stoughton	78th Pennsylvania
88th Indiana	18th Ohio	21st Ohio
15th Kentucky	19th Illinois	74th Ohio
3rd Ohio	11th Michigan	37th Indiana
104th Illinois	69th Ohio	

Artillery
Illinois Light, Bridge's
1st Ohio Light
1st Ohio Light, Battery G

Third Division: Brig. Gen. John Brannan

Connell's Brigade Col. J. Connell	2nd Brigade Col. J. Croxton	3rd Brigade Col. F. Van Derveer
17th Ohio	Col. W. Hays	9th Ohio
31st Ohio	4th Kentucky	35th Ohio
38th Ohio	10th Kentucky	2nd Minnesota
82nd Indiana	10th Indiana	87th Indiana
	74th Indiana	
	14th Ohio	

Artillery
1st Michigan Light, Battery D
1st Ohio Light, Battery C
4th U.S., Battery I

Fourth Division: Maj. Gen. Joseph Reynold's

First Brigade Col. J. Wilder's	Second Brigade Col. E. King's	Third Brigade Brig. Gen. J. Turchin's	Artillery
17th Indiana	Col. M. Robinson	11th Ohio	Indiana Light,18th Batt.
72nd Indiana	68th Indiana	36th Ohio	Indiana Light, 19th Batt.
92nd Illinois	75th Indiana	89th Ohio	Indiana Light, 21st Batt.
98th Illinois	101st Indiana	92nd Ohio	
123rd Illinois	80th Illinois	18th Kentucky	
	105th Ohio		

XX Corps: Maj. Gen. Alexander McDowell McCook
First Division: Brig. Gen. Jefferson Davis

First Brigade Col. Post	Second Brigade Brig. Gen. W. Carlin	Third Brigade Col. H. Heg	Artillery
22nd Indiana	21st Illinois	Col. J. Martin	Wisconsin Light, 5th Battery
59th Illinois	38th Illinois	15th Wisconsin	Minnesota Light, 2nd Battery
74th Illinois	81st Indiana	25th Illinois	Wisconsin Light, 8th Battery
75th Illinois	101st Ohio	35th Illinois	
		8th Kansas	

Second Division: Brig. Gen. Richard Johnson

First Brigade Brig. Gen. A. Willich	Second Brigade Col. Dodge	Third Brigade Col. P. Baldwin	Artillery
49th Ohio	77th Pennsylvania	Col. W. Berry	1st Ohio Light, Battery A
39th Indiana*	29th Indiana	6th Indiana	Ohio Light, 20th Battery
32nd Indiana	30th Indiana	1st Ohio	Indiana Light, 5th Battery
15th Ohio	79th Illinois	93rd Ohio	
79th Illinois			
5th Kentucky			

*Mounted & Detached

Third Division: Maj. Gen. Philip Sheridan

First Brigade Brig. Gen. W. Lytle	Second Brigade Col. B. Liabolt	Third Brigade Col. L. Bradley	Artillery
Col. S. Miller	2nd Missouri	Col. N. Walworth	Indiana Light, 11th Battery
88th Illinois	15th Missouri	22nd Illinois	1st Missouri Light, Battery G
36th Illinois	44th Illinois	27th Illinois	1st Illinois Light, Battery C
24th Wisconsin	73rd Illinois	42nd Illinois	
21st Michigan		51st Illinois	

XXI Corps
Maj. Gen. Thomas Crittenden
First Division: Brig. Gen. Thomas Wood

First Brigade Col. G. Buell	Second Brigade (not engaged in battle)	Third Brigade Col. C. Harker	Artillery
26th Ohio		3rd Kentucky	Indiana Light, 8th Battery
58th Indiana		64th Ohio	Ohio Light, 6th Battery
13th Michigan		125th Ohio	
100th Illinois		73rd Indiana	

Second Division: Maj. Gen. John Palmer

First Brigade Brig. Gen. C. Cruft	Second Brigade Brig. Gen. W. Hazen	Third Brigade Col. W. Grose	Artillery
1st Kentucky*	41st Ohio	36th Indiana	1st Ohio Light, Battery B
2nd Kentucky	124th Ohio	24th Ohio	1st Ohio Light, Battery F
31st Indiana	6th Kentucky	6th Ohio	4th U.S., Battery H
90th Ohio	9th Indiana	23rd Kentucky	4th U.S., Battery M
		84th Illinois	

*Five Companies detached as wagon guard

Third Division: Brig. Gen. H. Van Cleve

First Brigade Brig. Gen. S. Beatty	Second Brigade Col. G. Dick	Third Brigade Col. S. Barnes	Artillery
9th Kentucky	44th Indiana	51st Ohio	Indiana Light, 7th Battery
17th Kentucky	13th Ohio	99th Ohio	Pennsylvania Light, 26th Battery
19th Ohio	86th Indiana	35th Indiana	Wisconsin Light, 3rd Battery
79th Indiana	59th Ohio	8th Kentucky	

Reserve Corps: Maj. Gen. Gordon Granger
First Division: Brig. Gen. James Steedman

Whitaker's Brigade Brig. Gen. W. Whitaker	J. Mitchell's Brigade Col. J. Mitchell
40th Ohio	98th Ohio
89th Ohio	113th Ohio
84th Indiana	121st Ohio
96th Illinois	78th Illinois
115th Illinois	1st Illinois Light Artillery, Battery I
22nd Michigan	
Ohio Light Artillery, Battery M	

Cavalry Corps
First Division: Brig. Gen. Robert Mitchell

First Brigade	**Second Brigade**	**Third Brigade**
Col. E. McCook	**Col. D. Ray**	**Col. L. Watkins**
Col. A. Campbell's	2nd Indiana	4th Kentucky
2nd Michigan	4th Indiana	5th Kentucky
9th Pennsylvania	2nd Tennessee	6th Kentucky
1st Tennessee	1st Wisconsin	
	1st Ohio Light Artillery, Battery D (section)	

Second Division: Brig. Gen. George Crook

First Brigade	**Second Brigade**	**Artillery**
Col. R. Minty	**Col. E. Long**	Chicago (Illinois) Board
3rd Indiana (Battalion)	2nd Kentucky	of Trade Battery
4th Michigan	1st Ohio	
7th Pennsylvania	3rd Ohio	
4th U.S.	4th Ohio	

Confederate Forces
Army of Tennessee
Gen. Braxton Bragg
66,300 Men
Right Wing
Cheatham's Division

Jackson Brigade	**Smith's Brigade**	**Maney's Brigade**
Brig. Gen. J. Jackson	**Brig. Gen. P. Smith**	**Brig. Gen. G. Maney**
1st Georgia	Col. A. Vaugh, Jr.	6th-9th Tennessee
2nd Georgia Sharpshooters	11th Tennessee	1st-27th Tennessee
12th-47th Tennessee	4th Tennessee	24th Tennessee
5th Mississippi	13th-154th Tennessee	Dawson's Sharpshooters
8th Mississippi	29th Tennessee	

Wright's Brigade
Brig. Gen. M. Wright
8th Tennessee
16th Tennessee
28th Tennessee
38th Tennessee
51st-52nd Tennessee

Strahl's Brigade	**Divisional Artillery**
Brig. Gen. O. Strahl	Maj. Melancthon Smith
4th-5th Tennessee	Carnes (Tennessee) Battery

19th Tennessee   Scogin's (Georgia) Battery
24th Tennessee   Scott's (Tennessee) Battery
31st Tennessee   Smith's (Mississippi) Battery
33rd Tennessee   Stanford's (Mississippi) Battery

Hill's Corps
Lt. Gen. Daniel Hill
Maj. Gen. Patrick Cleburne's Division

Wood's Brigade	**Polk's Brigade**
Brig. Gen. S.A.M. Wood	Brig. Gen. Lucius Polk
16th Alabama	1st Arkansas
33rd Alabama	3rd-5th Confederate
45th Alabama	2nd Tennessee
18th Alabama	35th Tennessee
32nd-45th Mississippi	48th Tennessee
15th Mississippi Battalion S.S.*	

*Sharpshooters

Deschler's Brigade
Brig. Gen. James Deschler
19th-24th Arkansas
6th-10th Texas Infantry-15th Texas Cavalry (dismounted)
17th-18th-24th-25th Texas Cavalry (dismounted)

Divisional Artillery
Maj. Hotchkiss
Capt. Henry Semple
Calvert's Arkansas Battery
Douglas Texas Battery
Semple's Alabama Battery

Maj. Gen. John C. Breckinridge's Division

Helm's Brigade	**Adam's Brigade**	**Stovall's Brigade** Brig.
Gen. B. Helm	Brig. Gen. D. Adams	Brig. Gen. M. Stovall
Col. J. Lewis	Col. R. Gibson	1st-3rd Florida
41st Alabama	32nd Alabama	4th Florida
2nd Kentucky	13th-20th Louisiana	47th Georgia
4th Kentucky	16th-25th Louisiana	60th North Carolina
6th Kentucky	19th Louisiana	
9th Kentucky	14th Louisiana Battalion Sharpshooters	

Artillery
Maj. Rice Graves

Cobb's Kentucky Battery
Mebane's Tennessee Battery
Grave's Battery
Slocumb's Louisiana Battery

Reserve Corps
Maj. Gen. William H. T. Walker
Walker's Division
Maj. Gen. States Rights Gist

Gist's Brigade	**Ector's Brigade**	**Wilson's Brigade**
Col. Colquitt	**Brig. Gen. Ector**	**Col. C. Wilson**
46th Georgia	Stone's Alabama S.S.	25th Georgia
8th Georgia Battalion	Pound's Mississippi	29th Georgia
16th South Carolina	Battalion S.S.*	30th Georgia
24th South Carolina	29th North Carolina	1st Georgia Battalion
	10th Texas Cavalry	S.S.*
	(dismounted)	4th Louisiana Battalion
	14th Texas Cavalry	
	(dismounted)	
	32nd Texas Cavalry (dismounted)	

Artillery
Ferguson's South Carolina Battery
Howell's G. Battery

Liddell's Division
Brig. Gen. St. John Liddell

Liddell's Brigade	**Walthall's Brigade**	**Artillery**
Col. D. Govan	**Brig. Gen. E. Walthall**	**Capt. C. Swett**
2nd-15th Arkansas	24th Mississippi	Fowler's Alabama Battery
5th-13th Arkansas	29th Mississippi	Warren Light Artillery
6th-7th Arkansas	30th Mississippi	(Mississippi) Battery
8th Arkansas	34th Mississippi	
1st Louisiana Regulars		

Left Wing
Lt. Gen. James Longstreet
Hindman's Division
Maj. Gen. Thomas Hindman
Brig. Gen. Patton Anderson

Anderson's Brigade	**Deas' Brigade**	**Manigault's Brigade**
Brig. Gen. P. Anderson	Brig. Gen. Z. Deas	Brig. Gen. A. Manigault
Col. J. H. Sharp	19th Alabama	24th Alabama
7th Mississippi	22nd Alabama	28th Alabama
9th Mississippi	25th Alabama	34th Alabama
10th Mississippi	39th Alabama	10th-19th South Carolina
41st Mississippi	50th Alabama	Water's Battery (Alabama)
44th Mississippi	17th Alabama Batn. S.S.*	
9th Mississippi Batn. S.S.*	Dent's (Alabama) Battery	
Garrity's Alabama Battery		

Buckner's Corps
Maj. Gen. Simon Buckner
Stewart's Division
Maj. Gen. Alexander Stewart

Johnson's Brigade	**Bate's Brigade**	**Brown's Brigade**
Brig. Gen. B. Johnson	**Brig. Gen. W. Bate**	**Brig. Gen. J. Brown**
Col. J. Fulton	58th Alabama	Col. E. Cook
17th Tennessee	37th Georgia	18th Tennessee
23rd Tennessee	15th-37th Tennessee	26th Tennessee
25th Tennessee	20th Tennessee	32nd Tennessee
44th Tennessee	4th Georgia Batn. S.S.*	45th Tennessee
		23rd Tennessee Batn.

Clayton's Brigade
Brig. Gen. H. Clayton
18th Alabama
36th Alabama
38th Alabama

Artillery
Maj. J. Wesley Eldridge
1st Arkansas Battery
T.H. Dawson's Georgia Battery
Eufaula Artillery Alabama Battery
Company E., 9th Georgia Artillery Battalion (Everett's; formerly Billington York's Battery)

Preston's Division
Brig. Gen. William Preston

Gracie's Brigade	**Trigg's Brigade**	**Third Brigade**
Brig. Gen. A. Gracie, Jr.	**Col. R. Trigg**	**Col. J. Kelley**
1st Alabama Battalion	1st Florida Cav.	65th Georgia
2nd Alabama Battalion	(dismounted)	5th Kentucky
3rd Alabama Battalion	6th Florida	58th North Carolina
4th Alabama Battalion	7th Florida	63rd Virginia
43rd Alabama	54th Virginia	
63rd Tennessee		

9th Georgia Artillery Battery
Maj. A. Leyden
Company C, Wolihin's Battery
Company D, Peeple's Battery
Jeffress' Virginia Battery

Reserve Corps Artillery
Maj. Samuel Williams
Baxter's Tennessee Battery
Kolb's Alabama Battery
Darden's Mississippi Battery
McCant's Florida Battery

Johnson's Division
Brig. Gen. Bushrod Johnson

Gregg's Brigade	**McNair's Brigade**
Brig. Gen. J. Gregg	**Brig. Gen. E. McNair**
Col. C. Sugg	Col. D. Coleman
3rd Tennessee	1st Arkansas Mounted Rifles (dismounted)
10th Tennessee	2nd Arkansas Mounted Rifles (dismounted)
30th Tennessee	25th Arkansas
41st Tennessee	39th North Carolina
50th Tennessee	4th, 31st, 4th Arkansas Battalion (consolidated)
7th Texas	Culpepper's South Carolina Battery
1st Tennessee Battalion	
Bledsoe's Missouri Battery	

Longstreet's Corps
Maj. Gen. John Bell Hood
McLaw's Division
Brig. Gen. Joseph Kershaw
Maj. Gen. Lafayette McLaws

Kershaw's Brigade	**Humphrey's Brigade**
Brig. Gen. J. Kershaw	**Brig. Gen. B. Humphrey's**
2nd South Carolina	13th Mississippi
7th South Carolina	18th Mississippi
15th South Carolina	17th Mississippi
3rd South Carolina Battalion	21st Mississippi
8th South Carolina	
3rd South Carolina	

Hood's Division
Maj. Gen. John B. Hood
Brig. Gen. E. McIver Law

Law's Brigade	**Robertson's Brigade**	**Benning's Brigade**
Brig. Gen. E. M. Law	**Brig. Gen. J. Robertson**	**Brig. Gen. H. Benning**
Col. J. Sheffield	3rd Arkansas	2nd Georgia
4th Alabama	1st Texas	15th Georgia
15th Alabama	4th Texas	17th Georgia
47th Alabama	5th Texas	20th Georgia
44th Alabama		
15th Alabama		

Reserve Artillery
Maj. Felix Robertson
Barrett's Missouri Battery
Le Gardeur's Louisiana Battery
Havis's Georgia Battery
Lumsden's Alabama Battery
Massenburg's Georgia Battery

Cavalry
Maj. Gen. Joseph Wheeler
Wharton's Division
Brig. Gen. John Wharton

First Brigade	**Second Brigade**
Col. C. C. Crews	**Col. Thomas Harrison**

Malone's Alabama Regiment
2nd Georgia
3rd Georgia
4th Georgia

3rd Confederate
3rd Kentucky
4th Tennessee
8th Texas
11th Texas
White's Tennessee Battery

Martin's Division
Brig. Gen. William Martin

First Brigade
Col. J. T. Morgan
1st Alabama
3rd Alabama
51st Alabama
3rd Alabama
8th Confederate

Second Brigade
Col. A. Russell
4th Alabama
1st Confederate
Wiggins Arkansas Battery

Forrest's Corps
Brig. Gen. Nathan Bedford Forrest
Armstrong's Division
Brig. Gen. Frank Armstrong

Armstrong's Brigade
Col. James Wheeler
3rd Arkansas
2nd Kentucky
6th Tennessee
18th Tennessee Battalion

Forrest's Brigade
Col. G. Dibrell
4th Tennessee
8th Tennessee
9th Tennessee
10th Tennessee
11th Tennessee
Shaw's Battalion, P.P. Hamilton's
  Battalion & R. D. Allison's
  Squadron (Consolidated)
Huggin's Battery (Tennessee)
Morton's Battery (Tennessee)

Pegram's Division
Brig. Gen. John Pegram

Davidson's Brigade
Brig. Gen. H. B. Davidson
1st Georgia
6th Georgia
6th North Carolina
10th Confederate
Rucker's Tennessee Legion
Huwald's Tennessee Battery

Scott's Brigade
Col. J. Scott
Detachment of John Hunt
  Morgan's Command
1st Louisiana
2nd Tennessee
5th Tennessee
Robinson's Louisiana Battery
  (one section)

Between the 13th and 17th of September 1863, Union Major General William Rosecrans concentrated his divisions of the Army of the Cumberland that had been scattered between Chattanooga, Tennessee, and northwest Georgia. After prying Confederate General Braxton Bragg's army out of Chattanooga, Rosecran's troops followed it south, jockeyed with it at Dug Gap, then pulled back near Lee and Gordon's Mill.

Nightfall of the 17th found Maj. Gen. Thomas Crittenden's XXI Corps at Lee and Gordon's Mill, Maj. Gen. George Thomas XIV Corps nearby, and Maj. Gen. Alexander McCook's XX Corps in McLemore's Cove. Maj. Gen. Gordon Grangers reserve corps, called up from near Bridgeport, Alabama, went north to Rossville to guard the road to Chattanooga. Since Thomas and Crittenden had two close brushes with Bragg days earlier, Rosecrans was apprehensive, and facing south, he looked for the enemy.

Bragg marched his columns north on the east side of Chickamauga Creek, planning to cross it north of Lee and Gordon's Mill, block the road to Chattanooga, and either crush Crittenden's corps or hurl it back on Thomas. By mauling Rosecrans left (Crittenden and Thomas' positions west of the north-south La Fayette Road), Bragg could reoccupy Chattanooga and possibly destroy the Union army before it entered Tennessee. On the 18th Bragg was reinforced by Lt. Gen. James Longstreet and five brigades of Virginians, bringing his strength to over 66,000 men. On the 18th, Bragg ordered an attack on Crittenden's XXI Corps at Lee and Gordon's Mill. Bushrod Johnson's division was stopped at Reed's Bridge by Federal cavalry under Col. Robert Minty, just northwest of Crittenden and Thomas. Walker's corps was to take

the Federal center, but was engaged with John Wilder's cavalry at Alexander's bridge. Walker had to wade the creek at Lambert's Ford more than a mile to the north. Later Gen. John Bell Hood and his three brigades joined Johnson's divisions at Reed's Bridge and drove Minty's cavalry away.

On the morning of the 19th fighting began between Reed's Bridge and the La Fayette Road, Federals on the west, Confederates on the east. The battle started when Col. Dan McCook notified George Thomas that the Confederates were crossing the creek, and Thomas sent Gen. Brannan to attack the Confederate unit. Brannan sent the brigade of Col. John Croxton to Reed's Bridge, where at 8:00 a.m. Croxton faced Forrest's cavalry. Croxton drove Forrest back, and Walker's corps, under Confederate General States Rights Gist, ran into the Federals. Brannan sent the rest of his division to assist Croxton, but was swept away by the oncoming Confederates. Baird's division was brought up. Walker joined Brig. Gen. St. John Liddell. Again, the Confederates drove the Federals from their lines, pushing Brannan and Baird all the way back to their starting point. Liddell was captured, and Lt. George Van Pelt's six guns were captured, and he was killed.

Thomas now asked Rosecrans for help. Rosecrans sent Gen. Richard Johnson's division from McCook's corps. The Confederates fell back. Walker called for help and was sent Maj. Gen. Ben Cheatham's division. By 1:00 p.m., Rosecrans had moved his headquarters from Crawfish Springs to Lee and Gordon's Mill. Cheatham was counterattacked by Gen. Richard Johnson's division. Johnson's attack threatened the Confederate line, so Maj. Gen. Alexander P. Stewart's division was sent to support Cheatham. At 2:30 p.m., Stewart attacked Brig. Gen. Gen. Horatio Van Cleve's division, and sent it reeling back past the Brotherton House. Stewart lost 604 men in minutes. Reynold's joined Van Cleve. Negley stood in reserve. Stewart seized the La Fayette Road, which linked Thomas corps with Crittenden's corps. The Confederates now threatened the Dug Valley Road leading to Rosecrans Headquarters and Chattanooga.

Van Cleve's division reformed alongside Reynold's division in front of the Dug Valley Road as Stewart approached them. At 4:00 p.m., Hood aligned a division under Brig. Gen. Evander Law beside Brig. Gen. Bushrod Johnson and launched, without orders,

Maj. Gen. Thomas

Gen. Longstreet

a counterattack against the Federal right. Hood rode with his men, and struck Union General Jeff Davis. Davis flanks were unprotected and his regiments gave way under Hood's assault. Col. Hans Christian Heg was the last to leave of Davis division. He was killed along with 696 of his men. Brig. Gen. Thomas Wood moved into the gap on Davis right and now Hood's flank was threatened. Eli Lilly's artillery set up in a cornfield and fired at Johnson's left flank. Darkness was setting in and the fighting began to subside. Cleburne crossed the river, passed through Walker's lines, descended on Thomas, and captured three guns, 300 prisoners and gained a mile of ground. While the Federals northern line took a beating, there was no apparent victor.

On September 20th, at 9:45 a.m., Bragg resumed sledgehammer blows to the Union left. Gen. John C. Breckinridge, with three brigades, was to attack the Federal left. The Kentucky soldiers under Breckinridge got within 30 yards of the Union lines, but they took massive casualties. Confederate General Ben Hardin Helm was one of the fatalities. Helm was shot by a member of the 15th Kentucky Inf. U.S. Breckinridge seized the Chattanooga

Road, but couldn't hold on to it and Beatty called for Federal help. Negley's two other brigades couldn't help Beatty because Union General Thomas Wood's division hadn't replaced Negley in McCook's front line. Rosecrans ordered Wood to move his division into position, freeing Negley's remaining troops.

Breckinridge's attack was now followed by Cleburne division. Gen. James Deshler, under Cleburne was killed when a Federal shell ripped open his chest and took out his heart. The Confederates were under heavy fire from artillery and musket and fell back behind some trees. Confederate General Leonidas Polk now sent Walker and Cheatham's division in. The Confederates were driven back by the Federal troops who were protected by log breastworks. Rosecrans began to send all his units from the right flank to Thomas.

At 10:30 a.m., Capt. Sanford Kellogg reported to Rosecrans that a gap existed in his line. Unable to see a unit which was shielded by trees, he ordered Brig. Gen. Thomas Wood to move his men from their location on the right to fill the supposed hole. Wood protested, said there was no gap, then obeyed. Longstreet sent three divisions, under Brig. Gen. Joseph Kershaw, Gen. John Bell Hood, and Brig. Gen. Johnson to surge through the gap where Wood had been. Twenty three thousand Confederates poured through the quarter mile gap in the Union line. Rosecrans and half his army were swept from the field. Gen. Jeff Davis, Brig. Gen. Sheridan, and Gen. McCook all ran for the rear. Brig. Gen. William Lytle, of McCook's corps tried to stop the Confederate onslaught but was wounded four times, and his men broke and ran. Rosecrans ran for Chattanooga and arrived there by 4:00 p.m.. Thomas, the senior Union officer present, deployed brigades along the crest of Snodgrass Hill to the rear. Thomas' main line, which was held by Baird, Johnson, Reynold's and Maj. Gen. John Palmer's divisions, faced east. To the south was Brannan and part of Wood's, and to the rear were roads leading west to McFarland's Gap, and north to Rossville & Chattanooga. Gen. Steedman, and Maj. Gen. Gordon Granger arrived as reinforcements. In the face of savage attacks, these soldiers held their ground until dark, when Thomas withdrew most of his troops, leaving the field to the Confederates.

Rosecrans and many survivors began a march for Tennessee that afternoon. Thomas set up a rear guard at Rossville Gap, holding north through the 21st, then followed the rest of the army into Chattanooga.

Chickamauga was Bragg's greatest victory. To the frustration of many, he failed to follow it up, and losses were staggering. Bragg listed 2,312 dead, 14,674 wounded, and 1,469 missing or captured. Rosecrans reported 1,657 Union dead, 9,756 wounded, and 4,757 missing or captured. Chickamauga is second only to Gettysburg in the number of casualties.

BATTLE OF LOOKOUT MOUNTAIN
(CHATTANOOGA, TENNESSEE)

"Battle Above the Clouds"

November 24, 1863
Campaign: Chattanooga-Ringgold Campaign
Principal Commanders: Gen. Ulysses S. Grant (US); Gen. Braxton Bragg (CS)
Forces Engaged: Army of the Tennessee (US); Army of the Cumberland (US); Army of Tennessee (CS)

Union Forces
Maj. Gen. Ulysses S. Grant
Army of the Cumberland
Maj. Gen. George Thomas
Fourth Army Corps
Maj. Gen. Gordon Granger
First Division: Brig. Gen. Charles Cruft
Second Division: Maj. Gen. Philip Sheridan

2nd Brigade	3rd Brigade	1st Brigade	2nd Brigade
Brig. Gen. W. Whitaker	Col. W. Grose	Col. F. Sherman	Brig. Gen. G. Wagner
96th Illinois	59th Illinois	36th Illinois	100th Illinois
35th Indiana	75th Illinois	44th Illinois	15th Indiana
8th Kentucky	84th Illinois	73rd Illinois	40th Indiana
40th Ohio	9th Indiana	74th Illinois	51st Indiana
51st Ohio	36th Indiana	88th Illinois	57th Indiana
99th Ohio	24th Ohio	22nd Indiana	58th Indiana
		2nd Missouri	26th Ohio
		15th Missouri	97th Ohio
		24th Wisconsin	

Third Brigade	Artillery
Col. C. Harker	Capt. W. Edgarton
22nd Illinois	1st Illinois Light, Battery M
27th Illinois	10th Indiana Battery
42nd Illinois	1st Missouri Light Artillery, Battery G
51st Illinois	1st Ohio Light Artillery, Battery I
79th Illinois	4th U.S. Artillery, Battery G
3rd Kentucky	5th U.S. Artillery, Battery H
64th Ohio	
65th Ohio	
125th Ohio	

Third Division: Brig. Gen. Thomas Wood

1st Brigade	2nd Brigade	3rd Brigade
Brig. Gen. A. Willich	Brig. Gen. W. Hazen	Brig. Gen. S. Beatty
25th Illinois	6th Indiana	79th Indiana
35th Illinois	5th Kentucky	86th Indiana
89th Illinois	6th Kentucky	9th Kentucky
32nd Indiana	23rd Kentucky	17th Kentucky
68th Indiana	1st Ohio	13th Ohio
8th Kansas	6th Ohio	19th Ohio
15th Ohio	41st Ohio	59th Ohio
49th Ohio	93rd Ohio	
15th Wisconsin	124th Ohio	

Artillery
Capt. C. Bradley
Illinois Light, Bridge's Battery
6th Ohio Battery
20th Ohio Battery
Pennsylvania Light Artillery, Battery B

Eleventh Army Corps
Maj. Gen. Oliver Howard
2nd Division: Brig. Gen. Adolph von Steinwehr

1st Brigade	2nd Brigade
Col. A. Buschbeck	Col. O. Smith
33rd New Jersey	33rd Massachusetts
134th New York	136th New York
154th New York	55th Ohio
27th Pennsylvania	73rd Ohio
73rd Pennsylvania	

Third Division: Maj. Gen. Carl Schurz

1st Brigade	2nd Brigade	3rd Brigade
Brig. Gen. H. Tyndale	Col. W. Krzyzanowski	Col. F. Hecker
101st Illinois	58th New York	80th Illinois
45th New York	119th New York	82nd Illinois
143rd New York	141st New York	68th New York
61st Ohio	26th Wisconsin	75th Pennsylvania
82nd Ohio		

Artillery
Maj. T. Osborn
1st New York Light, Battery I
New York Light 13th Battery
1st Ohio Light, Battery I
1st Ohio Light Battery K
4th U.S. Battery G

Twelfth Army Corps
Second Division: Brig. Gen. J. Geary

1st Brigade	2nd Brigade	3rd Brigade	Artillery
Col. C. Candy	Col. G. Cobham, Jr.	Col. D. Ireland	Maj. J. Reynold's
Col. W. Creighton	29th Pennsylvania	60th New York	Pennsylvania
Col. T. Ahl	109th Pennsylvania	78th New York	Light, Battery E
5th Ohio	111th Pennsylvania	102nd New York	5th U.S.,
7th Ohio		137th New York	Battery K
29th Ohio		149th New York	
66th Ohio			
28th Pennsylvania			
147th Pennsylvania			

Fourteenth Army Corps: Maj. Gen. John Palmer
1st Division: Brig. Gen. Richard Johnson

1st Brigade	2nd Brigade	3rd Brigade
Brig. Gen. W. Carlin	Col. M. Moore	Brig. Gen. J. Starkweather
104th Illinois	Col. W. Stoughton	24th Illinois
38th Indiana	19th Illinois	37th Indiana
42nd Indiana	11th Michigan	21st Ohio
88th Indiana	69th Ohio	74th Ohio
2nd Ohio	15th U.S., 1st Battalion	78th Pennsylvania
33rd Ohio	15th U.S., 2nd Battalion	79th Pennsylvania
94th Ohio	16th U.S., 1st Battalion	1st Wisconsin
10th Wisconsin	18th U.S., 1st Battalion	21st Wisconsin

Military bridge over the Tennessee River at Chattanooga, built in October, 1863. From a photograph.

The army of the cumberland in front of Chattanooga. From a lithograph.

Panoramic view of the Chattanooga Region from Point Lookout, on Lookout Mountain. From a lithograph.

18th U.S., 2nd Battalion
19th U.S., 1st Battalion

Artillery
1st Illinois Light, Battery C
1st Michigan Light, Battery A
5th U.S., Battery H

Second Division: Brig. Gen. Jefferson Davis

1st Brigade	2nd Brigade	3rd Brigade
Brig. Gen. J. Morgan	Brig. Gen. J. Beatty	Col. D. McCook
10th Illinois	34th Illinois	85th Illinois
16th Illinois	78th Illinois	86th Illinois
60th Illinois	3rd Ohio	110th Illinois
21st Kentucky	98th Ohio	125th Illinois
10th Michigan	108th Ohio	52nd Ohio
14th Michigan	113th Ohio	
	121st Ohio	

Artillery
Capt. Hotchkiss
2nd Illinois Light, Battery I
Minnesota Light, 2nd Battery
Wisconsin Light, 5th Battery

Third Division: Brig. Gen. Absalom Baird

1st Brigade	2nd Brigade	3rd Brigade
Brig. Gen. J. Turchin	Col. F. Derveer	Col. E. Phelps
82nd Indiana	75th Indiana	Col. W. Hays
11th Ohio	87th Indiana.	10th Indiana
17th Ohio	101st Indiana	74th Indiana
31st Ohio	2nd Minnesota	4th Kentucky
36th Ohio	9th Ohio	10th Kentucky
89th Ohio	35th Ohio	18th Kentucky
92nd Ohio	105th Ohio	14th Ohio
		28th Ohio

Artillery
Capt. G. Swallow
Indiana Light, 7th Battery
Indiana Light, 19th Battery
4th U.S., Battery I

Engineer Troops
Brig. Gen. William Smith

Engineers	Pioneers
1st Michigan Engineers (detachment)	Col. G. Buell
13th Michigan Infantry	1st Battalion
21st Michigan Infantry	2nd Battalion
22nd Michigan Infantry	3rd Battalion
18th Ohio Infantry	

Artillery Reserve
Brig. Gen. John Brannan
1st Division: Col. James Barnett

1st Brigade	2nd Brigade
Maj. C. Cotter	1st Ohio Light, Battery G
1st Ohio Light, Battery B	1st Ohio Light, Battery M
1s Ohio Light, Battery C	Ohio Light, 18th Battery

1st Ohio Light, Battery E
1st Ohio Light, Battery F

Ohio Light, 20th Battery

Second Division

1st Brigade	2nd Brigade
Capt. J. Church	Capt. A. Sutermeister
1st Michigan Light, Battery D	Indiana Light, 4th Battery
1st Tennessee Light, Battery A	Indiana Light, 8th Battery
Wisconsin Light, 3rd Battery	Indiana Light, 11th Battery
Wisconsin Light, 8th Battery	Indiana Light, 21st Battery
Wisconsin Light, 10th Battery	1st Wisconsin Heavy, Company C

Cavalry
Second Brigade (Division): Col. Eli Long
98th Illinois (Mounted Infantry)
17th Indiana (Mounted Infantry)
2nd Kentucky
4th Michigan
1st Ohio
3rd Ohio
4th Ohio (Battalion)
10th Ohio

Post of Chattanooga
Col. John Parkhurst
44th Indiana
15th Kentucky
9th Michigan

Army of the Tennessee
Maj. Gen. William T. Sherman
Fifteenth Army Corps: Maj. Gen. Frank Blair, Jr.
1st Division: Brig. Gen. Peter Osterhaus

1st Brigade	2nd Brigade	Artillery
Brig. Gen. C. Woods	Col. J. Williamson	Capt. H. Griffiths
13th Illinois	4th Iowa	Iowa Light, 1st Battery
3rd Missouri	9th Iowa	2nd Missouri Light, Battery F
12th Missouri	25th Iowa	Ohio Light, 4th Battery
17th Missouri	26th Iowa	
27th Missouri	30th Iowa	
29th Missouri	31st Iowa	
31st Missouri		
32nd Missouri		
76th Ohio		

Second Division: Brig. Gen. Morgan Smith

1st Brigade	2nd Brigade	Artillery
Brig. Gen. G. Smith	Brig. Gen. A. Lightburn	1st Illinois Light, Battery A
Col. N. Tupper	83rd Indiana	1st Illinois Light, Battery B
55th Illinois	30th Ohio	1st Illinois Light, Battery H
116th Illinois	37th Ohio	
127th Illinois	47th Ohio	
6th Missouri	54th Ohio	
8th Missouri	4th West Virginia	
57th Ohio		
13th U.S., 1st Battalion		

Fourth Division: Brig. Gen. Hugh Ewing

1st Brigade	2nd Brigade	3rd Brigade	Artillery
Col. J. Loomis	Brig.Gen. J. Corse	Col. J. Cockrell	Capt. H. Richardson

Lookout Mountain

26th Illinois	Col. C. Walcutt	48th Illinois	1st Illinois Light, Battery F
90th Illinois	40th Illinois	97th Indiana	
12th Indiana	103rd Illinois	99th Indiana	1st Illinois Light, Battery I
100th Indiana	6th Iowa	53rd Ohio	
	15th Michigan	70th Ohio	1st Missouri Light, Battery D
	46th Ohio		

Seventeenth Army Corps
Second Division: Brig. Gen. John Smith

1st Brigade	**2nd Brigade**	**3rd Brigade**	**Artillery**
Col. J. Alexander	**Col. G. Raum**	**Brig. Gen. C. Matthies**	**Capt. H. Dillon**
63rd Illinois	Col. F. Deimling	Col. B. Dean	Cogswell's Illinois Battery
48th Indiana	Col. C. Wever	Col. J. Banbury	Wisconsin Light, 6th Battery
59th Indiana	56th Illinois	93rd Illinois	
4th Minnesota	17th Iowa	5th Iowa	Wisconsin Light, 12th Battery
18th Wisconsin	10th Missouri	10th Iowa	
	24th Missouri	26th Missouri	
	80th Ohio		

Confederate Forces
Army Of Tennessee
Gen. Braxton Bragg
Longstreet's Army Corps
McLaws' Division

Kershaw's Brigade	**Wofford's Brigade**	**Humphrey's Brigade**
2nd South Carolina	16th Georgia	13th Mississippi
3rd South Carolina	18th Georgia	17th Mississippi
7th South Carolina	24th Georgia	18th Mississippi
8th South Carolina	Cobb's Legion	21st Mississippi
15th South Carolina	Phillips' Legion	
3rd South Carolina Battalion		
3rd Georgia Battalion Sharpshooters		

Bryan's Brigade	**Artillery Battalion**
10th Georgia	Maj. Austin Leyden
50th Georgia	Georgia Battery (Capt. Peeples)
51st Georgia	Georgia Battery (Capt. Wolihin)
53rd Georgia	Georgia Battery (Capt. York)

Hood's Division

Jenkins Brigade	**Law's Brigade**	**Robertson's Brigade**	**Anderson's Brigade**
1st South Carolina	4th Alabama	3rd Arkansas	7th Georgia
2nd South Carolina	15th Alabama	1st Texas	8th Georgia
5th South Carolina	44th Alabama	4th Texas	9th Georgia
6th South Carolina	47th Alabama	5th Texas	11th Georgia
Hampton (South Carolina) Legion	48th Alabama	59th Georgia	
Palmetto Guard			

Benning's Brigade	**Artillery Battalion**
2nd Georgia	Col. P. Alexander
15th Georgia	South Carolina Battery (Fickling)
17th Georgia	Virginia Battery (Jordan)
20th Georgia	Louisiana Battery (Moody)
	Virginia Battery (Parker)
	Virginia Battery (Taylor)
	Virginia (Woolfolk, Jr.)

Hardee's Corps
Cheatham's Division

Jackson's Brigade	**Moore's Brigade**	**Walthall's Brigade**
1st Georgia	37th Alabama	24th & 27th Mississippi
5th Georgia	40th Alabama	29th & 30th Mississippi
47th Georgia	42nd Alabama	34th Mississippi
65th Georgia		
2nd Georgia. Battalion Sharpshooters		
5th Mississippi		

Wright's Brigade	**Artillery Battalion**
8th Tennessee	Maj. Smith
16th Tennessee	Fowler's Alabama Battery
28th Tennessee	McCants' Florida Battery
38th Tennessee	Scogin's Georgia Battery
51st & 52nd Tennessee	Smith's Mississippi Battery
Murray's (Tennessee) 8th Mississippi Battalion	

Hindman's Division

Anderson's Brigade	**Deas' Brigade**	**Manigault's Brigade**
7th Mississippi	19th Alabama	24th Alabama
9th Mississippi	22nd Alabama	28th Alabama
10th Mississippi	25th Alabama	34th Alabama
41st Mississippi	39th Alabama	10th & 19th South Carolina
44th Mississippi	50th Alabama	
9th Mississippi	17th Alabama	
Battalion Sharpshooters		

Vaughan's Brigade	**Artillery Battalion**
12th & 47th Tennessee	Maj. A. Courtney
13th & 154th Tennessee	Dent's Alabama Battery
29th Tennessee	Garrity's Alabama Battery
11th Tennessee	Scott's Tennessee Battery
	Water's Alabama Battery

Buckner's Division

Johnson's Brigade	**Gracie's Brigade**	**Reynold's Brigade**
17th & 23rd Tennessee	41st Alabama	58th North Carolina
25th & 44th Tennessee	43rd Alabama	60th North Carolina
63rd Tennessee	1st Battalion Alabama (Hillard's) Legion	54th Virginia
	2nd Battalion Alabama (Hillard's) Legion	63rd Virginia
	3rd Battalion Alabama (Hillard's) Legion	
	4th Battalion Alabama (Hillard's) Legion	

Artillery Battalion
Maj. S. Williams
Darden's Mississippi Battery
Jeffress' Virginia Battery
Kolb's Alabama Battery

Walker's Division

Maney's Brigade	**Gist's Brigade**	**Wilson's Brigade**
1st & 27th Tennessee	46th Georgia	25th Georgia

4th Tennessee
  (Provisional Army)
6th & 9th Tennessee
41st Tennessee
50th Tennessee
24th Tennessee Battalion
  Sharpshooters

8th Georgia Battalion
16th South Carolina
24th South Carolina

29th Georgia
30th Georgia
26th Georgia Battalion
1st Georgia Battalion.
  Sharpshooters

Artillery Battalion
Maj. R. Martin
Bledsoe's Missouri Battery
Ferguson's South Carolina Battery
Howell's Georgia Battery

Breckinridge's Army Corps
Cleburne's Division

Liddell's Brigade	**Polk's Brigade**
2nd & 15th Arkansas	1st Arkansas
5th & 13th Arkansas	3rd & 5th Confederate
6th & 7th Arkansas	2nd Tennessee
8th Arkansas	35th & 48th Tennessee
19th & 24th Arkansas	

Smith's Brigade
6th & 10th Texas Infantry & 15th Texas Cavalry (dismounted)
7th Texas
17th, 18th, 24th, 25th Texas Cavalry (dismounted)

Lowrey's Brigade	**Artillery Battalion**
16th Alabama	Maj. T. Hotchkiss
33rd Alabama	Calvert's Arkansas Battery
45th Alabama	Dougal's Texas Battery
32nd & 45th Mississippi	Semple's Alabama Battery
15th Mississippi. Battalion S.S.	Swett's Mississippi Battery

Stewart's Division

Adam's Brigade	**Strahl's Brigade**	**Clayton's Brigade**
13th & 20th Louisiana	4th & 5th Tennessee	18th Alabama
16th & 25th Louisiana	19th Tennessee	32nd Alabama
4th Louisiana	31st Tennessee	38th Alabama
14th Louisiana Battalion Sharpshooters	33rd Tennessee	58th Alabama

Stovall's Brigade	**Artillery Battalion**
40th Georgia	Capt. Semple
42nd Georgia	Dawson's Georgia Battery
43rd Georgia	Humphreys' Arkansas Battery
52nd Georgia	Oliver's Alabama Battery
	Stanford's Mississippi Battery

Breckinridge's Division

Lewis' Brigade	**Bate's Brigade**	**Florida Brigade**
2nd Kentucky	37th Georgia	1st & 3rd Florida
4th Kentucky	4th Georgia Battalion S.S.	4th Florida
5th Kentucky	10th Tennessee	6th Florida
6th Kentucky	15th & 37th Tennessee	7th Florida
9th Kentucky	20th Tennessee	1st Florida Cavalry
John. H. Morgan's	30th Tennessee	(dismounted)
(dismounted) men	1st Tennessee Batn.	

Artillery Battalion
Capt. Slocumb
Cobb's Kentucky Battery
Mebane Tennessee Battery
Slocumb's Louisiana Battery

Stevenson's Division

Brown's Brigade	**Cummings' Brigade**	**Petus' Brigade**
3rd Tennessee	34th Georgia	20th Alabama
18th & 26th Tennessee	36th Georgia	23rd Alabama
32nd Tennessee	39th Georgia	30th Alabama
45th & 23rd Tennessee	56th Georgia	31st Alabama
		46th Alabama

Vaughan's Brigade	**Artillery Battalion**
3rd Tennessee (Provisional Army)	Capt. Cobb

39th Tennessee
43rd Tennessee
59th Tennessee

Baxter's Tennessee Battery
Carnes' Tennessee Battery
Corput's Georgia Battery
Rowan's Georgia Battery

Wheeler's Cavalry Corps: Maj. Gen. Joseph Wheeler
Wharton's Division: Maj. Gen. John Wharton

1st Brigade	**2nd Brigade**
Col. T. Harrison	**Brig. Gen. H. Davidson**
3rd Arkansas	1st Tennessee
65th North Carolina (6th Cavalry)	2nd Tennessee
8th Texas	4th Tennessee
11th Texas	6th Tennessee
	11th Tennessee

Martin's Division: Maj. Gen. William Martin

1st Brigade	**2nd Brigade**
Brig. Gen. J. T. Morgan	**Col. J. Morrison**
1st Alabama	1st Georgia
3rd Alabama	2nd Georgia
4th Alabama (Russell's)	3rd Georgia
Malone's Alabama Regiment	4th Georgia
51st Alabama	6th Georgia

Armstrong's Division: Brig. Gen. Frank Armstrong

1st Brigade	**2nd Brigade**
Brig. Gen. W. Humes	**Col. Tyler**
4th Tennessee (Baxter Smith)	Clay's Kentucky Battalion
5th Tennessee	Edmunson's Virginia Battalion
8th Tennessee (Dibrell's)	Jesse's Kentucky Battalion
9th Tennessee	Johnson's Kentucky Battalion
10th Tennessee	

Kelley's Division

1st Brigade	**2nd Brigade**	**Artillery**
Col. W. Wade	**Col. W. Grigsby**	Huggins' Tennessee Battery
1st Confederate	2nd Kentucky	Huwald's Tennessee Battery
3rd Confederate	3rd Kentucky	White's, Jr. Tennessee Battery
8th Confederate	9th Kentucky	Wiggins' Arkansas Battery
10th Confederate	Allison's Tennessee Squadron	
	Hamilton's Tennessee Battalion	
	Rucker's Legion	

Reserve Artillery	**Detached**
Maj. F. Robertson	Roddey's Cavalry Brigade
Barret' Missouri Battery	4th Alabama
Havis' Georgia Battery	5th Alabama
Lumsden's Alabama Battery	53rd Alabama
Massenburg's Georgia Battery	Moreland's Alabama Battalion
	Ferrell's Georgia Battery

By September 22nd, the Federals were safe in Chattanooga. Bragg moved to the outskirts of town. He occupied Lookout Mountain to the west and Missionary Ridge to the east. He hoped to starve the Union troops into submission. Forrest was sent to an independent command in Western Tennessee, but his troops remained in Chattanooga. The siege was working. Over 10,000 pack animals had died. Food grew scarce. Bragg assigned Polk to Joseph Johnston, in exchange for Lt. Gen. William Hardee, and Hindman was relieved of command. Bragg's gener-

U.S. Grant

als tried to have him relieved of command on October 4th. Even President Jefferson Davis himself arrived in Chattanooga to try and settle the dispute. Davis and Bragg were friends, so Bragg remained in office. Buckner was made a division commander and given a leave of absence. Daniel Harvey Hill was suspended and sent home, and his corps was given to Maj. Gen. John Breckinridge. Hindman was returned to Breckinridge's command. Longstreet was sent to attack Ambrose Burnside at Knoxville. He took with him 5,000 cavalry under Wheeler and 10,000 infantrymen. This left Bragg with 40,000 men along an eight mile line.

Grant replaced Rosecrans and on October 23rd, Grant arrived at Chattanooga. Brig. Gen. William Smith informed Grant that his command could break the siege on Chattanooga. Smith's plan was to move against Brown's Ferry from Chattanooga with two forces, one marching across Moccasin Point, while the other drifted down the river in pontoon boats. The water borne force would surprise and overpower the pickets on the Confederate side of the river, then the combined forces would use the pontoons to build a bridge and move on to occupy the road to Kelley's Ferry. Hooker was to send three divisions across the Tennessee River on pontoons to Bridgeport. They were to march east along the railroad, around the flanks of the lightly held Racoon Mountain to Wauhatchie, just west of Lookout Mountain. There Hooker's men would be able to support attacks on the ferries.

On October 27th, at 3:00 a.m., Smith moved out. The Union forces were successful and secured a bridgehead across Brown's Ferry. By the 28th, Maj. Gen. Oliver Howard was in position a mile from Brown's Ferry. On October 28th, Longstreet's men fought Gen. Geary's troops at Wauhatchie. Longstreet withdrew from Wauhatchie and Lookout Mountain Valley. Grant was now able to send 20,000 men south of the Tennessee River and west of Lookout Mountain. The siege was over for Bragg.

Early in November, Gen. Ulysses S. Grant devised a broad plan for the battles of Chattanooga, Tennessee Troops under Maj. Gen. William Tecumseh Sherman would assault the right of Confederate General Braxton Bragg's Missionary Ridge line east of Chattanooga, Maj. Gen. George Thomas troops would hold the Federal center, facing Missionary Ridge. With two divisions, Union Major General Joseph Hooker would move on Rossville Gap, to the southwest. After securing the Missionary Ridge range at the Tennessee and Georgia border, Hooker would maneuver on Bragg's left and rear.

Hooker's part in Grant's strategy brought on the Battle of Lookout Mountain, on November 24, 1863. A 1,000 foot craggy tower southwest of Chattanooga, Lookout Mountain rose south of a bend in the Tennessee River opposite a finger of land called Moccasin Point. To reach Rossville Gap, Hooker's XII Corps would have to fight its way around or through Confederates occupying Lookout Mountain. Thomas was to give artillery support to Sherman and assault the enemy center.

On November 23, 1863, circumstances changed the particulars of Grant's plan of attack on the Confederates left. Earlier he had decided that four Federal divisions would cross the Tennessee River, west of Chattanooga, on a makeshift bridge at Brown's Ferry. (The bridge, connecting Moccasin Point with Lookout Creek and the entrance to Lookout Valley, had been thrown up during the October 1863 Cracker Line Operation). These divisions, after crossing the Brown's Ferry Bridge, would march up Moccasin Point, maneuver across the Union rear, and join Sherman's force for the attack on Bragg's right. On November 23rd the divisions began their movement, but the crude Brown's Ferry Bridge, under much stress and use, virtually collapsed after three divisions had crossed. Brig Gen. Peter Osterhaus' division was stranded on the Tennessee west bank, opposite Moccasin Point.

On that same day, as the three divisions maneuvered behind Chattanooga, an elaborate reconnaissance in force of the Confederate center by Thomas' troops resulted in the unexpected Battle of Orchard Knob, where the divisions of Brig. Gen. Thomas Wood, Maj. Gen. Philip Sheridan, and Brig. Gen. Abraham Baird seized

Orchard Knob. Union victory in this small battle allowed Chattanooga's entire Federal garrison to move to their front, to Orchard Knob, and the very foot of Missionary Ridge.

Bragg called back Cleburne's division off Lookout Mountain and placed it on Missionary Ridge.

Assessing the day's events, Grant decided to alter his strategy. He ordered Osterhaus's division to join Hooker for the latter's movement against Bragg's left, then he urged Hooker to show initiative: the general was to capture Lookout Mountain, if possible. By capturing the mountain, instead of merely fighting his way over or around it, Hooker would secure his rear when he entered Rossville Gap and, at the same time, shorten Bragg's defense line.

With his force now bolstered by three divisions under Brig. Gen. John Geary, Brig. Gen. Charles Cruft, and Brig. Gen. Peter Osterhaus, Hooker approached Lookout Mountain at 8:00 a.m., on November 24th and immediately met resistance. For twenty four hours the progress of the Battle of Lookout Mountain was a mystery to Federals around Chattanooga. Rain, mist, fog, and chill winds played on the mountain throughout the day. Because of the inclement weather, the fight, though heard, could not be seen from Grant's Orchard Knob headquarters at the Union center. Late in the day, when the fog lifted briefly to reveal Union troops firing and scaling the mountainside, Brig. Gen. Montgomery Meigs, watching from Orchard Knob, dubbed Hooker's fight the "Battle Above The Clouds."

Lookout Mountain was defended by Confederate Major General Carter Stevenson, whose small division, with a few cavalry and cannon, held the mountaintop plateau. A force of 2,694 men under Brig. Gen. Edward Waltham and Brig. Gen. John Moore held the mountain's slopes. Brig. Gen. Alfred Cumming's brigade, of Stevenson's division, and Brig. Gen. John Jackson's brigade, for that one day commanded in the field by Col. John Wilkinson, served as Moore's and Waltham's supports. Waltham and elements of his command were to fight as skirmishers along Lookout Creek at the mountains base. Jackson would be in overall command of a line established midway up the mountain's slopes.

Prior to November 23rd, Stevenson's superior, Lt. Gen. William Hardee, had been charged with the defense of Lookout Mountain. His force had included Maj. Gen. States Rights Gist's division, manning a line along Lookout Creek. But on the night of November 23rd, Hardee informed Stevenson that he and Gist's division had been ordered to the right of Bragg's Missionary Ridge line. Stevenson would command the defense of the mountain.

Stevenson complained that, as a division commander, he did not have sufficient knowledge of all the terrain in his front. Previously he had only been concerned with that part of the Confederate line held by his division. He informed his superiors that he had too few men to make an adequate stand against a Federal assault. Bragg, tacitly acknowledging these complaints, sent word that he would supply Stevenson with reinforcements if they were requested. But Bragg, concerned with Sherman's movements, did not believe an attack would be made against his left.

At about 8 a.m., November 24th, the first elements of Hooker's force, Union

Maj. Gen. E.C. Walthall

67

Brigadier General John Geary's division, having marched northeast up Lookout Valley from its Wauhatchie post, felled trees for use as crude bridges and forced a crossing of Lookout Creek to assault the northwest face of Lookout Mountain. Union Brigadier General Charles Cruft's division crossed the creek and hit the mountain on Geary's left. A short time later, Osterhaus' division crossed the creek and attacked on Cruft's left. Federals drove back Walthall's skirmishers, men sent forward from an established line at Craven's farm on the northeast face. Hit in the flank and rear, this portion of Walthall's force lost several men who were taken prisoner. Walthall's men then fell back to the Craven's farm line. There Walthall's and Moore's men fought around the Craven farmhouse (called the "white house" in initial Union reports), commanded by Jackson.

Maj. Gen. E. M. Law

Fog hindered both Union and Confederate infantry. At Moccasin Point, Union batteries supporting Hooker's three divisions had difficulty finding their range in the haze, as did Stevenson's few cannons atop Lookout Mountain. Confederate Brigadier General Edmund Pettus's brigade, detached from Stevenson's division, descended the mountain to the Craven farm line at about 1 p.m. After the arrival of Federal reinforcements commanded by Brig. Gen. William Carlin, and repeated Union assaults, the Confederate line was reestablished about 400 yards in the rear of the Craven House.

Meanwhile, atop the mountain, Stevenson repeatedly requested reinforcements from Bragg. The requests were not acknowledged. Then, at 2:30 p..m., word came from Bragg that Stevenson was to withdraw all his troops to the extreme right of the Missionary Ridge line. Stevenson's division was to take a place beside Gist's, and both were to support Maj. Gen. Patrick Cleburne's troops, then engaged with Sherman's advance at Tunnel Hill.

Distressed at having to move his entire force to a new front while already engaged with Hooker's troops, Stevenson received assistance from Maj. Gen. Benjamin Cheatham in supervising the withdrawal. Confederates on the plateau

Gen. Joseph Hooker

were removed first, while men fighting behind the Craven farm continued to hold their line. At 8:00 p.m. this last line of defense was withdrawn under cover of fire from Confederate Col. James Holtzclaw's brigade. This ended the day's fighting on Lookout Mountain.

On the morning of November 25th, members of the Federal 8th Kentucky Inf. raced for the unoccupied mountain summit and raised the United States flag, signaling victory to Union troops in the valley below. Hooker then moved on Rossville Gap.

Union and Confederate casualty figures at Lookout Mountain are difficult to ascertain, since both sides gave aggregate numbers for the battles of Chattanooga. Some report Federal losses at 480 men, and Confederate losses at 1,251 men, 1,554 being captured. On many maps and in many battle accounts, Moore's and Walthall's troops are listed as Cheatham's division. While they were members of that division, Cheatham was not present for most of the fighting at Lookout Mountain. Except for the period in which he helped Stevenson supervise the Confederate withdrawal, Cheatham executed duties on Bragg's right on November 24th.

BATTLE OF MISSIONARY RIDGE

"It's all right-if it turns out all right. If not, someone will suffer"-Grant's comments to George Thomas, as Phil Sheridan's men makes an assault on Missionary Ridge against orders.

(See Lookout Mountain for Order of Battle for Union and Confederate Forces).

November 25, 1863

Campaign: Chattanooga-Ringgold Campaign

Principal commanders: Maj. Gen. William T. Sherman (US); Gen. Braxton Bragg (CS)

Forces Engaged: Army of the Cumberland (US); Army of the Tennessee (US); Army of Tennessee (C.S.)

With Lookout Mountain in Federal hands, trains could run unimpeded from Bridgeport to Chattanooga and steamers could once again follow the river all the way into the city. After the Battle of Lookout Mountain, Hooker was to march to Rossville Gap in Missionary Ridge and was to attack Bragg's left flank, but retreating Confederates burned the Chattanooga Creek Bridge. Delayed midway to Rossville Gap, Hooker fell behind schedule and took little part in winning Missionary Ridge. Sherman's mission was to push skirmishers toward Tunnel Hill. Sherman had six divisions totaling 26,000 men against 10,000 men under Patrick Cleburne and Carter Stevenson.

Having acquired most of the Chattanooga garrision's cannons, Sherman started shelling his front at mid mourning on November 25th, and at 11:00 a.m. began a general assault on Tunnel Hill, led by Brig. Gen. John Corse and Col. John Loomis. The Confederate position was held by Stevenson's division and Cleburne's division. The Confederate position on Tunnel Hill was truly superior, Clebrune bolstering the line with artillery at three key positions: on the ridge directly above the tunnel, in the angle at the summitt, and on the north facing leg of the line. This position withstood the best Union efforts all day. For over two hours, the Federal troops attacked and counterattacked the Confederates without making any progress. Corse was wounded. At 3:00 p.m., Brig. Gen. Alfred Cumming wanted approval for a hand to hand attack and Gen. William Hardee gave permission. Cumming sent the 36th and 56th Georgia regiments through a narrow opening in the Confederate breastworks and led a charge that attacked Union Brigadier General Charles Matthies' brigade's left flank. At that very same moment, Cleburne led an attack against Matthies' center. After ten minutes, Matthies' men fled down the mountainside and the Union brigade of Col. John Loomis retreated. The Confederates captured eight flags and five hundred prisoners. Unable to progress, Sherman signaled Grant's headquarters several times, asking for Thomas to assault the center and weaken the Southern defense. Grant told Sherman to attack again and Sherman sent in two hundred men from Brig. Gen. Joseph Lightburn's brigade to attack the Confederates, but Lightburn was sent down the hill in defeat.

Hooker arrived at Rossville Gap and attacked the Confederate left around 3:00 p.m. Breckinridge was in command of the far left flank, which was defended by Brig. Gen. Henry Clayton's Alabama brigade. Bragg took control of Breckinridge's two divisions. Hooker drove two of Clayton's regiments from Rossville Gap, and Cruft's Federal division had gained a foothold on the southern slope of Missionary Ridge itself. Breckinridge was outnumbered when Cruft attacked again. Breckinridge fell back.

Gen. Sherman

While John Geary's division struck the Confederates from the west and Peter Osterhaus sent his troops around to the Confederate rear through the gap, Cruft's men drove north, onto the crest of the ridge. The Federal's routed Breckinridge's men and captured Breckinridge's son, Cabell. Finally, the destruction of the Confederate flank was under way, and Hooker, not Sherman was accomplishing it.

By this time, Grant had sent several reinforcements from Thomas' to Sherman's front. Grant advised Thomas to attack the first Confederate trench line with his remaining troops. Thomas sent 20,000 men belonging to the divisions of Brig. Gen. Thomas Wood and Maj. Gen. Philip Sheridan, Richard Johnson, and Brig. General Absalom Baird, to attack the Confederates. The Union division's under these four commanders drove the Confederate defenders from the first trench, then found themselves without cover under a heavy fire from the second line of trenches. Rather than stand under the severe fire, Wood's and Sheridan's men drove on up the hill, against orders. The Confederate earthworks were poorly constructed and the Confederates could not depress the muzzles of their cannons enough to fire down upon the advancing Union troops. The Confederates also would be exposed to Federal fire if they showed themselves. The Federals soon pushed the Southerners down the slope.

Hooker drove Breckinridge back two and a half miles from his position on the left; almost as far back as Bragg's headquarters on the center of the ridge. Bragg attempted to stop the rout, and tried to rally his men, but they no longer had any trust in their commander, and began to yell insults at Bragg as they were flying past him in full retreat. Bragg and Breckinridge barely missed being caught by the advancing Federals. Cleburne's division was pulled from its successful right wing defense and assigned as the rear guard for Bragg's defeated army. Sheridan's troops pursued, and Hooker's divisions, at last on Missionary Ridge, followed. On November 27th, Hooker and Sheridan caught up with Cleburne at Ringgold, Georgia, 15 miles from Chattanooga. Cleburne ambushed Hooker's men, who faltered, but recovered and a fierce engagement followed. For six hours, Cleburne held. When Bragg was at a safe distance, Cleburne slipped away during the night. Hooker lost 442 men and Cleburne lost 221 men in this engagement. Bragg's force retreated south to Dalton, Georgia. On November 28th, Grant called off the pursuit. The Confederates lost 6,700 soldiers killed, wounded, or captured at Missionary Ridge. Four thousand one hundred Confederates were captured. Five thousand eight hundred Federals were killed, or wounded at Missionary Ridge, and 350 were captured.

Union victory at Missionary Ridge won Grant a promotion to lieutenant general and prompted Bragg, after lambasting Breckinridge and the commanders of the center line division, to request that he be relieved from command. Jefferson Davis recalled him to Richmond, Virginia, and Bragg was made chief of staff.

Dug "U.S." marked chain from artillery piece found near Lookout Mountain, Tennessee. (BCWM)

Lt. Col. Michael Weidrich
1st New York Light Artillery, Battery I
15th New York Heavy Artillery

Michael Weidrich joined the army on August 8, 1861 and was assigned to the 1st New York Light Artillery, Battery I. He was the oldest battery commander in the Army of the Potomac. He was commissioned a captain on November 11, 1861 and would serve in some of the most important battles, both East and West. He would serve at the Battles of Second Bull Run, Look Out Mountain, Gettysburg, the Wilderness, Cold Harbor, and finally White Oaks Road. His career would be filled with intense action and gallantry.

The first major engagement that Capt. Weidrich was involved in was the Battle of Second Bull Run. On August 22nd, Weidrich's men were arriving near Freeman's Ford. Gen. Schurz immediately ordered Weidrich and his mostly German immigrants to advance their battery to relieve Capt. DeBeck's battery, which had been fighting the Confederates for some time, and was almost out of ammunition. When Weidrich arrived, Maj. Gen. Sigel ordered Weidrich to place two of his 10 pound Parrott's on a hill near some woods close to the river. His other two 10 pound Parrott's were placed to the right of Capt. De Beck's battery and his two 12 pound howitzers were held in reserve. As soon as his battery was in place, the Confederates fired heavily upon Weidrich's guns, and he lost five men killed and wounded. Weidrich also lost 10 horses, two of which were killed outright, and without his horses, Weidrich could not transport his cannons. As evening settled in, the firing from the Confederates ceased, and Weidrich managed to resupply during the night.

On August 24th, Weidrich was engaged near White Sulphur Springs, at Waterloo brigade. On August 29th, Weidrich's battery was ordered forward by Capt. Schimer, chief of artillery. Weidrich was to take a position on the right of the road to support the infantry. He was also sent to support Capt. Dilger's battery, because the Confederates had sighted Dilger's guns, and were laying a heavy fire on his position. Weidrich moved his four Parrott's into position and silenced the Rebel guns, but quickly ran out of ammunition. He went to the rear to pick up more ammunition and when he returned to his former position, he found his guns had been replaced by another battery. Weidrich then returned to where his two howit-

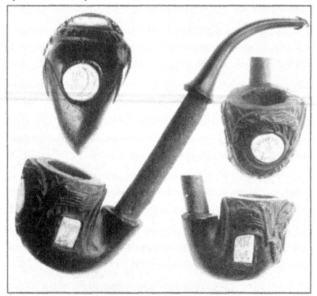

Ornate hand carved and inlayed smoking pipe belonging to Capt. Michael Weidrich, 1st New York Light Artillery. The pipe is engraved "Lookout Mountain". The pipe is made of laurel root found abundantly on Lookout Mountain. These pipes were sold as a commemorative and the inlays were blank and could be filled in at a later date with anyone's name. Weidrich's pipe includes bone inlays indicating his corps, regiment, and initials. (BCWM)

zers were being held in reserve and at the moment he arrived to recover them, enemy shells exploded nearby wounding two men from his battery. Lt. Schenhelberger had his leg shattered by a shell, and Pvt. William Moller's arm was wounded severely by another and had to be amputated. After Weidrich ran out of ammunition for the second time, he retired to Gen. Sigel's headquarters.

On August 30th, he was ordered to move his four Parrott guns to Col. McLean's position, which was on a low hill. Capt. Buell and his six pound bronze cannons limbered up and went with Capt. Weidrich's battery to assist. When they arrived at McLean's position, Col. McLean ordered Weidrich to a position on a hill to the left of the road, facing one of the Confederate guns directly in front of this new position. Maj. Gen. Irvin McDowell moved his infantry and artillery from the left to a new position directly in front of Weidrich's artillery and towards his right flank. Now Weidrich could not fire at the Confederate battery and infantry because McDowell's men were in his line of fire, and his left was now completely exposed to the Rebels. The Confederates advanced out of the woods directly towards Weidrich's position and his battery was soon attacked by the Confederate infantry. Col. McLean rushed to Weidrich's support with his brigade. Firing was heavy and the overwhelming number of Confederates forced Weidrich to fall back to another hill in the rear, where he remained until nightfall. He left for Centreville shortly after dark, arriving there the next morning, finally out of harm's way.

Weidrich next fought at the Battle of Gettysburg. On July 1st, his battery arrived on Cemetery Hill and was immediately ordered to the north side of the Baltimore Turnpike, near the cemetery and east of the city. By 5 p.m., the Union infantry had been pushed back towards the town of Gettysburg. Weidrich repositioned his guns so that he would be able to fire on the advancing Confederates. The Confederates quickly overran the town, and the Union infantry fell back behind Weidrich's guns, leaving his artillery to defend the hill alone. His artillery opened fire on the rapidly advancing Confederates with canister shot, and repulsed the Confederates long enough to allow the Union infantry to rally in the rear of his battery. The Union troops battled ahead and managed to push the Confederates back into the town. Weidrich's artillery kept up their fire until late in the afternoon.

On July 2nd, Weidrich's artillery exchanged fire with two Rebel batteries. One battery was directly to his front, and the other was to his left flank. Both sides kept up a heavy bombardment until 3:00 p.m. At 8:00 p.m., the 75 Confederates with the 6th North Carolina charged Weidrich's battery and pushing back the Union infantry, entered the entrenchments of his battery. The Union infantry rallied and fought off the Confederate attack. Weidrich then decimated the retreating body of Confederates with canister shot.

On the morning of July 3rd, Weidrich had several artillery duels with the Confederate artillery but at 1 p.m., the Confederates began to bring all their guns to bear on the Union lines, and his battery was exposed to a severe crossfire, but amazingly they received no injuries from the incoming projectiles. The losses that the battery did incur were from the Confederate sharpshooters that were hiding in the houses around the city of Gettysburg.

During the three day battle, Weidrich's battery lost three men killed, and 11 men wounded, two of them seriously.

After their harrowing experience at Gettysburg, Weidrich's battery was transferred to the Army of the Cumberland, 11th Corps, 2nd Division and arrived near the outskirts of Chattanooga on November 9th, and on November 23rd would participate in the Battle of Lookout Mountain. The battery was sent to the valley to assist Maj. Gen. Joseph Hooker's infantry which was preparing to make a major assault on the Confederate positions on Lookout Mountain. On November 24th, Weidrich's battery engaged the Confederates in the rifle pits at the foot of Lookout Mountain and the Confederates retreated before the heavy fire that Weidrich was directing on their position. The Confederates moved up the mountain until they reached their earthworks, under the peak of Lookout Mountain. Hooker's infantry laboriously pursued the retreating Confederates. Weidrich gave the order to cease fire when the Union infantry came within his sights. Hooker was not able to push the Confederates off Lookout Mountain, and Hooker's men stayed within the first set of Confederate entrenchments, ready to assault the Confederates in the second set of entrenchments the next day. During the night, Bragg pulled his troops from Lookout Mountain and when Hooker awoke the next morning, he found that the Confederates had retreated.

On November 25th, Weidrich's battery was ordered to cross the Lookout Creek, where it remained for several days before being ordered back to camp. Weidrich lost not a single man during the Battle of Lookout Mountain.

On March 1, 1864, Weidrich was promoted to lieutenant colonel and made commander of the 15th New York Heavy Artillery and was attached to an independent brigade. On May 3, 1864, Col. Weidrich and his new brigade crossed the Rapidan River at Ely's Ford. On May 5th, the brigade marched to Chancellorsville, toward the Wilderness. On May 6th, at 2:00 a.m., the troops marched forward and at 5:00 a.m., they took up a position in some woods on the left of the 2nd Corps. The brigade advanced, and the Confederates made an attack on their right wing, which was formed by the 2nd and 3rd Battalions. The Union troops were hampered by the thick undergrowth but they managed to beat back the first Confederate attack and followed the retreating Confederates for about 200 yards, until they reached a clearing. The Union forces prepared for another attack and formed in line of battle. Orders arrived telling the Union troops to take positions in the rifle pits, but they were soon relieved by the 5th Corps and ordered to build a second line of breastworks a short distance behind the first. After this was accomplished, the 15th Regiment New York Artillery stood by their guns, but no orders were given to advance. Evening soon fell, and the Battle of the Wilderness was over for the 15th Regiment New York Artillery.

On May 19th, the 15th was advancing on Spotsylvania Courthouse. The regiment was ordered to march to the right wing, when at 4 p.m., the Confederates made an attack on the Fredericksburg Road. The regiment which had been assigned to protect the railroad and trains took up a position in the woods, unprotected by any kind of works, and without assistance of artillery. The Confederates made several attacks but were repulsed each time. They were trying to flank his right wing and capture the trains, hoping to get badly needed supplies, but thanks to the 15th New York Heavy Artillery, the Confederates failed in their mission.

On May 29th, the regiment proceeded to New Bethel Church, then to Mount Carmel Church, on the North Anna River at Jericho Mills, and was told to take up positions overlooking the bridge as heavy fighting took place in their front.

On May 30th, the regiment advanced in line of battle at Bethesda Church. The Union infantry advanced under heavy fire and had to fall back to their line of rifle pits. The Confederates made an attack on their position and tried to break the communication lines between the Yankees and their support units. Weidrich's regiment lost five men and two officers and 57 men were wounded.

On June 2nd, the regiment was positioned along the Yorktown and Richmond Road. The Confederates attacked their right flank, and soon were fighting in the rear of the regiment, having passed them.

On June 11th, the 15th New York Artillery was near Cold Harbor and on the 18th, received orders to take their position in the first line advancing against Petersburg, and to link up on the right with Col. Hoffman's line. The regiment advanced under heavy Rebel fire, succeeded in taking its position, and hurriedly began to construct breastworks to help shield them from the deadly Rebel sharpshooters. Weidrich lost seven men killed and 43 wounded, including one officer.

On March 31, 1865, Weidrich's battery was placed into line of battle along the White Oaks Road. At 11:00 a.m., the order to advance was given, and the brigade moved to the attack. The Confederates were concealed along White Oak Road and their exact numbers could not be ascertained. The Confederates let loose a murderous fire upon the blue lines as the Union infantry advanced over an open field for one quarter of a mile and on reaching within 10 or 15 yards of the Confederate position, they were ambushed as two lines of yelling Confederates smashed into the thin single row of blue clad soldiers. The order was given to retreat quickly or the whole regiment might be captured. The Union troops fell back to their former position on the Gravelly Run. The Confederates rushed forward, but were beaten back. The Union troops rallied and advanced with the rest of the Union division. They recovered lost ground, gained the Rebels works, and managed to secure a position on the White Oaks Road.

On April 9, 1865, Confederate General Robert E. Lee surrendered to Union General Ulysses S. Grant, ending Grant's pursuit of Lee's army from Petersburg to Appomattox Courthouse. Weidrich took part in Grant's Appomattox Campaign, ending his glorious and battle weary career. Older than the typical soldier who joined the army, Weidrich showed that his age was not a hindrance, always acting with bravery and courage under fire.

Georgia Campaign

May-July, 1864
Campaign: Atlanta Campaign
Principal Commanders: William T. Sherman (U.S.); Joseph Johnston (C.S.), John Bell Hood (C.S.)
Forces Engaged: Army of the Ohio (U.S.), Army of the Cumberland (U.S.), Army of the Tennessee (U.S.). Army of Mississippi (C.S.), Army of Tennessee (C.S.)

Order of Battle
Union Forces
Federal Grand Army
Maj. Gen. William Tecumseh Sherman
98,000 men

Army of the Cumberland
Maj. Gen. George Thomas
IV Corps: Maj. Gen. Oliver Howard
          Maj. Gen. David Stanley

First Division: Maj. Gen. David Stanley
               Brig. Gen. William Grose
               Brig. Gen. Nathan Kimball

1st Brigade	2nd Brigade	3rd Brigade
Brig. Gen. C. Cruft	**Brig. Gen. W. Whitaker**	**Col. W. Grose**
Col. Isaac Kirby	Col. J. Taylor	Col. S. Post
21st Illinois	96th Illinois	Brig. Gen. W. Grose
38th Illinois	115th Illinois	Col. J. Bennett
81st Indiana	35th Indiana	59th Illinois
1st Kentucky	84th Indiana	75th Illinois
2nd Kentucky	21st Kentucky	80th Illinois
90th Ohio	40th Ohio	84th Illinois
101st Ohio	51st Ohio	30th Indiana
	99th Ohio	36th Indiana
		77th Pennsylvania

Artillery
Capt. S. McDowell
Capt. T. Thomasson
5th Indiana
Pennsylvania Light
Artillery, Battery B

Second Division: Brig. Gen. John Newton

1st Brigade	2nd Brigade	3rd Brigade
Col. F. Sherman	**Brig. Gen. G. Wagner**	**Brig. Gen. C. Harker**
Brig. Gen. N. Kimball	Col. J. Blake	22nd Illinois
Col. E. Opdycke	Brig. Gen. G. Wagner	27th Illinois
36th Illinois	100th Illinois	42nd Illinois
44th Illinois	40th Indiana	51st Illinois
73rd Illinois	57th Indiana	79th Illinois
74th Illinois	26th Ohio	3rd Kentucky
88th Illinois	97th Ohio	64th Ohio
28th Kentucky		65th Ohio
2nd Missouri		125th Ohio
15th Missouri		
24th Wisconsin		

Artillery
Capt. W. Edgarton
1st Illinois Light Artillery, Battery M
10th Indiana Light Artillery
1st Missouri Lt. Artillery, Battery G
1st Ohio, Battery I
4th U.S., Battery G
5th U.S., Battery H

Third Division: Brig. Gen. Thomas Wood
               Col. Sidney Post

1st Brigade	2nd Brigade	3rd Brigade
Brig. Gen. A. Willich	**Brig. Gen. W. Hazen**	**Brig. Gen. S. Beatty**
25th Illinois	6th Indiana	79th Indiana
38th Illinois	6th Kentucky	86th Indiana
32nd Indiana	6th Kentucky	9th Kentucky
68th Indiana	23rd Kentucky	17th Kentucky
8th Kansas	1st Ohio	13th Ohio
15th Ohio	6th Ohio	19th Ohio
49th Ohio	41st Ohio	59th Ohio
15th Wisconsin	93rd Ohio	
	124th Ohio	

Artillery
Capt. C. Bradley
Illinois Battery (Bridges)
6th Ohio (Ayres)
20th Ohio (Grosskopff)
Pennsylvania Artillery,
Battery B

XIV Corps: Maj. Gen. J. M. Palmer
          Brig. Gen. Richard Johnson
          Brig. Gen. Jefferson Davis

First Division: Brig. Gen. Richard Johnson
               Brig. Gen. John King
               Brig. Gen. William Carlin

1st Brigade	2nd Brigade
Brig. Gen. Carlin	**Brig. Gen J.King**
2nd Ohio	11th Michigan
10th Wisconsin	15th U.S., 1st Batn. 1 & 3 Batn. (9 companies)
15th Kentucky	15th U.S., 2nd Batn. (6 companies)
21st Wisconsin	16th U.S., 1st Batn. (4 companies)
33rd Ohio	16th US, 2nd Batn. (4 companies)
42nd Indiana	18th US, 1st & 3rd Batn. (8 companies)
88th Indiana	18th US, 2nd Batn. (8 companies)
94th Ohio	19th US, 1 Batn., Company A, 2nd Batn. (5 companies)
104th Illinois	

3rd Brigade
Col. B. Scribner
1st Wisconsin
21st Ohio
37th Indiana
38th Indiana
74th Ohio
78th Pennsylvania
79th Pennsylvania

Second Division: Brig. Gen. Jefferson Davis
               Brig. Gen. James Morgan

1st Brigade	2nd Brigade	3rd Brigade
Brig. Gen. J. Morgan	**Col. Mitchell**	**Col. D. McCook**
10th Illinois	34th Illinois	22nd Indiana
10th Michigan	78th Illinois	52nd Ohio
14th Michigan	98th Ohio	85th Illinois
16th Illinois	108th Ohio	86th Illinois
60th Illinois	113th Ohio	110th Illinois
17th New York	121st Ohio	125th Illinois

Artillery
2nd Illinois Light Artillery, Battery I
5th Independent Battery Wisconsin
Light Artillery
2nd Independent Battery, Minnesota
Light Artillery

Third Division: Brig. Gen. Absalom Baird

1st Brigade	2nd Brigade	3rd Brigade
Brig. Gen. J. Turchin	**Col. F. Van Derveer**	**Col. G. Este**
11th Ohio	2nd Minnesota	10th Indiana
17th Ohio	9th Ohio	10th Kentucky
19th Illinois	35th Ohio	14th Ohio
23rd Missouri	75th Indiana	18th Kentucky
24th Illinois	87th Indiana	38th Indiana
31st Ohio	101st Indiana	74th Indiana
82nd Indiana	105th Ohio	
89th Ohio		
92nd Ohio		

Artillery
7th Independent Battery, Indiana Light Artillery
19th Independent Battery, Indiana Light Artillery

XX Corps: Maj. Gen. Joseph Hooker
       Brig. Gen. Alpheus Williams
       Maj. Gen. Henry Slocum

First Division: Brig. Gen. Alpheus S. Williams
         Brig. Gen. Joseph Knipe
         Brig. Gen. A. S. Williams

1st Brigade	2nd Brigade	3rd Brigade
Brig. Gen. J. Knipe	**Brig. Gen. T. Ruger**	**Col. J. Robinson**
3rd Maryland	2nd Massachusetts	31st Wisconsin
5th Connecticut	3rd Wisconsin	45th New York
46th Pennsylvania	13th New Jersey	61st Ohio
123rd New York	27th Indiana	82nd Illinois
141st New York	107th New York	101st Illinois
	150th New York	143rd New York
		82nd Ohio

Artillery
1st New York Light Artillery, Battery I
1st New York Light Artillery, Battery M

Second Division: Brig. Gen. S. W. Geary

1st Brigade	2nd Brigade	3rd Brigade
Col. C. Candy	**Col. A. Buschbeck**	**Col. D. Ireland**
5th Ohio	27th Pennsylvania	29th Pennsylvania
7th Ohio	33rd New Jersey	60th New York
28th Pennsylvania	73rd Pennsylvania	78th New York
29th Ohio	109th Pennsylvania	102nd New York
66th Ohio	119th New York	111th Pennsylvania
147th Pennsylvania	134th New York	137th New York
	154th New York	149th New York

Artillery
13th Independent Battery, New York Light Artillery
Independent Battery E, Pennsylvania Light Artillery

Third Division: Maj. Gen. Daniel Butterfield
         Brig. Gen. William Ward

1st Brigade	2nd Brigade	3rd Brigade	Reserve Brigade
Brig. Gen. W. Ward	**Col. J. Coburn**	**Col. J. Wood**	**Col. J. Burke's**
70th Indiana	19th Michigan	26th Wisconsin	9th Michigan
79th Ohio	20th Connecticut	33rd Massachusetts	10th Ohio
102nd Illinois	22nd Wisconsin	55th Ohio	22nd Michigan
105th Illinois	33rd Indiana	73rd Ohio	
129th Illinois	85th Indiana	136th New York	

Pontoniers
Col. G. Buell
58th Indiana
Pontoon Battalion

Siege Artillery	**Artillery**
Sutermeister	Maj. J. Reynold's
11th Independent Battery,	1st Michigan Light Artillery, Battery I
Indiana Light Artillery.	1st New York Light Artillery, Battery M
	13th New York Artillery, Battery C
	1st Ohio Artillery, Battery E
	Pennsylvania Artillery, (Sloan)

XII Corps-Maj. Gen. Henry Slocum
2nd Division: Brig. Gen. John Geary

1st Brigade	2nd Brigade	3rd Brigade
Col. Candy	**Col. G. Cobham, Jr.**	**Col. D. Ireland**
Col. W. Creighton	29th Pennsylvania	60th New York
Col. T. Ahl	109th Pennsylvania	78th New York
5th Ohio	111th Pennsylvania	102nd New York
7th Ohio	137th New York	
29th Ohio	149th New York	
66th Ohio		
28th Pennsylvania		
147th Pennsylvania		

Artillery
Maj. J. A. Reynolds
Pennsylvania Light Artillery, Battery E
5th U.S. Artillery, Battery K

XI Corps: Maj. Gen. Oliver Howard
2nd Division: Brig. Gen. Adolph von Steinwehr

1st Brigade	2nd Brigade
Col. A. Buschbeck	**Col. O. Smith**
33rd New Jersey	33rd Massachusetts
134th New York	136th New York
154th New York	55th Ohio
27th Pennsylvania	73rd Ohio
73rd Pennsylvania	

Third Division: Maj. Gen. Carl Schurz

1st Brigade	2nd Brigade	3rd Brigade
Brig. Gen. H. Tyndale	**Col. W. Krzyzanowski**	**Col. F. Hecker**
101st Illinois	58th New York	80th Illinois
45th New York	119th New York	82nd Illinois
143rd New York	141st New York	68th New York
61st Ohio	26th Wisconsin	75th Pennsylvania
82nd Ohio		

Artillery
1st New York Artillery, Battery I
13th New York Light Artillery
1st Ohio Artillery, Battery K

Army of the Tennessee
Maj. Gen. James McPherson
Maj. Gen. John Logan
Maj. Gen. Oliver Howard

XV Corps: Maj. Gen. John Logan
         Brig. Gen. Morgan Smith
First Division: Brig. Gen. Peter Osterhaus
         Brig. Gen. Charles Woods

1st Brigade	2nd Brigade	3rd Brigade
Brig. Gen. Woods	**Col. Williamson**	**Col. Wangelin**
26th Iowa	4th Iowa	3rd Missouri
27th Missouri	9th Iowa	12th Missouri
30th Iowa	25th Iowa	17th Missouri
76th Ohio	31st Iowa	29th Missouri
		31st Missouri
		32nd Missouri

Artillery
2nd Missouri Light Artillery, Battery F
4th Independent Battery Ohio Light Artillery

Second Division: Brig. Gen. Morgan Smith
         Brig. Gen. J.A. J. Lightburn
         Brig. Gen. William Hazen

1st Brigade	2nd Brigade	Artillery
Brig. Gen. G. A. Smith	**Brig. Gen. Lightburn**	**Capt. Francis De Gress**
6th Missouri	30th Ohio	1st Illinois Light Artillery,
8th Missouri	37th Ohio	Battery A
55th Illinois	47th Ohio	1st Illinois Light Artillery,
57th Ohio	53rd Ohio	Battery B
111th Illinois	54th Ohio	1st Illinois Light Artillery,
116th Illinois	83rd Indiana	Battery H
127th Illinois		

Fourth Division: Brig. Gen. William Harrow

1st Brigade	2nd Brigade	3rd Brigade	Artillery
Col. R. Williams	**Brig. Gen. Walcutt**	**Col. J. Oliver**	1st Illinois Light
12th Indiana	6th Iowa	15th Michigan	Artillery, Batt. F
26th Illinois	40th Illinois	48th Illinois	1st Battery, Iowa
90th Illinois	46th Ohio	70th Ohio	Light Artillery
100th Illinois	97th Indiana	99th Indiana	
	103rd Illinois		

XVI Corps: Maj. Gen. Grenville Dodge
         Brig. Gen. Thomas Ransom

2nd Division: Brig. Gen. Thomas Sweeny
Brig. Gen. Elliot Rice
Brig. Gen. John Corse

1st Brigade	2nd Brigade	3rd Brigade	Artillery
Brig. Gen. Rice	Col. P. Burke	Col. Bane	Capt. Welker
2nd Iowa	9th Illinois	39th Iowa	1st Michigan Light
7th Iowa	Mounted Inf.	50th Illinois	Artillery, Battery B
52nd Illinois	12th Illinois	57th Illinois	1st Missouri Light
66th Indiana	66th Illinois	7th Illinois	Artillery, Battery H
	81st Ohio		1st Missouri Light
			Artillery, Battery I

4th Division:
Brig. Gen. James Veatch
Brig. Gen. John Fuller
Brig. Gen. Thomas Ranson

1st Brigade	2nd Brigade	3rd Brigade	Artillery
Brig. Gen. Fuller	Brig. Gen. Sprague	Col. T. Grower	1st Michigan Light
18th Missouri	25th Wisconsin	10th Illinois	Artillery, Battery C
27th Ohio	35th New Jersey	17th New York	14th Indiana Battery,
39th Ohio	43rd Ohio	25th Indiana	Ohio Light Artillery
64th Illinois	63rd Ohio	32nd Wisconsin	2nd US Artillery,
			Battery F

XVII Corps: Maj. Gen. Frank Blair
3rd Division: Brig. Gen. Mortimer Leggett
Brig. Gen. Charles Woods

1st Brigade	2nd Brigade	3rd Brigade
Brig. Gen. M. Force	Col. R. Scott	Col. A. Malloy
16th Wisconsin	20th Ohio	17th Wisconsin
20th Illinois	32nd Ohio	Worden's (Wisconsin &
30th Illinois	68th Ohio	Illinois) Battalion
31st Illinois	78th Ohio	
45th Illinois		

Artillery
1st Illinois Light Artillery, Battery D
1st Michigan Light Artillery, Battery H
3rd Independent Battery Ohio Artillery

4th Division: Brig. Gen. Walter Gresham

1st Brigade	2nd Brigade	3rd Brigade
Col. W. Sanderson	Col. G. Roger	Col. W. Hall
3rd Iowa	14th Illinois	11th Iowa
12th Wisconsin	15th Illinois	13th Iowa
23rd Indiana	41st Illinois	15th Iowa
32nd Illinois	53rd Illinois	16th Iowa
23rd Indiana		
53rd Indiana		

Artillery
Capt. Edward Spear
2nd Illinois Light Artillery, Battery F
1st Independent Battery, Minnesota Light Artillery
1st Missouri Light Artillery, Battery C
10th Independent Battery, Ohio Light Artillery
15th Independent Battery, Ohio Light Artillery

Cavalry Corps: Brig. Gen. Washington Elliot
1st Division: Brig. Gen. Edward McCook

1st Brigade	2nd Brigade	3rd Brigade
Col. Dorr	Col. LaGrange	Col. Watkin
1st Tennessee Cavalry	1st Wisconsin Cavalry	4th Kentucky Cavalry
2nd Michigan Cavalry	2nd Indiana Cavalry	6th Kentucky Cavalry
4th Kentucky Mounted Inf.	4th Indiana Cavalry	7th Kentucky Cavalry
8th Iowa Cavalry		

Artillery
18th Indiana, Light Artillery

2nd Division: Brig. Gen. Kenner Garrard

1st Brigade	2nd Brigade	3rd Brigade
Col. Minty	Col. E. Long	Wilder's Mounted Inf.
4th Michigan Cavalry	1st Ohio Cavalry	"Lighting Brigade"
4th U.S. Cavalry	3rd Ohio Cavalry	17th Indiana Mounted Inf.
7th Pennsylvania Cavalry	4th Ohio Cavalry	72nd Indiana Mounted Inf.

98th Illinois Mounted Inf.
123rd Illinois Mounted Inf.

Artillery
Chicago Board Of Trade Independent Battery

3rd Division: Brig. Gen. Judson Kilpatrick

1st Brigade	2nd Brigade	3rd Brigade
Lt. Col. Klein	Col. C. Smith	Col. E. Murray
3rd Indiana Cavalry	2nd Kentucky Cavalry	3rd Kentucky Cavalry
5th Iowa Cavalry	8th Indiana Cavalry	5th Kentucky Cavalry
	10th Ohio Cavalry	92nd Illinois

Artillery
10th Independent Battery, Wisconsin Light Artillery

Stoneman's Cavalry Division: Maj. Gen. George Stoneman

1st Brigade	2nd Brigade	3rd Brigade
Col. Garrard	Col. Biddle	Col. H. Capron
7th Ohio	5th Indiana Cavalry	8th Michigan Cavalry
9th Michigan	6th Indiana Cavalry	14th Illinois Cavalry
	12th Kentucky Cavalry	McLaughlin's (Ohio)
	16th Illinois Cavalry	Cavalry Squadron

Independent Cavalry Brigade
Col. A. Holeman
1st Kentucky Cavalry
11th Kentucky Cavalry

Army of the Ohio
(XXIII Corps)
Maj. Gen. John Schofield
First Division: Brig. Gen. Alvin Hovey

1st Brigade	2nd Brigade	Artillery
Col. R. Barter	Col. J. McQuiston	23rd Independent Battery,
120th Indiana	99th Ohio	Indiana Light Artillery
124th Indiana	123rd Indiana	24th Independent Battery,
128th Indiana	129th Indiana	Indiana Light Artillery
	130th Indiana	

Second Division:
Brig. Gen. Henry Judah
Brig. Gen. Milo Hascall

1st Brigade	2nd Brigade	3rd Brigade
Brig. Gen. N. McLean	Brig. Gen. M. Hascall	Col. S. Strickland
3rd Tennessee	23rd Michigan	14th Kentucky
6th Tennessee	45th Ohio	20th Kentucky
13th Kentucky	107th Illinois	27th Kentucky
25th Michigan	111th Ohio	50th Ohio
80th Indiana	118th Ohio	
91st Indiana		

Artillery
22nd Independent Battery Indiana, Light Artillery
1st Michigan Light Artillery, Battery F
19th Independent Battery, Ohio Light Artillery

Third Division: Brig. Gen. Jacob Cox

1st Brigade	2nd Brigade	3rd Brigade	Artillery
Col. J.Reilly	Brig. Gen. Manson	Brig. Gen. McLean	Maj. Henry Wells
8th Tennessee	5th Tennessee	1st Tennessee	15th Indiana Light
16th Kentucky	24th Kentucky	11th Kentucky	Artillery
100th Ohio	63rd Indiana	12th Kentucky	1st Ohio Light
104th Ohio	65th Illinois		Artillery, Batt. D
112th Illinois	103rd Ohio		
	65th Indiana		

Confederate Forces

Army of Mississippi
Lt. Gen. Leonidas Polk
Maj. Gen. W.W. Loring
Lt. Gen. A. P. Stewart
Maj. Gen. Benjamin Cheatham
Loring's Division: Maj. Gen. W. W. Loring
Brig. Gen. Featherstone

1st Brigade	2nd Brigade	Third Brigade
Brig. Gen. Featherstone	Brig. Gen. J. Adams	Col. T. Scott
3rd Mississippi	14th Mississippi	27th Alabama
22nd Mississippi	15th Mississippi	35th Alabama
31st Mississippi	20th Mississippi	49th Alabama
33rd Mississippi	23rd Mississippi	55th Alabama
40th Mississippi	43rd Mississippi	57th Alabama
1st Mississippi Battalion Sharpshooters	6th Mississippi	12th Louisiana
1st Mississippi		

Artillery
Maj. Myrick
Barry's Tennessee Battery
Bouanchaud's Louisiana Battery
Cowan's Mississippi Battery

French's Division: Maj. Gen. Samuel French

1st Brigade	2nd Brigade	Third Brigade
Brig. Gen. M. Ector	Brig. Gen. F. Cockrell	Brig. Gen. C. Sears
29th North Carolina	1st Missouri	4th Mississippi
39th North Carolina	2nd Missouri	35th Mississippi
9th Texas	3rd Missouri	36th Mississippi
10th Texas Cavalry (dismounted)	4th Missouri	39th Mississippi
14th Texas Cavalry (dismounted)	5th Missouri	46th Mississippi
32nd Texas Cavalry (dismounted)	6th Missouri	7th Mississippi Battalion
	1st Missouri Cavalry (dismounted)	
	3rd Missouri Cavalry (dismounted)	

Artillery
Maj. Storrs
Guibor's Missouri Battery
Hoskins' Mississippi Battery
Ward's Alabama Battery

Cantey's Division: Brig. Gen James Cantey
Maj. Gen. E.C. Walthall

1st Brigade	2nd Brigade	3rd Brigade
Brig. Gen. D. Reynolds	Col. V. Murphy	Brig.Gen. Quarles
1st Arkansas (dismounted rifles)		1st Alabama
2nd Arkansas (dismounted rifles)	17th Alabama	42nd Tennessee
4th Arkansas	26th Alabama	46th Tennessee
9th Arkansas	29th Alabama	55th Tennessee
25th Arkansas	37th Mississippi	48th Tennessee
		49th Tennessee
		52nd Tennessee

Artillery
Maj. W. Preston
Selden's Alabama Battery
Tarrant's Alabama Battery
Yate's Mississippi Battery

Cavalry Division: Brig. Gen. William Jackson

1st Brigade	2nd Brigade	Third Brigade
Brig. Gen. F. Armstrong	Brig. Gen. L. Ross	Brig. Gen. S. Ferguson
6th Alabama	3rd Texas	2nd Alabama
1st Mississippi	6th Texas	12th Mississippi
2nd Mississippi	9th Texas	56th Alabama
28th Mississippi	1st Texas	Miller's Mississippi Regt.
Ballentine's Mississippi Regt.		Perrin's Mississippi Regt.

Artillery
Croft's Georgia Battery
King's Missouri Battery
Waties South Carolina Battery

Army of Tennessee
Gen. Joseph Johnston
Gen. John Bell Hood
62,000 men
Hardee's Corps: Lt. Gen. William Hardee
Maj. Gen. Patrick Cleburne

Cheatham's Division: Maj. Gen. Benjamin Cheatham
Brig. Gen. George Maney
Brig. Gen. John Carter

Maney's Brigade	Wright's Brigade	Strahl's Brigade
Col. F. Walker	Brig. Gen. J. Carter	Brig. Gen. O. Strahl
1st Tennessee	8th Tennessee	4th Tennessee
27th Tennessee	16th Tennessee	5th Tennessee
4th Tennessee	28th Tennessee	24th Tennessee
6th Tennessee	38th Tennessee	31st Tennessee
9th Tennessee	51st Tennessee	33rd Tennessee
19th Tennessee	52nd Tennessee	41st Tennessee
50th Tennessee		
24th Tennessee		

Vaughan's Brigade
Col. M. Magevney, Jr.
11th Tennessee
12th Tennessee
47th Tennessee
29th Tennessee
154th Tennessee
13th Tennessee

Cleburne's Division: Maj. Gen. Patrick Cleburne
Brig. Gen. M. P. Lowrey

Polk's Brigade	Smith's Brigade	Lowrey's Brigade
1st Arkansas	6th Texas	16th Alabama
15th Arkansas	15th Texas Cavalry (dismounted)	33rd Alabama
5th Confederate	7th Texas	45th Alabama
2nd Tennessee	10th Texas	32nd Mississippi
48th Tennessee	17th Texas Cavalry (dismounted)	45th Mississippi
35th Tennessee	18th Texas Cavalry (dismounted)	7th Arkansas
	24th Texas Cavalry (dismounted)	8th Arkansas
	25th Texas Cavalry (dismounted)	19th Arkansas
		3rd Mississippi Batn.

Govan's Brigade	Granbury's Brigade
2nd Arkansas	6th Texas
24th Arkansas	15th Texas
5th Arkansas	7th Texas
13th Arkansas	10th Texas
6th Arkansas	17th Texas (dismounted)
3rd Confederate	18th Texas (dismounted)
7th Arkansas	24th Texas (dismounted)
8th Arkansas	25th Texas (dismounted)
19th Arkansas	

Walker's Division: Maj. Gen. William H. T. Walker
Brig. Gen. H. Mercer

Mercer's Brigade	Gist's Brigade	Steven's Brigade
Brig. Gen. H. Mercer	Brig. Gen. S. R. Gist	Brig. Gen. C. Stevens
1st Vol. Georgia	8th Georgia. Battalion	1st Georgia
54th Georgia	46th Georgia	25th Georgia
57th Georgia	65th Georgia	29th Georgia
63rd Georgia	5th Mississippi	30th Georgia
	8th Mississippi	66th Georgia
	16th South Carolina	1st Georgia Batn. S.S.
	24th South Carolina	2nd Georgia Batn. S.S.

Jackson's Brigade
Brig. Gen. Jackson
47th Georgia
65th Georgia
5th Mississippi
8th Mississippi
2nd Battalion Georgia Sharpshooters
5th Georgia

Bate's Division: Maj. Gen. William Bate
Maj. Gen. John Brown

Lewis' Brigade	Tyler's Brigade	Finley's Brigade
2nd Kentucky	37th Georgia	1st Florida Cavalry (dismounted)
4th Kentucky	15th Tennessee	3rd Florida
5th Kentucky	37th Tennessee	1st Florida
6th Kentucky	20th Tennessee	4th Florida

9th Kentucky   30th Tennessee   6th Florida
                   4th Georgia Batn. S.S.   7th Florida
                   10th Tennessee

Hood's Corps (Lee's)
Lt. Gen. John B. Hood
Maj. Gen. C. Stevenson
Maj. Gen. Ben Cheatham
Lt. Gen. Stephen Lee

Hindman's Division: Maj. Gen. Thomas Hindman
Brig. Gen. John Brown
Maj. Gen. Patton Anderson
Maj. Gen. Edward Johnson

Deas' Brigade	Manigault's Brigade	Tucker's Brigade
Col. J. Coltart	**Brig. Gen. A. Manigault**	**Col. S. Benton**
19th Alabama	24th Alabama	7th Mississippi
22nd Alabama	28th Alabama	9th Mississippi
25th Alabama	34th Alabama	10th Mississippi
39th Alabama	10th South Carolina	41st Mississippi
50th Alabama	19th South Carolina	9th Mississippi Batt.
17th Alabama Battalion Sharpshooters		Sharpshooters

Walthall's Brigade
Col. S. Benton
24th Mississippi
27th Mississippi
29th Mississippi
30th Mississippi
34th Mississippi

Stevenson's Division: Maj. Gen. Carter Stevenson

Brown's Brigade	Cumming's Brigade	Reynold's Brigade
Col. J. Palmer	**Brig. Gen. A. Cumming**	**Brig. Gen. A. Reynolds**
3rd Tennessee	2nd Georgia State Troops	58th North Carolina
18th Tennessee	34th Georgia	60th North Carolina
26th Tennessee	36th Georgia	54th Virginia
32nd Tennessee	39th Georgia	63rd Virginia
45th Tennessee	56th Georgia	
23rd Tennessee Battalion		

Pettus' Brigade
Brig. Gen. E. Pettus
20th Alabama
23rd Alabama
30th Alabama
31st Alabama
46th Alabama

Stewart's Division: Maj. Gen. Alexander Stewart
Maj. Gen. H. Clayton

Stovall's Brigade	Gibson's Brigade	Baker's Brigade
Brig. Gen. M. Stovall	**Brig. Gen. R. Gibson**	**Brig. Gen. A. Baker**
1st Georgia State Troops	1st Louisiana (regulars)	37th Alabama
40th Georgia	13th Louisiana	40th Alabama
41st Georgia	16th Louisiana	42nd Alabama
42nd Georgia	25th Louisiana	54th Alabama
43rd Georgia	19th Louisiana	
52nd Georgia	20th Louisiana	
	4th Louisiana Battalion	
	Austin's Louisiana Battalion Sharpshooters	
	30th Louisiana	

Clayton's Brigade
Brig. Gen. H. Clayton
18th Alabama
32nd Alabama
58th Alabama
36th Alabama
38th Alabama
Maj. Gen. Joseph Wheeler's Cavalry Corps
Martin's Division: Maj. Gen. William Martin

Allen's Brigade	Iverson's Brigade
1st Alabama	1st Georgia
3rd Alabama	2nd Georgia
4th Alabama	3rd Georgia
7th Alabama	4th Georgia
51st Alabama	6th Georgia
12th Alabama Battalion	

Humes Division: Brig. Gen. W. Humes

Ashby's Brigade	Harrison's Brigade	Grigsby's Brigade
1st (6) Tennessee	3rd Arkansas	**Col. Grigsby**
2nd Tennessee	4th Tennessee	1st Kentucky
5th Tennessee	8th Texas	2nd Kentucky
9th Tennessee Battalion	11th Texas	9th Kentucky
		2nd Kentucky Battalion
		Allison's Squadron
		Hamilton's Battalion

Kelley's Division: Brig. Gen. J. H. Kelley

Anderson's Brigade	Dibrell's Brigade	Hannon's Brigade
Col. R. Anderson	**Col. G. Dibrell**	**Col. W. Hannon**
3rd Confederate	4th Tennessee	53rd Alabama
8th Confederate	8th Tennessee	24th Alabama
10th Confederate	9th Tennessee	
12th Confederate	10th Tennessee	
5th Georgia	11th Tennessee	

Hannon's Brigade	Williams' Brigade
Col. M. Hannon	**Brig. Gen. John Williams**
53rd Alabama	1st (3rd) Kentucky
24th Alabama Battalion	2nd Kentucky (Woodard's Regt)
9th Kentucky	2nd Kentucky Battalion
	Allison's Tennessee Squadron
	Detachment Hamilton's Tennessee Battalion

Artillery
Brig. Gen. Francis Shoup
Hardee's Corps
Col. Melancthon Smith

Hoxton's Battalion	Martin's Battalion
Perry's Florida Battery	Bledsoe's Missouri Battery
Phelan's Alabama Battery	Ferguson's South Carolina Battery
Turner's Mississippi Battery	Swett's Mississippi Battery

Hotchkiss' Battalion	Cobb's Battalion
Goldwaite's Alabama Battery	Gracey's Kentucky Battery
Key's Arkansas Battery	Mebane's Tennessee Battery
Howell's Georgia Battery	Slocumb's Louisiana Battery

Hood's Corps
Col. R. Beckham

Courtney's Battalion	Eldridge's Battalion
Dent's Alabama Battery	Fenner's Louisiana Battery
Dougal's Texas Battery	Oliver's Alabama Battery
Garrity's Alabama Battery	Stanford's Mississippi Battery

Johnston's Battalion	Cavalry Corps
Corput's Georgia Battery	**Lt. Gen. Felix Robertson**
Marshall's Tennessee Battery	Ferrell's Georgia Battery
Rowans' Georgia Battery	Huggins' Tennessee Battery
	Ramsey's Tennessee Battery
	White's Tennessee Battery
	Wiggin's Arkansas Battery

Artillery Reserve
Lt. Col. James Hallonquest

Williams' Battalion	Palmer's Battalion	Waddell's Battalion
Darden's Mississippi Battery	Havis' Georgia Battery	Barrett's Missouri Battery
Jeffress' Virginia Battery	Lumsden's Battery	Bellamy's Alabama Battery
Kolb's Alabama Battery		Emery's Alabama Battery

First Division Georgia Militia: Maj. Gen. Gustavus Smith

1st Brigade	**2nd Brigade**
Brig. Gen. R. Carswell	**Brig. Gen. P. Phillips**
1st Georgia Regiment Militia	3rd Georgia Regiment Militia
2nd Georgia Regiment Militia	4th Georgia Regiment Militia
1st Georgia Battalion	6th Georgia Regiment Militia
5th Georgia Regiment Militia	

3rd Brigade	**4th Brigade**
Brig. Gen. C. Anderson	**Brig. Gen. H. McCay**
7th Georgia Regiment Militia	10th Georgia Regiment Militia
8th Georgia Regiment Militia	11th Georgia Regiment Militia
9th Georgia Regiment Militia	12th Georgia Regiment Militia

The campaign would pit Union Gen. William Tecumseh Sherman against Confederate General Joseph Eggleston Johnston. Sherman moved his army into Georgia, while Union General George Thomas would remain in Tennessee. Grant was transferred east to take on Gen. Lee. On March 18, 1864, Sherman became commander of all Union forces in the West. Sherman assembled 100,000 men against Joseph Johnston's 45,000 men. He amassed 100 locomotives and 1,000 cars crammed with supplies for his trip through Georgia. Sherman studied all the maps and censuses for Georgia, because he was going to have his men live off the land, and he needed to know where the most fertile regions were. It was up to Sherman to take Georgia. On May 5th-6th, Joseph Johnston placed his army on the Rocky Face Ridge, which runs north and south, and across Crow Valley, north of Dalton, Georgia. Rocky Face Ridge was 800 feet above the valley floor. Sherman sent Union General James McPherson and his Army of the Tennessee (24,465 men) to Snake Creek Gap, an opening through Rocky Face Ridge about 12 miles below Dalton. Sherman also sent George Thomas and his Army of the Cumberland (60,733 men) to Ringgold, about midway to Dalton on the Western & Atlantic Railroad. Maj. Gen. John Schoefield was sent with his Army of the Ohio (13,559 men) south via the Tennessee town of Cleveland and followed the east Tennessee & Georgia Railroad, which joined the Western & Atlantic at Dalton. On May 7th, Thomas attacked Tunnel Hill, seven miles southeast of Ringgold. On May 8th, Thomas sent one division to attack the Confederates four miles south of Mill Creek Gap. Dug Gap lay to the south of the main Confederate defenses and was guarded by 1,000 men. At 3:00 p.m., Brig. Gen. John Geary deployed two brigades at the base of Dug Gap and started them up the ridge. Geary's men ran into a 20-foot crest of rock from which the Confederates fired down upon the Union troops and successfully fought off Geary's attack. Toward evening, the Confederates received two fresh brigades of infantry under Gen. Patrick Cleburne and Gen. William Hardee. Geary then withdrew. Geary's losses were 357, Confederates lost 71.

On that same day, McPherson reached Villanow with no problems, and marched into Snake Creek Gap that night and occupied it. At the same time, Confederate Col. Grigsby's Kentucky Cavalry were sent to protect the approach to Snake Creek Gap.

Maj. Gen. William W. Loring

On May 9th, Grigsby's cavalry encountered McPherson's 9th Illinois Mounted Infantry. The Federals forced Grigsby's cavalry back to Resaca. McPherson then encountered Brig. Gen. James Cantey's skirmishers, who had recently arrived in Resaca. They were 4,000 men strong, and McPherson decided to fall back to Snake Creek Gap. Johnston had a force at Resaca, Georgia, which was a few miles east of the gap. That night John Bell Hood arrived in Resaca.

Sherman now decided to have George Thomas move towards

Gen. McPherson

Dalton with a larger force than McPherson's. He left one corps at Rocky Face Ridge, and sent the rest of his forces south through the gap. His goal was to place his troops between Johnston and Resaca.

On May 12th, Johnston discovered that Sherman was moving in his rear at Resaca, and Johnson abandoned Dalton that night, and redeployed north and west of Resaca. Confederate Gen. John Bell Hood held the right, Gen. William Hardee held the center, and Gen. Leonidas Polk held the left of the Confederate line. Johnston now had 66,000 men against Sherman's 104,000 and he controlled the high ground.

On May 13th, Sherman moved against Resaca, and on May 14th, the Battle of Resaca began. Schofield launched an attack with two divisions against Maj. Gen. Thomas Hindman's Confederate division on the other side of Camp Creek. Gen. Jacob Cox attacked on the left, Brig. Gen. Henry Judah attacked on the right. Cox captured Hindman's first line of entrenchments at 1:30 p.m., but Cox was halted by the Confederates and Cox lost 562 men. On Cox's right, Judah's division got entangled with a division from the Army of the Cumberland that was meant to support him on the right. He didn't halt to reorganize and didn't wait for support troops. Judah ordered a charge across 400 yards of open ground in the Camp Creek Valley and quickly lost 600 men. At 4:00 p.m., the Confederates in John Bell Hood's two divisions attacked Brig. Gen. David Stanley on his extreme left. Stanley's 35th Indiana ran but the 5th Indiana Artillery stopped the Confederates. Federal Gen. Alpheus Williams reinforcements helped halt the Confederate advance completely. The Confederates had come close to a victory. The fighting ended because of darkness.

On May 15th, Sherman ordered Brig. Gen. Thomas Sweeny to cross the Oostanaula River at Lay's Ferry. Sherman also ordered a push northwest of Resaca near the mouth of Camp Creek. Schofield moved around the extreme Federal left to make room for Maj. Gen. Joseph Hooker's XX Corps. Hooker would make the attack supported by Howard's IV Corps. Hooker instructed Maj. Gen. Daniel Butterfield's division to seize the Confederate earthworks and capture Capt. Max Van den Corput's four cannons. Col. Ben Harrison led his troops down the slope and into the open valley that separated the two ridges. The Indiana troops took the fort, but the Union troops soon found themselves under fire from the Confederate main line and had to fall back to the western edge of the fort. That night, under cover of darkness, the Federals took the four guns. Sweeny got across the Oostanaula River and built earthworks. He was attacked by Walker's Confederates, but Sweeny held his ground. Johnston soon realized that he was outflanked again, and his Confederate forces crossed the river and marched southward, abandoning Resaca. The Battle of Resaca cost Johnston 2,600 killed, wounded, or captured. Sherman lost 3,500 men, but he had forced Johnston out of his position twice.

On May 19th, Johnston unsuccessfully tried to concentrate his forces at Cassville, then he set up at Alltoona Pass. On May 23rd, Sherman crossed the Etowah River, west of Alltoona, and two days later he closed on Dallas, and attacked the Confederates at New Hope Church, northeast of town. Hooker, Geary, Butterfield, and Brig. Gen. Alpheus Williams all assaulted the well entrenched fort at New Hope. The Confederate's 16 cannons under Maj. Gen. Alexander Stewart rained down canister and solid shot on the approaching Union troops. The Federals reached within 50 yards of the Confederate main line, but the artillery fire was too much for them. The Union troops began to dig in, parallel to the six mile long Confederate line. Williams lost 745 men of his 7,500, and Hooker lost 1,665 men. Hood lost not quite half that many, and was victorious against Sherman. Two days later, Oliver Howard and

14,000 men from the IV Corps were to attack at Picket's Mill northeast of New Hope Church although without artillery support. Brig. Gen. Richard Johnston's division from the XIV Corps was to support the attack on the Federal left and a brigade from the Army of the Ohio was to shield his right. Wood's division was to lead the attack with 1,500 men under Brig. Gen. William Hazen. For two hours, Howard probed for the Confederate flank. In front of Howard waited the 4,700 men of Patrick Cleburne's division. Cleburne knew the attack was coming, and he readied his men. At 5:00 p.m., Hazen began his advance. He thought he saw a gap in the Confederate line and rushed forward. Cleburne fired point blank into Hazen's men. Hazen was then exposed to the cannon fire of Capt. Thomas Key's Arkansas Artillery. Hazen lost 500 men in 45 minutes. The survivors broke and ran.

Next, Col. William Gibson marched against Cleburne, and the 49th Ohio quickly lost 203 of their 400 men. Just before dark, Confederate artillery threatened the Union rear. Howard sent in Wood's brigade to hold the line. Union General Richard Johnson was wounded. Firing subsided after sundown as Wood's last brigade moved forward. That night, Brig. Gen. Hiram Granbury's Texans rushed down the ravine and captured 232 Union troops. Over 1,600 Federals lost their lives. The Confederates lost 500. The Battle of Pickett's Mill resulted in defeat for the Union troops.

On May 28th, Johnston ordered William Hardee to test the defenses of McPherson's army, which was south of Dallas. The task was given to the division under Maj. Gen. William Bate, which held the extreme left of the Confederate line. At 3:45 p.m., Confederate Brigadier General Frank Armstrong's cavalry hit the Federal right flank just south of Dallas and found McPherson's XV Corps well entrenched. Armstrong made it past the first line of fortifications and overran three guns of the 1st Iowa Battery. The Corps commander, Maj. Gen. John Logan rushed toward the front, leading his men to the seized cannon. A bullet hit him in the left forearm, but he managed to recaptured the guns.

At 4 p.m., Finley's Florida Brigade surged forward against the XV Corps and the XVI Corps farther north. The Florida brigade fell back, but Gen. Joseph Lewis's 1st Kentucky Brigade went over the Federals first line of works which were only 20 yards from the Federal main line. They didn't fall back until Lt. Col. Hiram Hawkins, a regimental commander, seized their colors and waved them back. The Orphan brigade lost 700 men. On June 1st, the Army of Tennessee disengaged and moved to the left, fighting as they moved.

Unable to defeat Johnston, Sherman moved east, shifting from right to left. In early June, the Union forces regained the railroad near Acworth. By June 10th, Sherman had received reinforcements, repaired the railroad, and advanced on Johnston. Sherman now had 100,000 men against Johnston's 70,000 men who occupied the hills north of Marietta. Sherman pushed Johnston to Kennesaw Mountain. There were four mountains in all facing Sherman. On the Confederate right was Brush Mountain, on the left was Lost Mountain, and in the middle was Pine Mountain. The last mountain was two miles behind the other mountains, and was the most imposing, standing 700 feet above the valley floor and was named Kennesaw Mountain. Kennesaw protected Johnston's headquarters at Marietta.

Maj. Gen. William B. Bate

On June 14th, Leonidas Polk was killed by a Union Parrott rifle and Confederate General Loring took over his command.

By June 22nd, the armies were strung out along a line that began north of Marietta, and swung to the west, and then south to a point several miles southwest of the town, near Alley's Creek. Sherman planned to attack at three places-Kennesaw Mountain, Cheatham's Hill west of Marietta, and along Alley's Creek. Sherman left Hooker's XX Corps and Schoefield's Army of the Ohio to advance towards Kolb's farm, which was three miles southwest of Marietta. At that same time, Johnston was sending Hood's Corps to advance on Kolb's farm. Hood, on his own orders, decided to attack the Federals. Late in the afternoon, two of Hood's divisions emerged from the woods on both sides of the Powder Springs Road. The Federals already knew of Hood's plans and were expecting his divisions. On the Federal line posted from left to right were the divisions of Brig. Gen. Milo Hascall, Alpheus Williams, and John Geary. Confederate General Carter Stevenson's division, supported by Hindman, attacked the Federals. The Union force had 40 cannons and outnumbered the Confederates by 11,000 men. Stevenson charged and fell back twice, getting within 50 yards of the Union line. Hindman also failed in taking the Federal position. Hood lost 1,000 men in this assault, 870 from Stevenson's division alone. Hooker lost 300. Hood never reported his losses to Johnston. Sherman brought 140 cannons to try and break the trench warfare around Kennesaw Mountain and decided to take the mountain by assault.

At 8:00 a.m., on June 27th, Sherman launched his attack with an opening salvo from 200 cannons. The Confederates replied in kind as McPherson's Army of the Tennessee made the assault on the Confederate right center. About 8:30 a.m., three brigades under Brig. Gen. Morgan Smith moved east, toward the southern slope of Little Kennesaw Mountain, just below Pigeon Hill. On Smith's right, the Yankees were able to take the rifle pits of Gen. William Walker's division, and capture 100 men. Then they started up Little Kennesaw on the left and Pigeon Hill on the right. The main Confederate line was 500 yards to their front. Smith retreated under heavy fire of cannon and musket and lost 500 men. At 9:00 a.m., two divisions of Thomas' Army of the Cumberland moved against the center of the Kennesaw Mountain line. Thomas ordered his five brigades, from Jeff Davis XIV Corps, and John Newton's IV Corps, to attack. On Newton's right, Brig. Gen. Charles Harper's attack had collapsed. Harper took a bullet through his right arm, then one in his chest. His men retreated. Newton's other three brigades lost 654 men and he also fell back. Two brigades under Jeff Davis attempted to take the Confederate earthworks on Cheatham's Hill. Maj. Gen. Ben Cheatham's troops were protecting the earthworks. Col. Daniel McCook's men got caught in a crossfire between 10 Confederate cannons. McCook tried to make a suicidal run at Dead Angle on Cheatham's Hill, and was bayoneted by a Confederate soldier. Capt. William Fellows, McCook's brigade inspector, took over command and was shot down. Col. Oscar Harmon then took command and he was also killed. Davis took 824 casualties. McCook's men were ordered to retreat. Sherman lost 3,000 men, and gained no ground. Only at Olley's Creek did Sherman claim any degree of success. Schofield already outflanked Kennesaw Mountain, having moved two brigades across Olley's Creek, a mile below Powder Springs road. This put Schoefield to Hood's extreme flank. Sherman next moved to the right, forcing Johnston to choose between giving up the Kennesaw line or being cut off from Atlanta.

Johnston started a new line at Smyrna, four miles below Marietta. On July 2nd-3rd, he moved to the Smyrna line. Union forces confronted Johnston on July 3rd. After a day of skirmishing, Sherman's right threatened Johnston's communications with Atlanta, and on July 4th-5th, the Confederates fell back to the north bank of the Chattahoochee, where they occupied a heavily fortified position. Sherman sent Kenner Garrards cavalry to capture Roswell, 16 miles upriver and planned to cross above Johnston's fortifications.

On July 8th, Schofield's men crossed the river. On July 9th-10th, Johnston crossed the Chattahooche and went into position along Peachtree Creek, a few miles from Atlanta. On July 17th, Joseph Johnston was replaced with John Bell Hood, because Jeff Davis was fearing the fall of Atlanta, the Federal advance into Georgia and the crippling effect it would have on the Confederacy, and felt that a more aggressive commander could beat back the Federals in Georgia.

On July 18th, Hood faced Sherman's army, which was north and east of Atlanta, and Thomas' army with it's right resting on the Chatttahooche River. Schofield and McPherson were to the east trying to reach the Georgia Railroad, Hood's direct link to the Carolinas and Virginia.

On July 19th, Hood saw a flaw in the Federal lines. He noticed that there was a two mile gap between Thomas and Schoefield's lines. Hood planned to attack the Federal gap by sending Hardee's Corps and Stewart to attack Thomas army when it was crossing Peachtree Creek. They were to drive Thomas into the creek, oblique left, and crush his remaining troops. Cheatham's corps was to hold off McPherson and Schoefield and then, after Thomas was defeated, Hardee and Stewart would join Cheatham in destroying the other two Federal armies. Because of mistakes in coordinating the attack, the battle didn't begin until two hours past the original time line. On July 20th, at 4 p.m., Hood sent 19,000 men into battle. Most of Thomas' Federals had made it across Peachtree Creek when Hardee attacked with four divisions on Thomas' left. Newton's men were hit by Walker's division, and by Bate's. Newton repulsed the Confederate attack on his left and front, but his right was vulnerable. He had a quarter mile gap between Newton's right and the next Union division. Brig Gen. George Maney, of Cheatham's division, poured through this gap. They were counterattacked by troops from Brig. Gen. John Coburn and Col. Ben Harrison and the Confederates fell back. Hardee was going to send Cleburne to attack Thomas' left, but he called off Cleburne's attack and sent him instead to take on McPherson's army when he learned that McPherson was moving on Atlanta, and was threatening to capture Confederate Gen. Joseph Wheeler's cavalry.

Hood failed to destroy the Federal army. He had lost 4,796 men. The Federals only lost 1,779 men and were now threatening Atlanta itself.

Lt. Barney Harwood
17th Kentucky Infantry (U.S.)

Lt. Barney Hardwood, at 24 years of age, joined the Union army for three years at Springfield, Kentucky, right after the Battle of Perryville. He was at first assigned to the 15th Kentucky Infantry on September 13, 1862, but was immediately transferred to the 17th Kentucky Infantry and was made a 2nd Lieutenant in Company C. In March 1863, Harwood was transferred to Company B, 17th Kentucky Infantry and made a 1st Lieutenant. Lt. Barney Harwood's diary covers the period from January 1st to August 4, 1864, and covers the battles from Chattanooga, Tennessee to Atlanta, Georgia. His diary is not a literary masterpiece, and the descriptions of the battles he was involved in are very short. His diary is more illuminating as to what the typical soldier faced while in camp. Illness takes up a large part of his entries. On January 2nd

Lt. Barney Harwood's Model 1851 Shako with Hardee hat eagle plate with embroidered infantry horn. Lt. Harwood's original hat box with manufacturing label "Brent & Bush's Fashionable hat establishment-corner of Court and Washington Streets Boston". Lt. Barney Harwood diary. (BCWM)

he reports, "Disease bad in camp. Many men unable to report for muster." On January 14th he again writes, "Disease bad in camp. Many men down with pox." On January 19th, Hardwood himself succumbs to disease, "Got dysentery. Went to Regt. Surgeon." On February 5th, he writes, "Only 60% of our troops are fit for duty." On March 6th, he writes, "Heard news of Pvt. friend. He died in hospital on March 2nd." On March 23rd he writes, "If Rebs fight today. Can only put 40% of my men in combat." On April 9th, Hardwood writes, "Quiet day in camp. Still many men ill with fever & pox." These reports of disease are not unusual considering that 60% of all deaths during the Civil War were caused by disease. The disease of dysentery accounted for as many as 7,000 deaths in the Union army, 13% of the mortality rate. There were inoculations for small pox, but many of the soldiers did not get their inoculations, and once the disease caught hold, it would spread like wildfire until every man who was not inoculated would come down with it. The men who had this disease were usually put into isolation tents where they were expected to die. A little over 4,000 deaths were attributed to different fevers in the Union army. Dysentery was caused by unsanitary conditions in camp. Soldiers very often would not bathe or would prepare food improperly.

His other entries pertain to camp life. Camp life for the soldier was filled with different ways to occupy his time. Drilling was one of them, and Lt. Harwood's diary has quite a few entries pertaining to drilling. On January 11th, he writes, "trying to drill our men today. Discipline hard to maintain." Jan. 15th, "Have review of troops today. Very pleased with my men." Feb. 8th, "drilled the men." Feb. 15, "drill, as usual. I missed services." May 2nd, "Drilled men, and had them clean the muskets." Many of the men also occupied their time with church service on Sundays. The soldiers on both sides usually belonged to some type of organized religion. Harwood writes, "The Regimental Cpl. soul service today. Men very inspired by sermon." Unfortunately, Lt. Harwood very often missed the services on Sunday, he writes that he missed so many services, "Guess I'm going to hell." Soldiers also filled their time by playing cards. Hardwood writes on March 3rd, "Rain today, men playing cards." There was even the occasional snowball fight in the winter. Harwood writes on Jan. 4th: " (Mon.) We had very bad snowfall during the night. Men playing with snowballs. Had to discipline." With so much time on a soldiers hands, he very often turned to the bottle to relieve tension and boredom. On Feb. 6th he writes: "Had two men put in jail today. Too drunk for muster." Feb. 18th, Harwood writes, "I got some brandy today. May get drunk." The next day he writes, "I did get drunk last night. I feel terrible today." Boredom even got to Harwood, he writes on April 19th, "I would rather stand up to a Reb musket, than to stay in camp one day longer." March 4th, "Thinking of home. Today very bored."

The soldier also looked forward to the time when the sutlers came to camp, although Harwood detested sutlers. He has many entries pertaining to the sutlers. March 17th "Suttlers wagons are coming into camp now. The damn bastards..." April 7th, "Wish I could draw and quarter every Sutler in this man's army. Not a bastard among them worth the price of rope to hang them." The reason for his animosity toward sutlers is that they would usually charge three times the going rate for the supplies and would very often show up when the soldiers were being paid. The sutlers sold every imaginable item that a soldier would want, including alcohol, pies, uniforms, and extra food.

Unfortunately, Barney Hardwood's diary only covers January 1, 1864 to August 4, 1864. From regimental histories, Hardwood's unit fought on both days at Chickamagua. On the first day of battle, the 17th Kentucky captured a battery and sent it to the rear. On the second day of battle, the 17th rallied on Snodgrass Hill on the right of the main line. The regiment fought all day, until ordered off the field at 7:30 p.m. The 17th Kentucky also participated in the battle of Missionary Ridge. After Missionary Ridge, the 17th moved from place to place during the winter. It was at Maryville, Knoxville, Strawberry Plains, Powder Springs, New Market, and Dandridge. On Jan. 23rd, Harwood writes: "Regiments scattered. Some men in Ga., some men in Tenn." On Feb 3rd, the regiment had been incorporated into the 4th Corps, Gen. Wood's Division, Beatty's brigade. Harwood writes: "Gen. Wood to receive our men today."

In April, the regiment moved to Cleveland, Tennessee, and was preparing to enter Georgia. On April 2nd, Harwood writes: " We hear Johnston is commanding the Rebels now." April 21st, "We hear that Reb. General Forrest and his cavalry are attacking our supply lines..." April 26th, "We have reports that our men outnumber the Rebs three to one, and if the Rebs are in a bad shape as the ones I have seen turn themselves in this winter, we would be in Atlanta by spring. If only our generals would give us the word to move our troops forward."

By May 4th, the regiment was at Catoosa Springs, and then it joined Sherman's Atlanta Campaign. On May 3rd, Harwood writes: "We hear rumors that this is an advance again to be made toward the enemy soon. I hope its true." On May 7th, he writes: "Finally battle 1 (won) today. We fought the enemy at a place called Tunnel Hill. The Rebs fell back entrenched at Rocky Face Ridge." On May 8th, the regiment advanced and suffered losses at Rocky Face Ridge. "We stayed at the base of the ridge and can move no further." May 10th, "the Rebs have marksmen on every point of advantage. Only ine man suffered any wounds from our engagement." May 12th, "The Regiment moved back & we can see the Rebs withdrawing toward Resaca." May 13th, "We are ordered to pursue the enemy and are glad to go this being the only battle we've been in for over three months. Alas who knows. We are the pursuing troops and see no more fighting." May 15th, "Cannot tell the horrors of the battle-

field. Men are torn to pieces in every considerable moment. We are only to pursue the retreating Rebs." May 16th, We are camped at the town called Calhoun and our men in the rebel rear." May 17th, "Two men wounded from fight." May 18th, "the Rebs moved out during the night & we broke camp at 6:00 to follow. Wish they would stand & fight." On May 19th, the regiment engaged at Cassville. Harwood writes: "Col. Stout sent three companies into action at Cassville today. The three companies lost several men and one officer, but fought valiantly." May 20th, "We awoke to find the Rebels had left Cassville in the night." May 21st, "Our company was assigned to bury the federal dead and mainly there were about 15 killed & many wounded left behind." On May 24th, the regiment fought at the battle of Altoona, where it lost Capt. W. J. Landrum. On May 27th, the regiment fought at Picket's Mill. Harwood writes: "What a battle we fought today. Many men killed on both sides. Several in my command wounded." May 28th, "Rain every where and the wounded are suffering from a lack of shelter. Not since Shiloh has our regiment suffered so many losses." May 30th, "Men killed & wounded everyday." May 31st, Sharpshooters are the bigger problem. We can't even bury our dead without being shot at. Truce flag were sent out for the purpose, but the Rebs know little about civilized warfare." June 3rd, "We are still in the face of the enemy & continue to take losses." June 6th, "Camp near the town of Ackworth, Ga. No fighting." June 14th, "Enemy entrenched around Kennesaw Mountain." On June 17th, the regiment lost Capt. R. Sturgis, who was killed by a bullet. June 18th, Harwood writes: "Advanced toward enemy at 7:00. Sharp contest. Enemy having entrenches." June 19th, "Cannon fire all day today." June 20th, "Damn Sherman assaulted Kennesaw Mt. today. Little gained as the Rebs have fortified the Mt. too well." June 23rd, "Still Rebs are retreating toward Atlanta. This hardship on the land is unbelievable. The God above scared that such a event never comes to Kentucky soil." July 6th, "Pushed toward Atlanta." July 15th, "Enemy campfires seen in our front, but no shots exchanged." July 18th, "Near Peachtree Creek. Very near Atlanta." July 20th, "Put to work today digging entrenchments. I guess Sherman plan to besiege Atlanta. Our commanders tells us nothing but what is absolutely necessary." July 22nd, " In front of Atlanta today. We're about to see action very soon." July 24th, "Rebs are pouring in shells as quickly as we throw them out." July 25th, "Several men hit by shells & fragments." July 26th, "Women and children of Atlanta came into our area almost daily." July 30th, "Fires are burning from every part of the city." Aug. 3rd, "How can the city still hold out. The fires from our shells have blanketed the city in flames & smoke."

Harwood may have had other diaries, but the last entry was for August 4th. On November 11, 1863, just before Atlanta fell, Harwood was court martialed. Lt. Col. James Hart, of the 71st Ohio Volunteer Infantry filed charges against Harwood for his contemptuous and disrespectful statements that he had made about the president and the war effort. Lt. Col. Hart claimed that Harwood said that "the south should hold out until the last man died before it should yield to Old Abe Lincoln." Hart also claimed that Harwood used words "expressing his contempt, disrespect and hatred of Abraham Lincoln. He also expressed "opposition in sentiment to the war. (and the) Policy of the Government of the U.S." Gen. Samuel Beatty found Harwood guilty of conduct unbecoming an officer and a gentlemen, and conduct prejudicial and disrespectful words against the President of the United States. He was fined $50.00 from his pay. Since Harwood had not been paid in four months, they decided not to pay him for his back salary for those four months. Lt. Barney Harwood was mustered out on August 23, 1865.

Lt. Barney Harwood's diary gave us a view of the common soldier. It was one filled with disease, death, and boredom. Harwood did his duty, however, and fought in some of the most intense battles of the Western Theatre, but as we have seen, the war finally got to Harwood. He had seen the carnage and couldn't understand it. He became frustrated with the war. Lt. Harwood's diary will forever be a testament of the common soldier.

BATTLES FOR ATLANTA

"Gateway to the South"
(Note: Please refer to Georgia Campaign for orders of battle for both Union and Confederate Forces)

Battle of Atlanta

July 22, 1864
Campaign: Atlanta Campaign
Principal Commanders: Maj. Gen. William Tecumseh Sherman (US); Gen. John Bell Hood (CS)
Forces Engaged: Army of the Tennessee (US), Army of the Ohio (US), Army of the Cumberland (US); Army of Tennessee (CS)

Despite his decisive defeat at Peachtree Creek, Confederate General John Bell Hood planned a second sortie against the armies invading Atlanta under Sherman. Hood was determined to recover ground lost in the July 20, 1864 battle and restore morale to his Army of Tennessee. He felt that under his predecessor, Gen. Joseph Johnston, the army had lost its will and ability to fight anywhere except behind breastworks. Hood felt that in order to cure this cowardice in his army, he would send his men into an open ground assault, east of the city, on July 22, 1864.

His plan of attack was bold but enterprising and promising. The corps of Lt. Gen. A.P. Stewart would occupy the Union armies north and northeast of Atlanta, Hood would send the rest of his main army, the two corps of Lt. Gen. William Hardee and Maj. Gen. Cheatham to strike the most vulnerable enemy force, Maj. Gen. James McPherson's Army of the Tennessee, then moving westward from Decatur toward Atlanta. Cheatham would strike McPherson frontally, while Hardee would make a 15 mile night march to the south and east, coming up beyond McPherson's left flank and rear. This plan not only exploited McPherson's relative isolation but also his lack of a cavalry screen, which might allow Hardees' approach to go unnoticed until too late to prevent it.

On the evening of July 21st, Hood began the offensive by withdrawing from his outer works, and slipping into the defenses of the city proper. Thinking Atlanta evacuated, McPherson's advance moved confidently along the Decatur Road on the morning of the 22nd until struck by Confederate skirmishers about two and a half miles from Atlanta. The attackers, two of Hardees divisions under Maj. Gen. W.H.T. Walker and William Bate, came on with great energy. But because of errors by Hardee and Walker, they had not marched far enough to the east to clear the Union line and had struck McPherson's left, held by Maj. Gen. Grenville Dodge's XVI Corps. Dodge and his men were also hard fighters, as they proved by repulsing two attacks. During one of the attacks Gen. Walker was killed and soon another casualty occurred. Gen. Blair reported that Brig. Gen. Giles Smith was under attack. McPherson immediately sent John Logan's reserve brigades to plug the gap between Dodge and Maj. Gen. Francis Blair's XVII Corps, on Dodge's right, McPherson rode out to see the gap himself, and on the way back met Patrick Cleburne's division. Capt. Richard Beard of the 5th Confederate Regiment ordered McPherson to surrender. McPherson tried to ride off, but Beard ordered his troops to fire on him. The general was hit in the lower back, and would soon die of his wound.

McPherson's death did not ensure a Confederate success. Confederate Gen. William Hardee committed his two other divisions, Brig Gen. George Maney's and Patrick Cleburne's, to a furious, coordinated assault against Blair. Thanks largely to a heavy cannonade, they pushed back Blair's left flank, then moved toward the gap between Blair and Dodge. At the last minute, however, the reserve brigade under John Logan, which had been ordered into the breach by McPherson, slammed the Confederates backward. Hardee's offensive was snuffed out when part of the XVI Corps formed and reestablished the line.

Lt. Gen. N.B. Forrest   *Maj. Gen. W.H.T. Walker*

At 3:00 p.m., Hood committed Cheatham's corps, bolstered by 5,000 Georgia militia under Maj. Gen. Gustavus Smith, against the Union front. Had this strike been timed to coincide with Hardee's, the Union Army of the Tennessee might have been destroyed, but with Hardee stalled, Maj. Gen. John Logan, who had temporarily replaced McPherson, secured the front with his own XV Corps and part of Blair's command. Cheatham and Smith penetrated below the line of the Georgia Railroad but were quickly repulsed. Sherman had ordered Wood's division to counterattack and Schofield to mass all the cannons from the Army of the Ohio, 20 in all, on a knoll near his headquarters. John Logan, now the commander of the Army of the Tennessee, personally led Col. August Mersy's four regiments to the new line north of the Georgia Railroad. Four divisions were now sending seven brigades to counterattack. Supported by 30 cannons, the Union troops overran the Confederate brigades under Arthur Manigault. The Federals managed to restore their original positions, and took back 10 artillery pieces that the Confederates had seized earlier.

As Cheatham retreated, Hardee regrouped south of Bald Hill, and Maney's division rallied. Cleburne brought up his reserve brigade as several regiments from Walker's division moved west from Sugar Creek. At 5:00 p.m., these units advanced against the southern flank of Giles Smith's division. Smith was hit from the east, west, and south. The Confederates were within 15 yards of the Federal defenses when the infantry under Col. Harris Lampley charged the earthworks, but Col. Lampley was killed, and Hardee's troops fell back.

At 6:00 p.m., Hardee mounted a final attack. Giles Smith pulled back and formed a stronger line. The Confederates charged this new line, but it held firm against them. Cleburne lost 40% of his men, including 30 of his 60 high ranking officers. Toward evening the fighting died out, but by then over 8,000 Confederates and 3,700 Union had been killed or wounded, and Hood's second sortie had failed.

Battle of Ezra Church
"Battle of the Poor House"

July 28, 1864
Though Confederate John Bell Hood's savage sortie on July 20th and 22th failed to wreck a portion of Maj. Gen. William T. Sherman's army and drive him away from Atlanta, it did, with the help of Atlanta's strong fortifications, block the Union drives on the city from the north and east. Consequently, Sherman looked to the west, deciding to move on the Macon & Western Railroad line, the last of John Bell Hood's supply lines still leading into the city. The focus of his attack would be on Lovejoy Station, 20 miles southeast of Atlanta. He would send two separate columns of troops to attack Lovejoy Station, while the Army of the Tennessee would march around Atlanta and attack the railroad between the city and East Point, threatening the Confederate supply line. Sherman hoped

Lt. Gen. S.D. Lee

that these movements would force Hood to either leave his fortification and fight him out in the open, or that he would abandon his fortifications and leave the city.

Sherman appointed Maj. Gen. Oliver Howard to take control of McPherson's Army of the Tennessee. Howard had marched half way around the city when he arrived at Ezra Church and knew there would be trouble from Hood, so he dug in. Grenville Dodge's XVI Corps and Francis Blair's XVII Corps took a north-south line facing east. On Blair's right, Logan's XV Corps extended the line southward in front of Ezra Church and then bent west at a right angle across the Lickskillet Road.

Howard was right about Hood. Hood sent four divisions to stop him, one corps was led by Lt. Gen. Stephen D. Lee, the other by Alexander Stewart. On July 28th, Lee met Howard's army. Lee attacked without orders from Hood. Lee sent Brig. Gen. John C. Brown against the right of Logan's Corps and Brown lost three commanders during the assault. Lee attacked again and sent Maj. Gen. Henry Clayton against Logan's left wing, but the Federals held.

At 2:00 p.m., Stewart arrived and ordered Maj. Gen. Edward Walthall to attack the Union right. At 3:00 p.m., Walthall attacked, and three charges were made, but all failed and Gen. Loring was severely wounded. At 5:00 p.m., Walthall and Lee withdrew. The fighting stopped. The Confederates lost 600 men. In 10 days, Hood had lost 18,000 men, or nearly one third of his 60,000 man force.

Battle of Utoy Creek

August 6, 1864

After failing to seize the Macon Railroad line which would cut off the Confederate supply line, Sherman decided to shift the Army of the Ohio counterclockwise on Howard's right near Utoy Creek, a couple of miles southwest of Ezra Chruch. On August 6th, Schofield with 12,000 men attacked the Macon & Western Railroad where they encountered William Bate's division blocking the Federals from within an entrenched line. At the Battle of Utoy Creek, Schofield lost 300 men before he called off the assault. The Confederates now fell back to their new line of fortifications at the railroad.

Battle of Jonesboro

August 31 to September 1, 1864

Sherman encountered earthworks all around the city, and felt that a direct assault would be impossible. On August 9th, he fired more than 5,000 shells into Atlanta. The people of Atlanta dug earthwork fortifications. Trench warfare had begun. Sherman decided that the only way to capture Atlanta was to throw his entire army at the Macon & Western Railroad, Atlanta's last lifeline for supplies.

During the night of August 25th, Sherman pulled his troops from the trenches north and west of Atlanta. One corps, the XX, fell back to the railroad bridge spanning the Chattahoochee River. With his other six corps-the IV, XIV, XV, XVI, XVII, and the XVIII-, 60,000 men in all, Sherman advanced from the northwest to strike the Macon & Western Railroad, between Rough and Ready and Jonesboro.

On August 30th, Howard was on the east bank of the Flint River, two miles from Jonesboro. Hood didn't realize that the entire Federal army was heading towards the Macon & Western line,

and would remain in Atlanta with Stewart and the Georgia Militia. Hardee would take the other two corps- his and Lee's- to Jonesboro, with orders to attack the Federals and drive them back across the Flint River.

Gen. Oliver O. Howard had only crossed a portion of his army. The Confederates outnumbered his forces, 24,000 to Howard's 17,000. The rest of Howard's troops were still on the far bank of the river. Lee attacked at 2:20 p.m., sending his three divisions against Logan's Federal XV Corps. Lee was supposed to wait for Cleburne's troops to engage first. Maj. Gen. James Patton Anderson led his troops across open terrain and got within 80 yards of the Federal breastworks where Logan's defenders were, but he was repulsed. Reinforcements expected from Col. Bushrod

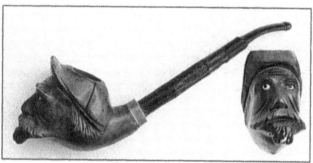

Hand carved smoking pipe with glass eyes, depicting an infantry soldier. Pipes such as this were carved in camp and smoked by soldiers. The aroma of their tobacco brought pleasure to many. This is a fine example of camp folk art. (BCWM)

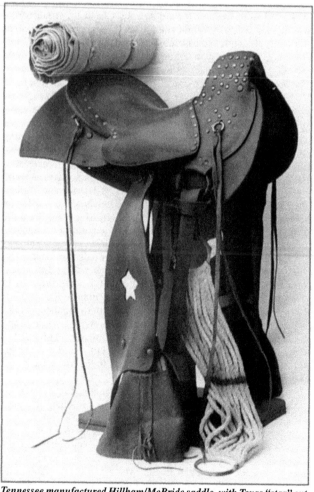

Tennessee manufactured Hillham/McBride saddle, with Texas "star" cut out of the side skirts. These saddles were used extensively in the Western campaigns. (BCWM)

Jones brigade never came. Patton tried to rally his men, but was wounded twice. Lee was being repulsed.

Hardee now advanced with Patrick Cleburne's troops. William Bate's division, now commanded by John C. Brown, charged forward, but was hit by a barrage from a half dozen 12 pound Napoleons. The Confederates took refuge from the cannon fire in a ravine, where they were promptly captured by the 66th Indiana. The division of George Maney on Brown's left fell back. On the far left, Cleburne's division, commanded by Brig. Gen. Mark Lowrey, hit the Federal right flank, but his left came under fire from Kilpatrick's cavalry division. Kilpatrick had four artillery pieces and his men were equipped with Spencer rifles. Lowrey charged the Federals, but only one of his units, under Hiram Grandbury continued to assault the Federals. Lowrey's other two brigades then followed suit. The Confederates were driving the Federals back, until Federal reinforcements stopped Lowrey's men and pushed them back. The assault by the other two Confederate divisions of Cleburne's troops had failed. The Confederates lost 1,725 men, 1,300 were lost by Lee alone. The Federals only lost 179 men.

During the afternoon, the Federal columns had managed to cut the Macon & Western Railroad line. By 3:00 p.m., Jacob Cox's division had reached the tracks a mile below Rough and Ready.

Hood still believed that the attack would come on Atlanta, so he ordered Hardee to stay in Jonesboro, but wanted him to send Lee's corps back to Atlanta. On September 1st, Lee's corps marched north, and left Hardee defending the army's only supply train. Sherman was planning to attack Jonesboro with his six corps.

Hardee only had 13,000 men and they were stretched out in a single line. Hardee's men dug in and built breastworks for the assault they knew would come. Sherman ordered Jeff Davis' XIV Corps to attack. At 4:00 p.m., Davis launched two brigades, but they were repulsed. He then brought up three divisions, and at 5:00 p.m., ordered a full assault across a cotton field. The Federals charge overran the earthworks. At this same time, Hood would give the order to abandon the city of Atlanta.

On the left, Govan's brigade began to give way under the massive Federal assault and Govan and his 600 men soon surrendered. The Federals managed to seize eight Confederate guns. Govan's surrender caused a gap in the line that the Federals rushed through, threatening Grandbury's Texans and Lewis' Kentuckians. The Confederates fell back, and with reinforcements and massed artillery, they formed a new line which held until darkness settled in and the fighting stopped. Sherman lost 1,300 men.

During the night, Hardee retreated to Lovejoy's Station, six miles farther down the Macon & Western Railroad. Stewart's corps and Lee's corps headed towards McDonough. Both were to link up with Hardee at Lovejoy's Station.

On September 2nd, the Confederate rearguard cavalry burned five locomotives, 81 rail cars, and 13 siege guns and shells. Union Major General Slocum, commander of the XX Corps marched into Atlanta, and at 11:00 a.m., on September 2nd, Mayor James Calhoun surrendered the city.

By capturing Atlanta, Sherman had not only deprived the Confederacy of a vital arsenal and rail hub, but he had strengthened the will of the Union to continue the War as well. After 128 days and a total of 35,000 casualties in the Confederate army, and nearly as many in his own army, Sherman and his men rested, for they would soon begin the long march to Savannah and the sea.

General William Henry Talbot Walker (C.S.)

William Henry Talbot Walker was born on November 26, 1816 in Augusta, Georgia. The son of a former United States Senator, Walker was educated in local schools before entering West Point at the age of 16 in 1837. He graduated 46th in the 50 man class of 1837. In 1837, Walker served as a lieutenant in the 6th U.S. Infantry and was severely wounded while fighting the Seminoles. During the Mexican War, Walker was twice breveted. In 1847, Walker was severely wounded by Mexicans at Molino del

Confederate General William Henry Talbot Walker's razors. The razors and case were part of Walker's personal effects that were sent home after his death at the Battle of Atlanta. (BCWM)

Rey and was not expected to recover. Walker did survive his wounds, but was placed on sick leave and light duty for the next five years. In 1849, the state officials in Georgia presented him with a sword of honor. From 1854 to 1856, Walker was Commandant of Cadets and instructor of tactics at West Point. On December 20, 1860, Walker resigned his Major's commission from the army and signed with the Confederacy. He left Minnesota, where he was serving, and went to Georgia.

Walker was appointed major general of State Volunteers in April of 1861, and became a brigadier general in May. As brigadier general in the Confederate Army, he served in Northern Virginia until his resignation on October 29, 1861. Within two months he was a major general of State Troops and served as such for over a year. In March 1863, Walker was reappointed in the Confederate service as brigadier general and was assigned to the forces under Joseph Johnston who was attempting to relieve the pressure on Vicksburg. Promoted to major general during that campaign, he fought twice at Jackson and then commanded the Reserve Corps at Chickamagua. After Chickamagua, Walker fought under Johnston from Resaca to the Chattahoochee River.

After the Chickamagua campaign, Gen. Walker, along with Confederate General Patrick Cleburne, supported and petitioned the Confederate government for the recruiting of black troops. On January 1, 1864, the plan was approved by the Army of Tennessee's Corps and Division Commanders. Forwarded to the authorities it was not acted upon until it was too late.

During the Atlanta Campaign, Walker commanded a division under Confederate General John Bell Hood's Army, until he was killed in the battle of Atlanta, proper, on July 22, 1864.

Battle of Franklin and Nashville

November 29-December 27, 1864
"It was a grand holocaust of death." - Private Sam Watkins
Location of Franklin: Williamson County
Location of Nashville: Davidson County
Forces Engaged at Franklin: IV & XXIII Army Corps (Army of the Ohio & Army of the Cumberland) (U.S.); Army of Tennessee (C.S.)
Forces Engaged at Nashville: IV Army Corps, Detachment of Army of the Tennessee, provisional detachment, and cavalry corps (U.S.); Army of Tennessee (C.S.)
Principal Commanders at Franklin: Maj. Gen. John Schofield (U.S.); Gen. John Bell Hood (C.S.)
Principal commanders at Nashville: Maj. Gen. George Thomas (U.S.); Gen. John Bell Hood (C.S.)

Order of Battle
Union Forces
Maj. Gen. John Schofield (Franklin)
Maj. Gen. George Thomas (Nashville)

4th Army Corps: Maj. Gen. David Stanley (Franklin); Brig. Gen. Thomas Wood (Nashville)
First Division: Brig. Gen. Nathan Kimball

1st Brigade	2nd Brigade	3rd Brigade
Col. I. Kirby	Brig. Gen. W. Whittaker	Brig. Gen. W. Grose
21st Illinois	96th Illinois	75th Illinois
38th Illinois	115th Illinois	80th Illinois
31st Indiana	35th Indiana	84th Illinois
81st Indiana	21st Kentucky	9th Indiana
90th Ohio	23rd Kentucky	30th Indiana
	45th Ohio	36th Indiana
	51st Ohio	84th Indiana
		77th Pennsylvania

Second Division: Brig. Gen. George Wagner (Franklin); Brig. Gen. Washington Elliott (Nashville)

1st Brigade	2nd Brigade	3rd Brigade
Col. E. Opdycke	Col. J. Lane	Col. J. Conrad
36th Illinois	100th Illinois	42nd Illinois
44th Illinois	40th Indiana	51st Illinois
73rd Illinois	57th Indiana	79th Illinois
74th Illinois	28th Kentucky	15th Missouri
88th Illinois	26th Ohio	64th Ohio
125th Ohio	97th Ohio	65th Ohio
24th Wisconsin		

Third Division: Brig. Gen. Thomas Wood (Franklin); Brig. Gen. Samuel Beatty (Nashville)

1st Brigade	2nd Brigade	3rd Brigade	Artillery
Col. Abel Streight	Col. S. Post	Col. F. Knefler	Maj. W. Goodspeed
89th Illinois	59th Illinois	79th Indiana	25th Indiana Light Battery
51st Indiana	41st Ohio	86th Indiana	1st Kentucky Battery
8th Kansas	71st Ohio	13th Ohio	1st Michigan Battery
15th Ohio	93rd Ohio	19th Ohio	1st Ohio Battery G
49th Ohio	124th Ohio		6th Ohio Battery
			Pennsylvania Light Artillery, Battery B
			4th U.S. Battery

23rd Army Corps
Brig. Gen. Jacob Cox (Franklin)
Maj. Gen. John Schofield (Nashville)

Second Division: Brig. Gen. Thomas Ruger (Franklin); Maj. Gen. Darion Couch (Nashville)

1st Brigade (Nashville only)	2nd Brigade	Artillery
Brig. Gen. J. Cooper	Col. O. Moore	13th Indiana Light Artillery
130th Indiana	107th Illinois	19th Light Ohio Battery
26th Kentucky	80th Indiana	
25th Michigan	129th Indiana	
99th Ohio	23rd Michigan	
3rd Tennessee	111th Ohio	
6th Tennessee	118th Ohio	
	91st Indiana	
	123rd Indiana	
	50th Ohio	
	183rd Ohio	

Third Division: Brig. Gen. James Reilley (Franklin); Brig. Gen. Jacob Cox (Nashville)

1st Brigade	2nd Brigade	3rd Brigade
Brig. Gen. J. Reilly (Franklin)	Col. J. Casement	Col. I. Stiles
Col. C. Doolittle (Nashville)	65th Illinois	112th Illinois
12th Kentucky	65th Indiana	63rd Indiana
16th Kentucky	124th Indiana	120th Indiana
100th Ohio	103rd Ohio	128th Indiana
104th Ohio	5th Tennessee	
8th Tennessee		

Artillery
23rd Indiana Light Artillery
1st Ohio Light Artillery, Battery D

Detachment Army of the Tennessee
Maj. Gen. Andrew Smith
First Division: Brig. Gen. John McArthur

1st Brigade	2nd Brigade	3rd Brigade
Col. W. McMillan	Col. L. Hubbard	Col. S. Hill (Nashville)
114th Illinois	5th Minnesota	Col. W. Marshall
93rd Indiana	9th Minnesota	12th Iowa
10th Minnesota	11th Missouri	35th Iowa
72nd Ohio	8th Wisconsin	7th Minnesota
95th Ohio	2nd Battery Iowa Light Artillery	33rd Missouri
Cogswell Light Artillery		2nd Missouri Light Artillery, Battery I

Second Division: Brig. Gen. Kenner Garrard

1st Brigade	2nd Brigade
Col. D. Moore	Col. J. Gilbert
119th Illinois	58th Illinois
122nd Illinois	32nd Iowa
89th Indiana	10th Kansas
9th Indiana Light Artillery	3rd Battery, Indiana Light Artillery

3rd Brigade
Col. E. Wolfe
49th Illinois
117th Illinois
52nd Indiana
178th New York
2nd Illinois Light Artillery, Battery G

Third Division: Col. Johnathon Moore

1st Brigade	2nd Brigade	Artillery
Col. L. Ward	Col. L. Blanden	11th Indiana Light Artillery
72nd Illinois	81st Illinois	2nd Missouri Light Artillery, Battery, A
40th Missouri	95th Illinois	
14th Wisconsin	44th Missouri	
33rd Wisconsin		

Provisional Detachment-District of the Etowah
Maj. Gen. James B. Steedman
Provisional Division: Brig. Gen. Charles Cruft

1st Colored Brigade	2nd Colored Brigade
Col. T. Morgan	Col. C. Thompson
14th U.S. Colored Troops	12th U.S. Colored Troops
16th U.S. Colored Troops	13th U.S. Colored troops
17th U.S. Colored Troops	100th U.S. Colored Troops
18th U.S. Colored Troops	1st Kansas Light Artillery
44th U.S. Colored Troops	

1st Brigade
Col. B. Harrison
Three Battalions from 20th Army Corps (detached)

2nd Brigade
Col. J. Mitchell
Composed of Men on Detached Duty From The Army of the Tennessee

Artillery
20th Indiana Light Artillery
18th Ohio Light Artillery

3rd Brigade
Lt. Col. C. Grosvenor
68th Indiana
18th Ohio
121st Ohio
2nd Battalion 14th Army Corps

Post of Nashville
Brig. Gen. John Miller

Brigade	**Unattached**
(20th Army Corps; 4th Division, 2nd Brigade)	3rd Kentucky
Col. E. Mason	28th Michigan
142nd Indiana	173rd Ohio
45th New York	78th Pennsylvania
176th Ohio	Veteran Reserve Corps
179th Ohio	44th Wisconsin
182nd Ohio	45th Wisconsin

Garrison Light Artillery
Illinois (Bridge's)
2nd Indiana
4th Indiana
12th Indiana
21st Indiana
22nd Indiana
24th Indiana
1st Michigan Light Artillery, Battery F
1st Ohio Light Artillery, Battery A & E
20th Ohio
1st Tennessee Light Artillery, Battery C & D
2nd U.S. Colored, Battery A

Quartermaster's Division
Bvt. Brig. Gen. James Donaldson
Composed of quartermaster's employees, used to man trenches.
First Division: Brig. Gen. Edward McCook

1st Brigade	**2nd Brigade**
Brig. Gen. J. Croxton	**Col. O. La Grange**
8th Iowa Cavalry	Detached in pursuit of Lyon's raid
4th Kentucky Mounted Infantry	into Western Kentucky
2nd Michigan Cavalry	
1st Tennessee Cavalry	
Board of Trade Battery, Illinois	
Light Artillery	

3rd Brigade
Bvt. Brig. Gen. L. Watkins
Detached in pursuit of Lyon's in Western Kentucky

Fifth Division: Brig. Gen. Edward Hatch

1st Brigade	**2nd Brigade**
Col. R. Stewart	**Col. D. Coon**
3rd Illinois Cavalry	6th Illinois Cavalry
11th Indiana Cavalry	7th Illinois Cavalry
12th Missouri Cavalry	9th Illinois Cavalry
10th Tennessee Cavalry	2nd Iowa Cavalry
	12th Tennessee Cavalry
	1st Illinois Light Artillery, Battery I

Sixth Division: Brig. Gen. Richard Johnson

1st Brigade	**2nd Brigade**	**Artillery**
Col. T. Harrison	**Col. J. Biddle**	4th U.S. Artillery, Battery I
16th Illinois Cavalry	14th Illinois Cavalry	
5th Iowa Cavalry	6th Indiana Cavalry	

7th Ohio Cavalry	8th Michigan Cavalry
	3rd Tennessee Cavalry

Seventh Division: Brig. Gen. Joseph Knipe

1st Brigade	**2nd Brigade**
Bvt. Brig. Gen. J. Hammond	**Col. G. Johnson (dismounted)**
9th Indiana Cavalry	12th Indiana Cavalry
10th Indiana Cavalry	13th Indiana Cavalry
19th Pennsylvania Cavalry	8th Tennessee Cavalry
2nd Tennessee Cavalry	
4th Tennessee Cavalry	

Artillery
14th Ohio Light Artillery

Confederate Forces
Army of Tennessee

Gen. John Bell Hood
Lee's Corps: Lt. Gen. Stephen D. Lee
Johnson's Division: Maj. Gen. Edward Johnson

Deas' Brigade	**Manigault's Brigade**	**Sharp's Brigade**
Brig. Gen. Z. Deas	**Brig. Gen. A. Manigault**	**Brig. Gen. J. Sharp**
19th Alabama	Lt. Col. W. Butler	7th Mississippi
22nd Alabama	24th Alabama	9th Mississippi
25th Alabama	28th Alabama	10th Mississippi
38th Alabama	34th Alabama	41st Mississippi
50th Alabama	10th South Carolina	9th Battalion Missis-
	19th South Carolina	sippi Sharpshooters
		44th Mississippi

Brantley's Brigade
Brig. Gen. W. Brantley
24th Mississippi
27th Mississippi
29th Mississippi
30th Mississippi
34th Mississippi
Dismounted Cavalry Company

Stevenson's Division: Maj. Gen. Carter Stevenson

Cumming's Brigade	**Pettus' Brigade**
Col. E. Watkins	Brig. Gen. E. Pettus
24th Georgia	20th Alabama
36th Georgia	23rd Alabama
39th Georgia	30th Alabama
56th Georgia	31st Alabama
	46th Alabama

Clayton's Division: Maj. Gen. Henry Clayton

Stovall's Brigade	**Gibson's Brigade**	**Holtzclaw's Brigade**
Brig. Gen. M. Stovall	**Brig. Gen. R. Gibson**	**Brig. Gen. J. Holtzclaw**
40th Georgia	1st Louisiana	18th Alabama
41st Georgia	4th Louisiana	32nd Alabama
42nd Georgia	13th Louisiana	36th Alabama
43rd Georgia	16th Louisiana	38th Alabama
52nd Georgia	19th Louisiana	58th Alabama
	20th Louisiana	
	25th Louisiana	
	30th Louisiana	
	4th Louisiana Battalion	
	14th Louisiana Battalion Sharpshooters	

Stewart's Corps: Lt. Gen. Alexander Stewart
Loring's Division: Maj. Gen. William Loring

Featherstone's Brigade	**Adam's Brigade**	**Scott's Brigade**
Brig. Gen. W. Featherstone	**Brig. Gen. J. Adams**	**Brig. Gen. T. Scott**
1st Mississippi	Col. R. Lowry	Col. J. Snodgrass
3rd Mississippi	6th Mississippi	27th Alabama
22nd Mississippi	14th Mississippi	35th Alabama
31st Mississippi	15th Mississippi	49th Alabama
40th Mississippi	20th Mississippi	55th Alabama
1st Mississippi Battalion	23rd Mississippi	57th Alabama
	43rd Mississippi	12th Louisiana

French's Division: Maj. Gen. Samuel G. French
Brig. Gen. Claudius Sears

Ector's Brigade	Cockrell's Brigade	Sears's Brigade
Col. D. Coleman	Brig. Gen. F.M. Cockrell	Brig. Gen. C. Sears
29th North Carolina	Col. P. Flournoy	Lt. Col. R. Shotwell
30th North Carolina	1st Missouri	4th Mississippi
9th Texas	2nd Missouri	35th Mississippi
10th Texas Cavalry	3rd Missouri	36th Mississippi
14th Texas Cavalry	4th Missouri	39th Mississippi
32nd Texas Cavalry	5th Missouri	46th Mississippi
(dismounted)	6th Missouri	7th Mississippi Battn.
	1st Missouri Cavalry	
	(dismounted)	
	3rd Missouri Cavalry Battalion	
	(dismounted)	

Walthall's Division: Maj. Gen. Edward Walthall

Quarles' Brigade	Cantley's Brigade	Reynold's Brigade
Brig. Gen. W. Quarles	Brig. Gen. C. Shelley	Brig. Gen. D. Reynolds
Brig. Gen. G. Johnson	17th Alabama	4th Arkansas
1st Alabama	26th Alabama	9th Arkansas
42nd Tennessee	29th Alabama	25th Arkansas
46th Tennessee	37th Mississippi	1st Arkansas Mounted
48th Tennessee		Rifles (dismounted)
49th Tennessee		2nd Arkansas Mounted
53rd Tennessee		Rifles (dismounted)
55th Tennessee		

Cheatham's Corps: Maj. Gen. Benjamin Cheatham
Cleburne's Division: Maj. Gen. Patrick Cleburne; Brig. Gen. James Smith (Nashville)

Lowrey's Brigade	Govan's Brigade	Grandbury's Brigade
Brig. Gen. M. Lowrey	Brig. Gen. D. Govan	Brig. Gen. H. Granbury
(Franklin)		
16th Alabama	1st Arkansas	Capt. E. Broughton
33rd Alabama	2nd Arkansas	5th Confederate
45th Alabama	5th Arkansas	35th Tennessee
5th Mississippi	6th Arkansas	6th Texas
8th Mississippi	7th Arkansas	7th Texas
32nd Mississippi	8th Arkansas	10th Texas
3rd Mississippi Battalion	13th Arkansas	15th Texas
	15th Arkansas	17th Texas Cavalry
	19th Arkansas	(dismounted)
	24th Arkansas	18th Texas Cavalry
		(dismounted)
		24th Texas Cavalry
		(dismounted)
		Nutt's Louisiana Cavalry
		(dismounted)

Smith's Brigade
Brig. Gen. J. Smith
Col. C. Olmstead (Nashville)
54th Georgia
57th Georgia
63rd Georgia
1st Georgia Volunteers

Brown's (Cheatham's Old) Division: Maj. Gen. John Brown (Franklin); Brig. Gen. Mark Lowrey (Nashville)

Gist's Brigade	Maney's Brigade	Strahl's Brigade
Brig. Gen. S. Gist	Brig. Gen. J. Carter	Brig. Gen. O. Strahl
(Franklin)	(Franklin)	(Franklin)
Lt. Col. Z. Watters	Col. H. Field	Col. A. Kellar
(Nashville)	(Nashville)	(Nashville)
46th Georgia	1st Tennessee	4th Tennessee
65th Georgia	4th (Provisional) Tennessee	5th Tennessee
2nd Battalion Georgia	6th Tennessee	19th Tennessee
Sharpshooters	8th Tennessee	24th Tennessee
16th South Carolina	9th Tennessee	31st Tennessee
24th South Carolina	16th Tennessee	33rd Tennessee
	27th Tennessee	38th Tennessee
	28th Tennessee	41st Tennessee
	50th Tennessee	

Vaughan's Brigade
Brig. Gen. G. Gordon (Franklin)
Col. W. Watkins (Nashville)
11th Tennessee
12th Tennessee
13th Tennessee
29th Tennessee
47th Tennessee
51st Tennessee
52nd Tennessee
154th Tennessee

Bate's Division: Maj. Gen. William Bate's

Tyler's Brigade	Finley's Brigade	Jackson's Brigade
Brig. Gen. T. Smith	Col. R. Bullock	Brig. Gen. H. Jackson
37th Georgia	Maj. J. Lash	25th Georiga
4th Battalion Georgia	1st Florida	29th Georgia
Sharpshooters	3rd Florida	30th Georgia
2nd Tennessee	4th Florida	1st Georgia Confederate
10th Tennessee	6th Florida	1st Battalion Georgia
20th Tennessee	7th Florida	Sharpshooters
37th Tennessee	1st Florida Cavalry (dismounted)	

Artillery
Lee's Corps: Col. Robert Beckham; Maj. John Johnston

Courtney's Battalion	Eldridge's Battalion
Capt. James Douglas	Capt. Charles Fenner
Dent's Alabama Battery	Eufaula Alabama Battery
Douglas' Texas Battery	Fenner's Louisiana Battery
Garrity's Alabama Battery	Stanford's Mississippi Battery

Johnson's Battalion
Capt. John Rowan
Corput's Georgia Battery
Marshall's Tennessee Battery
Stephen's Light Artillery

Stewart's Corps: Lt. Col. Samuel Williams

Truehart's Battalion	Myrick's Battalion
Lumsden's Alabama Battery	Bouanchaud's Louisiana Battery
Selden's Alabama Battery	Cowan's Mississippi Battery
	Darden's Mississippi Battery

Storr's Battalion
Guiborps' Missouri Battery
Hoskins' Mississippi Battery
Kolb's Alabama Battery

Cheatham's Corps: Col. Melancthon Smith

Hoxton's Battalion	Hotchkiss Battalion
Perry's Florida Battery	Bledsoe's Missouri Battery
Phelan's Alabama Battery	Goldwaite's Alabama Battery
Turner's Mississippi Battery	Key's Arkansas Battery

Cobb's Battalion
Ferguson's South Carolina Battery
Phillip's (Mebane's) Tennessee Battery
Slocumbs Louisiana Battery

Cavalry
Maj. Gen. Nathan Bedford Forrest
Chalmer's Division: Brig. Gen. James Chalmers

Rucker's Brigade	Biffle's Brigade
Col. Edmund Rucker	Col. J. Biffle
7th Alabama Cavalry	5 Mississippi Cavalry
7th Tennessee Cavalry	10th Tennessee Cavalry
12th Tennessee Cavalry	
14th Tennessee Cavalry	
15th Tennessee Cavalry	
Forrest's Regiment Tennessee Cavalry	

Buford's Division: Brig. Gen. Abraham Buford

Bell's Brigade	Crossland's Brigade
Col. T. Bell	Col. E. Crossland
2nd Tennessee Cavalry	3rd Kentucky Mounted Infantry
19th Tennessee Cavalry	7th Kentucky Mounted Infantry

20th Tennessee Cavalry	8th Kentucky Mounted Infantry
21st Tennessee Cavalry	12th Kentucky Mounted Infantry
Nixon's Tennessee Cavalry Regiment	12th Kentucky Cavalry
	Huey's Kentucky Battalion

Jackson's Division: Brig. Gen. William Jackson

Armstrong's Brigade	**Ross' Brigade**	**Artillery**
Brig. Gen. F. Armstrong	**Brig. Gen. L. Ross**	Morton's Tennessee
1st Mississippi Cavalry	5th Texas Cavalry	Battery
2nd Mississippi Cavalry	6th Texas Cavalry	1st Texas Legion
28th Mississippi Cavalry	9th Texas Cavalry	
Ballentine's Mississippi Regiment		

On November 22, 1864, Confederate General John Bell Hood's 39,000 Confederates left Florence, Alabama, in three columns commanded by Maj. Gen. Benjamin Cheatham, and Lt. Gen. Stephen D. Lee, and Lt. Gen. Alexander Stewart. Following a plan originated by Hood and approved by Jefferson Davis, they invaded Tennessee to draw Union military attention from the Deep South, and crushed Maj. Gen. Sherman's Western support for his operations in Georgia and perhaps take the war through Kentucky to the North.

After the fall of Atlanta, Hood had moved the Army of Tennessee northwest in September and October, drawing Sherman and a detached force from Atlanta, skirmishing and wrecking railroads, fighting at Alatoona, and then withdrawing into northwest Alabama. Sherman had followed them west of Rome, Georgia, and unwilling to pursue farther, ordered the IV, XVI, and XXIII Corps to Maj. Gen. George Thomas, at Nashville and returned to Atlanta to begin his March to the Sea. Sherman knew Hood's intent and believed that, reinforced, Thomas would repel him.

Early cadet grey Confederate infantry shell jacket, with pre war eagle buttons which were used extensively in the Western Theater. (BCWM)

Hood and Thomas spent more than 20 days preparing for their parts in the campaign. Hood gathered supplies, reorganized and waited for Maj. Gen. Nathan Forrest's cavalry; Thomas created a cavalry force under Brig. Gen. James Wilson and moved the IV and XXIII Corps from the Chattanooga area to positions west along the Tennessee and Alabama Railroad. The XVI Corps detachment Thomas awaited could not reach him until December. Forrest spent late October and early November raiding Nashville, Tennessee's supply lines and wrecking the railroad at Johnsonville.

Forrest joined Hood at Florence, the expedition entered Tennessee, and its columns, traveling miles apart, moved for Columbia, halfway to Nashville. The XXIII Corps, under Maj. Gen. John

Schofield and elements of the IV Corps were at Pulaski along the railroad, west of the invading columns. On George Thomas' orders, Schofield raced his force north to Columbia, arriving ahead of the Confederates on November 24th, and covered the bridges over the Duck River astride the invasion route. Federal cavalry sparred with Confederate horsemen from the Alabama line to Columbia. Schofield skirmished around Columbia from the 24th to the 26th until Hood's columns converged on his front. Bridges over the Duck River were destroyed and Schofield's troops withdrew north, covering the fords until Forrest's cavalry crossed at Henry's Mill, on Schofield's left, on the 28th. Wilson sent word to Schofield: "Get back to Franklin without delay."

Union Major General David Stanley, commanding IV Corps troops, hurried north to Spring Hill November 29th to hold the town until Schofield's troops passed through. Forrest, with his eastern crossing of the Duck River, threatened the Federal's right. Stanley's pickets held him off. Hood failed in his plan to hold the Federals there, circumvent them, and press on to Nashville. He blamed Cheatham for bungled enveloping maneuvers as Schofield slipped through, marching his men from midnight to noon from Spring Hill to Franklin, on November 30th.

When Hood found out that Schoefield and his Federals had escaped, he blamed Cheatham. He called all of his officers a bunch of

"Nashville Plow Works" manufactured sword made into a side knife. The sword has "Nashville Plow Works" and "C.S.A." cast into the guard. The Nashville Plow Works reversed the biblical quotation of turning swords into plowshares. This knife was found along the Confederate lines at Franklin, Tennessee. (BCWM)

cowards, and said the only way to cure a coward is to throw him into battle.

Schofield was now at Franklin and he began to dig trenches and rifle pits. He deployed two divisions of the XXIII Corps to dig in astride the turnpike, and then deployed one division from the IV Corps on the right flank. The headquarters were set up at the Fountain Branch Carter House which stood on the high point of a wide plain almost devoid of trees. If Hood planned to attack, it would be over two miles of open ground, starting from a low ridge to the south known as Winstead Hill. Schofield set up his dozen guns on the far side of the Harpeth River, at a place called Fort Granger.

Hood reached Franklin at 2 p.m., and sent Stewart's Corps forward to flank the hill and force the Federals off of it, then rode up and took a look at the Federal army. Against the advice of his generals, Hood decided to order a frontal attack on the Union position without artillery support. Hood was going to send Cheatham's and Stewart's divisions directly at the middle of the Union trenches. He thought that this would teach his men a lesson. He would send the units in one at a time, instead of en mass, and would only send seven of his 18 brigades at the Union position. The seven brigades belonged to Gen. John Brown's and Gen. Patrick Cleburne's Divisions. Brown put two brigades under Gen. States Rights Gist and Gen. George Washington Gordon, who made up the front line; two other brigades under Brig. Gen. John Carter and Otho Strahl would form the second line. From Cleburne's Division, Gen. Hiram Granbury's Texas brigade, would be on the left, and Daniel Govan's brigade would be in the center and Mark Lowrey's brigade would form on the right. The other division in Cheatham's Corps was made up of the three brigades in Bate's Division. Gen. Bate's brigades were on the left flank, and were to make an attack in conjunction with a division of Forrest's cavalry. On the far right flank, Loring's and Walthall's Divisions, in Stewart's Corps, were deployed with their right flank on the Harpeth River. Forrest and two of his divisions would try and drive back the Federal cavalry under Gen. Wilson, who was north of the river.

The Federals had dug two sets of trenches, to cover the gap left between the Columbia Turnpike and the breastworks. On both sides of the turnpike, the main line angled back in gradual steps conforming to the perimeter of the town of Franklin. A second line protecting the turnpike angled back similarly on higher ground and here more artillery were deployed to fire over the first line and sweep the field in front. The Confederates would attack the most vulnerable position that the Yankees had.

George Wagner's division, acting as the Federal rear guard, was pushed into the trenches by Stewart's flanking movement and abandoned Winstead Hill. Wagner formed a reserve near the Carter House. Wagner thought that he was supposed to hold where he was, no matter what happened to his exposed forward position. A half hour before sunset, Hood advanced. The Confederates charged Wagner's position, and Wagner's Yankees ran for the safety of the Federal lines. The Union artillery and rifleman in the Federal works were not able to fire upon the advancing Confederates because Wagner's retreating men got in their way and they were afraid that they would shoot their own men. The Confederates charged into the first works. The 104th Ohio panicked and ran, and that led to other units running. The guns on either side of the pike, and the works on the east and west of the pike were abandoned and Cleburne and Brown's men took possession of the recently vacated works.

Union Col. Opdycke's men were posted 200 yards behind the Carter House. When they heard the firing on the works they rushed forward with reinforcements, two Kentucky regiments and the remnants of Wagner's other two brigades. Hand to hand fighting broke out between the Confederates and Yankees. Hood had no reserves to back up the initial assault and the Confederates began to fall back inside the Federal trench line, then over the earthworks to huddle on the other side. Federal troops reoccupied the main line and threw up a barricade that plugged the gap. The assault by Stewart's men on the Federal left was going well until

they reached a railroad cut where Federal artillery from across the Harpeth River to the east, pounded their position. The Confederates got entangled in a grove of locust trees that the Federals had turned into an abatis. The Henry repeating rifles from Col. John Casement's brigade ripped large holes in the Confederate lines, and stopped them in their tracks.

One of Walthall's brigades, led by Brig. Gen. William Quarles, broke through the Federal earthworks, only to be pinned down by crossfire. Quarles was hit in the head. Artillery fire also decimated Maj. Gen. William Loring's Division, which was advancing on the far right. Other Confederate casualties included Brig. Gen. John Adams, who was shot when he tried to take the earthworks. He urged his men forward and led them directly into the Federal earthworks, and even tried to take the colors of the 65th Illinois. Adams later died of his wounds.

Farther to the right, Loring's other brigades under Brig. Gen. Winfield Featherstone, fell back. Loring himself rode out in front of his men and headed for the Federal earthworks. He tried to break the Yankee line, but he was pinned down by the Federal fire. Both Loring and Walthall were within a few hundred yards of the works, but they were both stalemated and could advance no farther.

The Confederate left also stalled. Gen. Bate's got close enough to order an attack on the works, but darkness had set in, and his force was small. The defenders, two divisions under Gen. Nathan Kimball and Thomas Ruger, kept the Confederates from advancing any farther.

The Yankees couldn't escape until the bridges over the Harpeth River were repaired. Now the Yankees and Confederates were separated by only a hundred yards in some areas, and in other areas only by a few feet. The attack cost the lives of Gen. Dams, Brig. Gen. Hiram Granbury, Gen. States Rights Gist, Gen. Patrick Cleburne, and Gen. Strahl. Gen. Gordon surrendered, and Col. F.E.P. Stafford was killed, and Maj. Gen. John Brown wounded. Hood also lost 7,000 men, 1,750 killed, the rest were wounded or taken prisoner. The Federals lost 1,222 killed and wounded, and 1,104 missing and presumed taken prisoner, mostly from Wagner's division. Schofield ordered a retreat, and tried to repair the bridges across the Harpeth River at their backs. The Union retreat, stalled by the destroyed bridges, began again at 11 p.m. and continued toward Thomas' Nashville lines the next day. At Franklin, Hood's last attempt to keep the IV and XXIII corps from reaching George Thomas at Nashville failed.

Hood woke up in the morning and saw that Schofield's men had evacuated Franklin and decided to pursue them and by 1 p.m., Hood's men were traveling north after Schofield, thinking that they had won a great victory.

Schofield reached Nashville on December 1st. Three divisions, 13,000 men strong, of the XVI corps, under Maj. Gen. Andrew Smith reached Nashville on November 30th, from the Trans-Mississippi. Schofield's arrival brought Thomas' strength to nearly 70,000. Hood arrived at the outskirts of Nashville on December 1st. At this point, Hood had only 30,000 men and this number was quickly diminishing. Hood's men were practically starving, they had no food, no clothes, no weapons, or ammunition. Hood faced a well fed, well clothed, and fresh army at Nashville. Nashville was also not an easy city to take. It was on a commanding elevation linked by miles of entrenchments. The south side of the city had a solid arc of trenches that extended from the Cumberland River east of the city to another west of town. These were backed by a reserve line.

Hood's men deployed on the Brentwood Hills, south of the city. His line was only four miles long, whereas the Federal line was 10 miles long. The Federal entrenchments covered all eight turnpikes spoking southward from the city. Hood only covered four of them, the Granny White Pike and the Franklin Pike toward his center, the Nolensville Pike to the east, and the Hillsboro Pike to the west. The flanks were unprotected, and within his lines, Hood's men were spread thin. Telegrams from Washington urged Thomas to finish the contest.

Thomas spent two weeks planning the attack and pursuit. On Dec. 6th, Lt. Gen. Grant wired a direct order "to attack Hood at once," but Thomas ignored it. Nine days later the Union force left the fortress city. Cheatham's Corps was on the Confederate right, across the Nolensville Pike; the eastern end of the line swung forward along a railroad cut that would make it difficult for enemy attacks to approach. The center was held by Stephen Lee's Corps. This position reached from the Franklin Pike to the Granny White Pike. Stewart's Corps held the Confederate left, reaching to Hillsboro Pike. Stewart's line bent back, the men building five redoubts of which only three were functional. The redoubts were small forts with four guns in each work, with 50 artillerists and 100 infantry. The redoubts were to protect Hood's left flank, which the Federals overlapped by several miles.

On December 15th, at 4:00 a.m., Thomas paid his hotel room bill and set out for the attack on Hood's army. His plan of attack was to launch an all out assault that was to begin with a feint from the Federal left, to hold the Confederate right in place, then to launch a main attack on the federal right and attack the left flank of Stewart's Corps.

On the Federal left, James Steedman and his colored troops from the 1st and 2nd Colored Brigade, along with two batteries, rushed the Confederates and overran the railroad cut. Steedman became bogged down once he reached the Confederate works, but he managed to keep Cheatham's Confederates in place all day. This charge also helped keep Stephen Lee's entire corps in the center.

On the Union right, Wilson's Cavalry pushed back Chalmers' single division of Confederate cavalry. At the same time, Andrew J. Smith pushed forward and approached Stewart's line. Confederate Brigadier General Matthew Ector's infantry fell back to the redoubts.

On the Federal center, Brig. Gen. Thomas Wood's IV Corps moved forward towards Montgomery Hill. Hood pulled back his men, and the 51st Indiana took Montgomery Hill. The men of the 59th Illinois disobeyed orders and attacked the earthworks beyond Montgomery Hill. They ran 300 hundred yards and captured the works, including two flags and four pieces of artillery. This broke Stewart's line and the Confederates ran for the rear.

On the Confederate left only two redoubts remained at Hillsboro Pike; Redoubts No. 2 and 3. Farther down the pike, well to the rear of the main line, were Redoubts No. 4 and 5. Gen. Walthall's division came to assist Stewart. Walthall's men were posted behind a stone wall that ran between Redoubts No. 3 and 4. Walthall put Ector's infantry on the extreme end of the line defending the stone wall. Redoubt No. 5 fell first to Gen. Edward Hatch's cavalry. Capt. Charles Lumsden saw that Redoubt No. 5 was captured and that Andrew Smith's corps was approaching. He told his men to run for their lives. The Federals now seized Redoubt No. 4. Col. Slyvester Hill ordered an attack on Redoubt No. 3, where Hill was killed when a bullet went through his head, but the Federals managed to take Redoubt No. 3. Col. Stibbs, and his 12th Iowa, along with the 7th Minnesota charged, then seized Redoubt No. 2.

By 1:30 p.m., Redoubt No. 1 was being attacked from both sides. Stewart pulled back. As Stewart was leaving Redoubt No. 1, Brig Gen. Claudius Sears was hit with a solid shot which severed his leg. As Stewart pulled back, so did Stephen D. Lee, and soon Cheatham pulled back. Hood moved his army to a new position that was now only two miles long and only covered two turnpikes: The Granny White on the left and the Franklin on the right. His lines were anchored on both ends by hills. On the left was Shy's Hill and on the right was Overton Hill or Peach Orchard Hill. Hood moved Stewart's corps to the center, and Cheatham to the left to cover Shy's Hill. Cheatham's left was bent back in a great arc around the hill to protect the Confederate left flank. Gen. Stephen Lee was on the right and fixed on Overton Hill. Hood posted his single cavalry division under Chalmer's at the end of Cheatham's line. The men began to dig in.

Two days later Thomas would attack the Confederates again. His plan was to pin down the Confederate right and overwhelm Hood's left. Col. Philip Sidney Post and his 2nd Brigade, and Col. Abel Streight's 1st Brigade were to attack Overton Hill from the west side, while Col. Charles Thompson's black soldiers were to attack the east side of Overton Hill. Heavy canister, grape shot and shell tore at the Federal troops as they climbed up the hill. On the far side of a cornfield, Federals approaching the Confederate main line came across a barrier of sharp stakes and abatis. The 13th Colored Troops reached the Confederate breastworks and mounted the rampart. Col. Post was hit by a bullet and severely wounded and his loss stopped the Federal charge. At this moment the Confederates poured fire into the Federals who then fell back, retreating back down the slope to the foot of Overton Hill. Hood pulled back Cleburne's division, now being led by Brig. Gen. James Smith, to a crucial position on Shy's Hill. He sent the division to the right to support Lee. Lee sent Cleburne's men back, but it was too late.

By early afternoon, Wilson had advanced across Granny White Pike, the Confederate line of retreat to the east. Chalmer's tried to hold off Wilson, but Wilson pressed harder against the rear of Shy's Hill. The Confederates were in a vulnerable position. Ector was to defend the hill, but Hood ordered Ector's men off the hill to confront Wilson's dismounted cavalry to the south. At the same time, Brig. Gen. William Bates division, of Cheatham's Corps, was ordered to hold Shy's Hill.

When Cleburne's division made its shift to the right, Bate's line was stretched to the left and the defense of the hill fell to Brig. Gen. Thomas Smith's brigade.

With Smith was Col. William Shy. Shy and Smith were appalled at what they saw on the hill. Ector's men had built the breastworks in the wrong place. The Confederates couldn't cover most of the slope; the approaching Federals would be sheltered from their fire. The Confederates also had erected no abatis. When the Federals came over the crest of the hill, no more than 20 yards from the breastworks, there would be nothing to stop them.

The main attack on Shy's Hill came when Gen. John McArthur, on his own, led his division of the XVI Corps towards the Confederate lines. Thomas saw McArthur advancing and ordered Schofield to advance his units. McArthur's three brigades proceeded under heavy fire as Schofield's men, off to the right, were going up Shy's Hill from the west. Smith's men broke the Confederate line just east of Shy's Hill and poured through the gap. On Shy's Hill, the Confederates were taking fire from the left, front and rear. Col. Shy held the line as Federal soldier's came over the crest of the hill and made for the breastworks. Shy was killed when a bullet struck him in the head. The Confederates broke and ran as Hood's lines disintegrated. Bate's, Walthall, then Brig. Gen. Daniel Reynolds ran for their lives. Stewart and Hood had already left. On the Federal left, at Overton Hill, Gen. Wood's troops overran the Confederate position but Lee slowly retreated in good order. On the Confederate left, Gen. Reynolds helped Cheatham's army escape down the Franklin Pike. Darkness set in and the Federals stopped their attacks. The Battle of Nashville was over and it had cost the Union 3,000 men killed, wounded or missing. The Confederates lost 6,400. In a day's fight, it wrecked and demoralized the Army of Tennessee in front of an enormous body of civilian spectators lining the hills around the battlefield. The Army of Tennessee was finished as a fighting force. The war in the West was over.

A 10 day pursuit followed, with Wilson's cavalry in the advance, and Forrest's cavalry providing the rear guard from Columbia south to the banks of the Tennessee River. The last of Forrest's men crossed the river on December 27th and two days later Hood's men marched on to Tupelo, Mississippi, ending the Campaign of Franklin and Nashville. The Army of Tennessee fragmented, and dispatched elements to Mississippi and Mobile, the remainder traveling east for the last campaign in the Carolina's.

SHERMAN'S MARCH TO THE SEA

November-December 1864
Campaign: March to the Sea
Principal commanders: Maj. Gen. William Tecumseh Sherman (US), Lt. Gen. William Hardee (CS), Maj. Gen. Gustavus Smith (CS), Maj. Gen. Joseph Wheeler (CS)

Forces engaged: Army of the Tennessee (US), Army of Georgia (formerly Army of the Cumberland) (US), Georgia Militia & State Troops (CS), Savannah Garrison(CS), Wheeler's Cavalry (CS)

After Atlanta's fall on September 2, 1864, Maj. Gen. Sherman occupied the city for 10 weeks, resting his army, damaging local communications, and plotting new strategy. Meanwhile, Gen. John Hood's Army of Tennessee began to range north and west on a march that would carry into Tennessee. Sherman briefly pursued but soon adopted a more productive course and resolved to send his trusted subordinate Maj. Gen. George Thomas, with two infantry corps and the majority of his cavalry, to Nashville for a showdown with Hood. The remainder of Sherman's command, some 62,000 troops of all arms with 64 cannons, he would lead through Georgia to the Atlantic Ocean.

Sherman had several reasons for waging such a campaign. He wanted to split the interior of the Deep South, "smashing things, generally," especially supply lines that supported the Confederates in Virginia. He also wished to "demonstrate the vulnerability of the South", by laying a heavy hand on a region thus far spared war's suffering, in brief, Sherman wished to "make Georgia howl."

His troops departed Atlanta on November 15th. Before he left Atlanta, he tore up railroad stations, warehouses, and factories. He burned the industrial area, and the flames spread to other parts of the city. Thirty seven percent of Atlanta was destroyed. His army would march simultaneously moving east toward Augusta and southeast in the direction of Macon, thereby deceiving the enemy as to his ultimate objective, Savannah. He accompanied the column taking the upper route, the XIV and XX corps of the Army of Georgia, commanded by Maj. Gen. Henry Slocum. They were to take Augusta. Maj. Gen. Oliver Howard commanded the Army of the Tennessee, consisting of the infantry of the XV and XVII corps, which would head towards Macon. Sherman also had the cavalry division of Brig. Gen. Judson Kilpatrick following his army. Union General Jeff Davis was in control of the XIV Corps, Brig. Gen.Alpheus Williams was in charge of the XX Corps. The XV Corps was led by Maj. Gen. Peter Osterhaus, and the XVII was led by Maj. Gen. Francis Preston Blair, Jr. He had 55,000 soldiers, 5,000 cavalry and 65 cannons. Wagons trains carrying pontoon boats and engineer units accompanied each wing, but the provision wagons were left behind, the troops would forage off the land.

With Hood gone, the nearest sizeable enemy force was the 18,000 man garrison under Lt. Gen. William Hardee at Savannah. The only others who remained to challenge him were 3,000 Georgia militia and state troops under Maj. Gen. Gustaus Smith, Maj. Gen. Joseph Wheeler's understrength cavalry corps (2,000 men), and miscellaneous local forces. Smith had concentrated at Macon.

Howard's wing circled northeast; the Federal army's other wing, under Slocum, approached Covington on its feint down the Georgia Railroad toward Augusta. Slocum marched to Madison and on November 17th, he set fire to the depots. On November 22nd, the Georgia militia approached Griswoldville. Gen. Smith had remained in Macon arranging for supplies and in temporary command of the troops was P.J. Phillips. In the path of the Confederates was the rear guard of Gen. Osterhaus' XV Corps. The brigade had 1,513 men-half the size of the Confederate force-but Osterhaus XV Corps was equipped with Spencer rifles. Their leader was Brig. Gen. Charles Walcutt. He ordered his men to construct temporary timberworks on a hill just beyond Griswoldville. Phillips was told not to engage the enemy but he deployed his men into an open field and prepared for an assault.

The Federals, who were cooking their noon meals, looked up as the Confederates came toward them. Walcutt waited until the Confederates were very close, then he let a Federal volley rip through the first line, but the Confederates kept coming. The Spencer rifles opened up and the Confederates fell in large numbers, but they still advanced, and their charge came within 50 yards before it broke, just as the Federals ran out of ammunition. The Confederates retreated to the east. Phillips lost 51 killed and 472 wounded.

The Confederates began to evacuate Milledgeville, whose defenders, commanded by Brig. Gen. Harry Wayne were comprised of schoolboys and prisoners and numbered 650 men. Wayne ordered his men to the east. On November 22nd, the American flag was waving over Milledgeville, the capital of Georgia. The Union troops now destroyed the military utility of Milledgeville and between November 22nd through the 24th they sacked state government buildings. On November 24th, Sherman rode southeast, his left wing heading towards Savannah. Howard's right wing had already turned toward Savannah. Sherman marched between 10 and 15 miles a day and along the way, made sure that all railroad tracks, mills, cotton gins, and such, were destroyed.

Slocum, with his pontoon bridges across the Oconee and Ogeechee Rivers, crossed into a much different land. Gone were the rich fields with large plantations. These were now replaced with marshy swamps and barren land. Foraging for food became much more difficult. In 10 days, Sherman covered nearly half the distance to Savannah with no opposition and now moved his headquarters with Howard's right wing, traveling with Frank Blair's XVII Corps. While Howard rode with Osterhaus' corps, Kilpatrick moved to the left wing to demonstrate against Augusta, threatening the garrison there and preventing those troops from moving

Sherman's troops destroyuing railroads at Atlanta.

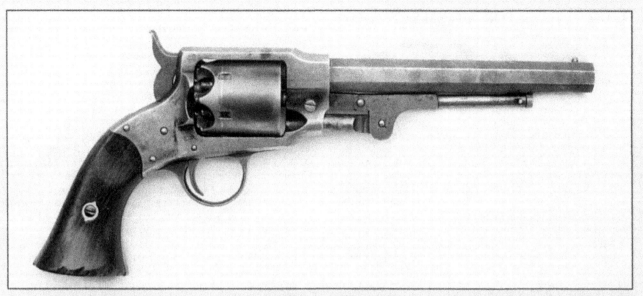

Rogers & Spencer pistol-.44 Army - Rogers & Spencer of Utica, New York, produced this well designed, six shot, single action revolver for a US government contract, but they did not deliver their 5000 revolvers until the end of the war. The Army accepted them but most were sold off as government surplus in 1901 without ever having been fired. (BCWM)

out to harass the Federal rear. The only major Confederate forces to confront the Yankees were Hardee's 10,000 men at Savannah and Joe Wheeler's men.

On November 26th, near Augusta, Wheeler overrode a Federal cavalry campsite at Sylvan Grove, galloped among the sleeping men and took them prisoner and captured 50 horses, but Kilpatrick escaped.

Fighting continued for three days in a series of skirmishes known as the Battle of Waynesboro. On November 27th, Kilpatrick and his men had to fight for their lives, barely holding off attacks by Wheeler. On November 28th, Kilpatrick had to escape again when he and a single regiment, the 9th Michigan Cavalry, were surprised by Wheeler and had to fight their way out to get back to the Federal main body. Kilpatrick asked for infantry support. Two brigades of infantry came, and with Kilpatrick's cavalry, they managed to drive Wheeler back to Waynesboro and then through the town itself. Kilpatrick kept other Confederate cavalry in check at Reynold's Plantation and then joined Slocum's column heading to Savannah.

On December 3rd, Slocum was approaching Millen, a railroad junction on the far side of the Ogeechee River and the site of a prisoner of war camp called Camp Lawton, which was now deserted, the prisoners having been previously removed. During the two days that the XIV and the XX Corps rested in Millen, the troops saw the horrible conditions at Camp Lawton. The soldiers were hardened towards the Confederates after seeing this, and the Federals burned a good part of Millen.

The forage parties grew meaner and rougher. Sherman's right wing approached Sandersville and his men were shot at from the buildings and street corners. Sherman was going to burn the whole town, until he discovered that the shots had come from Wheeler's men. The courthouse was the only building burned because it was fortified by the Confederates.

By December 10th, when they pulled up outside Savannah, having come 250 miles in 26 days, Sherman's soldiers had done $100 million dollars in damage. He had torn up over 200 miles of railroad track and to make sure the South never used them again, he built huge bonfires and laid the rails on top of them and when they were red-hot, the soldiers would bend them around a tree. These rails became known as Sherman's neckties. Sherman reduced Georgia's midsection to debris and desolation.

Fort McAllister was atop a bluff on the south bank of the Ogeechee River and was the key to the defenses of Savannah, 15

miles to the north. Fort McAllister was protected by 22 large caliber cannons, and was constructed of logs and dirt. It was filled with bombproofs and traverses, and was very strong. On December 12th, Sherman ordered his right wing commander, Maj. Gen. Oliver Howard to capture the fort. Once the fort was taken, the Union army could land all the rations the men needed, unhindered.

Howard assigned the mission to Brig. Gen. William Hazen's division of the XV Corps. On December 13th, Hazen deployed 1,500 troops for the assault. Awaiting them were 150 Confederates under Maj. Gen. George W. Anderson of Savannah. Determined "to defend the fort to the last extremity," they had spent several days strengthening the fort on its leeshore side.

With just one hour of daylight remaining, Hazen's veterans rushed forward, and without a pause, made their way over the fallen trees, rows of abatis and Chevaux-De-Frise, a large ditch, and numerous 13 inch shells that had been converted into land mines. Reaching the parapet, they scrambled to the top, then into the fort, where after ferocious hand to hand fighting they overwhelmed the tiny garrison. Sixteen Confederates were killed and 55 were wounded; the Union losses totaled 134, mainly from the land mines. The defenders simply lacked the firepower to stop the attackers, whose sharpshooters had neutralized the fort's cannon. Sherman now had his "cracker line" ready to bring in supplies.

Savannah was protected by a garrison of 10,000 men under Lt. General William Hardee. The troops occupied formidable fortifications covering all sides of the city, which was surrounded by swamps, rivers, and rice fields. Perceiving that the city was strongly defended, Sherman brought up siege guns and other equipment. On December 17th, Sherman called on Hardee to surrender, threatening otherwise to destroy Savannah. Hardee, however, refused. Sherman thereupon ordered his troops to prepare to storm the Confederate fort. But at the same time he went to the headquarters of Maj. Gen. John G. Foster, commanding Union forces in South Carolina, and arranged for Foster to seal off Savannah from the east. In this way Sherman hoped to trap Hardee and make it unnecessary to carry out a costly assault on Savannah.

Before this plan could be executed, Confederate General William Hardee, more concerned with preserving his army than attempting a hopeless defense of Savannah, evacuated his troops and escaped into South Carolina on the night of December 20th. On December 21st, a Union division occupied Savannah, bringing the March to the Sea to a triumphant close.

Last Battle for Sherman's Army

The Battle of Bentonville, North Carolina

Campaign: Carolina's Campaign (1865)

Principal commanders: Maj. Gen. William T. Sherman(US); Maj. Gen. Joseph Johnston(CS),

Forces Engaged: Army of the Tennessee(US), Army of Georgia(US), Army of Tennessee(CS)

Once Sherman had Savannah, he would move up through the Carolina's and cut off Joseph Johnston's army from reaching Robert E. Lee's Army of Northern Virginia. Grant and his Army of the Potomac were now engaging General Robert E. Lee's Army of Northern Virginia and preventing their escape. Sherman caught up with Joseph Johnston's army at Bentonville, North Carolina. Slocum's advance towards Bentonville was slowed by Hardee's troops at Averysboro. Sherman's right wing, under Maj. Gen. O.O. Howard marched toward Goldsboro. On March 19th, Slocum encountered the entrenched Confederates of Gen. Joseph Johnston who had concentrated to meet his advance at Bentonville. Johnson attacked in late afternoon, crushing the line of the XIV Corps. Only strong counterattacks and desperate fighting south of the Goldsboro Road blunted the Confederate offensive. Elements of the XX Corps were thrown into the action as they arrived on the field. Five Confederate attacks failed to dislodge the Federal defenders and darkness ended the first day's fighting. During the night, Johnston contracted his line into a V to protect his flanks with Mill Creek to his rear. On March 20th, Slocum was heavily reinforced, but fighting was sporadic. Sherman was inclined to let Johnston retreat. On the 21st, however, Johnston remained in position while he removed his wounded. In the morning, Mower sent the 64th Illinois forward into town, where skirmishing began immediately. Col. Robert J. Henderson, commanding Cummings Georgia brigade, stopped the Federal advance. The 64th Illinois was driven into the woods to the east of Bentonville. The rest of the two skirmish companies were driven into the woods by Col. Baxter Smith's 8th Texas and 4th Tennessee cavalry. Six hundred men from Brown's Division, comprised of Maney's, Strahl's, and Vaughan's Tennessee brigades, plus Gist's Brigade of South Carolina and Georgia troops, advanced through the woods towards the Federals. Union Col. John Tillson's men formed a new line of defense with the 32nd Wisconsin on the right, the 25th Indiana in the center, and the 10th Illinois on the left. Gen. Mower ordered Brig. Gen. John Fuller to form on his left. Mower then brought up his division from the XVII Corps and put it into the line of battle. Sherman did not want a full scale engagement, so he sent Maj. Gen. Frank Blair, Mower's superior, to stop Mower's advance. Sherman ordered a general attack by the skirmish line along Maj. Gen. Oliver Howard's entire front.

Mower ordered Tillson to pass around Fuller's rear, form on his left, and make a connection with Force's division. Mower's position now overlooked the Sam Howell Branch.

The Confederates counterattacked and Mower was driven in on all sides and forced back. The Confederates won a victory, but at a cost, as Gen. William Hardee's son, Willie, was mortally wounded in the attack. Mower withdrew, ending the fighting for the day. During the night, Johnston had to retreat across the bridge at Bentonville. He realized that the initial Union breakthrough showed the vulnerability of his position. Union forces pursued at first light, driving back Wheeler's cavalry's rear guard and saving the bridge. Federal pursuit was halted at Hannah's Creek after a severe skirmish. Sherman, after regrouping at Goldsboro, pursued Johnston toward Raleigh. On April 18th, Johnston signed an armistice with Sherman at the Bennett House, and on April 26th, formally surrendered his 89,000 man army. At a place called Appomattox Courthouse, Grant would receive the surrender of Gen. Robert E. Lee's Army of Northern Virginia on April 9, 1865. The Civil War was over, and now it was time for the country to mend it's wounds and become one country again.

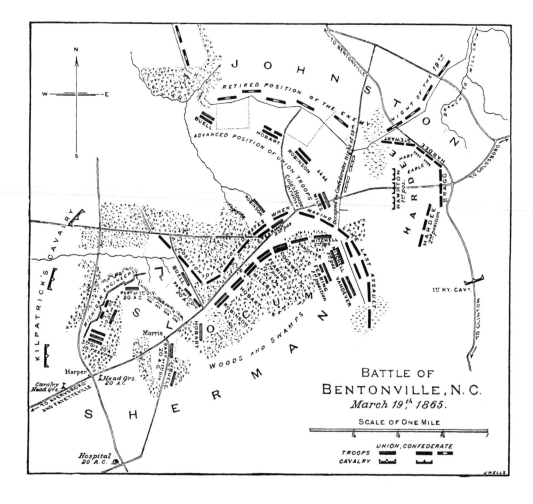

BATTLE OF
BENTONVILLE, N.C.
March 19th 1865.

SCALE OF ONE MILE

UNION, CONFEDERATE
TROOPS
CAVALRY

Orphan Brigade
Soldiers without a Home

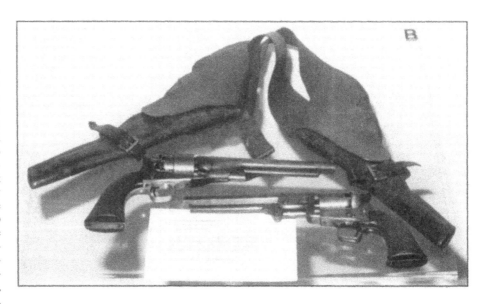

In the summer of 1861, Kentucky was forming the 1st Kentucky Brigade, and 4,000 men signed up for the Confederate cause. Union General Ulysses Grant entered Paducah in 1861 and forced the 3rd Kentucky to Camp Burnett in Bowling Green, Kentucky along with the rest of the 1st Kentucky Brigade. By February 1862, the 1st Kentucky Brigade was forced to train at Camp Boone, in Tennessee. Arming the 1st Kentucky Brigade was difficult. The guns supplied to Kentucky Brigade were the old flintlock muskets, Models 1808-1822, .69 caliber Belgian muskets, which many soldiers didn't like because they had a tendency to burst, and sometimes the Kentucky long rifle. Many Confederate soldiers had no weapons at all in 1861. The lack of clothing was also a problem. In 1861, the 1st Kentucky Brigade wore pretty much what they brought with them. Col. Lloyd Tilghman who was commander of the 3rd Kentucky Infantry in 1861, wrote constantly to Albert Sidney Johnston for uniforms and weapons, but to no avail. Lloyd Tilghman mentions in one of his reports that some of the uniforms were being made by several ladies. Just prior to and after the Battle of Shiloh, in April 1862, the 1st Kentucky Brigade managed to re-arm itself with the .577 caliber British Enfield. Uniforms were also being shipped to the 1st Kentucky Brigade by the different government supply depots.

After the Battle of Perryville, in October 1862, Kentucky would remain in Union control. Because of this, the 1st Kentucky Brigade would be in exile, and never saw their home state again until the war had ended.

The 1st Kentucky Brigade became part of the Army of the Tennessee, and were known as a hard fighting unit. It participated in the battles of Shiloh, Corinth, Vicksburg, Baton Rouge, Stone's River, Jackson, Chickamagua, and Missionary Ridge, as well as throughout the Atlanta campaign and against Sherman during his March to the Sea. During the final months of the war, the 1st Kentucky Brigade became mounted and served in the eastern theatre. The last of the 1st Kentucky Brigade surrendered in May 1865 at Washington, Georgia. Because the 1st Kentucky Brigade was not allowed to recruit from its home state after 1862, the numbers of the Orphan Brigade dwindled quickly, only 500 of the original 4,000 members of the brigade remained when they surrendered in 1865.

During the battle of Stone's River from December 31, 1862 to January 2, 1863, Confederate Division commander of the 1st Confederate Brigade, Gen. John C. Breckinridge coined the famous phrase "the Orphan Brigade," when he lost 400 men, out of his 1,200 in the fatal charge on the last day of battle. Breckinridge was riding among the survivors crying, "My poor Orphans! My poor Orphans!" During that same battle, the 1st Kentucky Brigade would lose Gen. Roger Hanson. Another famous Confederate general of the 1st Kentucky Brigade, Ben Hardin Helm, who was Lincoln's brother-in-law, was killed at the Battle of Chickamauga on September 1863.

One of the best biographers of the Orphan Brigade was Ed Porter Thompson. Because of his work, the history of the Orphan Brigade remains intact. His two books; **The History of the First Brigade**, published in 1868, and **The History of the Orphan Brigade**, published in 1898 is a good record of each member of the Orphan Brigade and includes short biographies, and photos.

Confederate General John Cabell Breckinridge's Colt .36 caliber Navy revolver and .44 caliber Army revolver, with holsters. John Cabell Breckinridge was born on January 15, 1821 in Lexington, Kentucky. John came from a prominent Kentucky family. He studied law at the Transylvania Institute and settled in Lexington. During the Mexican War, John served as a Major in the Third Kentucky, but saw no action. After the war, John resumed his legal practice but soon entered politics. He was elected to the state House of Representatives in 1849 and was elected twice to the U.S. Congress (1851-55). In 1856, the Democratic party nominated John to run with James Buchanan in the presidential election. At the age of 35, he became the youngest vice president in U.S. history. After serving his term as vice president, he was named to the U.S. Senate. In 1860, the Democratic party split. John was selected as the presidential candidate for the Southern faction of the Democratic party, and Stephen Douglas was nominated for the Northern Democratic party. Breckinridge was against secession but insisted that Southerners be allowed the rights guaranteed them in the Constitution. Breckinridge came in second in the electoral vote. After Lincoln won the election, and the Southern states started to secede, John tried to keep Kentucky's neutrality and retained his seat in the Senate. An order was issued for his arrest for being a suspected Confederate sympathizer, even though he had committed no treasonous act. Breckinridge fled Washington to his home state, and joined the Confederacy. On November 2, 1861, he was appointed Brigadier General of the First Kentucky Brigade, Buckner's Division, later known as the Orphan Brigade, and sent to reinforce Fort Donelson. On April 14, 1862, he was appointed Major General. Breckinridge commanded his corps at Shiloh, led an attack on Baton Rouge in August, and played a significant role at Stone's River on the third day in December. From this battle arose a controversy between Bragg and Breckinridge, that would never be healed. In the spring of 1863, Breckinridge served under Confederate General Joe Johnston in the attempt to relieve the pressure on Vicksburg. Breckinridge later fought at Jackson, Mississippi, and led his division under Bragg at Chickamauga. He commanded a corps at Missionary Ridge; then went east to command the Department of Southwestern Virginia. On May 15, 1864, Breckinridge won the Battle of New Market winning one of the most important small battles of the war. He also commanded at Cold Harbor, in Lt. Gen. Jubal Early's Washington Raid, and against Maj. Gen. Philip Sheridan in the Shenandoah Valley campaign of 1864.

In February 1865, Breckinridge was appointed Secretary of War and held that position until the end of the war. He organized the evacuation of Richmond, Virginia, accompanied President Jefferson Davis from Richmond to Charlotte, North Carolina, and took part in the negotiations for surrender between Maj. Gen. William T. Sherman and Confederate General Joe Johnston. He escaped to Cuba at the close of the war, and then traveled to Europe and Canada before returning to Lexington in 1868. Exhausted by the war, and distraught over losing so many of his men during the war, he died seven years later at the age of 54. The war has taken its toll on a man who loved his Orphans. [Reference: Who Was Who in the Confederacy, Civil War Cards, John C. Breckinridge, and Historical Times Illustrated Encyclopedia of the Civil War.] (Kentucky Military History Museum)

(1)   (2a)   (2b)

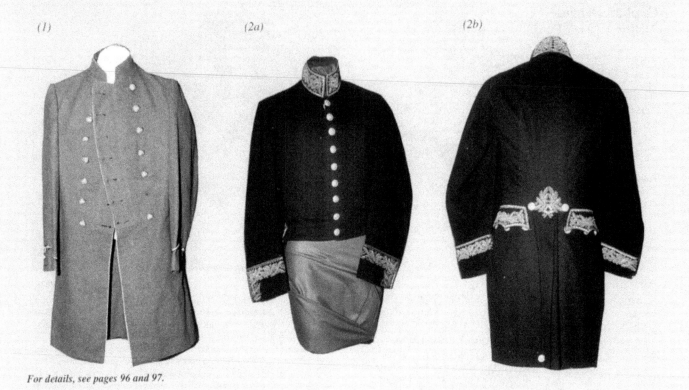

For details, see pages 96 and 97.

(3)   (4)

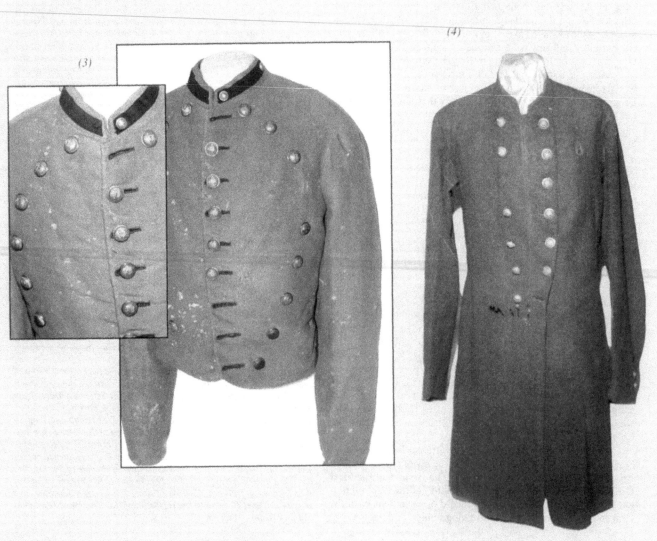

(5)

(6)

(7a)

(7b)

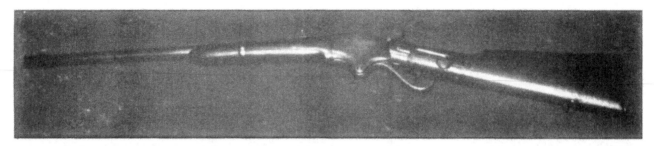

Above: Lt. Col. Hervey McDowell's Spencer Carbine—Hervey McDowell was born near Lexington, Kentucky on April 15th, 1835. When Hervey was twelve years old, his family moved to Owen County, Kentucky and settled on the Green River. He took a preparatory course at Drennon Springs, and went to the Kentucky Military Institute, where he graduated in 1856. He then studied medicine at Lexington, attending the annual sessions of the Missouri Medical College, at St. Louis, where he graduated in 1858. He located to Cynthiana, and practiced until the summer of 1861, when he recruited Company F., 2nd Kentucky Infantry and was its first Captain. He was promoted to major after the Battle of Chickamagua on September 20th, 1863 and was promoted to Lt. Colonel after the Battle of Jonesboro, Georgia on August 31st, 1864.

At the Battle of Fort Donelson in February of 1862, McDowell was severely wounded in the head and side as was captured with the rest of his command and kept in prison on Johnson's Island Prison for six months. When exchanged, he returned with his command to Vicksburg, where it was reunited with the other regiments of the Orphan Brigade. He was in the battles of Hartsville, Stone's River, Chickamauga, Missionary Ridge, Resaca, Dallas, Dalton, Jonesboro, and fought Sherman's men from his march to the Sea campaign to Sherman's Carolina campaign.

At the Battle of Stone's River, McDowell was wounded through both arms and struck in three other places. He also was wounded at Chickamagua.

After the war, he continued his medical studies, and attended two courses of lectures as a post graduate of Missouri Medical College. In 1868, he married a second cousin, Miss Louise Irvine McDowell. They both permanently located in Cynthiana, where he practiced medicine. He would have six sons. For twenty-four years he would be a member of the Board of Education and in 1878, was president. (Reference: Ed Porter Thompson; The History of the Orphan Brigade) (Ken Hamilton, Blue Grass Historic Trust)

Photos on pages 94-95

(1) Capt. Charlton Morgan's officer frock coat. Charlton Morgan was Adjutant to Confederate General John C. Breckinridge, and to Confederate General John Hunt Morgan. Charlton Morgan was the brother of Confederate General John Hunt Morgan. Charlton was wounded at the Battle of Shiloh, and was captured at the Battle of Huntsville. He was later exchanged but was again captured near Lexington, Kentucky while on a reconnoitering mission in 1863. Morgan's uniform is a double breasted grey wool frock coat. It has two rows of eight gold U.S. Army eagle buttons. It has three same pattern buttons at the cuffs. It has an upright collar with yellow cotton piping up the front and around the collar. It has a pleated and split tail with four buttons. The coat has a dark wool lining. The uniform also has copper and yellow cotton chevrons. (Kentucky Military History Museum)

(2a & b) Charlton Morgan's Ambassador Coat. Charlton Morgan was U.S. Council to Italy in 1859. (Blue Grass Historic Trust, Hunt-Morgan House)

(3) Pre-Civil War Militia Short Coat. This short coat is a non-regulation style typical of the pattern that was used by Home Guards and local Militia organizations of the period. This particular coat is made of cotton wept with wool weave. Originally located in Lexington, Kentucky, this coat is believed to have been Kentucky made due to the historic location and the Kentucky State Seal buttons that adorn the coat. Due to the history, it is also believed that this coat would be typical of the uniforms of the men, which went into the Confederate service, and became known as the "Orphan Brigade." (Chaplin Hill Properties, Inc.)

(4) Unidentified Confederate uniform frock coat-Three quarter length dark blue-gray wool double breasted uniform oat manufactured of Irish wool broadcloth. It has a 14 button double breasted front with standing collar. Rank insignia has been removed but four diagonal cuts exist in the collar where the gilt cloth insignia for a first lieutenant was present. Buttons are die stamped brass, where the gilt cloth insignia for a first lieutenant was present. Buttons are die stamped brass, three piece U.S. Staff Officer pattern marked "superior quality." Two are missing from the front, one from the left sleeve and one from the rear waist, the uni-form coat is lined in black polsied cotton with white cotton sleeve lining. Breast is quilted lain being of regulation cut and pattern but unadorned with any cuff or collar facings, piping or sleeve rank insignia. This uniform coat was most likely manufactured by the firm of P. Trait & Co., Limerick, Ireland for export to the Confederate States. (Hunt-Morgan House, Ken Hamilton)

(5) Private Elizah Woodward's shell jacket. Elizah Woodward enlisted in the 9th Kentucky Infantry, Company C, on September 22, 1861, in Hopkinsville, Kentucky for one year of service. He fought at the Battle of Shiloh in April of 1862, even though his rifle was stolen. He deserted from camp near Murfreesboro, Tennessee on November 14, 1862. Woodward's shell jacket was made from grey wool although time has faded the uniform to brown. It has a five button front, with blue trim at the collar and cuffs. It has a stand up collar, with a full white cotton lining. (Kentucky Military History Museum)

(6) Confederate grey kepi with Kentucky state seal buttons, and tarred leather brim. (BCWM)

(7a & b) Capt. William T. B. South's wool shell jacket. Captain of the 5th Kentucky Mounted Infantry, Company A and B. William T. B. South enlisted in the 5th Kentucky Infantry on January 8, 1862, in Prestonburg, Kentucky for one year. On May 10, 1862, South was made 1st Lieutenant. He was elected Captain on September 18, 1862 and enlisted for three years. In July of 1862, South was sent to Kentucky for recruiting and enlisted 79 men from Breathitt County. From January to February of 1864, South was sent to recruit for Confederate General Joe Johnston. South served with one of the most famous of all Confederate units; the Orphan Brigade. South would participate in all the major engagements the 5th Kentucky was involved in. At the Battle of Jonesboro, Georgia, in 1864, South was acting Lt. Colonel. At the Battle of Sandersville, the 5th Kentucky was a mounted unit and South's unit was sent forward to hold a hazardous position and prevent a flank movement of the Yankees till reinforcements arrived, which he successfully executed. [Reference: Ed Porter Thompson, The History of the Orphan Brigade] (Kentucky Military History Museum)

Brother Against Brother

The American Civil War has been given many names, but perhaps the most fitting is "The Brother's War," for its history is filled with the stories of families divided by their loyalties to both the Union and the Confederacy.

Divided loyalties befell even the White House, as for four years President Lincoln's brother-in-law, Ben Hardin Helm, served the Confederate cause. Ben Hardin Helm, turned down a personal offer from Lincoln of a commission in the Union army and was later killed as a Confederate general in the Battle of Chickamagua. Lincoln's wife, Mary Todd, was from an aristocratic family, and the Washington gossip spoke of her as being proslavery and in favor of Southern secession. When senate members of the Committee on the Conduct of the War met to consider charges of treason against her, Lincoln made a surprise appearance and gave assurances that headed off further deliberation of the charges.

Border states naturally endured many divided families in the conflict. Kentuckian Henry Clay who tried for many years to soothe the sectional strife that led to the war, had three grandsons fighting for the Union and four serving the Confederate cause. Kentucky Sen. John Crittenden had two sons serving as general officers during the war: Maj. Gen. Thomas L. Crittenden with the Union army and his brother Maj. Gen. George B. Crittenden for the Confederate army.

Another example of a divided family were the Hanson brothers of Kentucky. Lt. Col. Charles Hanson served with distinction on the Union side, as commander of the 20th Kentucky Infantry and the 37th Kentucky Mounted Infantry. His brother Confederate General Roger Hanson served as commander of the Orphan Brigade. Unfortunately, Roger Hanson was killed at the Battle of Stone's River.

Oil painting of President Abraham Lincoln taken from a war time photograph. (BCWM)

Lincoln & Davis

Abraham Lincoln was born near Hodgenville, Kentucky on February 12, 1809. Jefferson Davis was born in Christian City, Kentucky on June 3, 1808. Both men would become Presidents. Abraham Lincoln would become President of the United States of America, and Jefferson Davis would become President of the Confederates States of America. They were born only 90 miles apart. Abraham Lincoln would lose a child in his White House. Willie Lincoln died in 1862. Jefferson Davis lost a child in his White House in Virginia. His son fell out of the second story window. Abraham Lincoln has a memorial in Washington, DC, and Jefferson Davis has a monument in Fairview, Kentucky. The Jefferson Davis monument looks very much like the Washington Monument, and is the largest Confederate monument in the world.

Mexican War photo of Jefferson Davis in his military uniform. (BCWM)

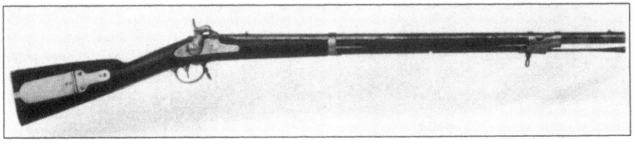

Mississippi Rifle made famous by Jefferson Davis during the Mexican War. (BCWM)

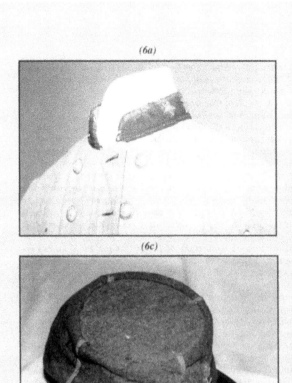

(6a)

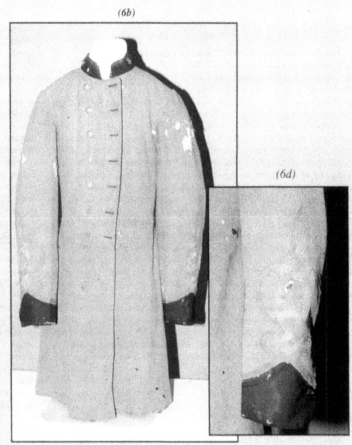

(6b)

(6d)

(6c)

Presentation Sword of Confederate
General John C. Breckinridge
Inscribed on scabbard:
From Finley's & Bates Brigade to
Gen. J. C. Breckinridge.

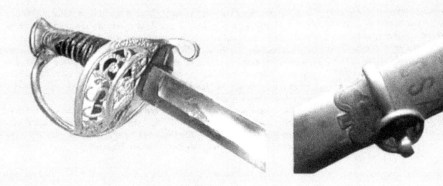

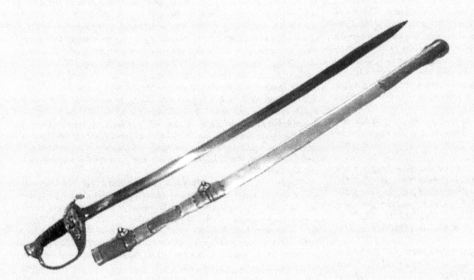

Photos on pages 98 & 99.

(1) New York Zouave Uniform, "Ellsworth's Zouave's" (BCWM)
(2) New York Zouave Uniform. (BCWM)
(3) Chasseur Uniform. (BCWM)
(4) New York Zouave kepi. (BCWM)
(5 a,b,c,d) Private David Fenimore Cooper Weller's shell jacket, vest, and overcoat. David Weller was born on March 11, 1843 in Louisville, Kentucky. He was 18 years old when he enlisted in Company C, 22nd Kentucky Infantry on August 16, 1861 at Camp Boone, Tennessee. He signed up for three years. According to Ed Porter Thompson, Weller fought at the Battle of Fort Donelson and was wounded seven or eight times, one of which was in the shoulder, which disabled him from carrying a rifle. He was paroled at Camp Chattanooga on November 1862. On February 15, 1863, Weller is ordered by Confederate General Braxton Bragg to be stationed at Tunnel Hill Hospital and serve as a nurse. He did nursing duties under Dr. Stout in the spring and summer of 1863, but rejoined the company and fought at the Battle of Chickamauga. He was captured at the Battle of Chickamauga and paroled and placed in Camp Chattanooga, Tennessee and declared exchanged on January 11, 1863. From January 1864 till the close of the war, Weller served as a hospital nurse. He died in Louisville. Weller's shell jacket was made from grey wool, although time has changed the color from grey to brown. The jacket has a stand up collar, with blue trim on collar and cuffs. The front has six buttons, and has a full white cotton lining. The vest is made of grey wool with two split front pockets, with a roll collar. It has a ten button front, with a belt at back with square buckle. The back of the vest has a unusual black and tan pattern. (Kentucky Military History Museum)

Photos on pages 98-99

(6) Uniform and Kepi of Col. Joseph Preyer Nuckols
4th Kentucky Infantry, C. S.

Joseph Preyer Nuckols was born in Barren County, Kentucky on April 20th, 1826. He was described as being "6'2", with dark hair, dark eyes, and a certain settled, stern expression of countenance, which was due more to his health than his disposition." Joseph attended the common schools in Glasgow, Kentucky until he was seventeen, when he made a trip to Texas to bring back the wife and baby of his brother, Andrew Nuckols, who had joined the U.S. Army under Gen. Zachary Taylor in the war with Mexico. In 1849, he went to California in search of gold. He worked in the gold mines for a few years, with some success that enabled Joseph to return to Glasgow prior to the Civil War and buy a farm of 365 acres near town.

On his return to Kentucky in 1856 he took up the study of law and entered practice at Glasgow, Kentucky, although it is not clear that he ever practiced law as a profession. In 1859, Nuckols married Linda Carr and took up residence in Glasgow.

On August 24, 1860 Nuckols organized and was elected captain of a company of Barren County, Kentucky men called the "Glasgow Guards." Nuckols took his company to Louisville for the first encampment of the Kentucky State Guard in August of 1860. There he met the new commander of the State Guard, Simon Bolivar of Munfordville. The State Guard trained diligently in close order drill, manual of arms, and other skills.

In 1861, the company paraded through the streets of Glasgow under the Confederate flag. By August he had recruited a total of 83 men, all single except Nuckols. The 2nd and 3rd regiments under J. M. Hawes of Paris, and Lloyd Tilghman of Paducah already had moved into bivouac at Montgomery County, Tennessee, where various units of the Army of Confederate States of America were forming at Camp Boone. Nuckols remained in Glasgow until August elections for the Kentucky General Assembly so they could help elect a pro-Southern member of the House to represent Glasgow in the legislature. Before they proceeded to Tennessee they boxed their arms and equipment, property of the state of Kentucky, and turned them over to the county judge for the Home Guards.

Nuckols and his company arrived at Camp Boone on August 9th, where he met with Col. Robert Trabue of Columbia, Kentucky. Trabue formed the 4th Kentucky Regiment for three years of service. Nuckols was offered a promotion to major, but he opted to remain commander of Company A, 4th Kentucky Infantry.

Simon Buckner was appointed by Confederate General Albert Sidney Johnston to command the Confederate Kentucky troops, and was ordered to take Bowling Green, Kentucky. After the fall of Forts Henry and Donelson, the Kentucky troops, along with Johnston, left Bowling Green, and fell back to Nashville, Tennessee.

At the Battle of Shiloh, Nuckols was placed in command of the left of his regiment as acting Major. Nuckols was mounted most of the day and was constantly was exposed to danger. On April 6th, they moved into a thickly wooded area at the base of a small hill. As they advanced over the rise, they found themselves at the rear of the Confederate line of battle and shortly the regiment aligned in front broke ranks and retreated, passing through the 4th Kentucky on it's way. In a few minutes Nuckols noticed a long line of muskets pointing through a line of trees on their left. Tall in the saddle, Nuckols could see a Federal regiment forming at right angles in front of him. Actually they were arrayed against the 46th Ohio. As the 4th Kentucky engaged the Ohio regiment, another regiment of reserve was brought up to aid the Ohio unit. The 4th Kentucky charged the woods and drove out the Federals.

On April 7th, Nuckols troops were arrayed against a division led by Union General Don Carlos Buell. Nuckols was wounded in the ankle, a musket ball lodged between the bones and brought great pain, later removed by a field surgeon. As Nuckols was being carried from the field, his troops suddenly began to sing the "Kentucky Battle Song" in his honor.

Nuckols was taken to Corinth, Mississippi the following day. Confederate General John C. Breckinridge praised Nuckols for his valor at Shiloh. Nuckols joined the command at Knoxville around October 1st, 1862, and Breckinridge sent them to Kentucky to precede the division and recruit for the Confederate army. They got as far as Barbourville, where they met the head of Bragg's retreating army. Nuckols and the other officers turned back toward Knoxville. they rejoined the division on it's way to Murfreesboro, where Nuckols was promoted to Major in November, to date from April 7th, the second day of Shiloh.

Nuckols was promoted to Lt. Colonel on December 18th, 1862. Nuckols was ordered by Breckinridge to move one mile in front of the division. Nuckols remained in command of the advance line until December 31st, watching Union movements and reporting back to the division. Nuckols reported to Breckinridge, recommending that a regiment be moved to a hill which the fight had earlier raged. On January 2nd, Bragg sent word to Breckinridge to take the same hill and place artillery in position there. Nuckols knew the risk involved in the effort to take the hill. Attempting to encourage his men in the heat of battle, Nuckols reached for the regimental colors, to use them as a rallying point, when he was struck in the arm by a bullet. His horse was also injured, but Lt. Col. Nuckols continued. He tried to reform his lines, but his horse was shot again, and Nuckols was forced to limp from the field on foot. Nuckols returned to command in February at Manchester. Because Col. Trabue was killed, Nuckols was promoted to Colonel of the 4th Kentucky.

Nuckols took his troops into battle on the first day at Chickamaugua where the regiment was protecting the artillery near Glass' Mills. During the battle, the regiment was under heavy fire from shot and shell. If it were not for Nuckols, the men would have not marched over the open field. The next day, Nuckols went forward to find the enemy and reported their position. They found the Yankees entrenched. Nuckols dismounted in the center of the line, intending to stand until reinforcements could arrive. Nuckols was hit by a minnie ball which pierced his left arm below the elbow, shattering the bones. The wound was so serious, it forced Nuckols to retire from active service.

Nuckols returned to Glasgow financially ruined. After the war, he was elected three times as county clerk of Barren, in 1866, 1870, and 1874. Nuckols first wife, Linda, died after the war, and in 1870, Nuckols remarried to Caron Donaldson. On May 1st, 1876, he resigned as county clerk to accept the appointment as Quartermaster General by Gov. James McCreary. Nuckols was in charge of the state arsenal. He was awarded the rank of Brig. General by Gov. Blackburn by executive order on October 1st, 1879 to serve as both adjutant general and inspector general.

The sleeve on the uniform pictured shows the bullet wound received by Col. Nuckols at the Battle of Chickamauga. [Reference: Ed Porter Thompson: The History of the Orphan Brigade, Kentucky Military History Museum] (Kentucky Military History Museum)

Zouave Uniforms

(1) Zouave Uniforms-The French Connection

The most popular nonstandard apparel of the soldier during the war was the brightly colored Zouave garb modeled after the uniforms worn by the North African army of Emperor Napoleon III of France. The Algerian soldiers in these French infantry units were known not only for their flashy uniforms and quick-spirited drill, but also for military excellence and bravery. The exotic attire became popular and was adopted by many militia units throughout the United States. One unit, Col. Elmer Ellsworth's United States Zouave Cadets, toured the country on the eve of the war, entertaining audiences with their acrobatic drill.

Zouave uniforms came in several variations, but most included a brightly colored short jacket that did not close at the front, baggy red trousers bloused at the ankle, white gaiters, and a tasseled, brilliant red fez. Sashes and trim and sometimes turbans of contrasting bright colors completed the uniforms. Officers in many Zouave units believed their smart uniforms boosted morale and confidence, and helped them become well known as fierce and dependable fighters, conspicuous in hard fought battles. Other Zouave officers found that the garb made them much too conspicuous on the battlefield and soon adopted the standard-issue uniform in an effort to avoid enemy fire.

Most Zouave regiments came from the North-Eastern states, but at least one Zouave unit did fight in the West, they were the 33rd New Jersey Volunteers/2nd Zouaves U.S.A. This particular unit fought with Sherman's army. Their uniforms were dark blue pantaloons in the baggy style, matching their short jackets, and both sporting colorful red trim. The regulation kepi capped their heads instead of the fez. The few Confederate Zouave regiments, such as the Louisiana Tigers or Wheat's Tigers, were mostly from Louisiana and were known as hard fighters both on and off the battlefield.

(2) New York Zouaves-Ellsworth Zouaves

When the war began, Elmer E. Ellsworth, well known in mid-19th century military circles as the organizer, trainer, and popularizer of Zouave units in several Northern states, raised a regiment from the firemen of New York City. In it's early months the regiment adopted the zouave dress (scarlet trousers and blue jacket) and took the name 1st New York Fire Zouaves or Ellsworth Zouaves. Officially the unit was the 11th New York Infantry. The zouave uniform proved to be much too conspicuous on the battlefield and was replaced by regulation uniforms.

Ellsworth was elected it's colonel, and on April 20, 1861 the regiment was accepted into state service. Mustered into U.S. service for two years on May 7th, the unit spent virtually it's entire wartime service in the area around the District of Columbia, probably due to the fact that Ellsworth was a friend and favorite of President Abraham Lincoln. The Zouaves acquired a reputation for rowdy conduct, but they also helped extinguish a fire that threatened serious damage to the capital. Ellsworth became the first Union martyr when he was killed May 24, 1861 after removing a Southern flag from atop a hotel in Alexandria, Virginia.

The regiment fought at First Bull Run, on July 20, 1861 as part of Brig. Gen. Samuel Heintzelman's division, and distinguished itself while supporting the Federal Artillery. In that battle the Zouaves lost 177 men.

Charles Leoser was colonel of the 11th New York from August 1861, until April 1862. In June 1862, the regiment was mustered out of service, despite the fact that it still had almost a year of its original term of service left.

(3) **French Chasseur uniform**-There were over 10,000 of these French uniforms imported before the Civil War. The belt buckle is an English snake buckle. Col. John Hunt Morgan wore uniforms very similar to the Chasseur uniform when Morgan commanded the Lexington rifles.

Cap box and rifle cartridge box. The cartridge box has "Col. Mann's Patent, E. Gaylord, Chicopee, Massachusetts stamped in the leather. (BCWM)

Type of hat worn by Lincoln, type of .41 caliber Derringer used by John Wilkes Booth, reading glasses from the period, and clipping from a Washington paper offering rewards for the murderers of the President. (BCWM)

Camp Scene

Officer's desk belonging to the 15th Kentucky Union Infantry. Wagon- Model 1857. These wagons were normally 10 feet wide and would have been covered with a canvas top, with the unit designation stenciled on the canvas. Wagons were very important, and transported everything the army needed for their campaigns. Rifle box containing three Tower muskets from England, three officer's folding chairs, and a hand made banjo.

Militia Items

Before there was any centralized Federal army, America relied on its local militia groups to help protect their communities from Indian attacks, or from civil disobedience. Millitia units wore a variety of colorful uniforms, and carried a hodge-podge of weapons. Before the Civil War, many of the militia units carried old muskets left over from the War of 1812, or even carried the Kentucky long rifles. The

Tintype of Southern plantation owner, also containing a stick pin made of porcelain depicting his beloved mother. (BCWM)

Photo of two young Kentucky Military Institute cadets. K.M. I. sent officers both North and South to the conflict. Truly this was brother against brother. Many of the cadets enclosed in the album didn't return to their Kentucky homes after the war. (BCWM)

Kentucky Plantation saddle. A favorite of Confederate General John Hunt Morgan and the 2nd Kentucky Cavalry, who preferred comfort of the plantation saddle and in it's gentleness on the backs of thoroughbred horses. The Kentucky cavalry regiments used these extensively at the beginning of the war. (BCWM)

cannons owned by the various militia groups could also range from those used during the War of 1812, to the newer and lighter cannons such as the Model 1840, six pound smoothbore, the Model 1841, six pounder rifled cannons, the model 1840, smoothbore 12 pounders, and the model 1857, 12 pounder smoothbore, known as the Napoleon.

Many of the communities that formed these local militia groups had great pride in their units and during the spring and summer, the states would hold militia competitions. Each militia group vied for the position of best militia group in the state as they showed their skill with artillery, rifle, and drill. It was a grand affair for the whole community to watch these colorful groups in action.

When the Civil War broke out, many of these militia organizations were automatically absorbed into the Regular Army, uniforms and all, which early in the war, made for a great amount of confusion on the battlefields as to who were Confederate and who were Union. The commissary department also had a very difficult time coming up with all the different types of ammunition needed for the muskets used by the militia groups. By 1863, the Union government had started to standardize the uniform and weapon to be used by the soldiers of each army.

Double barreled shotgun-In 1860 the overwhelming majority of American households owned at least one shotgun. Throughout rural America all manner of shotguns and fowling pieces were in use, mainly in either 10 or 12 gauge. Although most were assembled in America, many parts were imported from Europe. English made barrels were very common since their quality and price could not be matched by U.S. gun makers until well after the war. Shotguns were pressed into military service by ill armed volunteer units early in the war and were retained by many Confederate cavalry outfits. It is unlikely that shotguns were ever manufactured by the Confederate government. [1]

Mexican War period coat, with silver epaulettes, and gold washed coin buttons. Worn by Tennessee Colonel at the beginning of the war. (BCWM)

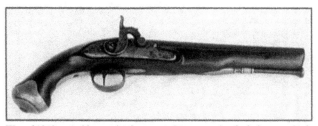

War of 1812 period horse pistol converted to percussion by bolster method. This pistol was common among many Southern militia soldiers. (BCWM)

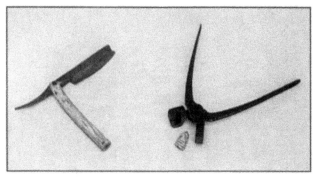

On the left is a shaving razor with a hand made bone handle. On the right is his .58 caliber bullet mold and bullet. The .58 caliber bullet was the most frequently used projectile for rifles used during the Civil War. (BCWM)

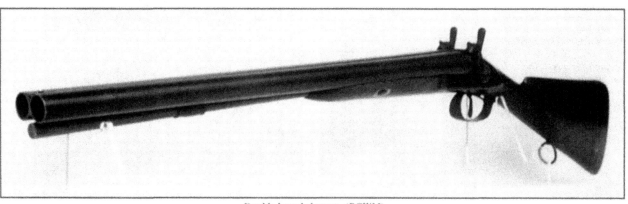

Double barrel shotgun. (BCWM)

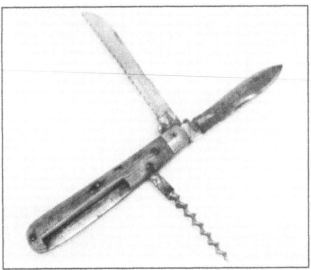

Early multiple blade pocket knife, featuring a saw blade, cutting blade and a cork screw. It also has a bone handle. The pocket knife was a favorite of the enlisted men's accouterments. (BCWM)

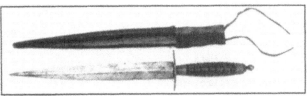

Early spear point knife with leather scabbard and turned ebony handle. This side knife dates back to the early 1800's and was carried by many Southern soldiers throughout the war. (BCWM)

C.D.V. of a unknown Western private from Kentucky.

C.D.V. of Ohio Volunteer infantryman. (BCWM)

Pre war Sergeant armed with a Colt police model, side knife in his belt, and his model 1840's style knight's head militia sword, and .69 caliber Springfield musket. This typical studio photograph was sent home by early enlists wearing studio props armed to the teeth. Privates were not allowed to carry pistols or swords. (BCWM)

Tintype of Militia infantrymen wearing typical shell jacket of the Western theater. (BCWM)

ARTILLERY

Deadly Thunder

Battery

The basic unit of artillery is the battery, which has four to six guns, is commanded by a captain, and has four lieutenants, 12 or so noncommissioned officers, and about 120 privates. In the South, it had four, usually dissimilar guns, typically a 12 pound Napoleon smoothbore and a pair of 10 Pound Parrott Rifles and a six pounder smoothbore. In the North, the make up was similar, all 10 Pound Parrotts, all 12 pound Napoleons or all three inch ordnance rifles. Batteries were subdivided into gun crews of 20 or so, and into sections of two gun crews, two or three sections per battery. A gun crew was commanded by a sergeant and a section by a lieutenant. Typical artillery crews were intelligent and they were required to learn technical skills, like the mathematics of trajectory. Many of

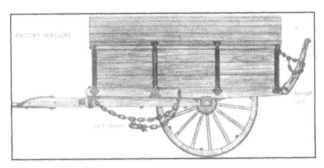

Model 1832 Foot artillery short sword with scabbard, made by the Ames Manufacturing Company, Chicopee, Massachusetts. These swords were tactically useless but the artillerymen could use these swords to chop branches and cut wood. Their design was based on a Roman pattern sword used centuries before. (BCWM)

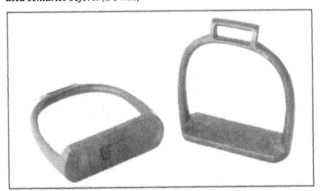

These artillery stirrups are made of brass, with U.S. stamped on the base of each stir-up. It was used on artillery drivers saddles. (BCWM)

the artillerymen were college graduates, clerks, and businessmen before the war. Artillery crews had to be calm under fire and be able to work together, and be in tune with their movements, like all trained soldiers. Batteries were an auxiliary branch of the armies. Their role was defensive. Cannons were positioned at 14 yard intervals, so a six gun battery occupied a frontage of 80 yards. The gunner personally aimed the gun and inspected the fuses.

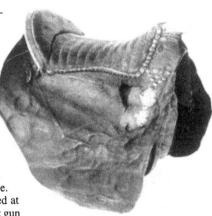

Confederate copy of a Grimsley saddle. (BCWM)

Battalion or Brigade

At the start of the Civil War, each side was assigned one battery to each infantry brigade, plus an artillery reserve under the army commander. By mid-1862, larger organizations were used. The basic unit contained three or four artillery batteries; it was called a battalion in the South and a brigade in the North (same unit, just a different name) and was commanded by a colonel, lieutenant colonel, or major.

Artillery Reserve

After 1862, it was typical for each infantry division to have an artillery battalion attached, and each corps or army to have a reserve of two to five battalions. Each division's artillery usually fought along side the infantry, while the corps/army reserves were used to form the massed batteries. The artillery reserve was commanded by a brigadier general or colonel.

Pair of short swords. The sword on the right is a French manufactured double edged blade with brass mounted leather scabbard. The sword on the left is a Model 1832 Foot Artillery sword manufactured by the Ames Manufacturing Company, Chickopee, Mass. Based on the French pattern, this sword was in continuous use until 1870. (BCWM)

Heavy Artillery

The Union organized some "heavy artillery" units, regiments containing 10 artillery batteries (about 180 men) which had training both as infantry and as artillerists. They were organized in much the same way as infantry units, but were quite a bit larger to provide enough men to man the guns. Originally raised to man the defenses of Washington, in 1864 they joined Grant's army, where they served primarily as infantry.

Field Artillery

The smallest regulation gun caliber during the Civil war was the six pounder which had a 3.67 inch bore. The six pound bronze, models 1839 and 1841, the U.S. six pound cast iron, models 1819 and 1831, and the U.S.-Confederate six pound were all variations of this gun. The Confederate six pound was either made from bronze or iron, and based on the Model 1841 pattern, and were either smoothbored or rifled. The rifled six pounder was called the "James Rifle."

The next size of cannon were the 12 pounders, Model 1839, which all have 4.62 inch bores. The 12 pounder could be used as a field weapon and siege/garrison weapon. This model came in a smoothbore or rifled version in James or Brooke style.

The next class in 12 pounders was the Gun Howitzer, Light 12 pounder or 12 pound gun model

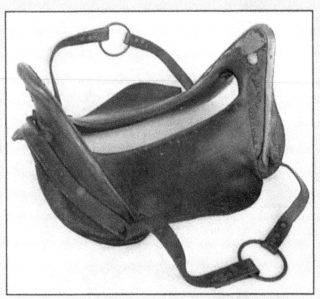

Model 1859 McClellan artillery valise saddle. (BCWM)

Union enlisted Bummer's cap, with crossed brass artillery insignia (BCWM)

1857, known as the Napoleon. The first Napoleon was made by Ames Manufacturing Company of Chickopee, Massachusetts, and had handles on the sides of the tube. The later Federal style had the handles omitted and had a swell at the end of the muzzle. The Napoleon was a favorite on both sides, and could fire grape, shell, spherical case, and canister shot.

The next class was the howitzer. Howitzers were smoothbores which were designed to throw projectiles with light charges of powder that were concentrated in a chamber at the bottom of the tube. They were lighter and had a shorter range but with shell, grape, and canister shot they were more effective than the larger calibers. The caliber of howitzers followed standard cannon sizes and were expressed in terms of weight of solid shot, for the lighter guns, and inches for larger bores. There were 12, 24 pounders, and the 32 pounders. The rifled guns were known as the eight inch 32 pounder, and the10 inch, 42 pounder seacoast howitzers.

(1) The 12 Pound Mountain Howitzer (Model 1841) was a smoothbore gun made of bronze, and was designed to throw large projectiles with comparatively light charges of powder concentrated in a chamber at the bottom of the

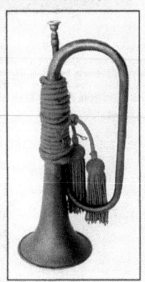

This artillery bugle with red artillery bugle cord was used by both Union and Confederate artillery. (BCWM)

This Grimsley artillery saddle has a artillery driver's personal valise tied to it. Also shown is the standard Model 1863 U.S. bit. (BCWM)

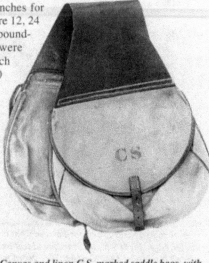

Canvas and linen C.S. marked saddle bags with red artillery piping. (BCWM)

(1) 12 lb. Mountain Howitzer. (BCWM)

(2) Six lb. smoothbore, U.S. stamped.

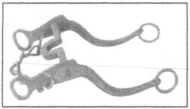

Hand forged Confederate artillery horse bit. (BCWM)

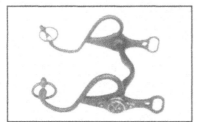

French Artillery bit. (BCWM)

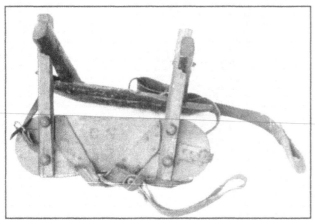

This is a Confederate mountain howitzer pack saddle. It was used to carry the bronze 12 pound tube. It is also C.S. marked on it's base. (BCWM)

tube. They were lighter than other guns of the same caliber and at short ranges could fire shell, grape, canister, and case shot. They were considerably more effective than the larger guns. They also had a higher trajectory and their shells were able to reach targets in greater numbers than could other guns. The Mountain Howitzer had 2.67 inch diameter trunnions and had it's own carriage.

The Mountain Howitzer was a dual purpose weapon used in the highly contrasting terrains of mountain and prairie. Although having the standard 12 pound bore of 4.62 inches, the tube is but 37.21 inches long and weighs only 220 pounds, a convenient load for a pack animal. The carriage, a smaller, simplified version of the field carriage, breaks down into several parts which may be loaded on another mule. With ammunition and other battery equipment similarly packed, the entire unit could operate easily in mountainous country that would be extremely difficult if not impossible for a field outfit. When mounted on the carriage, no limber was used. Instead the howitzer was hauled by a single animal using two shafts attached to the stock near the trail plate.

The particular model shown was the model 1841, made by the Cyrus Algers & Company.

(2) Six Pound Mountain Howitzer Model 1836-iron barrel, possibly made by the West Point Foundry.

Rifled Cannon

Invented by Robert Parrott (1804-1877), the 10 pound, 20 pound, 100 pound, 200 pound, and 300 pound, and finally the 60 pound rifled cannon were inexpensive, tough, and could be produced quickly and in quantity. They were not of the best design and the larger heavy rifles had a tendency to burst. The Parrott consisted of a long tube, and a cast iron piece with a wrought iron reinforcing band over the breech. The band was made by cooling a wedge shaped iron bar around a mandible, then upsetting the coil and pounding the joints together until welded solid. The tube was rotated horizontally on rollers with a stream of water sprayed inside to keep it cool. The band was slipped on, and because of the tube rotation, cooled and adhered itself uniformly to the breech. Even with the strength of the reinforced band around the Parrott's tube, the tube would very often rupture where the seam of the band ended.

(3) Three Inch Ordnance Rifle-The most important cannon both in number and general achievement was the three inch, wrought iron field rifle Model 1861 known and admired on both sides of the line as the Ordnance rifle or Ordnance gun. Col. William Allan, Chief of Ordnance, 2nd Corps, Army of Northern Virginia, remarked: "We especially valued the three inch rifles which became the favorite field pieces." Union Brigadier General George D. Ramsay, chief ordnance said: "The experience of wrought iron field guns is most favorable to their endurance and efficiency. They

Three inch ordance rifle

12 pound Grape shot.

30 pound Grape shot

Mosby's Cannon (BCWM)

(5)

6 lb. iron cannon

Left: 12 pound canister shot. Right: Hotchkiss three inch canister shot. (BCWM)

and was used during the Atlanta campaign. This gun has been spiked.

Spiking the gun-When an artillery crew felt that there was no other way to remove their gun from the field, or if the field piece was about ready to be overrun and captured by the enemy, the artillerists could spike the gun. This was done only as a last resort. Spiking the gun consisted of driving a jagged, hardened steel spike flush with the top of the tube, then the soft point was driven into the vent flush with the top of the tube, then the soft point clinched in the bore below by hitting it with the rammer. If the spikes were mislaid, heavy nails with the heads cut off would serve as a substitute.

Spiked vents could be cleared in several ways. If the spike was not clinched and the bore open, a one third charge packed with junk wads could be set off by laying a board down the bore with a groove on the under side filled with a length of quick match. This generally blew the spike out. If not, it might be drilled out if the barrel was iron or a new vent bored. If the weapon was bronze, sulfuric acid poured around the spike loosened it enough to be blown out by a charge.[1]

(4) One Pound cannon made by J. R. Anderson & Co. or better known as the Tredegar Iron Works in Richmond, Virginia- This particular cannon belonged to Gen. Mosby's Rangers.

(5) Six lb Iron Cannon with carriage made by the Bellona Foundry near Richmond, Virginia-This Confederate cannon has been spiked and redrilled. It was captured at the battle of Shiloh by the 37th Indiana Infantry.

Smoothbore Artillery Projectiles

Cannonballs were fired by prepared cloth cartridges containing a measured quantity of black powder. Solid shot was usually supplied on a wooden sabot, secured to it with tin straps. Spherical shells for smoothbore guns had straps and a sabot. It had a hole for the fuse to be inserted in the shell. Rifled guns also fired solid shot, called bolts, the most accurate projectiles. Field artillery fired four types of ammunition: Solid shot, common shell, spherical case, and canister. The older forms of chain shot and grape shot had been done away with by the time of the Civil War, although some rounds were used because government warehouses were full of these projectiles. Chain shot was two cannon balls attached to each end of a chain. Two cannons were loaded with one ball in each tube, the chain extending between them. The goal was to fire both guns at the same instant and for the balls to rotate with the chain staying in the middle. Originally used to destroy a ships' rigging sails, chain shot was a devastating when used against infantry. The problem with bar shot or chain shot is that both cannons must fire at exactly the same time for it to be successful.

12 Pound Grape Shot- Grape shot was also originally used by the Navy to de-rig enemy ships, but was later used by field

Left: 12 pound solid shot with wooden sabot. Top right: 12 pound Confederate solid shot. Bottom right: 32 pound solid shot. (BCWM)

cost less than steel and stand all the charge we want to impose on them."

Toward the end of the war, Hotchkiss shells and Schenkl projectiles were mainly used with Ordnance rifles, although some Dyer shells were also used. The diameter of the rifled bore was three inches, the bore length was 65 inches for an overall length of 73.3 inches, and the weight was 820 pounds. With a one pound charge at a 10 degree elevation it could fire up to 2,788 yards away. The three inch Ordnance rifle shown was made by the Phoenix Iron Company, Phoenixville, Pennsylvania. It was built in 1864,

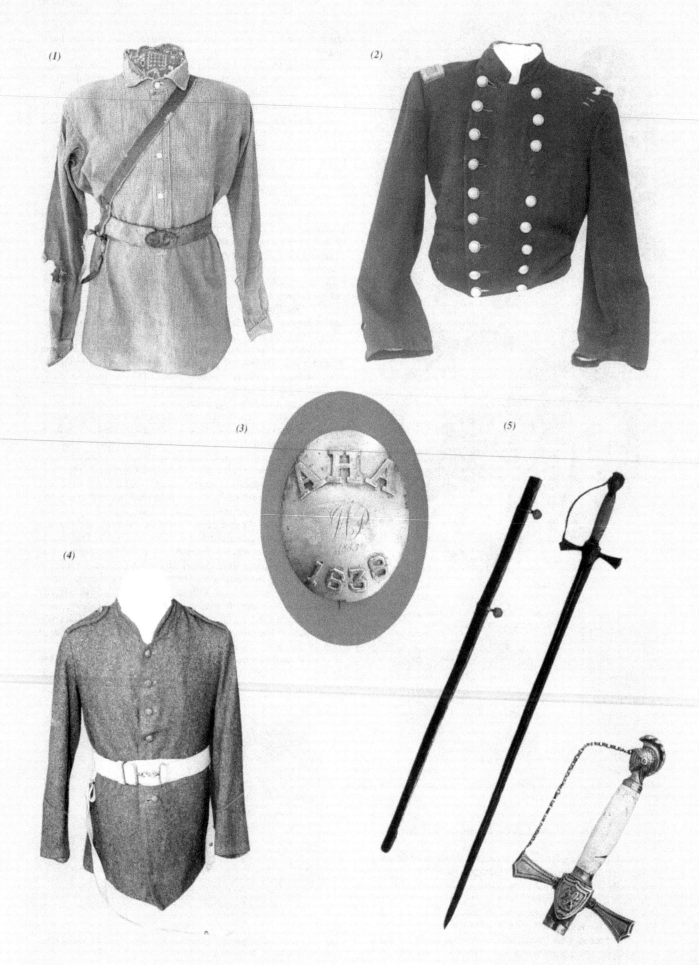

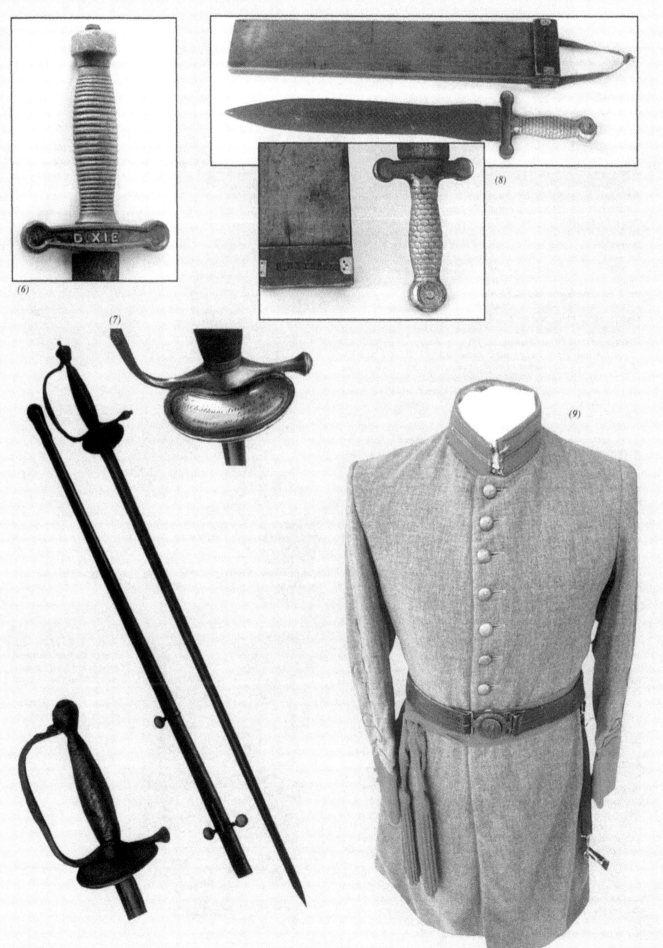

(6)

(7)

(8)

(9)

Photos on pages 110-111

(1) This is a hand loomed all cotton shirt with white milk glass buttons. Also shown is a white buffed belt, and red shoulder strap with sword hangers. The belt buckle is a U.S. belt buckle, but it has been turned upside down, which now reads "S.N." or Southern Nation. Southern Soldiers refused to wear any U.S. insignia and turned their buckles upside down and generally took off any U.S. markings. (BCWM)

(2) Colonel's double breasted non-regulation shell jacket. The epaulette on the left shoulder was lost when an artillery fragment pierced his left shoulder. The uniform has the regulation 18 buttons on the front, and the remaining shoulder strap with bullion eagle and red background denotes the artillery branch of service. (BCWM)

(3) Breast Plate belonging to William Pratt, Inscription reads: A.H.A., WP, 1855, 1638. William Pratt was born in Boston, Massachusetts on October 9, 1814. He was the son of Obed and Harriet Millet Pratt. He married Lucy Ann Galloway of Boston, on January 1, 1838. He spent his boyhood in Boston, graduating at the Mayhew School in 1828. He learned the watchmaker's trade, and in 1834 went into that business on his own account, and followed it during his life.

William Pratt first joined the Lafayette Guards, organized about 1827, which was disbanded at the time of the Broad Street riot in 1837. Afterward, for several years he was a member of the Boston City Greys. In 1850 he moved to Winchester, and assisted in forming the Winchester Light Guard, which was originally Company A, Seventh Regiment, Fourth Brigade, Second Division, Massachusetts Volunteer Militia. He was commissioned Third Lieutenant of this company on March 27, 1851, and served four years. The company disbanded on March 27, 1855 and March 30, 1855, Lieutenant Pratt was commissioned Captain of Company E, Fifth Regiment, Third Brigade, Second Division, Massachusetts Volunteer Militia. On May 28, 1855 William Pratt joined the Ancient and Honorable Artillery Company (A.H.A.) and was eleventh sergeant. He was discharged on August 4, 1856, but rejoined the company on May 21, 1860.

The Ancient and Honorable Artillery Company formed in 1637, seven years after Boston and four communities had formed. Although Boston had militia units, they were usually poorly trained. Some of the men in Boston petitioned the General Court to form a military group to train officers for the existing and future militia units. The petition was not granted because of religious and political reasons. But in 1638, the men reapplied and the military training group was allowed. It was given a generous grant, they were given pieces of land in New Hampshire and the western part of Massachusetts to train, were allowed to elect their own officers, and no other military activities could take place on their training days. Their charter was granted in March 1638.

During the Civil War, the Ancient and Honorable Artillery Company became a training organization and sent men to other military organizations. It never fought as a unit during the Civil War, but many members went on to be awarded the Medal of Honor, such as Major George Maynard, Corporal Lowell Maxham, Col. Francis Hasseltine, and Lt. George Harkins.

After the Civil War, William Pratt was eleventh sergeant in 1866, and fourth sergeant of artillery in 1880. He was a fireman, having been a member of both Hancock and Melville Engine Companies , also a member of William Parkman Lodge, St. Paul's Chapter, and Boston Commandery, Knights Templars. William Pratt died on January 13, 1897, and his funeral was attended by Boston Commandery, Knights Templars on Sunday January 17th.

The Ancient and Honorable Artillery company is still in existence and celebrated its 300th Anniversary in 1988.

Special thanks to John McCauley, Curator of Ancient and Honorable Artillery Company of Massachusetts, Boston, Massachusetts. (BCWM)

(4) This uniform belonged to Private Joseph Alexander, Co. E, 1st (Butler's) South Carolina Infantry. On April 12 and 13th, 1861 he was temporarily assigned to Beauregard's Battery, Fort Moultrie, Sullivan Island, and was present at the Battle of Fort Sumter. This artillery coat is made of a coarse hand loomed wool construction with red piping to denote artillery service. It has the 1850's period eagle buttons. The white buff belt with two piece snake belt buckle was smuggled into the Confederacy through the blockade in Charleston harbor. (BCWM)

(5) Col. Eschelman's Militia Staff Officer's sword has a straight double edged blade, and engraved brass scabbard. This sword features the Louisiana state seal in the cross guard. The handle is made of bone, and has the large brass knight's head pommel. This sword was issued to staff officer's and state militias, like the Washington Artillery which is one of the oldest organizations in Louisiana. (BCWM)

(6) This Confederate short sword with "Dixie" cast into the guard was made in London, England and was imported to the Confederacy through the Union blockade. (BCWM)

(7) Model 1833 Staff Officer's Presentation grade sword belonging to Henry K. Washburn, Chatham artillery. (BCWM)

(8) This Confederate manufactured short sword with wooden scabbard belonged to H. Reinbold. The blade is made from a large metal rasp. (BCWM)

(9) This Lieutenant's Artillery Confederate frock coat was custom made in Europe from the highest quality European wool. The pre-war eagle buttons feature the "A" on the breast of the eagle to denote artillery service. It also has the single strand gold braid to denote the rank of Lieutenant, which is embroidered from the wrist to the elbow. The two piece belt plate is from the 1850's period, and features the Kentucky state seal. (BCWM)

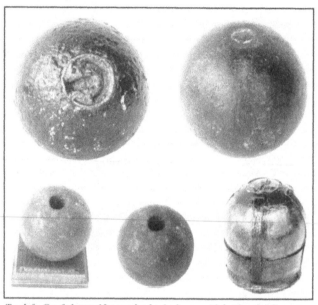

Top left: Confederate 12 pound spherical case with lead sealed Bormann time fuse. Top right: Confederate 6 pound spherical case with wooden fuse plug. Bottom left: Confederate 12 pound shell, with wooden fuse plug. Weight is 8.5 lb., and measurement 4.52 inches. Excavated at Munfordsville, Kentucky. Bottom center: 6 pound spherical shell with wood plug. Bottom left: U.S. 12 pound spherical shell with fuse and wooden sabot. (BCWM)

Left: U.S. 10 pounder Parrott bolt, which was dug at Dalton, Georgia. Weight is 11.5 lb., diameter 2.88 inches, length 8.5 inches.
Right: Parrott flat nose three inch projectile. (BCWM)

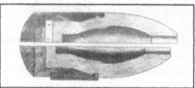

4-inch Hotchkiss Shell

artillery. You need very level ground in order for grape shot to work effectively. Grape shot had been discontinued for field use several years before the Civil War broke out and it was felt that canister could do a more efficient job. Grape shot normally consists of nine iron balls, top and bottom plates, two rings, and a bolt, all of iron, and a rope handle on top.

12 Pound Canister-A canister round consisted of iron top and bottom plates, over which were bent the ends of a cylinder formed from sheet tin. Inside were iron balls of calculated size for the caliber, arranged in four tiers, the interstices solidly packed with sawdust to prevent the balls from moving. Six pounder through 42 pounder guns had seven balls in each layer-one in the center surrounded by six. To leave room for the rivets of the handle, the center ball of the top tier was omitted giving a total of 27 balls per round. A wooden block or sabot was attached to the bottom of the canister. The sabot helped keep the round in the middle of the bore and also prevented the explosive gases from shooting out around

2.75 inch Whitworth bolt. Weight 12.75 lb., diameter 2.75 inches, length 8.875 inches. (BCWM)

Left: Solid three inch Hotchkiss shell with no fuse. (BCWM)
Right: 12 pounder James rifle "Bird Cage" projectile. This projectile would whistle when the air passed through the ribs. (BCWM)

Three inch Hotchkiss projectile. (BCWM)

the sides of the canister. Attached to the bottom of the sabot was the cloth bag that contained the propellant powder that set off the round. When the powder was ignited, the force of the explosion would disrupt the can and the shot would spray out of the muzzle of the cannon with murderous effect.

Canister rounds were the smoothbore cannon's most lethal load and probably killed more Civil War soldiers than all other types of artillery rounds combined. Canister was effective only at short ranges, 600 yards or less, acting like the blast from a giant sawed-off shotgun, the mass of slugs from the round would spread out and decimate anything downrange. When the enemy was within 150 yards, soldiers would load the guns with two or three rounds of canister and fire them all off at one time.[2]

Solid shot was used against masonry fortifications. Solid shot's effectiveness relied on a steady cannonade rather than the accuracy of individual rounds. It would not inflict major losses on entrenched infantry.

Shells were hollow spheres filled with powder, and were fired by most forms of ordnance to achieve the long range destruction of men and equipment. Shells used low grade black powder and exploded into small fragments.

Spherical case or Shrapnel was developed by Gen. Henry Shrapnel (1761-1842) of the British Army. It consisted of a thin walled shell loaded with small lead or iron balls, a small bursting charge and a time fuse. The Bormann time fuse was used the most to explode the shell at a calculated distance from the gun. The bursting charge was sufficient only to rupture the shell and release the balls, which continued along the trajectory with the momentum of the projectile. It was also called case shot. U.S. Regulations called for case shot to have 78, .58 caliber balls in a 12 pound round. Spherical case was not very useful against advancing troops because it was very difficult to figure the degrees and elevation needed to fire accurately at a stationary target, let alone a moving target. Precise timing was needed for the fuse, or the round would explode too far in front of, or too far behind the advancing troops.

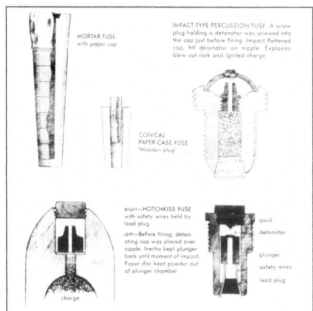

MORTAR FUSE with paper cap

IMPACT-TYPE PERCUSSION FUSE. A screw plug holding a detonator was screwed into the cap just before firing. Impact flattened cap, hit detonator on nipple. Explosion blew out cork and ignited charge

CONICAL PAPER-CASE FUSE Wooden plug

RIGHT---HOTCHKISS FUSE with safety wires held by lead plug
LEFT---Before firing, detonating cap was placed over nipple. Inertia kept plunger back until moment of impact. Paper disc kept powder out of plunger chamber

anvil
detonator
plunger
safety wires
lead plug

charge

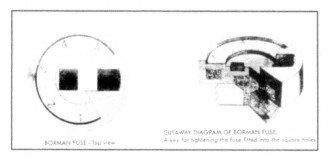

BORMAN FUSE-Top view

CUTAWAY DIAGRAM OF BORMAN FUSE. A key for tightening the fuse fitted into the square holes

Rifled Artillery Projectiles

Rifled projectiles generally took the name of their inventor and were made in numerous calibers and various forms including solid, case, shell, and canister. They differed mainly in methods of providing rotation to the projectile.

Parrott shells, or **bolts** as they were sometimes called, were of two types–the indented brass cup and a flat variety in which the brass was cast flush around the projectile base. They were made in all calibers from 2.9 to 10 inch. Bolts also fit all calibers and came in two flat nose varieties — one with a rounded groove, the other with a marked step to the flat surface. Some Parrott projectiles could fire incendiary materials. In this shell the interior was cast so that there were two separate compartments for the incendiary material. The top compartment of the shell held a small bursting charge. The bottom was packed with cotton through a hole in the base, then filled with incendiary composition and then the hole was closed with a copper washer and a bolt.

Hotchkiss projectiles were the most used type of field ammunition and various calibers up to 12 inch were made. It consisted of three parts- a cast iron body, and a cast iron cup, with a lead band in between. Discharge forced the cup forward squeezing the lead into the rifling. Pressure of the cup prevented slipping. Time fused shells and cases had longitudinal grooves, usually three, which permitted access of the discharge flame to the fuse. Grooves were normally absent on shot.

James projectiles. When the Civil War broke out, there were hundreds of old smoothbore cannons that were in government warehouses and also being used by militia groups. The Model 1841 was a smoothbore, but before and during the war a number of them were grooved by the North in what is known as the James System of rifling. Gen. Charles Tillinghast James was the inventor of this type of shell that would fit the now rifled cannons. He also invented a gun of his own, a 14 pounder. The Ames Manufacturing Company began to make James projectiles to fit the newly rifled smoothbores. The types of rounds manufactured varied from six through 42 pounder cannons, as well as 3.8 inch, 5.1 inch, 8 inch, and 12 inch rifled cannons. The Confederacy later rifled the 32 and 42 pounders. James projectiles usually are double the weight of similar caliber spheres. For example, a six pound shell for a six pounder weighs six pounds, but the James projectile for a rifled six pounder weighed 12 pounds. James projectiles came in shot, shell, and canister. The James projectile consisted of a cast iron

body shaped like a football with a cage of slanted iron ribs starting near the middle and extending beyond the lower end. The soft metal covering was composed of light tin plate.

Fuses

The Borman time fuses was a five second fuse made of lead and tin in equal parts and was considered to be the most reliable. The complete fuse was 1.65 inches in diameter and .45 inches thick. The fuse had time increments from one to four minutes on the top of the fuse. Beneath the time markings was a horizontal powder train in the shape of a horseshoe. Before firing the spherical case, the artillerists would cut through the thin metal at any mark and expose the black powder train to the flame of discharge. The black powder would burn at a uniform rate, and when it burned to the time set on the shell, it ignited a cylindrical powder magazine, or booster, in the center of the fuse, which flashed into the bursting charge through a small hole in a plug beneath the fuse. These plugs were made of brass or iron, and their function was to form a solid base for the fuse which might be driven into the shell by the pressure of air bearing down on the shell as it exited the tube at discharge. The major feature was the horseshoe train of black powder, which burned horizontally, eliminating the layer effect, which contributed to irregular performance in other time fuses.

Hotchkiss percussion fuse-It had a metallic base closed at the front by a flat screw cap with a small "V" shaped anvil on the inner side. The fulminate was affixed to the nipple on a lead plunger retained, prior to firing, by a thin wire anchored in a tapered lead safety plug which closed the base of the fuse like a cork. Setback at discharge sheared the wire and dropped the safety plug into the shell clearing a passage for the flame and leaving the plunger free to drive the cap into the anvil at impact.

Whitworth cannon-British import-it had a hexagonal barrel. The Confederates were quite fond of them, although they saw little use in the North. The weapon was made of steel, and both muzzle loaders and breech loaders were made. It was made in various calibers. The main calibers were the 12 pounder (2.75 inch), both breech and muzzle loading, and the 70 pounder (five inch). Most were purchased by the South, but one of the first batteries to arrive in America went North. This was a six piece battery of 2.75 inch breechloaders complete with carriages, ammunition, and machinery for making more projectiles. The 12 pounder could deliver a round 2,600 yards with a five degree elevation, 4,500 yards with a 10 degree elevation, 7,000 yards with a 20 degree elevation, and a 10,000 yards with a 35 degree elevation. The North didn't like the Whitworth because it was too sensitive, and the gun was prone to jamming.

How a cannon was fired

Field guns were operated by a gunner and seven artillery men. The gunner standing behind the trail gave the order to load. The #1 man would sponge the tube, the #6 & #7 men managed the limber, where they cut the fuses and handed shells to the #5 man, who carried them to the gun. He passed the round to the #2 man who inserted it into the barrel. When #1 had finished sponging out the tube, he then rammed the shell down the barrel, while the # 3 man held his thumb, which was covered with a thumbstall, over the vent hole as he stood to the right of the breech. He then lifted the breech and moved to the trail. The #5 man headed back to the limber to collect the next round. The Gunner said, "Pick and Prime." The #1 man & #2 man

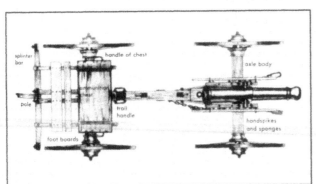

Whitworth cannon with limber chest. (BCWM)

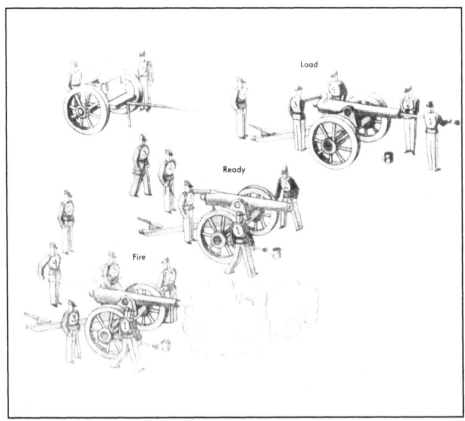

How a cannon was fired.

stepped aside from the muzzle as the # 3 man pricked open the cartridge, and the #4 man hooked a lanyard to the friction primer and inserted it in the vent. The #4 man then moved to the rear. When the command "Ready" was given, #1, # 2, and #3 men would stand clear of the wheels. When the command was given to "fire", the #4 man yanked the lanyard. To accelerate fire the # 5 & #7 men could alternate forming a human chain to pass ammo. Gunners preferred shooting from the crest of a hill, so they could protect the horses, limbers, and caissons. A good artillery crew could fire two rounds every minute.[3]

Friction Primers-They were used by the North and South on most cannon. The friction primer was simple and quick to use, yet extremely effective. It consisted of two small brass tubes, a serrated wire, friction composition, and musket powder. In use, the wire was bent upward, hooked to the lanyard and the long tube inserted into the vent. A steady, quick pull on the lanyard dragged the serrated wire across the friction composition igniting it and setting off the musket powder which flashed down the tube and vent to the main charge. It was a convenient and generally reliable method of ignition, and had the added advantage of giving little flash to betray the piece during night firing.[4]

Pendulum Hausse sight-Adopted from the Russians, it was a breech sight suspended to permit front and rear as well as lateral movement. This was accomplished by replacing the foot beneath the brass sight column with a bulb filled with lead and attaching it at a single point to a horizontal pin. This permitted the column to swing right or left. The pin extended into tiny journals. In use, the journals fitted a bracket bolted to the rear of the breech and permitted the column to swing back and forth in line with the axis of the bore. Consequently, with the column able to swing in four directions, the bulb centered it exactly vertical regardless of whether the trunnions were level, and allowed sighting without distortion. The sight was removed prior to firing. It was also made to fit a particular caliber of weapon.[5]

Limber Chest-A limber was used to carry different types of rounds for the cannon. When the cannon was being transported, the limber chest was attached to the cannon. The caisson was similar to a limber chest, except that it carried an extra wheel, implements, and rounds. The caisson shuttled back and forth between the cannon and the ammunition wagon. When the limber chest was running low on rounds, the artillerist would send the caisson back to retrieve more rounds. Each limber chest carried 50 rounds of ammo, 32 rounds for a 12 pound, 23 rounds for 24 pound howitzer. U.S. regulations stated that a six pound cannon carried 25 rounds of solid shot, 20 rounds of spherical case and five rounds of canister. A 12 pound carried 20 rounds of solid, eight spherical case, and three rounds of canister.

Washington Artillery-Composed of wealthy and prominent men of the city, the Washington Artillery of New Orleans was the most famous of the Confederate artillery organizations. According to Civil War author Jennings C. Wise, "At the out-

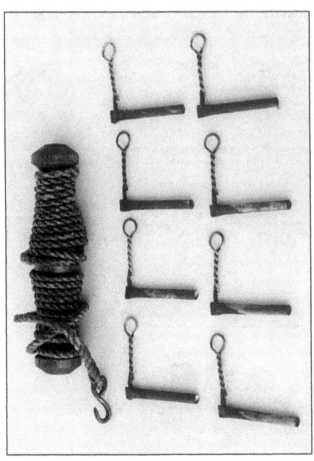

Friction primers with lanyard. (BCWM)

Lanyard and friction primer. (BCWM)

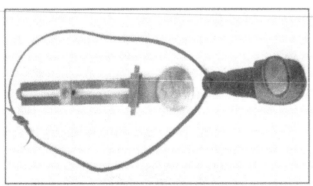

Pendulum Hausse with thumbstall. (BCWM)

break of the Civil War, there was not a finer organization of citizen soldiery in America." Organized in 1838, it had fought in the Mexican War as Company A of Persifor Smith's regiment. The unit was comprised of five companies that were ready to fight when the firing began in 1861. Much of its equipment for the Civil War, including six, six pounder guns and ammunition was obtained in the seizure of the Baton Rouge Arsenal on April 11, 1861.

Accepted into the Confederate army in May 1861, the first four companies went to Virginia immediately and took part in the first Battle of Manassas, where they were commanded by Col. James B. Walton. From that time on they served with the Army of Northern Virginia throughout all its major campaigns. The unit especially distinguished itself in the defense of Marye's Heights during the Fredericksburg and during the Chancellorville campaign. The Washington Artillery, in the East, was commanded successfully by Walton Benjamin F. Eschelman and William Miller Owen. Owen later wrote about his experiences with the unit in "A Hot Day On Marye's Heights."

The 5th Company, Washington Artillery Battalion, also referred to as Slocumb's Battery, participated in the battles of Shiloh, Perryville, Murfreesboro, Chickamagua, and Chattanooga, the Atlanta, and Tennessee Campaign's, and Spanish Fort. Their first commander was W. Irving Hodgeson, then Capt. Slocumb, and

then later Capt. Josef Charlron. The 5th Company was a mainstay of Anderson's/Adam's brigade of the Army of the Tennessee's 2nd Corps through the Spring of 1863. For the next nine months it was attached to Breckinridge's command and from February 1864 on was again in the Army of the Tennessee's 2nd and 1st Corps, largely in Cobb's Artillery Battalion. The Civil War Memoirs of Philip Dangerfield Stephenson, DD, edited by Nat Hughes are the exploits of the 5th Company of the Washington Artillery from the start of 1864.

The 6th company was disbanded in New Orleans shortly after being formed. After the war, members of the unit formed the "Washington Artillery Veterans Charitable & Benevolent Association." They held secret infantry drills, assembled weapons, and in 1870, as a protest against carpetbag rule, appeared with two miniature brass cannons to drive former Confederate General James Longstreet's Metropolitan Police off the streets of New Orleans. Later, the Washington Artillery fought in the war with Spain in 1898 and fought in both WW I and WW II. [6]

Dixie short sword- The word Dixie stems from the French word meaning 10(Dix), which was seen on the money of French immigrants in Lousiana. The song Dixie, which ironically was written by the son of an abolitionist, became the most popular song in the South. Short swords were used not only for decoration, but also as a defensive weapons by artillerymen who would hack at the horses legs if they were overrun by cavalry, in order to unseat the riders.

Henry K. Washburn

Chatham Artillery & the 22nd Georgia Heavy Artillery

The oldest and one of the best known of the military commands of Georgia is the Chatham Artillery. The artillery unit formed on April 16, 1751, although the battery also claims that it formed in 1746. The unit consisted of four independent companies of volunteer militia, three infantry, one mounted. On June 13,

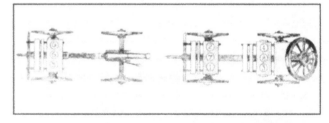

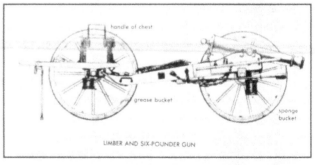

LIMBER AND SIX-POUNDER GUN

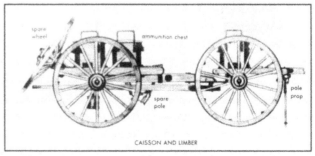

CAISSON AND LIMBER

TABLE OF FIRE
12-pdr. field gun, Napoleon

ELEVATION in Degrees	powder	Ball		Range	Time Of Flight in Seconds
0 30	2.5 lbs.	Sph. Case		300	1
1 0		shot.		575	1 3/4
1 30		"		633	2 1/2
2 0		"		730	3
3 0		"		1080	4 3/4
3 45		"		1135	5
0	2.0	Shell		300	0 3/4
0 30		"		425	1 1/4
1		"		616	1 3/4
1 30		"		700	2 1/4
2 0		"		787	2 3/4
2 30		"		925	3 1/2
3 0		"		1080	4

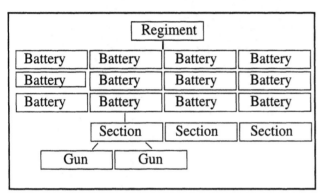

1751, the unit was put under the command of Captain Noble Jones in Savannah, Georgia. On April 2, 1757, it reformed as the 1st Regiment of Foot Militia, Division of Savannah, Col. Noble Jones commanding. On February 6, 1777, it was predesignated as the 1st (or Chatham County) Regiment of Militia to include the volunteer militia companies of the Savannah area. The Artillery Company was organized on May 1, 1786, and was assigned to the regiment; after about 1796, this unit was designated as the Chatham Artillery.

During the War of 1812, the Heavy Artillery Company and Chatham Artillery were in Federal service from October-November 23, 1812 at Fort Jackson, South Carolina, under Capt. William Bullock. The entire regiment was in Federal service from January 22-Feb. 23, 1815.

The Chatham Artillery was in state service at Picolata, Florida in 1836.

Their original pledge called more than military efforts from them, and their members added to the civic and business life of Savannah. Every year in January, the infantry and artillery units in Savannah would have competitions to win trophies of honor within their units. The units would perform feats of marksmanship and the artillery would show their expertise in cannonading. Pvt. Henry K. Washburn on January 8, 1847, competed for the sword given by the Chatham artillery for best ability in artillery marksmanship. Washburn won the sword for hitting a target dead on at 450 yards.

On January 20, 1852, the Independent Volunteer Battalion of Savannah was to include the units of: Chatham Artillery, Savannah Volunteer Guards, Republican Blues, Phoenix Riflemen, Irish Jasper Greens, German Volunteers, and De Kalb Riflemen. On May 17, 1856, the battalion was redesignated as the 1st Regiment, Georgia Volunteers. On January 2, 1861, the 1st Regiment was ordered to take Fort Pulaski in the Savannah Harbor. In May-July 1861 the regiment was mustered into Confederate service by companies. The

Chatham artillery detached from the regiment on September 28, 1861, and was commanded by Capt. Joseph Claghorn, and Capt. John Wheaton.

Henry K. Washburn entered Confederate Service and became a captain of the 22nd Battalion Georgia Heavy Artillery and was designated as their Quartermaster. The 22nd Battalion Georgia Heavy Artillery was at Camp Roberts, Chatham County, Georgia, near the Thunderbolt Battery, four miles below Savannah, and served here from May 1863 until October 1863. Washburn later became General and Staff Quartermaster for the Confederate service.

During the Civil War, the Chatham Artillery went on to fight at the Battles of Grimball's Landing, James Island, on July 16, 1863; Charleston Harbor on August through September, 1863; Olustee, Florida on February 20, 1864; the Carolina's Campaign from February through April 1865, and finally the Battle of Bentonville on March 19 - 21, 1865.

After the war, the Chatham Artillery could not have any weapons, so they became a social club. In 1872, the Chatham Artillery reorganized in all their glory in their grey uniforms, cocked hats, and gold lace. The Chatham Artillery were known for their famous Chatham Artillery punch which became popular all over the U.S.

In 1898, they joined the military and were designated as the Light Battery B, U.S.V., but they did not serve in the fighting in Cuba. In 1913, they were expanded into two batteries and a battalion headquarters. In 1917, the unit became the nucleus for the two light regiments of the 31st Division, the 116th and 117th Field Artillery.

In 1921, the Chatham Artillery became the Second Battalion Headquarters Battery and Combat train, 118th and 117th F.A. Battery A. and Battery C.

In 1942, the regiment was broken up and redesignated as Headquarters and Headquarters Battery and the 1st Battalion as the 118th Field Artillery Battalion. The 2nd Battalion as the 230th Field Artillery Battalion. In 1959, the 118th Artillery and 230th consolidated to form the 118th Artillery. In 1969, the unit was reorganized and redesignated and became part of the 48th Armored Division.

The Chatham artillery takes pride not only in its long service record, but in its civic leaders, governors, mayors, judges, and statesmen, who were the builders and policy makers of Savannah. [7]

Chatham Artillery Punch

New York Herald Tribune, circa 1930's. Information provided by Elizabeth Edgerton

"Originated with the Chatham Artillery, Savannah, Georgia, who served in that city for more than 100 years. It is delicious, seductive,and powerful. This is the punch that knocked out Admiral Schley when he visited Savannah in 1899 after the Spanish War. Adm.l Cervera's Spanish shells were harmless to the brave American admiral, but Artillery Punch scored a direct hit which put him out for two days."

For 100 people or Ten Admirals
1 1/2 gallons Catawba Wine
1 1/2 quarts Rye Whiskey
1/2 gallon St. Croix Rum
1/2 pint Benedictine
1 quart Gin
1 quart Brandy
1 1/2 gallons strong tea
2 1/2 pounds brown sugar
Juice 1 1/2 dozen oranges
Juice 1 1/2 dozen lemons

INFANTRY

Bayonets

At the beginning of the civil war the battlefield tactics that were accepted and taught were those of the Napoleonic Wars in Europe. In Napoleon's day, infantry warfare was based in a large part on the bayonet charge. The muskets of that era were accurate for little more than 100 yards; therefore, an attacking force could expect to reach that distance from an enemy's position in relative safety. That last 100 yards would be crossed quickly in a furious charge, with the attacker relying upon the bayonet to rout the enemy out of his position. In making the charge, the attacking force could expect to receive but one volley from the slowly loaded muskets of that day, and that one volley would not usually knock out enough attackers to deter them from their mission.

In the Civil War, however, the mass charge was often disastrous for attacking forces, as was seen at the Battle of Franklin, Tennessee. These charges all failed because firearms had improved between the wars of Napoleon and the Civil War. Rifling added to the musket and cannon barrels and the development of ammunition for these field weapons greatly increased their range and accuracy. Forces attacking across cleared areas were now easily within range at 400 yards or more, and by the time they fought their way across that added distance, too few men were left standing to complete the mission. Sadly, some Civil War generals never learned this lesson.

Though there were many mass

Colonel's uniform designed by Confederate General Simon Bolivar Buckner. This frock has the pleat style pattern in the front of the coat, large fold down collar with the three stars denoting colonel's rank. The balloon sleeves measure 11 inches width at the elbow. The buttons are standard 1850's eagle buttons. This frock coat is made of a woolen/ cotton blend and has a cotton lining. It is very light weight and comfortable. (BCWM)

Union Major's frock coat with Kentucky state seal buttons. (BCWM)

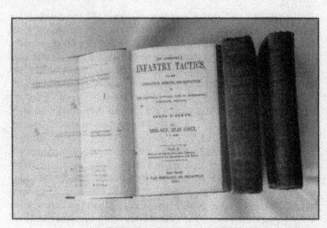

A set of Casey's infantry tactics. (BCWM)

charges in Civil War battles, there were few hand to hand bayonet fights, and those were usually of short duration. Although infantry soldiers were issued bayonets and received bayonet drill, they found the weapon more useful for other purposes. Bayonets made excellent tent stakes and candle holders, and when a charge petered out, they were useful for digging a hole to hide in. Bayonet wounds accounted for less than four percent of battlefield wounds; Artillery fire caused five percent; bullets, on the other hand, caused more than 90 percent of the wounds. [1]

Tactics Books

Early in the war most of the officers were using translations of French books. Winfield Scott wrote a tactics book in 1835. William Hardee, who later became a Confederate General, wrote a two volume manual in 1854 called Hardee's Rifle and Light Infantry Tactics, which was very popular on both sides. The book adopted tactics that fit in with the new rifled musket and stressed that men should march in two ranks, one behind the other. Skirmishers should move ahead of the main infantry body, and were divided into four man squads. He also devised a double quick step, in which the soldiers would move at a pace of 180 steps a minute. He stressed that target practice was needed and that units marching should move five miles an hour in good order. He also laid out how a rifle should be fired in 20 separate motions using only nine steps. Unfortunately, his book still had the old Napoleonic tactic where men stood upright in the open and fired by volley.

In 1862, Silas Casey wrote System of Infantry Tactics. This book came in three volumes, and was adopted by both sides. It covered individual, company, and battalion drill, and Casey expanded his book to include evolutions for brigade and division units, something that Hardee's didn't have. It was the first manual adapted and designed for the types of military organizations then in the service. Casey simplified his descriptions of maneuvers by using everyday language instead of the French words in some of the old

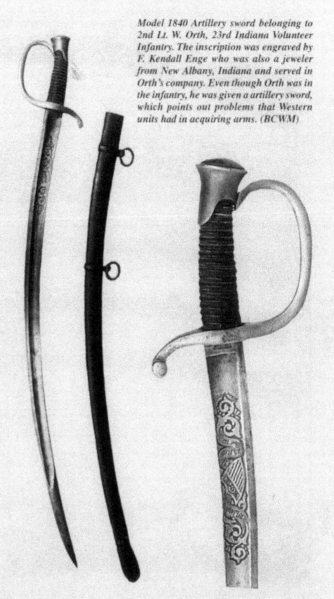

Model 1840 Artillery sword belonging to 2nd Lt. W. Orth, 23rd Indiana Volunteer Infantry. The inscription was engraved by F. Kendall Enge who was also a jeweler from New Albany, Indiana and served in Orth's company. Even though Orth was in the infantry, he was given a artillery sword, which points out problems that Western units had in acquiring arms. (BCWM)

First Lieutenant William Orth,
23rd Indiana, Company A.

The 23rd Indiana Regt. was organized and mustered into service for three years, at New Albany, Indiana on July 29, 1861, with William L. Sanderson as colonel. At the age of 24, William Orth, who had immigrated from Darmstadt, Germany, and settled in New Albany, was mustered into service there, on August 15, 1861. On July 27, 1861, William Orth was made a first lieutenant. Early in August the 23rd Indiana moved to St. Louis, and from there to Paducah, Kentucky. In the attack on Fort Henry the regiment was placed on gunboats, and several of the men of Company "B" were lost when the boilers of the gunboat Essex exploded. On the second day of Shiloh the 23rd was engaged as part of Gen. Lew Wallace's Division, losing one officer and 50 men in killed, wounded and missing. During the siege of Corinth it formed part of the reserve stationed at Pea Ridge. After the siege was lifted the regiment moved to Bolivar and remained there during the summer of 1862. In September it marched to Iuka and participated in the recapture of that place, after which it was ordered to proceed to Hatchie Bridge, but arrived too late to take part in the engagement there. In November it marched down the Mississippi Central Railroad, and after the capture of Holly Springs by Van Dorn, moved back to Memphis. On February 21, 1863, it proceeded down the river to participate in the Vicksburg campaign, landing at Lake Providence. The regiment was engaged in the various movements made by Grant's army prior to its march to the rear of Vicksburg, and on the 21st of April 21st, volunteers were accepted from the various companies and placed on board the steamer J. W. Cheesman to run by the Vicksburg batteries. In accomplishing this run, the boat was badly damaged, but no lives were lost.

During the march in the rear of Vicksburg the 23rd was engaged in the battle of Thompson's Hill, losing one officer, and nine men; and again in a skirmish on May 3rd, having one officer, and three men wounded. On May 12th it participated in the battle of Raymond, charging the enemy and capturing many prisoners, but losing one third of their number engaged. The 23rd was the first regiment to arrive to reinforce Hovey's Division at Champion Hill, soon after the battle opened, and lost four officers and 14 men wounded in the engagement. On May 24th it took part in the attack on, and capture of Jackson. The regiment was in the front line at the siege of Vicksburg, and lost, during the investment, five officers and 50 men killed and wounded. During the fall and most of the following winter, it was not actively engaged with the enemy, but on February 3, 1864, the 23rd marched through Mississippi with Sherman's great raiding army as far as Meridian, and aided in destroying the railroads on the line of march. During the winter the regiment re-enlisted at Hebron, Mississippi, and soon after its return from the Meridian raid, came home on veteran furlough. William Orth did not re-enlist and was mustered out on August 1, 1864. The 23rd Regt. became part of Sherman's army and was involved in the capture of Atlanta, and the March To The Sea Campaign. The 23rd Indiana Regiment also fought at the battle of Bentonville, and when Joe Johnston surrendered, it was sent to Louisville, Kentucky and was mustered out on July 23, 1865.

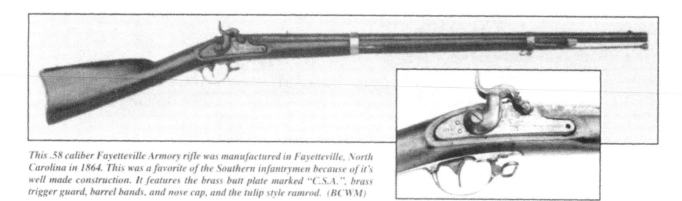

This .58 caliber Fayetteville Armory rifle was manufactured in Fayetteville, North Carolina in 1864. This was a favorite of the Southern infantrymen because of it's well made construction. It features the brass butt plate marked "C.S.A.", brass trigger guard, barrel bands, and nose cap, and the tulip style ramrod. (BCWM)

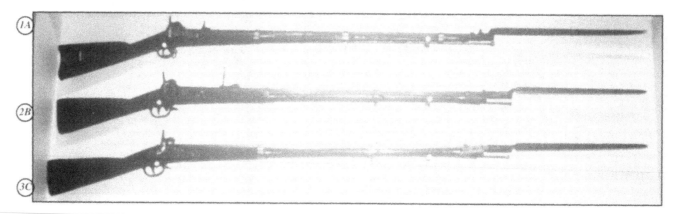

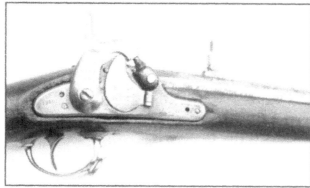

(1A)   Model 1855 U.S. Harper's Ferry (Maynard)

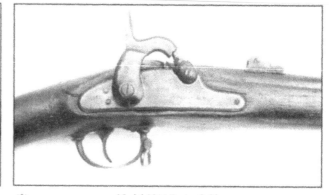

(2)   Model 1861 Springfield

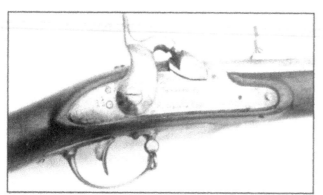

(3)   **Hughes-Phillips conversion**

weapon. At "Draw rammer," the soldier removed the ramrod from his rifle. The next order was "ram," and the soldier rammed the bullet down the barrel of the rifle. At the next order, "Prime," the soldier picked up the rifle, took out a percussion cap from his pouch and placed it on the nipple of the rifle. The next was "Shoulder arms," and the soldier brought the butt of his rifle up to his shoulder, and cocked the hammer into the first position. The next order was "Ready," and the soldier cocked the hammer all the way back. The last two orders were "Aim," "Fire." (2)

Rifles Used By Both Armies

When the Civil War began both the North and South had a vast array of weapons to chose from. They ranged from flintlock muskets and old double barrel shotguns to the newest innovations in field weapons, the Springfield Rifle and the British Enfield Rifle. One of the first uses of the new rifled weapons came during the Mexican War, when Jefferson Davis, soon to become President of the Confederate States of America, equipped his men with the Model 1841 US Rifle. It was .54 caliber, and weighed about nine pounds, and it would forever be called the Mississippi Rifle. It was accurate up to 500 yards, and used the new Minie bullet, which

manuals. His language was clear and concise, and he greatly simplified the steps in loading a muzzle loader. On the order "Load," the soldier properly positioned the butt of the rifle between his feet. The next order was "Handle cartridge" and the soldier took out the paper cartridge from his cartridge box, tore it open with his teeth and poured the black powder and bullet into the muzzle of the

had a hollow base that expanded to fill the grooves in the rifle barrel.

The Union began to import rifles from Belgium and Austria. They were .54 caliber to .70 caliber, bulky and heavy, and sometimes were of poor quality. The Confederacy had about 150,000 shoulder weapons, but almost all of them were antiques.

The government of each side adopted the U.S. Springfield and the British Enfield rifles. The 1861 Model was manufactured at the U.S. Armory in Springfield Massachusetts. Demand for the new rifle was so great that the U.S. government had to award private contracts to other companies to make them. They were:

Alfred Jenks and Sons-Bridesburg & Philadelphia, Pennsylvania

Eagle Manufacturing Co., Mansfield, Connecticut

"Manton" marked muskets made by the Eli Whitney factory-New Haven, Connecticut

William Mason-Taunton, Massachusetts

Millbury Contract-by A.H. Waters & Co.-Millbury, Massachusetts

James D. Mowry-Norwich, Connecticut

William Muir & Co.-Windsor Locks, Connecticut

Sarson & Roberts- New York-Subcontracted by Alfred Jenks & Sons

Norfolk Contract-Welch, Brown & Co.-Norfolk, Connecticut

Norwich Arms Co.-Norwich, Connecticut

Parker, Snow & Co.-Meridian, Connecticut

Providence Tool Co.-Providence, Rhode Island

E. Remington & Sons-Ilion, New York

E. Robinson-New York

Savage Revolving Firearms Co.-Middleton, Connecticut

C.D. Schubarth & Co.-Providence, Rhode Island

S. Norris & W.T. Clement-Springfield, Massachusetts

Trenton Contract-J.T. Hodge and A. M. Burton at the

Trenton Locomotive and Machine Works-Trenton, New Jersey

Union Arms Co.-New York City

German Contract- Suhl, Germany

Watertown Contract-by Charles B. Hoard- Watertown, New York

Whitney Contracts (6 various markings)-Eli Whitney Factory-New Haven, Connecticut

Windsor Locks Contract-believed made by either Dinslow & Chase or William Muir & Co., both of Windsor Locks, Connecticut

Special Contract 1861 musket-Amoskeag Mfg. Co., Manchester, New Hampshire Colt Firearms Co.-Hartford, Conn.-Lamson, Goodnow & Yale Co.-Windsor, Vermont-E.G. Lamson & Co.-Windsor, Connecticut

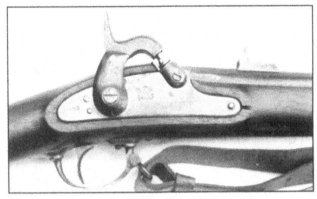

(1)   *Model 1863 U.S. Trenton*

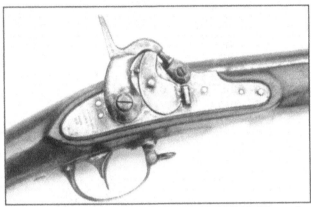

(2B)   *Remington conversion rifle & bayonet Model 1816. (Maynard)*

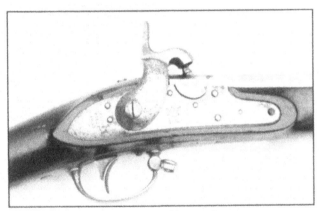

(3C)   *Model 1816 smoothbore musket.*

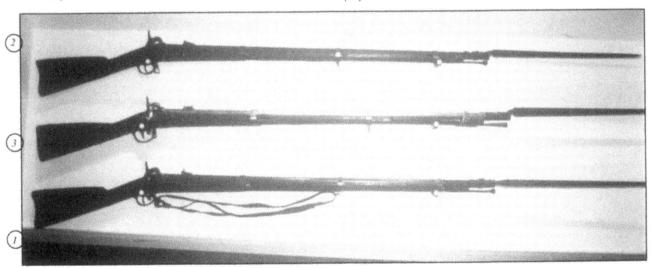

Top: Period engineers transit , type used at Vicksburg. (BCWM)
Left:Engineers Surveyors Tangent-Model 1840's period tangent with 1860 modifications added, manufactured by Henry Ware, Cincinnati, Ohio. Union engineering corps used transients extensively in Vicksburg trying to tunnel under Confederate fortifications to slip into the city. At one point, the Union engineers tried to blow a hole into the fortifications. (BCWM)

The 1863 muskets type I were all made at the U.S. Armory in Springfield, Mass. There were no contracts. The 1863, Type II, were made at Springfield and by J.P. Linsey-New York. The 1863 Remington "Zouave" rifle was made at Ilion, New York.

There were 1.5 million 1861 and 1863 rifles made during the Civil War. The Springfield is .58 Caliber, has three barrel bands, weighs nine pounds, and is four feet, eight inches long, and has a 40 inch long steel barrel. It took 60 grains of black powder to fire its conical Minie ball. A trained soldier could fire off 10 shots in five minutes. The Springfield could also penetrate through 11 inches of pine board at 100 yards.

The Enfield was one pound lighter than the Springfield and two inches shorter. It could also take the Springfield's .58 caliber bullet in its .57 inch bore. The British Enfield became the Confederate weapon of choice during the Civil War. The Confederacy bought over 120,000 of these weapons. The Union bought about 500,000 them. The Enfield was accurate up to 1,000 yards.

In 1863, the Union government recognized 79 different models of shoulder arms, 23 models of carbines, and 19 different pistols and revolvers. The Confederacy recognized every weapon under the sun, which made life difficult for the ordnance sergeant that had to order the bullets to fit the weapons. Late in 1862, the Army of the Tennessee captured 27,500 mixed rifles and muskets. Some men were carrying shotguns and old British Tower Muskets left from the War of 1812. In the Confederate Army of

the Tennessee, during August 1863, 45% of the men carried Enfields and captured Springfields. Another seven percent carried .54 caliber Mississippi Rifles and other models, 30% of the army carried the old Model 1817 and later .69 caliber smoothbores, 10% had .52 caliber and .53 caliber Hall Rifles, and three percent carried .70 caliber Belgian rifles.

The Confederacy also manufactured their version of the popular Yankee rifles. When the war broke out the South didn't have even one pistol factory, but within one year, the South had set up their industries, public and private, and started to turn out weapons similar to the Yankees, and also converted the older smoothbores into rifled muskets. They even started to make the carbines, breechloaders, and pistols that were so popular in the North. These weapons were equal to, or sometimes better, than their counterparts. This was a herculean task considering the South was short of steel and very often had to make their weapons from brass church bells and candlesticks.

The Confederate soldier who carried an old smoothbore weapon quickly discovered that his optimum load was what was called "buck and ball." The soldier loaded three smaller buckshot wadded behind the full sized ball. This was done because the smoothbores were erratic and inaccurate at long ranges, and this loading procedure increased the odds that at least one round might hit the enemy, and at close range it would prove to be devastating.

Because of the wide variety of weapons used by the Confederates, many soldiers began to collect bullet molds or made bullet molds of their own from thimbles, and did not have to rely on the ordnance sergeant to replenish their rounds. [3]

Artifacts

(1) 1863 U.S. Trenton Contract, Model 1861-A refinement of the Springfield Musket, Model 1861, the .58 caliber Model 1863 retained the fundamental features of the original but substituted the modified barrel bands, simplified bolster (percussion chamber), redesigned hammer, and streamlined ramrod of the Special Model 1861.

(2) U.S. 1861 Springfield Musket with Bayonet. It was the most widely used shoulder arm during the Civil War and saw more action from 1862 through 1865 than any other Federal arm. Over 700,000 of these rifles were made by the Springfield factory and with the government contracts about 1.5 million guns were made. [4]

(3) Hughes-Phillips Conversion Musket. This model 1816, .69 caliber smoothbore musket was rifled and bored by Hughes-Phillips. After rifling, a long range sight was affixed to the barrel. This was commonly done to the old smoothbore muskets that were lying around in government warehouses.

(1A) Model 1855 U.S. Harper's Ferry Musket with Bayonet, .58 caliber. The U.S. Arsenal in Harper's Ferry, Virginia first produced the Harper's Ferry rifle, or Mississippi rifle, and produced about 25,296 rifles between 1846-55. It was the first U.S. Army Standard issue rifle small arm using percussion caps. In the butt of the rifle was a space that could carry an extra nipple and caps. This rifle also used the Maynard Tape Priming System. As a child you may have played with a cap gun. The Maynard was based on this principle of a paper roll with black powder. The major problem with the Maynard Priming system was that when the paper would get wet the gun would not discharge.

(2B) Remington Conversion Rifle. This model 1816 smoothbore musket was rifled and fitted with a long range sight by the Remington Rifle Company. It also had a new lock and plate, and used the unique Maynard Tape Priming System.

(3C) Model 1816 Smoothbore Musket. This musket was converted from flintlock to percussion, was not rifled, and it had no long range sight. The type of round fired from this weapon was the previously mentioned "Buck and Ball."

How Armies were Organized

The following paragraphs will explain how the typical infantry units were made up. Please keep in mind that up to 50% of a company could be missing because of disease or battlefield losses.

Company

The basic unit is the company, commanded by a captain.

100 men=2 platoons=4 sections=8 squads

A company has the following officers(commissioned and non-commissioned): Captain(1), 1st Lieutenant(1), 2nd Lieutenant(1), 1st Sergeant(1), Sergeant(4), and Corporals(8).

When the company was divided into platoons, the captain commanded one and the 1st Lieutenant the other. There was a Sergeant for each section, and a Corporal for each squad. The 1st Sergeant "ran" the whole company.

Battalion and Regiment

Battalions and Regiments were formed by adding companies together. In the volunteers(Union and Confederate), 10 companies would be organized together into a regiment, commanded by a Colonel. A regiment has the following staff(one of each): Colonel, Lt. Colonel, Major, Adjutant (1st Lt.), Surgeon (Major); Assistant Surgeon (Captain), Quartermaster (Lieutenant), Commissary (Lieutenant, Sergeant-Major, Quartermaster Sergeant.

There were also volunteer organizations containing less than

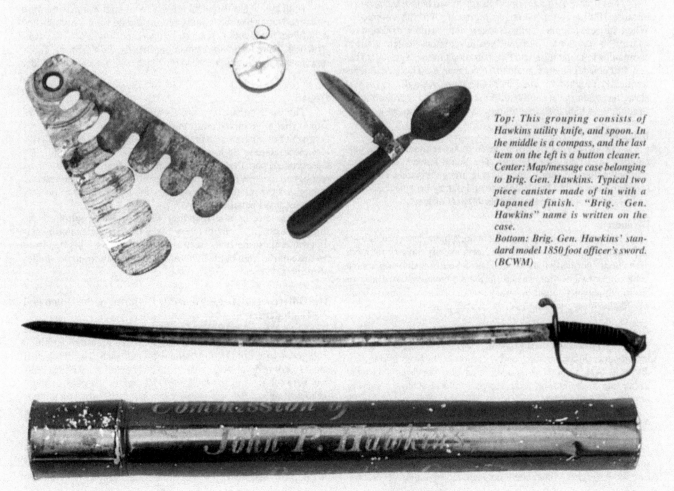

Top: This grouping consists of Hawkins utility knife, and spoon. In the middle is a compass, and the last item on the left is a button cleaner.
Center: Map/message case belonging to Brig. Gen. Hawkins. Typical two piece canister made of tin with a Japaned finish. "Brig. Gen. Hawkins" name is written on the case.
Bottom: Brig. Gen. Hawkins' standard model 1850 foot officer's sword. (BCWM)

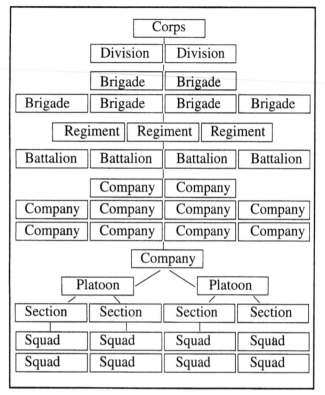

the North, and usually by full generals in the South. Corps and armies usually had some artillery and cavalry attached. Each army would also have a varying number of staff officers.

To summarize, the nominal strength and commanding officers were:

Unit	Men	Commander	Example Name
Company	100	Captain	Co. A
Regiment	1000	Colonel	5th N.Y. Infantry
Brigade	4000	Brigadier General	3rd Brigade(US)**
Division	12000	Major General	Cleburne's Division(CS)**
Corps	36000	Major General*	III Corps(US)**
Army		Major General+	Army of Tennessee(CS)++

* or Lt. General in the South

+ or General in the South

** Numerical designation was used in the North, The Commander's name was typically used in the South, e.g. Forrest's Corps.

++ The South mainly used the name of the area or state where the army operated. Rivers were used primarily as names in the North, e.g. Army of the Cumberland.

Sharpshooters

Both sides raised special sharpshooters units. The Confederate units tended to be independent companies, but the Union raised two sharpshooter regiments (Berdan's 1st and 2nd US Sharpshooters). These regiments were organized as infantry. Usually they were assigned to skirmish duty, or they would be allowed to roam around the battlefield to find good positions from which to shoot at enemy officers.

Engineers

Both sides raised special regiments of engineers. They were organized much like the infantry regiments and were accomplished in building forts, entrenchments, bridges, and similar military construction. They were combatants but usually didn't do any fighting, instead continuing to work on construction even when under fire.

Legion

The Confederacy organized a number of units known as legions. They were mixed arms units, usually containing six to eight companies of infantry, two to three of cavalry, and a couple of artillery pieces. Generally, as soon as they reached the battlefield, they were broken apart, the infantry forming a battalion, the cavalry being reassigned to some other unit, and the artillery joining the reserve. Sometimes the infantry retained the name legion, more frequently it was renamed battalion.

Please keep in mind that there were always exceptions to the rule. For example, colonels very often lead brigades and brigadier generals sometimes were leading divisions. This occurred because of the high battlefield losses, especially for lower grades of officers. [5]

The Differences Between Generals Uniforms of the Union and the Confederacy

U.S. Army regulations during the Civil War called for the general officer's uniform to include a double breasted dark blue frock coat with gold buttons, epaulets, and sash. The frock coat had a standing collar and a skirt front and back that extended halfway between the hip and the knee. The rank of the general could be identified by the arrangement of the double row of buttons down the front. A brigadier general's buttons were arranged in four groups of two and a major general's in three groups of three. For field duty, generals usually wore the looser fitting sack coat. The button arrangements remained the same on the sack coat, but the sash and epaulets were generally not worn. Rank was denoted on gilt edged shoulder straps: one star for a brigadier general, two

10 companies: if they contained from four to eight companies, they were called battalions, and usually were commanded by a Major or Lieutenant Colonel.

The (Union) Regular regiments organized before the war (1st through 10th) were 10 company regiments like the volunteers. When the new Regular regiments were authorized, a different organization was used. The new Regular regiment contained eight companies to a battalion and two battalions to the regiment. This new Regular regiment contained 16 companies. These regiments frequently fought as battalions rather than as single regiments. However, often the second battalion could not be recruited up to strength, in which case they fought as a single regiment.

Brigade

A brigade is formed from three to six regiments and commanded by a Brigadier General. The South tended to use more regiments than the North, thus having bigger brigades. At times, some artillery would be attached to an infantry brigade. Each brigade would have a varying number of staff officers.

Division

A division is commanded by a major general and is composed of from two to six brigades. In the North usually three or four, but in the South normally four to six. Thus, a Southern division tended to be almost twice as large as its Northern counterpart. Artillery, or less often, cavalry might be attached to a division. Each division would also have a varying number of staff officers.

Corps

A corps is commanded by a major general (Union) or a lieutenant general(Confederate) and is comprised of from two to four divisions. Again, the North tended to have two or three, while the South had three or four. Each Corps would also have a varying number of staff officers.

Armies

Corps within a geographic department were aggregated into armies. The number of corps in an army could vary considerably: sometimes an army would contain only one corps and other times as many as eight. Armies were commanded by major generals in

Ballot Box

used for electing officers in volunteer companies, and it was also used to select men for guard duty. Every soldier had to do guard duty, and to keep it fair, the ballot box was used. A marble was tipped forward into the small cup, if you got a white marble you didn't have guard duty, if you got the black marble you had guard duty.

Brig. Gen. John P. Hawkins- John Parker Hawkins was born in Indianapolis, Indiana on September 29, 1830. For 42 years, Hawkins held positions in the Quartermaster and Commissary departments. After graduating 40th in the 43 man West point class of 1852, he waited almost two years to be promoted from Brevet 2nd Lieutenant in the 6th Infantry to full 2nd Lieutenant in the 2nd Infantry. From 1858 to 1861 he served as Regimental Quartermaster in the Northwest as a 1st Lieutenant.

At the beginning of the war, Hawkins joined the army's Commissary Department as a captain and served in several posts throughout Missouri as Assistant Inspecting, and then Chief Commissary.

While serving as Chief Commissary of the Army of the Tennessee in 1863, Hawkins fell ill and missed three months service. On his return to duty he was transferred to Louisiana, placed in command of the District of Northeastern Louisiana and a black brigade, and promoted to Brigadier General of Volunteers on April 13, 1863. In February 1864, Hawkins joined the Federal garrison near Vicksburg, Mississippi, as the commander of an all black division, that he led in the siege and capture of Mobile in March 1865. He attained the brevet of major general for "gallant and meritorious service" during the siege, and the ranks of brigadier general and major general in the Regular Army and major general of volunteers.

After the war, Hawkins joined the Subsistence Department as a captain in the Regular Army and served for 28 years until he retired in 1894 as Commissary General of Subsistence. He retired to Indianapolis, where he died on February 7, 1914. [7]

Capt. Isaac S. Dains
50th Regiment Indiana Volunteer Infantry

At the age of 30, Isaac Dains entered the Union Infantry on August 28, 1861, in Monroe County, Indiana and was mustered into service on December 31, 1861, at Camp Morton, Indiana. He was commissioned captain of Company D, 50th Indiana Volunteer Infantry. The 50th Indiana was organized at Seymour September 12, 1861, with Cyrus L. Dunham as Colonel. On October 25th it left Seymour and marched through Jackson, Lawrence, Washington, Orange and Floyd counties to New Albany, stopping at several places on the route to enlist recruits. Leaving New Albany on December 25th for Kentucky, it marched to Bardstown, where it went into a camp of instruction. From there it proceeded to Bowling Green and after the occupation of Nashville the regiment was distributed along the line of the Louisville and Nashville Railroad, remaining on that duty until September 1862. While on this duty, a detachment of 20 men under the command of Capt. Atkinson were attacked while in a stockade near Edgefield Junction, on August 20th by 1,000 of John Hunt Morgan's cavalry. The Rebels were repulsed three times by the gallant little band and finally, after three hours fighting were driven from the field, leaving behind the dead bodies of Morgan's Adjutant and seven privates. Eighteen others were wounded. On March 13, 1862, Dains resigned his commission, but was recommissioned on April 1, 1862.

In September the regiment moved to the relief of Munfordsville and was surrendered with the forces at that place to Gen. Bragg on September 14th. On being paroled, the regiment proceeded to Indianapolis, where it remained in parole camp until exchanged. On November 1st it left for the field, arriving at Jackson, Tennessee, on November 10th, where it was attached to Gen. Jere Sullivan's Division, of the 16th Corps. On December 31st, it engaged the enemy under Gen. Forrest during the whole day at

for a major general, and three for a lieutenant general. The highest rank of all, lieutenant general commanding the army, wore a three star shoulder strap with the middle star larger than the other two. On full dress occasions, generals would replace the shoulder straps with gold fringed shoulder epaulettes. General officers wore varied types of hats but the most popular were slouch hats, kepis, and forage caps. Regulations also called for generals to wear plain dark blue trousers and Jefferson boots.

In contrast, Confederate officers were expected to provide their own uniforms, and while they were certainly better dressed than most of the enlisted men, their clothing was equally nonuniform. Colors for Confederate uniforms could vary from butternut to gray, and brown. Simon Bolivar Buckner even invented his own style of uniform, although never adopted by the Confederate military, it was brown in color and had pleats and large sleeves on the coat. Officers in the Confederate military service could wear tunics, frock coats, shell jackets, and sometimes civilian coats. The uniforms usually had standing collars and were double breasted, with two rows of seven buttons down the front. Generals could be distinguished from other officers by the eagle buttons, which were distinctively spaced in pairs. The regulations made no distinction among different grades of generals, but some major generals adopted the federal custom of spacing their buttons in groups of three. The rank for general was found on the collar; for all grades, it consisted of three stars encircled by a wreath. Cuffs, collars, edging, and sash of a buff color also denoted the rank of general, although lower ranking officers wore color of the unit they belonged to on their collars, blue denoting infantry, red for artillery, and yellow for cavalry. Officers gold braiding on their sleeves were in the configuration of the "Austrian knot." Generals uniforms had four strands of the braiding; lesser ranks had fewer strands. Dark blue trousers trimmed in buff were standard for Confederate generals, although there were variations. Lower ranking officers sometimes wore light blue, grey, and butternut with a colored stripe going down the trousers, denoting their branch of service. Soldiers in all ranks wore a variety of hats, with no particular distinction for generals, except possibly the four star stranded gold braid on the top of kepis. [6]

Infantry Artifacts

Ballot Box (The box contained black marbles and white marbles. The ballot box has a long history, and it was originally used by the Masons during elections. During the Civil War it was

Oval framed, hand colored, Cartes De Vista of Capt. Dains. This photo was taken in Indianapolis, Indiana, the home state of Capt. Dains.

Capt. Dains Federal regulation single breasted infantry frock coat. Buttons are the regulation eagle with "I" and the shield with the "superior quality" back mark. The belt and keeper are the Model 1851 rectangular cast brass eagle sword plate and belt. Also shown is the regulation burgundy colored sabre sash.
At left: Capt. Dains Presentation sword. (BCWM)

Parker's Crossroads, Tennessee, capturing 500 prisoners and seven pieces of artillery. During the Winter of 1863, the regiment remained in the vicinity of Jackson, and the following spring it moved to Collierville, and then to Memphis.

From Memphis the 50th was transferred to Arkansas, engaging the enemy at Little Rock. Moving from Little Rock on September 10th, 1863, to Lewisburg, Arkansas, it remained there on garrison duty until May 17, 1864. On March 2, 1864, Capt. Dains and 350 men of the regiment re-enlisted as veterans.

Joining Steele's command the regiment marched with it on the Camden expedition, engaging in the following battles: Terre Noir, April 2nd; Prairie Leon, April 10th; Red Mound, April 17th; Camden, April 17th, and Saline River April 30th; returning from

Regimental flag of 16th Kentucky. Note 35 stars.

Standard regimental regulation drum from the 16th Kentucky Infantry. (BCWM)

this expedition to Little Rock on May 5th, the regiment remained there until the latter part of July. Capt. Isaac Dains came down with an illness and died at Little Rock, Arkansas on July 18, 1864.

The regiment went on to march with Gen. Carr's expedition to the Saline River in January 1865 and was involved in the siege of Spanish Fort from March 27th to April 8, 1865, and was present at the capture of Mobile on the 10th of April. The 50th regiment was later consolidated with the 52nd regiment, and was finally mustered out of service on September 10, 1865 in Montgomery, Alabama. [8]

16th Kentucky Union Regimental Flag and drum

The 16th Kentucky was recruited and organized in the Fall of 1861 by Col. Charles A. Marshall, at Camp Kenton, Mason County, Kentucky. Col. Marshall was the son of Capt. Thomas Marshall, who was a brother of Chief Justice John Marshall. The men that formed the unit came from Mason, Fleming, Bracken, Lewis, and Whitley counties, Kentucky. The 16th Kentucky accompanied Gen. Nelson into eastern Kentucky, and fought in the battle of Ivy Mountain., November 8, 1861. Confederate General John S. Williams was defeated at this battle, and fell back into Virginia. The regiment was finally mustered into service on January 27, 1862. In May 1862, Col. Marshall became ill and was replaced by Col. J. W. Craddock. In December and January, the regiment chased Confederate General John Hunt Morgan through Springfield, Lebanon, Campbellsville, and Columbia, Kentucky. The regiment returned to Lebanon and protected the city from Confederate raids until the Spring of 1863. Col. Craddock died in Louisville and was replaced by Col. J. W. Gault of Mason County, on June 2, 1863. In August the regiment was in Col. O. H. Moore's brigade, 23rd Corps, and it participated in Gen. Ambrose Burnside's expedition into east Tennessee. In October it met Confederate General

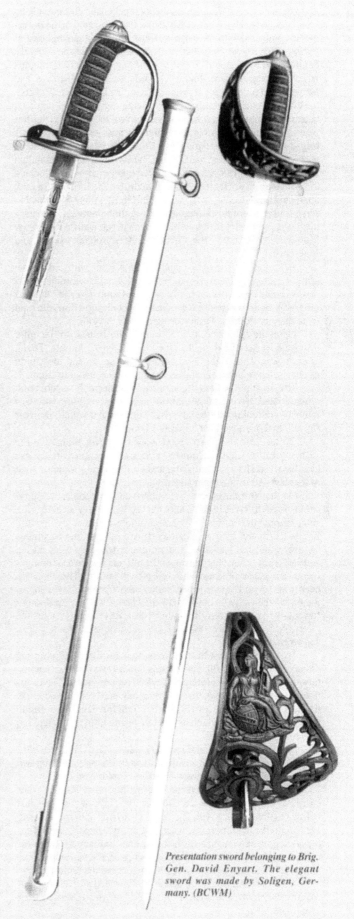

Presentation sword belonging to Brig. Gen. David Enyart. The elegant sword was made by Soligen, Germany. (BCWM)

Longstreet's force. The 16th Kentucky repelled an attack made by Confederate cavalry while at Kingston. It participated in the movements connected with the siege on Knoxville, and then on December 29, 1863, it was engaged in a severe battle in which the Federals, commanded by General's Elliot, and Strugis, successfully fought a large Confederate force under Generals Martin, Armstrong, and Morgan, and pursued them from the field. On December 27, 1863, the 16th Kentucky re-enlisted as a veteran regiment and was sent back into Kentucky, and in 1864 was moved to Georgia to participate in Sherman's Georgia Campaign. It was assigned to Riley's brigade (1st) Cox's Division, 23rd Corps. On May 14th, the 16th participated in the Battle of Resaca, where Lt. Laurie was killed and Capt. Pumpelly was wounded. Two other men were killed and 27 wounded. Col. Gault became ill and Lt. Col. J. S. White took command until the end of the war. The 16th Kentucky continued to serve under Sherman throughout his entire campaign. The regiment was engaged at Cartersville, Etowah River, Dallas, Kennesaw Mountain, crossing of the Chattahoochee, around Atlanta, and Jonesboro.

After the capture of Atlanta, the 16th went with Sherman's army in pursuit of Gen. Hood. When the pursuit was abandoned and Sherman began his March To The Sea Campaign, the 16th was sent with the troops under Gen. George Thomas to Nashville, and from there to Pulsaki, Tennessee under Gen. Schofield.

Upon the approach of Hood's army, the 16th, with the other troops under Schofield, made a forced march to Columbia. There, in the midst of the fight between the Confederate and the Union cavalry's, the infantry skirmishers soon put the enemy to flight.

The night of the 25th the regiment was hurriedly ordered out, crossed Duck River and encamped on high ground opposite Colombia, overlooking a tree covered valley around which the river flowed, making an almost horseshoe bend.

On the 26th its men were at work on fortifications. On the 27th several of Capt. Hammer's companies occupied the works near the river. Heavy skirmishing and artillery firing went on most of the day, part of the night and all of the 28th.

On the 29th the enemy were observed descending the opposite bank of the river in force and, backed by a heavy artillery fire, soon charged the advanced Federal positions occupied by the 16th Ky. and 12th Ky. Infantry Regiments. A portion of the regiments gave way and fell back on the main line where they were rallied and reformed. They charged down the hill and reinforced the regiments that had stayed, and who were slowly retiring. They kept the enemy at bay and reached some fallen timber where they were rejoined by the rallied troops. Here the enemy was checked and a furious battle raged until the rebels were driven back under the cover of the river bank, leaving the ground stewn with their dead and wounded.

This battle, which had the important result of delaying the crossing of Hood's artillery and trains, has had less mention in history than is due. The holding of Duck River prevented Hood's artillery and trains from passing that entire day, and until three o'clock the next morning, and caused Hood to fight the battle of Franklin with but two batteries which he had taken with him on his flanking movement to Spring Hill.

Late in the afternoon, Gen. Cox directed Gen. Riley to withdraw his command at dark and move toward Franklin, leaving two regiments to keep the enemy in check until midnight.

After an all night march and passing the enemy in plain view, en route, they camped in the fields on the right of the road just before reaching Spring Hill. The regiment arrived at Franklin about 11:30 a.m. the next morning, worn and weary. Here the 16th Kentucky Regiment was placed on the reserve line about 100 yards behind the main line, with its right resting on the Columbia pike and its left reaching a point immediately behind the cotton gin.

The Confederate army appeared on Winstead's Hill about half past three o'clock. The soldiers of the Federal army could see their every movement.

About half a mile in front of the main line, two brigades of Wagner's division had been stationed and as the Confederates approached, these brigades commenced firing, instead of withdrawing as they should have. Their firing checked the advance immediately in their front, but the enemy was passing each flank, and there was nothing to do but to rush back to their main line, rapidly pursued by the Confederates. As they crowded over the breastworks with the enemy close behind, the men in the works became demoralized to some extent and a portion of the line, for a moment, was undefended. Capt. M. C. Hutchins, of the 16th Kentucky was on Gen. Riley's staff, and though thrown down while attempting to rally the breaking men, regained his feet and continued his work. The reserves, consisting of the 12th and 16th Kentucky, and the 8th Tennessee, saw the danger, and promptly charged forward and engaged in a hand to hand fight at the works. The rally of the men who had given way strengthened the line and though the pressure was tremendous the position was held, and within an hour the repulse was complete. The 16th Kentucky suffered severely in this battle, its actual loss in killed, wounded and missing was 83 men. Col. White was severely wounded in the face, but with a bloody bandage about his head, continued with his command.

Among the killed were Capt. Henry Palmer, Company H, and Lt. Joseph Heiser, Company C. Lt. Brown and Lt. Courtney were wounded. Capt. Jacob Miller's company led the regiment out of Franklin that night and they arrived at Nashville the next morning

On the 15th and 16th days of December, the 16th Kentucky attached to the 23rd Corps, was engaged in the great battle of Nashville, and moved upon and attacked the left flank of Hood's army. After the battle it joined in the pursuit through Franklin and Columbia and then marched to Clifton on the Tennessee River.

The 16th was removed from Clifton and sent to Alexandria Virginia, and then boarded a steamer for Fort Fisher on the coast of North Carolina. After several unsuccessful efforts to advance directly toward Wilmington, a force under Gen. Cox was sent by way of Smithville up the south side of the Fear River. The 16th was with this command and engaged in severe fighting on the way, having an all day skirmish with the 2nd South Carolina Cavalry and driving them down the road leading to Wilmington. The next day they took part in the victorious battle of Town Creek. On February 23rd the regiment was the first Federal troop to enter the city of Wilmington, simultaneously with the evacuation of the place by the enemy. The 16th Kentucky was then ordered to march on Kingston, then Goldborough, and finally Raleigh to take part in the review of Sherman's army by Sherman and Gen. Grant. A few days later it arrived at Greensburg and from there marched to Company Shops, North Carolina, where the regiment was mustered out of military service June 1, 1865, and sent to Louisville, Kentucky where it was paid off and disbanded, having served four years on active duty. [9]

Lt. Col. David Enyart
1st Kentucky Infantry

Because of Kentucky's neutrality in 1861, the1st Kentucky infantry, had to recruit on the other side of the river, in Indiana. Col. James Guthrie persuaded David Enyart to join the 1st Kentucky Infantry at Camp Clay on May 3, 1861. The 1st Kentucky Infantry was mustered into service on June 4th, 1861. David was made a lieutenant colonel of the 1st Kentucky Regiment on June 28, 1861 at Camp Dennison. The regiment was immediately ordered, along with the 2nd Kentucky under Col. Woodruff, to proceed to what is now known as West Virginia. On July 2, 1861, Gen. George B. McClellan, who was then commander of the Union forces in West Virginia, ordered Gen. Jacob .D. Cox, to take command of the 1st and 2nd Kentucky Infantry, and proceed up the Kanawha River. On July 25th, Gen. William Rosecrans, who was then commanding all Union forces in West Virginia, from Grafton, was organizing his forces into the 4th Brigade, to consist of the 1st

Kentucky and 2nd Kentucky, with the 12th, 19th and a portion of the 18th and 21st Ohio, to be called the Brigade of the Kanawha, under the command of Gen. Jacob D. Cox.

On July 16, 1861, the 1st Kentucky fought at the Battle of Red House. Maj. Gen. George B. McClellan ordered Lt. Col. Enyart to join his force. McClellan was trying to control the roads converging at Charleston from Parkersburg to Guyandotte and reported that constant skirmishing was occurring along the hills. McClellan complained in his official report that the rifles that the units were using were converted muskets and that his men were at a disadvantage because the range of their rifles was poor. McClellan was moving towards Charleston and figured the force at Charleston was superior to his own. He ordered the 1st Kentucky to make a demonstration towards Gauley to cut off the retreat of the Confederates. By September 1st, Rosecrans reported that 500 rebels were 12 miles up from Loop Creek, and 2,000 more were at Lafayette. Col. Guthrie, who was camped at Charleston, reported that 500 more were at Peytona. Guthrie ordered Lt. Col. Enyart, who was at Witcher's Creek, to cross the river and attack the Rebel force at Peytona. On September 2nd, Enyart, with six companies attacked a force at Boone Courthouse and routed the Rebel force. On November 13, 1861, Brig. Gen. Jacob Cox ordered Lt. Col. Enyart to cross the river below the falls with 200 men and occupy the mills and the spurs of the mountains near there, and to reconnoiter the Fayette road and hold the position which had been previously held by Rebel artillery opposite the 1st Kentucky's camp. A battle soon erupted when 50 of the Rebels were encountered at Blake's farm. The Rebels were soon reinforced by about 200 men. The remainder of the 11th under Col. De Villiers arrived and the Rebels were driven back up the hills. The Yankees then formed a defensive line leading diagonally up the hills, from Blake's house to the crest above the battery, opposite the point.

After dark, six companies of the 2nd Kentucky crossed the river and reinforced Col. De Villiers. The Rebels were also reinforcing on a ridge, and at 9 o'clock the left wing of the 11th Ohio was driven back from Blake's farm about a quarter of a mile, but upon being reinforced by two companies of the 2nd Kentucky, Maj. Coleman drove back the Rebels and reoccupied their former position. The Rebels made a succession of attacks upon the remainder of the Union forces as they tried to push their way up the mountain crest along the whole line from Blake's farm to Kananwha. Fighting continued past midnight.

At daybreak the 11th Ohio was ordered to drive the enemy back to Cotton Hill and the 11th slowly pushed the Rebels toward New River. The advance was stopped at Cotton Hill because the Rebel force was superior to De Villiers.

On November 11th, the 11th Ohio and the 1st Kentucky Regiment under Maj. Leiper followed the enemy up the Fayette Turnpike, crossed Cotton Hill, and took up positions at Laurel Creek, where they remained until evening. They then retired half a mile after dark. During the fighting at New Mountains, Cox lost two killed, one wounded and six missing, all from the 11th Ohio. He estimated that the Rebels lost one killed and about 20 or 30 wounded.

The 1st Kentucky Regiment remained in West Virginia for most of the winter. In December 1861, Col. Guthrie resigned and Enyart was made colonel of the regiment. Early in January 1862, the 1st Kentucky Infantry was ordered to join the Army of the Cumberland. In February, the regiment was at the Green River on their way south with Buell's army. Upon the fall of Fort Donelson in February, the regiment moved to Nashville. The 1st Kentucky was in Bruce's brigade, Nelson's division and accompanied Buell's army to Pittsburg Landing. The brigade consisted of the 1st Ky., 2nd Kentucky, and the 20th Kentucky. Enyart's men arrived at Pittsburg Landing on April 6th, at 5:30 p.m. and were immediately marched up to the lines at dusk and were instructed by Gen. Nelson to sleep on their weapons and be ready for any emergency that might arise during the night. Two of his companies were sent ahead as skirmishers. At 4:00 a.m., Enyart was instructed to prepare his lines for battle, his skirmishers advancing 300 yards in front of his main line. After marching a half mile, Enyart encountered Rebel pickets and drove them back under a "galling fire for about one mile, when they took to the woods, where they had a battery of about three guns, which they opened on us, without doing much damage." Enyart's pickets from Company A, and Company G, 1st Kentucky Infantry and the 9th Indiana, charged and took the guns, but they could not hold on to them, as a regiment of Rebel infantry opened up a deadly fire on them from the bushes and forced the Yankees to fall back. The Federals kept up a steady fire while falling back, until they were relieved by the 19th Brigade and three pieces of artillery. Enyart's pickets and the 9th Indiana advanced with the 19th Brigade until they reached their old position and were told not to bring on a general engagement until more reserves arrived.

As the engagement became more intense, Enyart was ordered to sustain the 19th Brigade, which they approached from the left and front. Enyart was instructed to halt and send out more skirmishers, since the Rebels had fallen back. He sent out Company I, and Company C. All four of Enyart's companies were ordered to advance and take a position on a ridge in an open field. As his companies arrived on the ridge they recieved a deadly fire from two or three Rebel infantry regiments and a battery of artillery. Enyart was ordered to fall back into the woods just as the Rebels charged into his left flank. He immediately shored up his left flank but the Rebels were reinforced as Enyart was changing his position, and were determined to turn his left flank. Two companies from the 2nd Kentucky and part of the 12th Kentucky and three pieces of artillery came to Enyart's assistance and beat back the Rebel force. Enyart's men were driving the Rebels before them, until he was ordered to halt and rally his men. Once this was accomplished, Enyart again advanced and his men occupied the Rebel camps and the hills on the extreme left of their lines, throwing pickets and skirmishers a half mile in advance of any position they had before occupied. Enyart then reformed and marched back to camp.

From Shiloh, the regiment marched to Corinth and was in the trenches from May 30 to June 4th. Brig. Gen. Mahlon Manson, who was commanding the 22nd Brigade, commended Col. Enyart's, along with other regiments "for the prompt manner in which they have carried out the orders of the brigade commander." From Corinth, the regiment followed Buell's army in all its movements in Tennessee and Northern Alabama and in the long, severe march to Kentucky, where they took part in the pursuit of Bragg from that state.

On October 23rd, Enyart and his regiment were ordered to destroy five salt works located at Goose Creek, and Collin's Fork in Manchester, Kentucky. Upon arriving at each salt works, Enyart's men along with the 20th Kentucky, and the 2nd Kentucky destroyed the pumps, wells, and pipes conveying the water to the salt works and destroyed about 30,000 pounds of salt. Enyart was given permission by Brig. Gen. Cruft to give some salt to the loyal citizens around Manchester. It had taken 550 men 36 hours to destroy all the salt works.

The regiment then returned to Tennessee ,and was with the army under Rosecrans. On November 26th, the 1st Kentucky left Nashville and proceeded on to Murfreesboro. The regiment arrived one mile from La Vergne about 4 p.m. A large Rebel force had been discovered on the left of the road, and the 1st Brigade, Second Division, left wing, was ordered to engage the Rebels. Gen. Cruft ordered the 1st Kentucky to the front, and after "considerable skirmishing with the enemy we charged and drove him across the creek into the woods near the town, with a loss of two men wounded."

The regiment was ordered to picket the position that they had won earlier that day. Soon after dark, a Rebel cavalry unit attacked the left of Enyart's picket line, but were repulsed by Companies I and C, losing one man.

On November 27th, the regiment was marched with the division to Stewart's Creek. On the 29th, the regiment proceeded slowly towards Murfreesboro and camped two and one-half miles from that city.

Above: Brig. Gen. Enyart's Lt. Colonel's double breasted frock coat. Early war custom tailored coat. Having a watch pocket made into the waist area of the coat. The buttons are the standard eagle "I" buttons, with the "superior quality" back mark. The "I" in the center of the eagle button denotes infantry. The shoulder straps bear the Lt. Col. rank designation.
Inset: Brig. Gen. Enyart's early two piece Kentucky belt, with the Kentucky state seal emblem, his cap box and silk sabre sash.

Above, right: Standard collapsible drinking cup belonging to Brig. Gen. Enyart, and his traveling lap desk.
Above, left: 18 karat gold pendant with tintype of Enyart that belonged to his wife. This type of broach was commonly worn by officer's wives. (BCWM)
Below: This type of desk was used by most officer's to write their orders in the field and letters home to loved ones.

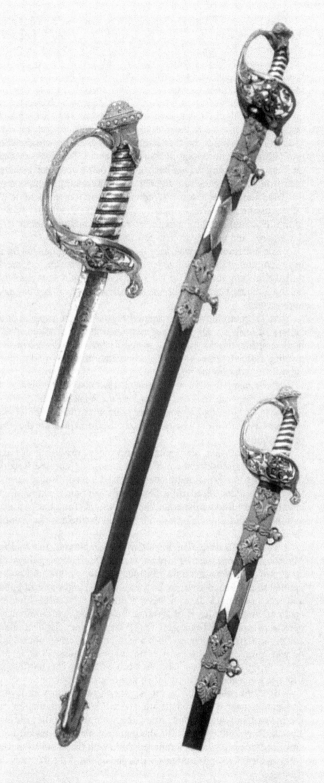

Right: Sword Presented to Lt. Col. Charles Hanson-This officers sword is an elegant specimen displaying the very finest of quality and has a brass hilt with a heavy gilt finish. The workmanship is extremely delicate, detailed and elaborate. The half basket guard is made of numerous separately applied, intertwining pieces of scroll and leaf motifs, all delicately engraved as is the knuckle bow. The pommel cap is large and handsome with a high relief eagle and shell designs, etc. The grips are solid silver. The 32 inch, exceptional quality, single edge, curved blade is etched and engraved with such quality and skill that it is almost like a fine steel bank note engraving. On the blade are large military motifs, floral patterns, a full standing figure of a female Liberty holding an American shield, and a full figure of a Civil War Zouave soldier and it's marked by the famed "Schuyler, Hartley, and Graham-New York." Very handsome all iron sheath with matching heavy gilt brass mounts with high relief delicate detailed leaf and scroll patterns. Large silver plaque affixed to scabbard is beautifully inscribed "Shiloh- Corinth- Chaplin Hills- Presented to Lt. Col. C. S. Hanson- 20th Kentucky Vols as a token of friendship and esteem by J. (or I.) M.- May 1863." (Sword Courtesy of Lyle Sloan)

On November 30th the regiment was assigned a position in the line of battle, on the right of the second line of Cruft's brigade, which was on the right of Palmer's division and was under the overall command of Gen. Crittenden. The 19th Ohio was on the 1st Kentucky's left and the 31st Indiana was to the 1st Kentucky's front in the first line. Enyart's men laid on their arms during the day.

On November 31st at 8 o'clock, Gen. Negley's division took position on their right and soon after the Battle of Stone's River began. About 9 o'clock their front was hard pressed and the brigade moved forward, the first line to the edge of the woods with the 1st Kentucky in support of Standart's battery. The right wing of their army was being driven back, and the battle was approaching their front when Gen. Cruft ordered the 1st Kentucky to move forward and march over to the 31st Indiana's position in the corn field, 300 yards ahead. The regiment was exposed to the fire of two pieces of artillery, supported by a regiment of Rebel infantry, about 100 yards away, and directly to their left flank.

The 1st Kentucky was soon in danger of being cut off by a heavy column of the Rebels advancing on their right. The regiment pulled back in good order to the woods, and took a new position behind a fence. The regiment was then ordered to slowly fall back to the road.

At 12 noon, the 1st was ordered forward to the support of a battery of artillery. The regiment remained there for about a half hour and then the brigade was moved to the railroad, and in the evening formed a new line in the rear of the division, where they slept fitfully during the night.

On January 1, 1863, the regiment was moved to the left to a new position, with their left resting on the bank of the Stone's River. At 12 noon the regiment was ordered farther to the left to support Capt. Swallow's battery where they remained for the rest of the night.

On January 2nd, the regiment threw up a breastwork of rails and stones, fighting from cover in an attempt to stop the Rebels from turning the left of their line. After the defeat of Bragg's army they were ordered forward by Gen. Cruft. Coming in range of an enemy battery the regiment laid down until the firing had ceased, and then retired to their former position and remained there until January 4th.

On July 10, 1863, Col. Enyart was made provost marshall in Manchester, Tennessee. His orders were to "reprise and punish all straggling, pillaging and other disorder." On July 18th Col. Enyart applied for a leave of absence. Enyart claimed that he was fatigued and was granted 15 days of leave. On August 21, 1863, Enyart again applied for a leave of absence. Enyart said that on his way back to Manchester, Tennessee, he fell from his horse and strained and contorted his left ankle. His leave of absence was granted and he was given 30 days to recover. Enyart would miss some of the most important battles of the Western Theatre; The battles of Chickamagua and the Ringgold-Chattanooga Campaign.

By September 3rd, the 1st Kentucky regiment was at the Sequatchie, near Jasper; on the 4th, at Shell Mound; on the 8th, at the base of Lookout Mountain; on the 10th at Rossville; on the 11th, at Ringgold. On the 12th, the regiment marched toward Lee and Gordon's Mills, and skirmished there with the enemy. On the 14th, again at Lee and Gordon's Mills, and on the 18th, at Crawfish Springs.

The 1st Kentucky engaged the Rebels both days at Chickamagua, on the 19th and 20th of September, losing 86 men in killed and wounded. After the battle of Chickamagua, the 1st remained on duty at Chattanooga.

On October 6, 1863, Col. Enyart applied for another leave of absence. Enyart's left ankle was continuing to cause him great pain. The recommendation was 20 more days of leave.

By December, Enyart had returned to his regiment. The 1st Kentucky was placed in the 4th Corps, 1st Division, 1st Brigade, under Brig. Gen. Charles Cruft. In February 1864, the regiment was stationed at Ooltewah, near Blue Springs, Tennessee. On February 22, 1864, it moved out of Blue Springs and marched nine miles to Red Clay, Georgia. On February 23rd, the 1st along with 17 other regiments moved eight miles to the farm of Dr. Lee, near Catoosa Springs, an area encompassing Catoosa Platform, Stone Church, Ringgold, and Tunnel Hill. In the night the regiment moved two miles towards Stone Church. The 1st Kentucky fought at Buzzard's Roost gap on the 25th. After the battle they returned to Chattanooga. In May the regiment pulled out of Chattanooga and participated in Sherman's Atlanta Campaign, going as far as the Etowah River. From Northern Georgia the 1st Kentucky was sent back to Kentucky and stationed at Covington under the command of Gen. Hobson. In June 1864, Hobson reported the 1st and 2nd Kentucky were part of his force engaging Morgan's raiders.

By June the 1st Kentucky's three years of service had expired and it was mustered out at Covington on July 18, 1864. Col. Enyart wrote to Gen. Burbridge on July 20, 1864, asking that he be relieved as commandant of the Post at Covington and suggested that whoever Burbridge sent to replace him, must be "strict and counting" since "the Rebs here want to be treated with a firm and determined rule." Col. Enyart's replacement arrived, and Enyart returned home. On June 22, 1867, Col. Enyart, by Special Order No. 65, was breveted a brigadier general "for his meritous services," to be post dated to March 13, 1865. [11]

Lt. Col. Charles Hanson

Lt. Col. Charles Hanson was born in 1829, in Clark County, Kentucky and was the son of Samuel Hanson, a lawyer, and the brother of Confederate General Roger Hanson of Orphan Brigade fame. Charles was raised to be a lawyer like his father and was County Attorney of Clark County, Kentucky until the war broke out. On October 1, 1861, Hanson took down his shingle and unlike his brother Roger, cast his lot with the Union. On January 6, 1862, he was mustered in at Smithland, Kentucky and became lieutenant colonel of the 20th Kentucky Regiment of Infantry. Following the fall of Fort Donelson in February 1862, the regiment moved to Nashville with Don Carlos Buell's army, where Lt. Col. Hanson was given command of the 20th Kentucky. From Nashville they marched to Shiloh and encountered their first real taste of war. Formed into line of battle on April 6th, the 20th Kentucky was heavily engaged. Hanson's regiment was assigned to the Fourth Division, Brig. Gen. William Nelson's 22nd brigade. The 1st Kentucky, 2nd Kentucky, and the 20th were under Col. Sanders Bruce. Hanson, in his report of the battle of Shiloh, says that he had about 300 men in his regiment, and that the 20th Kentucky was originally slated to be held in reserve, but was immediately ordered forward and to the left to support and prevent the turning of Col. Ammne's left flank. Col. Hanson says: "In these last three positions we were in a galling and destructive fire of the enemy's cannon and musketry. The regiment moved to them in good order, and maintained their positions with steadiness and coolness ..." Hanson's men were assigned as skirmishers and protected the left flank. The 20th Kentucky drove the enemy from their position and secured the ground, but the Rebels quickly counter attacked. The regiment, along with four companies of the 1st Kentucky and one of the 2nd Kentucky were to protect Capt. Terrill's battery from being overrun. The 20th Kentucky, along with the battery, beat back the second attack mounted by the Confederates on the left flank, and Hanson and his units held on to their ground. Their last assignment at Shiloh was for them to move to the right, to hold a position on the flank, but the Confederates had retreated by that time. Hanson won great praise from his other commanders. Col. Sanders Bruce reported that Hanson's 20th Kentucky "was in full range of the enemy's fire, and at all times maintained their formation with the steadiness and tenacity becoming veterans ... Hanson deserves very high commendation for the manner in which he managed his regiment at this crisis."

After Shiloh, Hanson moved with the army to Corinth, Mississippi and was involved in the siege of Corinth, where he and his men took part in many skirmishes. On May 21, 1862, the 1st Kentucky was deployed on the left of the road leading to Corinth, and the 20th Kentucky on the right. They were to skirmish ahead, and as soon as the skirmishers were deployed the Confederates, who were hidden in the woods poured volley after volley into the 20th and 1st Kentucky, driving them back to widow Serratt's house. The enemy was trying to turn the Union left flank. Hanson was sent in with his remaining companies to the left to support the 1st Kentucky and stem the tide of graybacks who were raining down shot and shell upon his men. Artillery was brought up and fired into the Confederate ranks. The battle raged for three quarters of an hour and the Confederates rallied three times, but the Union line held firm. The 20th Kentucky pushed the enemy back and gained a position across a small creek beyond widow Serratt's house. The Rebel fire stopped and the Union forces held their ground until nightfall, then Buell recalled the 1st and 2nd Kentucky, while the 31st Indiana remained on the field to deceive the enemy into thinking the Federals remained on the field in force. Sedwick reports that Hanson "evinced the greatest bravery, gallantly leading and encouraging his men amid the greatest dangers."

On May 28th, Hanson was involved in the battle, three fourths of a mile beyond their entrenchments, at Corinth, Mississippi. Col. Sedwick reported that on the morning of May 28th, the 20th Kentucky, and 2nd Kentucky were formed into line of battle and made up the first line. The regiments quickly began to advance and had only gotten 50 yards or so when the Confederate forces opened up on them. The line shuddered and then slowly began to gain ground, driving the Confederates back across Bridge Creek. The bridge was hotly contested by both sides, with the Federal troops finally gaining control. Maj. Buckner, with two companies of the 20th Kentucky, crossed over the bridge and deployed on the left and Company B, 2nd Kentucky, and the main body of the 20th Kentucky, under Lt. Col. Hanson was ordered forward on the right. The 1st Kentucky was being driven back, and Hanson deployed his men and ordered them to fire on the Confederates. The 20th Kentucky put down such a withering and destructive fire upon the Confederates that the gray clad troops grudgingly began to fall back. Capt. Mendenhall's battery rolled its guns closer to the front while the Confederate and Union troops attacked and counterattacked. The Union forces did not advance any farther than the bridge, but managed to hold onto it. The Confederates finally broke off the fight, and the victorious but dog-tired Union troops began to dig rifle pits. By 9:00 p.m., the exhausted brigade was pulled out and were given a rest and a chance to lick their wounds. Sedwick's report commended Col. Hanson for "displaying great coolness and judgment both in manner of handling his regiment and in his efforts to assist me in the discharge of my duties."

On May 30th, Col. Hanson's troops followed the army into an abandoned Corinth. On June 4th, they pursued the enemy until they reached Baldwyn and remained there for two days. Then the 20th followed Buell's army into Northern Alabama, being at Huntsville and then on to McMinnville, Tennessee. In August, the regiment moved with Buell to Kentucky and marched with Nelson's division from Louisville to Perryville. It engaged in the skirmishing of that battle on October 8th, and then moved in pursuit of Bragg's army going as far as Mt. Vernon. It then marched through Somerset and Glasgow to Nashville and remained there until the month of December, when it was ordered to Bowling Green, Kentucky, guarding the railroad at various points until about the first of July, when it was sent to Lebanon, Kentucky. It just so happened that Confederate General John Hunt Morgan was headed in this same direction on his famous July 1863 raid.

Lt. Col. Hanson reported that "on the morning of the 4th, instant, I received reliable information that a force, 5,000 strong with six pieces of artillery, under the command of John Hunt Morgan; was approaching on the Columbia Road, and that the advance was within eight miles of town." Hanson had about 360 men, and no artillery. Hanson set about trying to get horses since he had no cavalry with him. He sent out scouts, and they soon found Morgan's scouts who were at first pushed back by Hanson's, but an overwhelming force under Morgan soon drove Hanson's men back to

their pickets. Hanson then encountered Morgan's scouts along the Columbia Road and the Bradfordville Road, and after a skirmish pushed Morgan's men back to Muldraugh Hill. Hanson was ordered to stay and fight until reinforcements came. No fighting occurred until the next morning. At 6:30 a.m., Hanson saw Morgan's men covering the Bradfordsville road across the Columbia Pike and the railroad to the Saint Mary's Road. His line stretched for nearly two miles. His position was about one and a half miles from town. Hanson threw out 280 skirmishers in a semi circle covering the front of the enemy, and about 50 more under Capt. Wolcott were placed in the Bradfordsville road and to the left with directions to hold the town until overcome; they were then to take cover in two buildings on Main Street that had previously been prepared for defense, and which best covered that part of Lebanon. At 7 o'clock Morgan's artillery opened up on Hanson's camp, and at the same moment Confederate Lt. Col. R. A. Alston was sent with a flag of truce. Alston demanded that Hanson surrender but Hanson refused. Morgan then continued his shelling of the town, and his men moved to Hanson's right and left, surrounding him. The fighting now intensified. Skirmishers from the 20th Kentucky fought for two hours but finally fell back to the L & N train depot. Hanson ordered the ordnance and commissary stores destroyed. Fighting broke out in the streets of Lebanon. Hanson's men who had not reached the depot took shelter in the houses. Morgan directed his cannon to fire upon the depot, and the roof soon caught on fire. With their Springfield and Enfield rifles, Hanson's men managed to keep Morgan's artillery from getting any closer than 1,000 yards from the depot, but by now the Rebels occupied about two thirds of the town. At 12 noon, the citizens of the town sent a flag of truce to the depot and said that if Hanson's men did not surrender in 10 minutes that Morgan would burn the town to the ground. General Morgan took advantage of the cease fire and moved his artillery within 300 yards, and moved his men closer to the depot. Col. Hanson immediately ordered his men to fire, without giving the towns folk any message. Morgan knew that Union reinforcements were coming and he did not want to be caught up in a major engagement since his main objective was to reach the Ohio River. Morgan decided to storm the depot by a frontal assault. Morgan's 2nd and 5th Kentucky moved across the open ground firing at the windows to keep the defending bluecoats down. Lt. Thomas Morgan, who was Gen. John Hunt Morgan brother, was shot through the heart during the final charge on the depot. He fell dead in the arms of another brother, Calvin. "Brother Cally, they have killed me" were his last words. At 1:20 p.m., Hanson's men were running out of ammunition, having fired 125 rounds per man. They were worn out, and most of their weapons were badly fouled. After a valiant stand lasting almost seven hours and against overwhelming odds, Lt. Col. Charles S. Hanson surrendered. When the 2nd Kentucky found out that Thomas Morgan had been killed, they were overcome by emotion and were going to kill Hanson and his men, but John Hunt Morgan, still grieving and in shock over his brother's death, rode out in front of his men and at gun point, told them he would shoot anyone who tried to harm Col. Hanson or any of his men. Laying down their arms, Col. Hanson and his men were paroled. As he was leaving the building, Morgan turned to Hanson and said, "Charles, when you go home, if it is any source of gratification to you, tell Mother you killed brother Tom." John Hunt Morgan and Thomas Morgan knew Charles before the War, when they had been friends. Union losses were 13 killed and 28 wounded. The Confederates lost 13 killed, and 30 wounded. The 300 captured Federals were then ordered at the double quick to Springfield.

Most of you will not have heard of Lt. Col. Charles S. Hanson, the 20th Kentucky, or this nasty little battle that took place in Lebanon, Kentucky, on a hot day in early July 1863. It did not make the history books, because a couple of days earlier, on other battlefields far from Kentucky, other battles raged, at places called Gettysburg and Vicksburg.

Gen. Ambrose Burnside was very upset with Hanson for being paroled on the spot, telling Col. Hanson that he should have waited until he got to City Point. Burnside put Hanson under arrest and sent him to Louisville to do Provost Marshall duty. Hanson objected, stating he was a paroled prisoner and should not be forced to perform such duty. His objections were overruled and Col. Hanson was forced to take the post under penalty of court-martial and arrest if he refused. Maj. Gen. Burnside sent Hanson to Camp Nelson without arms, where he was then given garrison duty and finally notified that he was officially exchanged.

On December 29, 1863, Hanson was promoted to colonel and given a new command, the 37th Kentucky Volunteer Mounted Infantry. In March 1864, Hanson and the 37th were ordered to Columbia, Kentucky with all available troops in the state, for the purpose of moving into eastern Kentucky for an all out pursuit of John Hunt Morgan and his raiders.

About June 1, 1864, Col. Hanson's brigade was ordered to Irvine, Kentucky to aid in checking the movement of Morgan into Kentucky. Gen. Burbridge knew of Morgan's plans and moved to Pound Gap, but Morgan eluded him and moved on to Mt. Sterling where Hanson's brigade skirmished with Morgan's men and lost, and then recaptured, one of Hanson's mountain howitzer's.

On July 12th, Morgan's Cavalry, with 2,300 troopers attacked Cynthania, Kentucky, which was defended by Gen. Burbridge and 5,000 Union cavalry. Hanson and the 37th again played a major part in the battle. Morgan's men were exhausted and the bluecoats managed to take back prisoners that Morgan had captured at Mt. Sterling. Morgan and his troopers then skedaddled for the relative safety of Virginia. In September 1864, Burbridge mounted another attack against Morgan at Saltville, Virginia, where Col. Hanson and the 37th Kentucky fought against Morgan once more, during Burbridges expedition to destroy the salt works. During the battle, on October 2, 1864, Col. Hanson was severely wounded when he was shot in the left side just above the hip. The bullet lodged in his right side after knocking off the outer part of his spine. Col. Hanson was taken prisoner and sent to Emory and Henry Hospital in Washington County, Virginia. In a report dated October 26, 1864, Surgeon W. H. Gardner, 30th Kentucky Infantry, states "On Monday morning, October 3rd ... several armed men, as I believe soldiers in the Confederate service, took five men, privates, wounded (negroes), and shot them ... on Friday evening, October 7th, at Emory and Henry College Hospital, Washington County Virginia, to which place our wounded had been removed, several armed men entered the said hospital about 10:00 p.m. and went up stairs into the rooms occupied by the Federal wounded prisoners, and shot two of them (negroes) dead in their beds ... on Saturday, October 8th, armed men entered the hospital about 4 p.m., overpowered the guard, and shot Lt. E. C. Smith, 13th Regt. Kentucky Cavalry, dead in his bed, where he lay severely wounded. They at the same time called out for the other Federal officers confined there, particularly Col. Hanson, 37th Regt. Kentucky Volunteers ... swearing that they intended to kill all of them; and I believe that they were only prevented doing so by the exertions of surgeon Murfree, the surgeon in charge, the steward Mr. Acres, and the other surgeons, and the hospital attendants did all in their power, even to the risk of their lives, to prevent the perpetration of these outrages; and that they assisted in removing Col. Hanson and Capt. Degenfeld, as well as myself, to a place of safety."

Col. Hanson was then transferred to College Hospital in Lynchburg, Virginia. On October 12th, Gen. Burbridge reported that Hanson had died at Emory and Henry Hospital, and on the 14th, he requested Hanson's body. This was probably a surprise to Hanson since he was still very much alive, although severely wounded.

While he was held prisoner, charges were filed against Hanson by Confederate Lt. Col. Alston, of Morgan's command, who remembered him from the Battle of Lebanon. He charged Hanson with cruelty to Confederate prisoners and violation of his parole. Ambrose Burnside came to the defense of Col. Hanson and wrote

Col. William Fenton's shaving box with sharpening stone and razors. Painted on the lid of the box is Col. Wm. Fenton Eighth Michigan. (BCWM)

to Charles Dana, the Assistant Secretary of War, a list of statements in his defense. On November 14th, G. A. Stone wrote to Gen. Jas. H. Lane, requesting that his brother in law, Charles Hanson of the 37th be exchanged. Secretary of War, E. A. Hitchcock, in a letter to the Asst. Adjutant. Gen., stated that he did not think that Hanson should be exchanged and that the charges against him by the Confederate government should be ignored since the Confederacy "has no legal case." The Confederates finally decided not to bring him up on charges, and as soon as he was able to be moved, transferred him to Libby Prison in Richmond, Virginia, where he was finally paroled on March 6, 1865.

After the war, Col. Hanson returned to Kentucky and made an unsuccessful run for Congress. He then moved to Paris, Kentucky, and resided there until his death on November 8, 1875. Hanson was survived by his wife, Carrie, and his three children; Carloine W., Sarah Carter, and Charles Roger. Col. Charles S. Hanson was truly a great soldier and worthy of praise. In the November 16, 1875, issue of the Kentucky Yeoman, the paper declared Hanson "a fine disciplinarian, and was very popular of his soldiers. He had a great dash and decision of character. Few men had finer social qualities, and no one better deserved the high character that he enjoyed for honor and integrity. Of a quick, active intellect, a lively, vivacious disposition and possessed of much "Bon Hommie" and a fine sense of humor, he had great popularity. He was a brave, gallant gentlemen, and a true friend, a kind husband and affectionate father." What more can be said for this great man? [10]

Col. William Fenton
Eighth Michigan Infantry
"The Wandering Regiment"

At the age of 50, William Fenton, who was from Flint, Michigan, entered service with the Eighth Michigan Infantry on August 7, 1861. When most men his age were thinking about retiring and enjoying the golden years, William Fenton heard the call of Father Abraham Lincoln and felt it was his duty to serve his country. The Eighth Michigan was mustered into service on September 23, 1861 at Grand Rapids, Michigan, and was later transferred to Fort Wayne in Detroit. On September 27th, the regiment left Detroit and was transferred to Washington, DC It arrived in Washington on September 30th, with 915 officers and men. The regiment was assigned to William Tecumseh Sherman's "Expeditionary Corps." Sherman and the Eighth Michigan were sent to Hilton Head, Beaufort, South Carolina.

On January 1, 1862, the Eighth Michigan would encounter it first real battle at Coosaw River, South Carolina. The Eighth Michigan was transported by flat boat from Brickyard Point, Port Royal Island to the mainland near the Adams House. Upon arrival, Fenton ordered his men to march towards a Rebel battery at the Adams House. On their approach to the ferry the Eighth Michigan were ordered to attack as skirmishers and a masked battery opened fire on them from the right. Fenton immediately detached the first two and the tenth companies, and directed their march to the left and front of the battery. His additional four companies followed to the right and front. The fire of the battery continued to batter Fenton's line until the skirmishers reached the right, and the fire was turned on them. As they approached, right, left, and front, to within 75 yards of the Rebel position, the Rebel infantry opened up on Fenton's men. The force of Rebel infantry and their battery were concealed by trees, brush, and undergrowth. Fenton surmised

that the Rebel force consisted of two mountain howitzers supported by a regiment or more of infantry, and some cavalry. Fenton's skirmishers were protected by brush and furrows, and continued to fire upon the Rebel's, who replied with volleys of musketry and shells from the battery. Fenton's fire was well directed and seemed to be effective. One mounted Rebel officer was seen to fall from his horse, where upon the Rebel troops on the right were thrown into confusion. The Rebel position seemed to be changing to the rear, and Fenton called back his skirmishers and formed his regiment into line as the Rebel fire stopped. The regiment was then marched to its position in line of battle in the rear of the fort. Lt. Col. Graves led the Eighth on the left and Major Watson led the men on the right of the skirmishers. While urging on his line, the major received a severe flesh wound in the leg. Fenton calculated that the Rebels lost about 40, while he had lost seven wounded and two missing.

On April 16, 1862, the Regiment had a sharp engagement with Confederate forces on Wilmington Island, Georgia. Fenton and seven companies of the Eighth Michigan acted as an escort for Lt. J. H. Wilson, of the Topographical Engineers, on a reconnaissance of Wilmington Island. Two companies under the command of

Col. William Fenton's officer chair. The back would fold down to become a writing desk. (BCWM)

Capt. Pratt were landed at Screven's Plantation, and the other five companies were landed at Gibson's Plantation. Two of these companies were ordered by Lt. Wilson to skirt Turner's Creek. A third was to take the road to the right toward the ferry at Carston's Bluff and to protect a boat and a party of men who were up Oatland Creek, and the remainder were to secure the landing. After one company of the five was landed Lt. Wilson proceeded in a boat up Turner's Creek. The troops under Fenton were delayed in disembarking from their steamer because the steamer had gotten stuck in the channel, and the small number of boats on the ship allowed only few men to be transported to the Island. Fenton directed Lt. Col. Graves to follow with the second company and skirt Turner's Creek, but Graves took the road to the right toward Carston's Bluff. Landing with the remaining companies Fenton then received word from Graves that the Rebels were in force at Fleetwood's Plantation and to the left of the woods. This rendered the reconnaissance up Oatland Creek by boat as unsafe and Fenton ordered the companies to return to the landing and prepare for an attack and sent out strong pickets on both roads. If it weren't for Graves taking the wrong road, Fenton's forces may have been wiped out. Fenton now had the information on the approach of the Rebels and posted his men in a position where the Rebel approach could be observed. The Thirteenth Georgia, about 800 strong, and armed with Enfield rifles appeared at 4 o'clock, approaching with a strong body of skirmishers in the skirt of woods below where Fenton had stationed his companies to the right and left of the road. When the Rebels got close enough, Fenton's men let out a thunderous volley. Fenton then called for a charge that would advance the companies in the rear of the first line. The first line misunderstood Fenton's signal, and fell back to the next cover. A constant and effective fire was kept up on both sides from the cover of trees and brush for an hour or more. Lt. Wilson had returned with the boat party, and was ordered to the left, as Fenton ordered another company to the right to try and flank the Rebels. Both operations were successful and in a few moments the Rebels retreated in confusion, leaving several dead on the field, and pursued by Fenton's wildly cheering men.

As the sun began to set, Fenton recalled his troops and gave Lt. Wilson the command of the pickets acting as sentries. Wilson formed his companies into line and posted them. He also ordered his dead and wounded sent to the ships first, and gradually and very quietly under cover of night the men were sent on board the ships as fast as their limited transportation allowed. When the last transport picked up the last of his men, Fenton, along with Lt. Wilson, Lt. Col. Graves, and the remainder of his command left the island and were transported to the steamer **Honduras**.

During the engagement Fenton lost his adjutant Pratt and also lost 10 men killed and 35 men wounded out of a command of 300.

On April 12, 1862, Fenton took command of the 1st Brigade, Second Division, under Brig. Gen. Isaac Stevens. The brigade was made up of the Eighth Michigan, the 7th Connecticut, and the 28th Massachusetts. On June 16, 1862, Col. Fenton fought at Secessionville, James Island, South Carolina. Fenton and his command were ordered to move out at 1 o'clock a.m. and at 2 o'clock to advance into line, and move to the second row of houses in the town of Secessionville. Brig. Gen. Stevens advanced with Fenton and the regiments were ordered to march by the right flank and not make a sound. Two Companies, C and H, of the Eighth Michigan, were to advance as skirmishers and attacking party. The remaining eight companies of the Eighth were under command of Lt. Col. Graves. The Seventh Connecticut, under Lt. Col. Hawley, followed with a section of artillery. The Twenty-Eighth Massachusetts, was under Lt. Col. Moore.

As the brigade passed quietly by the house beyond the marsh the advance was fired on by the Rebel pickets and two men of Company H, Eighth Michigan, were wounded. Silence was maintained by the men, and no shots were returned, but four of the

Rebel's pickets were captured and sent to the rear. The two advance companies were deployed into line and were joined by the Eighth Michigan as they formed into line of battle in the open field, in view of the Rebels works. Fenton observed the Rebels position and thought it would be desirable to obtain ground to the right for the purpose of flanking the Rebels left during the assault, and advanced his other regiments into position for effective fire on the Rebel infantry, supporting the works. He ordered an oblique march, which was carried out with no major problems. Fenton then dispatched Lt. Belcher, his acting aide, to bring up the Seventh Connecticut to form on the left of the Eighth Michigan. Lt. Brackett, acting assistant adjutant general, was to bring up the Twenty Eighth Massachusetts to support the two regiments, taking his position on the front and center to receive and direct the other regiments as they advanced.

The order was not to fire, but to use the bayonet. Fenton's advance companies reached the parapet of the works at the angle on their right front, engaging the Rebels at the point of the bayonet. They were closely followed by the remaining companies of the regiment. During this advance the Rebels opened up on Fenton's lines with an enormous, destructive fire of grape, canister, and musketry but Fenton's regiments pushed on as veterans, divided only to the right and left by a sweeping torrent from the Rebels main gun in their front. This brought a portion of the regiment to the left near the tower or lookout, and a brisk fire of musketry was soon opened up on both sides. The Rebel fire proved so galling and destructive, according to Fenton, that his troops on the parapet were compelled to retire under the cover of a ditch and slope on their right at the marsh, and a slope and trees on their left. His men maintained their position, partially protected, doing a much better job acting as sharpshooters.

The Seventh Connecticut formed into line as they advanced, reaching a point in the open field in front of the tower with their left resting on the bushes skirting the marsh. Fenton ordered a march by the right flank across the field to support the troops on the right. Fenton personally directed the movement, which was carried out in good order under a continuing shower of grape and canister and the infantry raked them with musket fire as they neared the works. Meanwhile, one section of the Connecticut battery had opened up on the Rebels from their left and in the early part of the march this regiment was caught in the middle of an artillery duel.

The Twenty-Eighth Massachusetts filed through the first hedge and came up rapidly, following the advance of artillery, forming a column of companies and coming into line, they arrived near the Seventh Connecticut's position, and then filled in on the left of the flank. For a short time, the left of the two regiments clustered together in the bushes, but the march of the Seventh Connecticut cleared them. The Twenty-Eighth then filed up to the obstructions a short distance from the Rebel entrenchments near the tower, and opened fire on the Rebel defenders.

All the regiments were subjected to galling and raking fire until they retired. The storm of grape, canister, and musketry continued and many of Fenton's officers and men were wounded. Orders came down to withdraw his men and his command was rapidly pulled back, and reformed behind the main hedge. An advance was again made to the cover of the ditch or second hedge in support of a field battery which was being pushed forward.

Posted in the woods on their right and near the angle of the fort, were some of the Rebel sharpshooters. They were also in rifle pits and under cover in the rear and the house, was filled with them. From these and other positions in and about the fort and on its right a constant fire of musketry was kept up by the Rebels. The Second Brigade of this Second Division, was rushed forward to Fenton's support, and at all accessible points the Rebels were catching hell.

The Rebels now brought up a floating battery on their right front, from which four shots were fired. Once again the order to withdraw was given. An aide to his extreme right and front were to recall the men there. The aide, Lt. Fenton, found them near the angle of the fort and directed them to fall back, which was done by most of the troops; but after the regiments were reforming behind the hedge 100 or more of the Eighth Michigan still remained at the angle and were recalled by Lt. Belcher, who had ridden over the field to bring in all who remained able to move. The field of battle was furrowed across with cotton ridges, and many of the men lay there loading and firing as deliberately "as though on their hunting grounds at home."

Fenton reported that all the horses in his command were either killed or wounded, and all his aides and orderlies were hit in some way. During the engagement the Eighth Michigan's colors were carried on the parapet, and as the men withdrew it was unfurled to protect them from friendly fire from the rear.

At 9:00 a.m., the order was given to withdraw and return to camp. Fenton lost 341 killed, wounded, and missing, 132 from the Eighth Michigan alone. The Seventh Connecticut lost 85, and the 28th Massachusetts lost 74. Fenton's total force was 1,676 men.

In July the regiment left James Island, and after a series of long marches reached Manassas, Virginia, where it was engaged in the Second Battle of Manassas on August 29th and 30th. The regiment was then heavily engaged at South Mountain and Antietam from September 14th through September 17th. In March 1863, the Eighth Michigan was ordered to Louisville, Kentucky. On March 15, 1863, Col. Fenton was honorably discharged and returned home to Flint, Michigan. The Eighth Michigan was then sent on to Vicksburg, Mississippi where it arrived on March 17th. The regiment was engaged in the marches around Vicksburg, especially Jackson, Mississippi, after which it headed for Knoxville, Tennessee, by way of Crab Orchard and Cumberland Gap, arriving there on September 26th.

When Confederate General James Longstreet marched through Tennessee, the Eighth was among the troops that met him at Campbell Station. During the siege of Knoxville, the Eighth was in advanced works suffering along with the rest of the Union troops in Knoxville. After Longstreet withdrew his troops from Knoxville, the Eighth pursued Longstreet and went as far as Rutledge, Tennessee, then retired to Blain's Cross Roads. At this camp, the regiment decided to re-enlist as a veterans regiment, with 283 men re-enlisting. The regiment was then marched 200 miles across the Cumberland Mountains and arrived in Nicholasville, Kentucky on January 19, 1864. The Eighth was then sent home and they arrived in Detroit, Michigan on the 25th and were given a furlough of 30 days. After the furlough the Eighth was sent to Annapolis, Maryland. On May 4, 1864, the regiment started with Grant on his campaign through Virginia. The Eighth was engaged in the Battle of the Wilderness and lost 99 men killed, wounded or missing. Col. Graves was killed in the battle. On May 12th, the regiment assaulted the Rebel works at Spottsylvania and suffered heavily, losing 49 men and officers killed. On June 3rd, the regiment fought the Rebels at Bethesda Church and lost 52 killed, wounded and missing. On the 15th, the Eighth crossed the James River and was engaged on the 17th and 18th assaulting the earthworks at Petersburg, and lost another 49 officers and men. When Petersburg fell the Eighth Michigan was one of the first regiments to enter the city.

After the surrender of Confederate General Robert E. Lee on April 9, 1865, the Eighth Michigan moved to City Point, where it left by boat for Alexandria, Virginia, and reached Washington, DC on May 9th. On August 1st, the Eighth Michigan started for home after a long four years of fighting. The regiment arrived in Detroit on August 3, 1865. The Eighth Michigan began its career with 1,715 men, and by 1865 they had lost 687 men, a full 40 percent of their Regiment.

Col. Fenton led a regiment that fought not only in the Eastern theatre but also in the Western theatre. Col. Fenton served three years, and became a central figure in the history of the Eighth Michigan. Col. Fenton proved that age was no factor when it came to leadership, courage, and bravery. [11]

Col. John Thomas Wilder

John Thomas Wilder was born in Greene County, New York, on January 31, 1830. In 1849, Wilder moved to Columbus, Ohio, and was hired as an apprentice in a foundry. Wilder later moved to Greensburg, Indiana, in 1857 to start his own foundry and millwright business. In four years, Wilder's business expanded and eventually employed one hundred people in five states.

When the Civil War began, Wilder immediately cast two six pound cannons and raised a company of men. The men became Company A of the 17th Indiana Infantry, and Wilder became their regimental Lieutenant Colonel. In April 1862, the 17th arrived too late to be involved in the Battle of Shiloh, but were involved in the siege of Corinth, Mississippi. Wilder made a brave stand during Confederate General Braxton Bragg's invasion of Kentucky in September and October of 1862. Wilder was commander of Fort Craig, in Munfordville, Kentucky. Against overwhelming forces, Wilder finally surrendered the fort to Bragg's army. Wilder later sought permission to procure horses from the local countryside in order to mount his men. The horses would be used for transport and the men would fight on foot. Wilder also bought the seven shot Spencer repeating rifle for his men, making his brigade the first of the Western armies to be equipped with the Spencer. This was a heavy expense considering each rifle cost $35.00 dollars a piece. The money was borrowed from the Greensburg, Indiana bank. The brigade now became known as "The Lightening Brigade". The Brigade went on to fight at Hoover's Gap, Tennessee, Chickamugua, Georgia, and Sherman's march to Atlanta. Wilder was given a brevet Brigadier General's commission on August 7, 1864, but resigned on October 4, 1864, because of reoccurring typhoid fever. In 1866, Wilder moved from Greensburg to Chattanooga, Tennessee. He later became mayor of Chattanooga. Later he moved to Johnson City, Tennessee where he capitalized on the future of coal and the railroads. He also bought the water rights along the Tennessee River. Wilder died in Jacksonville, Florida on October 20, 1917 and was buried in Forest Hills Cemetery in Chattanooga.

Shell jacket has the high collar, and was originally a cavalry jacket lined with yellow trim on the collar and cuffs, but according to legend, Wilder did not want to be identified as cavalry so he made his men tear off the yellow trim on their uniforms. The uniform still has the stitching where the yellow trim used to be.

Photos on pages 138-139

(1) Union Shell Jacket Belonging to one of Col. John Thomas Wilder's men, Commander of the "Lightening Brigade", 17th Indiana Mounted Infantry. (BCWM)
(2) Sergeant Major's shell jacket made of a coarse cotton with a lining of cloth known as osnaburg. Featuring CSA buttons with Hyde & Goodrich New Orleans, LA. (BCWM)
(3) Model 1858 militia privates uniform coat with detachable brass shoulder scales only worn early in the war. Also has the standard U.S. belt, cap box, .58 caliber bayonet and sheath. Over his shoulder is the standard cartridge box and sling with the eagle breast plate on the sling itself, and the U.S. belt plate on the cartridge box. (BCWM)
(4) Standard officer's infantry slouch hat. The gold bullion horn insignia indicates infantry and the gold "20" within the horn indicates his regiment. It also features the gold braid hat cord with acorns. (BCWM)
(5) Union Major General's Frock Coat-Typical early Major General's Frock coat is denoted by three spaced of nine buttons on each side, and two stars on the shoulder boards. The uniform also has early extra side elbows, with a velvet collar. The uniform used to have velvet cuffs, which were removed during the war. (BCWM)
(6) This is a regulation enlisted men's infantry shell jacket, blue in color, with the standard twelve buttons in the front and two buttons on each sleeve. These are "Superior Quality" buttons with the standard eagle motifs. (BCWM)
(7) This regulation tarred billed kepi has the standard eagle buttons with the brass horn insignia indicating infantry. This was a favorite among the enlisted men. (BCWM)
(8) This is a standard infantry officer's kepi, which features the gold bullion branch insignia of the infantry, and the "I" eagle buttons on the sides of the kepi for the chin strap. (BCWM)

(1)

(3)

(2)

(4)

(5)

(6)

(7)

(8)

This relic condition embossed "CS" in oval cartouche cap box, with the rare double belt loops was manufactured in the Baton Rouge, Louisiana Arsenal, and are extremely rare. (BCWM)

Early tin type of a Western theatre Arkansas infantry man. Identified by his uniform which has the ball buttons, turn down collar, and small ribbon tie.

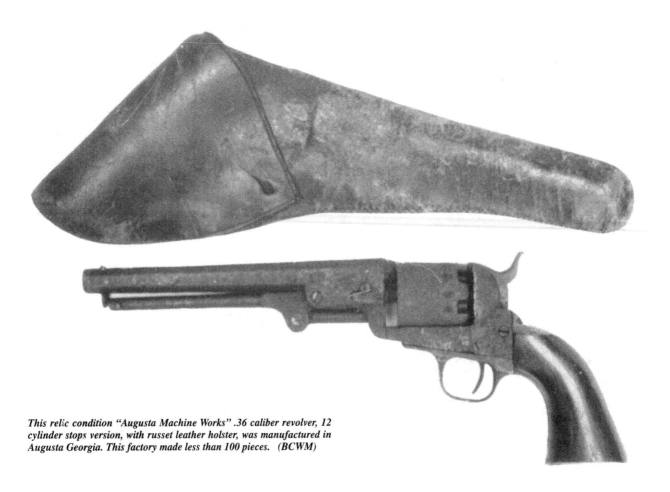

This relic condition "Augusta Machine Works" .36 caliber revolver, 12 cylinder stops version, with russet leather holster, was manufactured in Augusta Georgia. This factory made less than 100 pieces. (BCWM)

This Militia style box knapsack reads "23d Separate Co. N. G. S. N. Y.", which stands for the National Guard State of New York. (BCWM)

Militia style knapsack used by the 9th Indiana Infantry. The ribbed style knapsacks are reinforced with wood and paste board to give it a neat appearance for official occasions and parades. (BCWM)

This massive 1840's style double edged, spear point bowie knife with hexagonal tiger stripped curly maple handle, was used by a Tennessee infantrymen. The overall length is 18 inches. (BCWM)

Early war style knapsack used by the 11th Regiment of the Ohio Volunteers. This box type knap sack was shunned by the men because of it's weight and was replaced by the later style soft back pack which became standard issue in late 1861. (BCWM)

This 1830's style bowie knife, with sheath, is similar to the bowie knives that Resin Bowie, Jim Bowie's older brother, presented to his friends. Bowie knives were a favorite side arm of the Southern soldier. (BCWM)

Top left: This tarred bill infantry forage cap has the brass infantry horn insignia and brass letter "C". It also features the Kentucky state seal buttons on the side of the forage cap for the chin strap. (BCWM)

Top right: Confederate Canteen captured by Union soldier and hand painted with American eagle. These type of items were sent back to their Northern homes as trophies of war. (BCWM)

Above left: This Confederate brown colored, bound brimmed officer's slouch hat has the gold bullion infantry insignia, and tan colored hat cords. This was a favorite style of hat worn by the Confederate line or foot officer. (BCWM)

Above right: This tan colored, bound brimmed Confederate officer's slouch hat, has an unusual large gold bullion infantry horn. The number "2" indicates his regiment. The hat also features gold bullion hat cords with acorns. (BCWM)

Bottom right: Confederate General John Hunt Morgan's 2nd Kentucky Guidon. (Chaplin Hills Properties, Inc.)

Left: This small thirty four star flag was used by civilians to wave during parades in their home towns. It also was used to hang in windows of families that had loved ones that were serving in the war. (BCWM)
Below right: This water color portrait depicts a Union officer in the mounted infantry, note his leather gauntlets and mounted infantry sword. He was from a Kentucky regiment. Center: The sword is a model 1850 foot officer's sword. (BCWM)
Bottom right: A silver identification badge from Assistant Provost Marshall Gilliss from Louisville, Kentucky. Rare marked Horstmann & Sons of Philadelphia provost marshall whistle. The provost marshall were the police force of the army. Provost marshall items are extremely rare. (BCWM)
Bottom left: This Star Single Action Revolver, .44 caliber, with leather holster, was made by the Starr Arms Company of New York. There were 25,000 of these pistols purchased by the government for $12.00 a pistol. (BCWM)

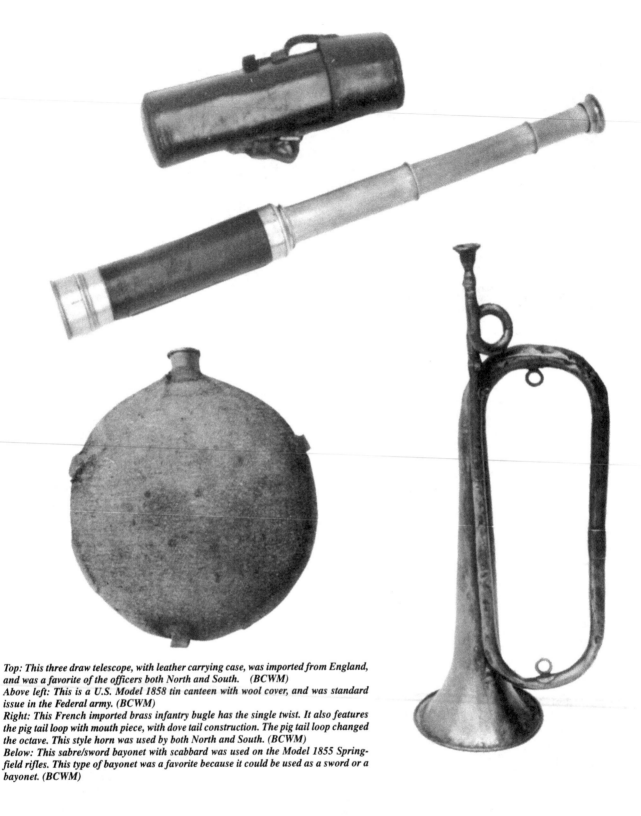

Top: This three draw telescope, with leather carrying case, was imported from England, and was a favorite of the officers both North and South. (BCWM)

Above left: This is a U.S. Model 1858 tin canteen with wool cover, and was standard issue in the Federal army. (BCWM)

Right: This French imported brass infantry bugle has the single twist. It also features the pig tail loop with mouth piece, with dove tail construction. The pig tail loop changed the octave. This style horn was used by both North and South. (BCWM)

Below: This sabre/sword bayonet with scabbard was used on the Model 1855 Spring-field rifles. This type of bayonet was a favorite because it could be used as a sword or a bayonet. (BCWM)

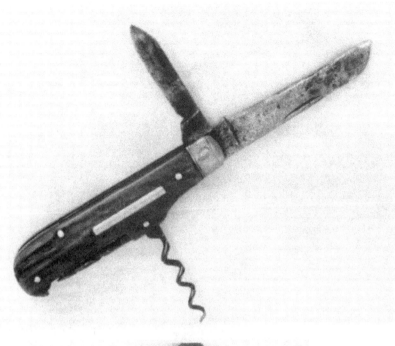

Top right: This stag handled pocket knife has the multiple blades, which was "a must have" for the individual soldier of both North and South. (BCWM)

Center left: This period straight razor, with leather case was used by enlisted men and officer's alike. The razor was manufactured by Wade and Butcher, Sheffield, England. (BCWM)

Center right: This Confederate Cartridge box, for the standard .58 caliber rifle, features the brass Georgia state seal emblem, which is affixed onto the flap. (BCWM)

Bottom: Confederate wooden sole shoes, with iron horse shoes applied to the wooden base to insure steadiness in inclement weather. (BCWM)

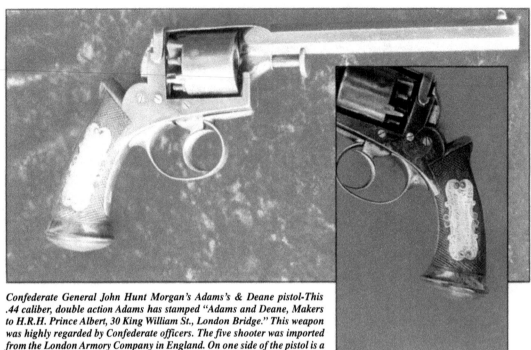

Confederate General John Hunt Morgan's Adams's & Deane pistol-This .44 caliber, double action Adams has stamped "Adams and Deane, Makers to H.R.H. Prince Albert, 30 King William St., London Bridge." This weapon was highly regarded by Confederate officers. The five shooter was imported from the London Armory Company in England. On one side of the pistol is a silver plate studded by eight rubies, the plate bearing the inscription, "Presented by F.K. Hunt to Capt. J.H. Morgan, 1854." Francis Key Hunt was a wealthy industrialist and was at one time the mayor of Lexington, Kentucky. He had also built the Gothic Revival mansion "Loudon." Hunt was one of the richest men in Kentucky at the time. The pistol was presented to Morgan, when he was leader of the Lexington Rifles militia. (Waveland State Historic Site)

Confederate General John Hunt Morgan's sword-Model 1833 Dragoon cavalry Saber. Stamped 1836, Ames Manufacturing Co. The sword has John H. Morgan engraved in script on the sword handle. (Blue Grass Historic Trust, Hunt-Morgan House)

This is a modified Confederate McClellan style saddle with saddle bags used by a member of General John Hunt Morgan's Second Kentucky Cavalry. (BCWM)

This eleven star flag of the first national model was captured at Lisbon, Ohio in 1863 from General John Hunt Morgan's men during his great Ohio Raid which was the most northern penetration of the United States during the Civil War. (BCWM)

Confederate General John Hunt Morgan's Shako from the Lexington Rifles. (Ken Hamilton, Hunt-Morgan House)

This U.S. Cavalry Slouch Hat was popular with the Western troops, and is similar to the one worn by General Phil Sheriden and is made of beaver. (BCWM)

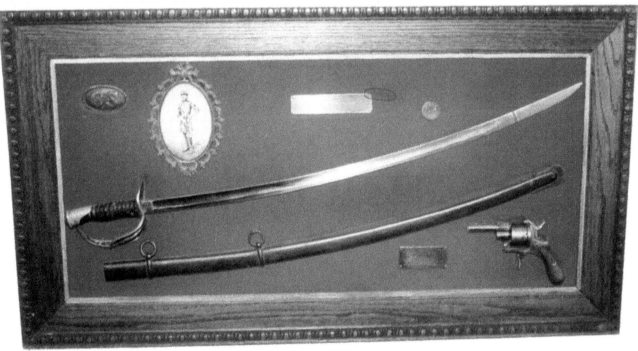

Col. George Sheary's cavalry saber, pistol, C.S. belt plate, and painting-Col. George Sheary rode with Confederate John Hunt Morgan and was a close personal friend. Sheary rode with Morgan on daring raids into Union territory. (Ken Hamilton)

CAVALRY
"Those Dashing Cavaliers"

When the Civil War broke out there wasn't a single company of organized cavalry in the North. Cavalry hadn't progressed much since Napoleonic times. The old Napoleonic tradition was for massed cavalry of as many as 12,000 men, to storm down the field with sabers flashing. Once the cavalry had reached the infantry lines, they would slash away with their sabers. The Union saw cavalry not only as being outmoded but also as being a very expensive proposition. In order to equip a mounted regiment, it would cost the government a half million dollars. They also believed that in order to have a well trained company of cavalry, it would take at least three years to properly train the officers, and at least that long for the men. Lincoln's generals also thought that the job of forming a cavalry should be left up to the regulars and not the volunteers.

In 1861, when the Battle of Bull Run was fought with disastrous results for the Union, Lincoln rethought his position on cavalry and by December 1861, the Union had raised and equipped 82 regiments, and 90,000 cavalrymen. Why did he change his position? At Bull Run, the Confederate cavalry in Turner Ashby's command proved that cavalry was a much needed element in any army. His cavalry performed a wide range of tasks, which included scouting the enemy's movements, masking the movements of the infantry, harassing enemy communications, gathering intelligence, and moving quickly wherever needed. Not to mention that they also fought like devils and for over two years the Southern cavalry would reign supreme over the battlefields of both theatres. The main reason for this was the Southern cavalryman himself, as almost all Southerners had grown up around horses with most having ridden since early childhood. Often the Southern cavalryman brought his own horse with him into the cavalry. Many of the new Union cavalrymen had never even ridden a horse. The Union Army also purchased their horses from private contractors and the cavalryman that recieved one of these horses had no idea what kind of temper it had, or if it was even healthy. The Union cavalrymen had to learn

Federal-issued soldier's boots favored by both mounted and foot soldiers. The boots extended up to the base of the knee. (BCWM)

how to ride an unfamiliar horse, but the Southerner was already familiar with his mount and he knew how to properly feed his horse, groom it and even tend to it when it was sick. These were skills his Northern counterpart had yet to learn. The South was still a very rural area in 1861 and the only way to get around in the vast areas of the South was by horse, and this too proved to be an advantage, since not only did the future Southern cavalryman become a skilled rider, but he also became very familar with the area.

Yankees from the West had an advantage over their Eastern cousins. Large areas of Illinois and Indiana were still rural and were based pretty much on farming and the men were familiar with horses, but the Union cavalry in the Western theatre had major problems with the leadership supplied by their officer corps.

By 1862, the South had produced some of the greatest cavalrymen in history. Names like John Hunt Morgan, Nathan Bedford Forrest, and Joseph Wheeler filled the newspapers on both sides. Their daring raids in 1862 and 1863 would bring pride to the South, and mortal fear to the North.

There were differences and similarities between the cavalries North and South. Both cavalry groups wanted to get in the enemy's rear; burn railroad bridges and tear up railroad track; hit supply bases and attack wagon trains; cut telegraph lines or "tap" into them to learn the enemy's intentions. Morgan was famous for doing this. His telegraph expert was called "Lighting" Ellsworth. Both sides also wanted to force the enemy to weaken his main army to deal with the raiders. Both sides also gathered information and would avoid a pitched battle unless certain of victory.

There were differences between them also. The South had problems with equipping their cavalry. Uniforms were scarce. Many troopers carried an old shotgun instead of a modern military carbine. All types and calibers of pistols were used. While many a trooper did receive a saber, most threw them away in favor of a bowie knife, and some Confederate cavalrymen wore no cutlery at all. The Union cavalry were well equipped with the latest inventions, but it did not take long before the new arms and equipment of the Union cavalry had found their way into the grateful hands of the cavaliers from Dixie.

Fighting in the Western Theatre was also much different than the fighting in the East. In the West, because of wooded landscapes, hills, rivers, and bluffs, the old Napoleonic tactics were

Model 1859 U.S. Cavalry bit with original gold G.A.R. paint. (BCWM)

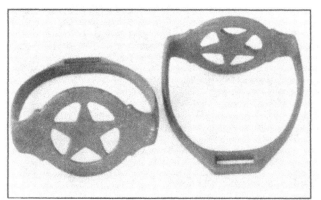

Pair of Texas stirrups featuring the cut out Texas Star in the foot sole dug at Franklin, TN (BCWM)

ruled out. No longer could you charge across open fields with thousands of men. The landscape made that impossible. Dense woods, and rural areas made communication and supply lines difficult to maintain. Western cavalry was now based on lighting fast raids, with quick, deep penetrations, speedy destruction, and a hasty withdrawal. The Confederates quickly adopted this type of fighting and were very successful with it and did more real damage to the Union army than all the bold strikes that Jeb Stuart made in the East. Millions of dollars worth of Federal supplies, and material were destroyed on Morgan's and Forrest's raids.

In 1863, the Union cavalry began to catch up with the Confederate cavalry. Albert Lee, David Stanley, and John Wilder became famous Union cavalry leaders. In 1863, Ulysses S. Grant sent Grierson on a raid through Mississippi to divert Confederate troops from Vicksburg. Grierson rode 600 miles in 16 days. He tore up 60 miles of railroad track and telegraph wire, destroyed 12,000 or more rifles and other Confederate supplies, captured 1,000 horses and mules, and caused 600 casualties. Grierson became an overnight hero in the North. For the first time, the North proved it could go one on one with the Confederate cavalry and hold its own.

In the far west, cavalry fighting took on a new form and became more vicious. Confederate cavalrymen like William Quantrill George Todd, and Bloody Bill Anderson massacred people. Union cavalry leaders John Chivington, and Charles Jennison were no better than their Confederate counterparts. There were executions, torture, scalping, robberies, rape, pil-

lage, and mutilations. Guerilla warfare would be used extensively in the Civil War.

By 1864, the most glamourous men in the Confederate cavalry were dead, John Hunt Morgan was killed in Greenville, Tennessee, Jeb Stuart was killed at Yellow Tavern. They were replaced by men like Phil Sheridan and Nathan Bedford Forrest. Forrest didn't like pomp and flair. He was a serious man who knew that war was "fighin' and killin' and that's all that mattered." You were there to get the job done, whatever the task demanded. Forrest used horses to get to a battle, but usually fought dismounted. They rode in fast, struck hard, and then left just as fast. No one used sabres. Pistols were their weapons.

In the far west, the Confederate cavalry remained active until the end of the war. Confederate raiders invaded Missouri, and Arkansas. Maj. Gen. Sterling Price led a raid into Missouri in 1864. He left Arkansas with 12,000 cavalry determined to drive the Federals out of Missouri. This was the greatest assembly of Confederate cavalry during the Civil War. Ready to greet them were 20,000 Union troops, 8,000 of them cavalry. On October 23, 1864, at Westport, near Kansas City, 17,000 cavalrymen engaged. Price and his Confederate cavalry were defeated in

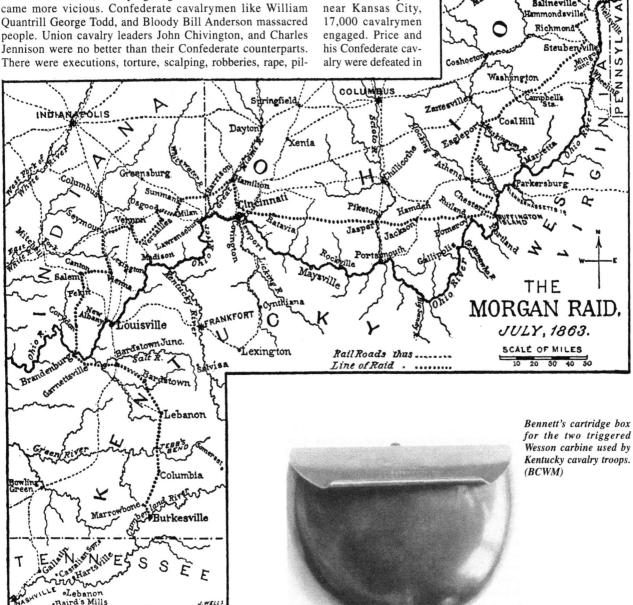

THE
MORGAN RAID,
JULY, 1863.
SCALE OF MILES
10 20 30 40 50

Rail Roads thus ....
Line of Raid . ...

MAP OF MORGAN'S OHIO RAID.

Bennett's cartridge box for the two triggered Wesson carbine used by Kentucky cavalry troops. (BCWM)

the second largest cavalry engagement of the war, behind only the battle of Brandy Station.

By 1865, cavalry had evolved into a totally new form. On March 22, 1865, James Wilson led three divisions of Federal cavalry across the Tennessee River and into Georgia and Alabama. Forrest tried to beat back Wilson, but the task proved to be too much for him. Wilson managed to destroy Selma, and then rode on to Montgomery and the capital. Wilson's 13,000 cavalry had taken Columbus and Macon, Georgia. Wilson had made a 525 mile march in which he had beaten Forrest twice, captured more than half their number and killed or wounded 1,000 or more men. Wilson destroyed seven ironworks, seven foundries, seven machine shops, two steel mills, five collieries, thirteen factories, three arsenals, a powder works, a navy yard and five steamboats, 35 locomotives, and 565 rail cars. The raid destroyed the industrial capability of the South. The last of the Confederate cavaliers was defeated.

The evolution of the cavalry in the field went from idealized heroes, glitz and glamour, and parade style pomp and chivalry to swift, lightly equipped, destructive and quite un-chivalrous raiders.[1]

Troop or Company

The basic unit of cavalry was the troop or company, organized along the same lines as an infantry company. The nominal strength was 100 men. If the troop dismounted for battle, one man in four would stay behind to guard the horses.

Battalion and Regiment

In the Union volunteers, 12 cavalry troops formed a regiment commanded by a colonel. The Confederate cavalry employed a 10 company regiment. The Union had a different organization: in the Regular units two troops formed a squadron, two squadrons formed a battalion, and three battalions formed a regiment.

This is a Carte de Viste of General John Hunt Morgan from Lexington, KY. The Carte de Viste depicts General Morgan in his full Confederate General's dress uniform and is hand colored and autographed. (BCWM)

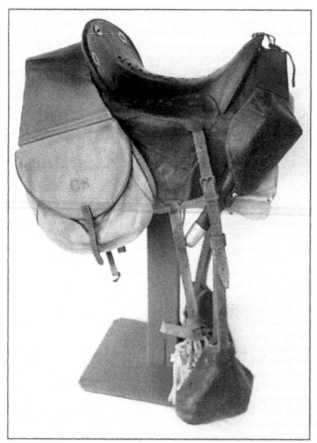

Richmond Arsenal manufactured McClellan type saddle with pommel holsters and CS marked canvas saddle bags used by a member of General Hood's Texas division. (BCWM)

Brigade, Division, and Corps

Initially, each Union cavalry regiment was assigned to an infantry division. The Confederates brigaded their cavalry together. The Union eventually adopted this organization as well. As the war progressed, both sides formed cavalry divisions(again the South took the lead). The North also formed cavalry corps, and the South later also adopted this innovation.

Confederate General John Hunt Morgan was born in Huntsville, Alabama on June 1, 1825. A member of a prominent Kentucky family, Morgan attended Translvania College in Lexington, Kentucky for two years. He left the college in 1842 under suspension for trouble he had gotten into with another student. From 1846 to 1847, he served in the Mexican War as a Lieutenant of Volunteers. After the war he purchased a hemp factory and woolen mill on his return to Kentucky. In 1857, he organized the Lexington Rifles, a local militia unit that followed him into the Confederate Army in September 1861. Serving first under Maj. Gen. Simon B. Buckner, Morgan was promoted to colonel of the 2nd Kentucky Cavalry on April 4, 1862, and to brigadier general on December 11th the same year.

Morgan was Kentucky's contribution to the ranks of legendary Southern cavalry commanders, and was noted for his daring, headline-producing raids. Like his counterpart in the East, Maj. Gen. J.E.B. Stuart, Morgan was the epitome of a cavalry leader. He stood arrow-straight, more than six feet tall, and was always impeccably dressed and finely mounted, with the manner of a polished gentlemen. While his military background was limited, innate talent offset any lack of formal training. Shrewd and fearless, he firmly established a reputation as a winner and earned the devotion and dedication of his men.

Morgan's cavalry operated in the Western theatre under the command of Maj. Gen. Joseph Wheeler. Morgan's primary contribution to the war lay not so much in what his own raids accomplished but in what they added to the total impact of cavalry operations in the West. He conducted a series of raids into Tennessee and Kentucky, the raid of July 1862 lasting three weeks as his cavalry rampaged through Kentucky, seemingly invincible to the Union cavalry sent against him. In alarm, federal military leaders in Kentucky asked the War Department for help and warned of imminent Confederate uprisings in the state. In exasperation, Abraham Lincoln wired Maj. Gen. Henry Halleck, the ranking federal commander in the department: "They are having a stampede in Kentucky. Please look in to it."

Morgan's final cavalry exploit in July 1863, was a wild, 24-day ride through southern Indiana and across Ohio, ending with Morgan's capture and confinement in the Ohio State Penitentiary. Although he escaped, the incurable adventurer was killed in a surprise cavalry encounter at Greenville, Tennessee on September 3, 1864. [2]

Basil Duke

Basil Duke was born in Georgetown, Kentucky on May 28, 1838. Many in the Confederacy's high command became able historians of the conflict, but none more able than Duke. Duke attended Centre College in Danville, Kentucky and studied law before the war, and was practicing in St. Louis, Missouri when the crisis came. Associated briefly with partisan ranger M. Jeff Thompson, he soon returned to Kentucky, where he enlisted in the Lexington rifles, which was commanded by his brother-in-law, Brig. Gen. John Hunt Morgan.

This Captain's Confederate Cavalry jacket, made of the cadet gray wool jersey material and CSA superior quality buttons, belonged to a trooper from General N. B. Forrest's command. (BCWM)

Confederate General Basil Duke's frock coat-Double breasted 3/4 frock coat of English wool broadcloth dyed a deep gray blue color. It has 16 double breasted front with buttons grouped in four groups of two, three cuff sized buttons on each cuff and four at the rear waist and tail pockets. All buttons are United States Army General Staff, three piece gilt brass backmarked "Superior Quality." Six buttons are missing from the breast. The coast is constructed with a padded and ballooned arms measuring four inches at the cuff and eight inches at the elbow. Standing collar is two inches high with separately applied Confederate General's insignia of gilt wire wreath encircling three embroidered stars, the central star being slightly superior in size. The upper body of the frock is lined with wool broadcloth in the breast, the back being a diagonally woven loose worsted wool dyed midnight blue. The tails are lined with a dark green polished cotton, with sleeves and tail pockets having unbleached linen within. The coat is of late war (1864-65). (Blue Grass Historic Trust, Hunt-Morgan House)

Private Meredith Perkins cut down Springfield rifle-Meredith Perkins enlisted in the 11th Kentucky, Company B, on September 10, 1862 at Richmond, Kentucky. He was captured on July 20, 1863, at Cheshire, Ohio during Confederate General John Hunt Morgan's raid through Kentucky, Indiana, and Ohio. He was taken to Camp Chase Prison, Ohio on July 26, 1863. In August 1863, he was transferred to Camp Douglas, Ohio. On March 2, 1865, Perkins was transferred to Point Lookout, Maryland. He was released from prison and took the oath of allegiance on May 23, 1865. (Ken Hamilton)

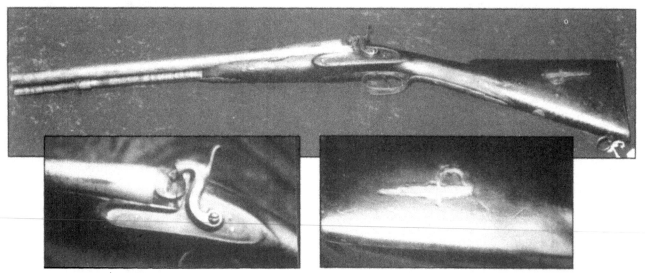

10 Gauge Greener Shotgun. The shotgun has a silver plated sword set into the butt of the rifle with 2nd Kentucky Cavalry engraved onto the sword plate. (Ken Hamilton)

Duke rose rapidly in rank first to 2nd lieutenant, then to lieutenant colonel of the 2nd Kentucky Cavalry. He served with distinction throughout Morgan's campaigns, including the raid into Indiana and Ohio, where both were captured. He did not take part in Morgan's celebrated escape from the Ohio State Penitentiary, on November 26, 1863, and was exchanged in 1864. Duke returned to the Kentucky Cavalry that fall, serving in southwest Virginia, and on Morgan's death was promoted to brigadier general, taking over Morgan's Cavalry.

Duke accompanied President Jefferson Davis and the fleeing Confederate government during April and May 1865, his being the last organized command answering to the War Department.

Following the surrender Duke returned to the law, moved to Louisville, and for the rest of his life took a prominent role in Kentucky affairs. A moderate, advocating reconciliation with the North, he devoted much of his time to preserving the history of the Confederacy. He edited Southern Bivouac, one of the best veterans magazines of the 1880's, and wrote two first rate books, A History of Morgan's Cavalry(1867) and Reminiscences of Gen. Basil W. Duke(1911). He died in New York City on September 16, 1916. [3]

Nathan Bedford Forrest was born in Bedford City, Tennessee on July 13, 1821. The son of a poverty-stricken, backwoods blacksmith. No man had more to overcome during his rise to fame than Forrest. Forced to assume responsibility for a large family at 16, Forrest, who always made the most of meager resource had become a successful slave trader and planter by the age of 40, in 1861.

In 1861, Forrest enlisted in the Confederate army as a private, but was soon made a colonel. He was promoted to brigadier general on July 21, 1862, and to major general on December 4, 1863. By war's end, in spite of a lack of military education, he displayed extraordinary capability as a tactician with a firm grasp of strategic considerations. He applied this belief with such imagination and ferocity that he became the most feared of all Confederate cavalry leaders.

Forrest's escape with all his men from Fort Donelson and his performance

This is a Carte de Viste of Lieut. Gen'l Nathan Bedford Forrest. (BCWM)

at Sacramento, Kentucky and the Battle of Shiloh brought him to prominence early in the war, and allowed him to develop the raiding tactics that made his cavalry a superb strike force. Time after time, he led his men on raids behind enemy lines and invariably accomplished far more than could have been expected from the resources committed. At the Battle of Murfreesboro, in July 13, 1862, Forrest, with only 1,400 troopers captured 1,200 Yankees and took one million dollars worth of supplies. Though such outstanding successes caused his other capabilities to be overlooked

This is an ambrotype of Lieut. Gen'l Nathan Bedford Forrest. (BCWM)

for much of the war, he was far more than a raider, which he clearly demonstrated at Brice's Crossroads. There, in a head-on engagement, he inflicted one of the most humiliating defeats in the history of the United States Army.

Forrest killed 30 Union Officers and had 29 horses shot out from under him. Forrest was the popular conception of a cavalry leader, but the war was no longer pomp and flair. As Forrest said himself, war was "Fightin' and Killin'" and that's all.

block to keep it from dropping loose from its bed. Eight hundred were produced. The Type 3, was the first to use a forestock. Type 4 had a hinged, double-pivoting breech block patented by Issac Hartshorn in March 1864. A total of 55,567 carbines of Types 2,3,4

This is a CDV of Lieut. Gen'l Nathan Bedford Forrest. (BCWM)

After the war, Forrest was ruined financially, and returned to farming and railroading business interests, although he would never recover the wealth he had before the Civil War. Maj. Gen. William Tecumsheh Sherman summed up the accomplishments of this charismatic leader and magnificent field commander when he said: "After all, I think Forrest was the most remarkable man our Civil War produced on either side." Forrest died on October 29, 1877. [5]

Cavalry Weapons-The Carbine

The carbine was the short-barreled cousin of the rifle and musket. It was the basic shoulder weapon of the cavalry.

(1) 1860 Spencer carbine-.52 caliber-Yankee officers cited the Spencer as one of the single greatest factors in winning the War. On March 6, 1860, Christopher Spencer patented the repeating carbine. It fired seven copper cartridges, positioned end on end in a metal tube, loading through the buttstock. It fired down a 22 inch barrel and it could empty its magazine in less than 30 seconds. It weighed 10 pounds and took hexagonal primed rimfire cartridges. The Spencer carbine was issued to Federal cavalrymen in late 1863, although it had been invented much earlier. By the war's end it was the most widely used carbine in service. Large scale use of the Spencer gave the Union troops a decided advantage over the Confederates, and substantially helped to shorten the war. The day of the muzzleloading weapon was over. An estimated 200,000 breechloading carbines were used in the Civil War. The Spencer Manufacturing Company went belly up in 1869, and was sold to the Winchester Repeating Arms Company.

(2) Starr Percussion Carbine-.54 caliber-From July 1863 to the end of the War, the United States government purchased 25,000 of these carbines: .54 caliber 20,000, .52 caliber 5,000. [6]

It was a single shot breechloader which fired a .54 caliber bullet from a linen cartridge. Patterned on the more famous Sharps, the Starr lacked its look-alike's sturdy reliability. According to one Federal assessment of the weapon: "The mechanism is too light and complicated. It works well enough while perfectly new but the least dirt deranges it." [7]

(3) Burnside Carbine-.54 caliber-Patented in 1856 by its inventor Union General Ambose Burnside. It was the first metallic cartridge breechloader adopted by the Federal government. On the whole an accurate and reliable weapon, it was produced in four different models. Type 1 used a tape priming device similar to a Maynard. Only 250 were produced. The Type 2 eliminated the tape primer and a catch spring was installed on the breech

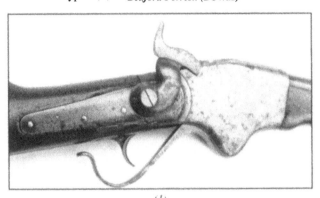

(1)

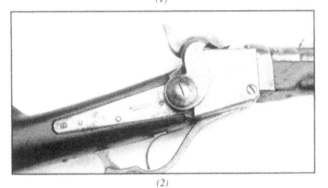

(2)

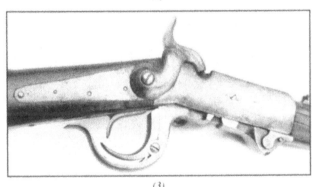

(3)

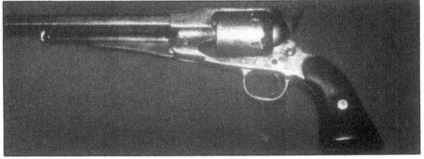

Private William Crowder's 1858 New Model .44 Remington-Private William J. Crowder was a member of the 9th Tennessee Cavalry, Morgan's Brigade, C.S.A. (Ken Hamilton)

153

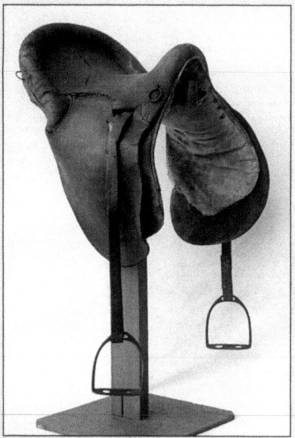

This is a modified plantation saddle used by a Tennessee plantation owner in the first years of the Civil War. (BCWM)

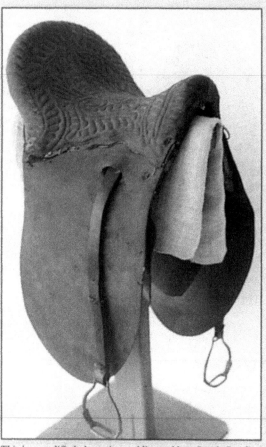

This is a modified plantation saddle used by a South Carolina plantation owner from the Charleston area. (BCWM)

Confederate modified McClellan. (BCWM)

Gen. John H. Morgan's saddle. (Bluegrass Historical Trust)

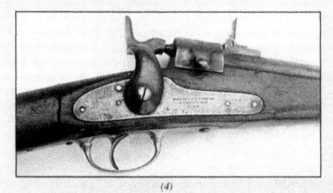

(4)

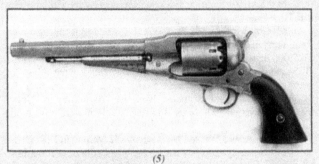

(5)

(6)

were delivered to the government, along with 22 million distinctive cone-based cartridges. Numerous Cavalry units used the Burnside. [8]

(4) Joslyn Rimfire Carbine/ Model 1862-Between July 1864 and February 1865, the Joslyn Firearms Company of Stonington, Connecticut, supplied the Federal government with some 11,000 rimfire Josyln carbines, 4,000 were the 1862 model. The six pound ten ounce weapon used a .52 caliber Spencer rimfire cartridge. The Joslyn carbine was one of the most widely used cavalry carbines of the war, the United States forces taking deliveries of them right up to 1865. Some of the very first Model 1862 Joslyn carbines had percussion ignition. A small proportion of the Model 1864 carbines were manufactured in .44 rimfire. Standard barrel length was 22 inches, but some of the later ones varied. To operate the Joslyn, a hooklike hatch on the top of the semi-cylindrical breechblock was flipped up, uncovering the firing chamber into which the cartridge was inserted. The hammer struck a firing pin at the rear of the breech and pushed it into the rim of the cartridge, detonating the explosive material in its base. [9]

Pistols

(5) Remington Army Revolver-.44 caliber- It was made in two calibers and several models. The New Model 1863 was purchased in greater quantity by the United States government than any other handgun except the Colt. In fact, by 1863 Remington's prices were so favorable and the weapons so good that Colt, whose prices were higher, no longer received government contracts. Over 115,563 were sold to the Union government. [10]

(6) Double Action Starr Revolver-Designed in both double action and single action by Eben T. Starr, it was produced in three models in factories located in Yonkers, Binghampton, and Morrisania, New York. The Model 1858 Navy Revolver was a double action, .36 caliber, six shot weapon produced between 1858-1860. What appears to be the trigger is actually a cocking lever. When pulled, the cylinder rotates and the hammer is pulled back. The real trigger is concealed on the inside rear of the trigger guard. It is fired either in the conventional manner with the index finger or by the use of an adjustable stud located on the back of the locking lever. Approximatively 3,000 of these navy revolvers were produced.

Col. W.W. Ward's Presentation Lefaucheux revolver-.41 caliber pinfire-Col. W.W. Ward was member of the 9th Tennessee Cavalry, Morgan's Brigade, C.S.A. This pistol has Col. W.W. Ward, 1st Kentucky Cavalry engraved on the silver plated shield on the pommel of the gun. (Kentucky Military History Museum)

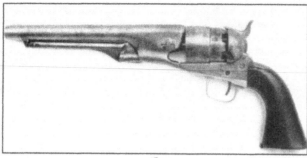

(7)

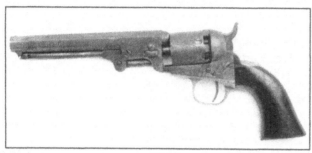

(8)

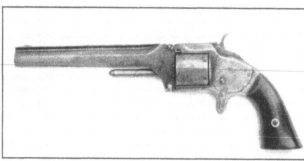

(9)

(10)

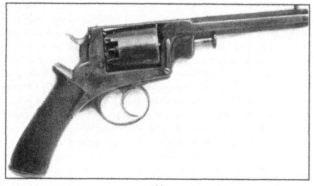

(11)

The 1858 Army revolver was essentially the same as the navy but in .44 caliber. Over 25,000 of the .44 caliber weapons were bought by the Union Government. The Model 1863 Army revolver eliminated the double action system in favor of a single action because Remington and Whitney were selling their single action revolvers at $15.00 each, so to be competitive, Starr priced theirs at $12.00, and sold about 31,000 to the government. Many were supplied to and used in the Western theatre. [11]

(7) 1860 Colt Army Revolver-.44 caliber- Six shot precussion revolver-It fired a paper cartridge loaded from the front of the cylinder, and had to be capped before the weapon could be fired. It weighed 2 lb., 11 oz. Altogether, there were 200,500 made between 1860-1873. The Federal government bought 127,156, and the Navy bought 4,800. It was the major revolver used by the Union during the Civil War. [12]

(8) Colt Model 1849 Pocket Revolver- This is the most common version of the Model 1849, of which Colt manufactured over 325,000 between 1850 and 1873. Essentially a reduced size Model 1851 navy, more of these pistols were produced than any other Colt percussion firearm. There were many minor variations-over 200 according to the best estimates. None were issued by the United States government. Those used in the Civil War were private purchase items. [13]

(9) Smith and Wesson No. 2 Army-.32 caliber-In 1857 Daniel B. Wesson managed to buy the patent that had blocked manufacture in the United States. For 12 years Smith & Wesson enjoyed a monopoly, producing a range of metallic cartridge revolvers that spelled the end of percussion pistols. The No. 2 Army fired a .32 rimfire cartridge and the barrel hinged upward to allow the cylinder to be withdrawn. The fixed pin beneath the barrel was then used to push out the empty cases one by one. During the war, the state of Kentucky purchased 700 of the No. 2's from the arms dealer B. Kittridge & Company of Cincinnati, Ohio and issued them to the 7th Kentucky cavalry. Thousands more were privately obtained by Union enlisted men and officers, who found the gun a serviceable, well crafted sidearm. [14]

(10) Lefaucheux 11 mm French Pin-fire Revolver-This French revolver was the first to use metallic cartridges. Produced in 1853, the Lefaucheux cartridge was made of copper and held a charge of black powder behind the bullet. A brass pin projected from the base and ignited the primer when it was struck by the hammer. Adopted as the service arm of the French Navy in 1855, the Lefaucheux was immediately available to federal purchasing agents in 1860. They bought 10,000 for the United States Army. [15]

(11) Massachusetts Adams revolver-.32 caliber- Robert Adams was partner in the London company of Deane, Adams, & Deane. The revolver was a double action. The frame and barrel were made in one piece and the cylinder was easy to detach. Produced in .32, .44, and .50 caliber, the Adams design was modified in 1857 to allow the gun to be fired single or double action. Both sides imported the Adams during the war, and some were manufactured under license in Massachusetts. Around 700 of them had been produced by the Massachusetts Arms Company of Chicopee Falls and acquired by the Federal government between 1857 and 1861. Each pistol weighed a little over two and a half pounds and had a six inch long rifled barrel. [16]

(12)Whitney Navy Revolver (belonging to a soldier in Company D, 11th Kentucky Union cavalry)-.36 caliber-Some 11,000 of these revolvers were bought by the United States ordnance department for issue to cavalrymen. The pistol was highly regarded and its design was copied by a number of arms manufacturers.

W.B. Middleton 4th Corporal

Company F, 3rd Regiment Kentucky Mounted Infantry C.S.

W.B. Middleton enlisted at Ballard County, Kentucky in the Confederate Cavalry on April 27, 1864. He was not in the service for long. Middleton was severly wounded in the foot at the Battle of Tishomingo Creek, Guntown, Mississippi (also known as Brice's

Soldier from 11th KY. Union Cavalry.

Crossroads), while serving in Maj. Gen. Nathan Bedford Forrest's command on June 10, 1864. He was transported to a hospital and survived his wounds and lived until the 1920s.

The Battle of Brice's Crossroads was an important victory for Nathan Bedford Forrest, and was a dismal failure for the Union army under Sherman. On March 16, 1895, Mr. Samuel Agnew of Bethany, Mississippi wrote an article explaining the battle in vivid detail. Mr. Agnew lived where the battle occurred. In his own words, Agnew explains the battle:

"The battle occurred about six miles from Guntown at the crossings of the Ripley and Fulton Road with the road leading from Pontotoc to Jacinto. ... At this crossroads, in 1864, were the residence of Mr. William Brice, a large two-story building .... On the 7th of June, we had positive assurance that on Sabbath night the 5th, three Federal regiments of cavalry passed through Ripley taking the Rienzi Road, and camped three miles from Ripley and fed off of Yancey who was said to be ruined. They went on to Rienzi and were reported at Hatchie Turnpike Monday evening. This force was estimated at from 1,500 to 3,000 men. A large force, said to be at Salem coming on ... Russell's Tennessee regiment was following this cavalry force, watching their movements.

"Forrest, with his force passed up by the Crossroads Tuesday evening the 7th. The trains on the Mobile & Ohio Railroad that night and the next morning brought up his artillery and it was evident that he was moving towards Corinth, regarding that as the point of danger.

"On Tuesday evening the 7th, Rucker's brigade consisting of Duckworth's Tennessee, and Duff's and Chalmers' Mississippi regiments had a fight four miles south of Ripley and fell back and camped at Kelley's mill on Tallahatchie, and thence on Wednesday they went to Baldwyn. (The Federal) force on Muddy Creek above Ripley was said to consist of seven regiments of infantry, four of which were negroes, 2,500 cavalry, 250 wagons, 150 ambulances and large quantities of artillery. On Thursday, the 9th, we learned that Rucker's brigade had gone from Baldywn towards Rienzi. Forrest force was all above us and we felt our neighborhood would not be a scene of conflict. Late Thursday, however, we heard that the Federal force was coming from the direction of Ripley towards our country, but we discredited the rumor, unconscious of the proximity of danger Thursday night.

"Friday, the eventful 10th of June, dawned peacefully. The morning was cloudy. For several days had had much rain. While sitting at the table a negro man

came in and reported that the Yankees had camped the night before at Stubb's farm, seven miles from us in the direction of Ripley ... As soon as a few mouthfuls were swallowed ... (we) went into a dense thicket a mile and a half southwest of our home ... We were in a branch bottom back of my father's farm. We heard roaring northward which we could not explain. Afterward we knew it was the noise made by the advancing Federal army.... we were now certain that the Federal force had come down the Ripley and Fulton Road. We did not dare communicate with home ... (we) anxiously

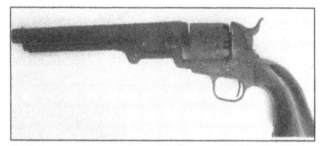

Confederate revolver manufactured by "Augusta Machine Works", Augusta, Georgia. This is a .36 caliber revolver, featuring a 12 stop cylinder, and the cryptic number "7" and the letter L on various parts of the gun. There were less than 100 of these weapons made. (BCWM)

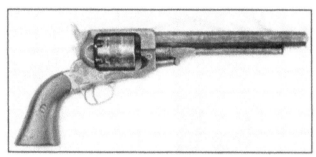

(12) Whitney Revolver. (BCWM)

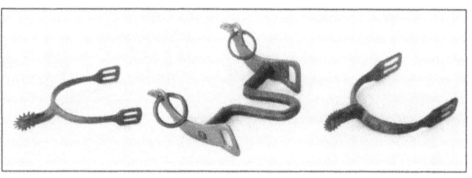

Above and below: Assortment of Civil War spurs and bits. (BCWM)

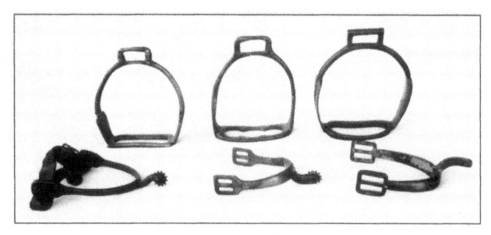

Capt. Waller Overton-Adjutant to Confederate General Adam Rankin Johnson, Adjutant of the Eighth and Twelfth Kentucky Cavalry Regiments, and Sybert's Battalion under Confederate General Nathan Bedford Forrest-Overton's butternut wool shell jacket has an eight button front with upright collar. The uniform has a red and black wool lining. The jacket has right and left side inside pockets. The butternut wool trousers have a five wooden button fly, with suspender buttons. The trousers also have a cloth waistband. (Kentucky Military History Museum)

awaited the developments. We did not have long to wait, a volley of small arms was heard—it was the first shots of the day, when the advance guards of (Brig. Gen. Samuel D.) Sturgis force encountered a squad of cavalry which had been sent from Baldwyn to reconnoiter — this occurred in Dry Creek bottom ... They fell back and reported the advance to the Federal force. We did not have long to wait before we heard the cannon roaring in southeastern direction ... it was near the Cross Roads. The battle raged on long ... about 10:00 a.m. and it was after 5 o'clock before the Federals were forced to retreat.

"Sturgis had moved early from Stubb's but was much impeded by muddy roads. He established his headquarters in Mr. Brice's house. His cavalry was under the command of (Brig.) Gen. B(enjamin) H. Grierson and consisted of two brigades, Warren's and Winslow's, numbering 3,300 men with six pieces of artillery and four mountain howitzers. His infantry consisted of three brigades, Wilkin's, Hoge's and Benton's. The last was a colored brigade. The infantry numbered 4,400 men with twelve pieces of artillery. Sturgis estimated his force at 8,000 men in round numbers and the estimate is regarded as a low one. He had 23 regiments in all.

"Forrest's force consisted of 3,500 men comprised in four brigades, commanded by Lyons, Rucker, Johnson, and (Col. Tyree H.) Bell, all cavalry. With the main part of his force he was in Booneville the night of the 9th. I have understood that the movements of Sturgis were so covered that Forrest was not sure where he was until during that night, when scouts reported him camped at Stubb's farm. Some of his troops expected to move northward early Friday morning, as orders had been issued to cook two days rations and be ready to move very early. But the developments of that night led to a change of purpose and the next morning he moved southward before day to intercept Sturgis. Forrest moved very rapidly coming, according to Gen. Chalmer's, eight miles in a gallop. His wagon train was hurried south on roads east of the railroad. (Maj.) Gen. (Stephen D.) Lee, the commanding officer, had come up and it had been decided that it was best to fall back before the enemy, delaying their advance as much as possible, and to gather a force south of him and blockade his advance force about Okalona which might successfully oppose Sturgis. And Lee had gone down to make the needful preparations sometime during Thursday night. Notwithstanding Forrest's haste, Sturgis succeeded in getting his force south of him and blockaded his advance at the Cross Roads ... Forrest moved with his command to the left of the Baldwyn Road and advanced flanking the enemy's right. The Federal force was placed in the form of a fan, beginning in the blackjack thicket little north of the Baldwyn road, touching on that road a bald prairie ... the movement of Forrest to the Guntown Road was very difficult, owing to a thick undergrowth of blackjack which covered the surface all around the Cross Roads. But his men were dismounted and fought as infantry, every fourth man being left to hold horses. The Federal cavalry held their front until their infantry came up. Forrest's rapid ride from Booneville had doubtless fagged his horses, and therefore it is possible that it was best for his men to fight on foot. They were brave men and fought with spirit. Midway between the two roads and back of the Porter Field, the conflict was very sanguinary. At the opening of the battle Forrest ordered Gen. Buford to send a regiment (Barteau's) from Old Carrollville across the country into the rear of the enemy. They moved accordingly and entered the Creek, five and a half miles from the Cross Roads and, moving down the road a mile and a half, they deployed into the woods and fired into the enemy, who were beginning to fall back. This attack in the rear served to increase the discomfiture of the enemy. About the middle of the afternoon, in my place of concealment, I heard firing of this attack of Batteau' on the enemy.

"While the battle was in progress it became evident about 5 o'clock that the firing was nearer, that the Federals was manifestly falling back and that Forrest was pressing them in this direction. About 6 o'clock, when this long, hot and anxious day was drawing to a close, to my surprise shells began to fall in the woods where we were hidden. I was a little east of where our stock was concealed and, as the shells passed over my head whizzing and sputtering, I couldn't help dodging ... We were evidently in an unsafe place and retreated, going south, while the shells were flying over us. The battle was raging (over the fields at my house) ... The ground all around the Cross Roads was covered with the wounded and dead. Forrest was in the front pursuing them with vigor and the last reports were that a desperate stand had been made at my father's house.

"That night was a showery one, the next morning, as soon as I could see, I started to find out what happened at home .... I found out that the Yankees had been driven away. Our once pleasant home was a wreck. Thanks to Providence the lives of the family had been preserved, although they had been in great danger .... The public road in both directions was lined with wagons as far as could be seen. As I came home, for more than half a mile, I saw hundreds of shoes and articles of every description which had been thrown away by the Yankees in their retreat .... When I saw these things I knew that Forrest had gained a great and complete victory, but my heart sunk within me at the prospect of our own losses .... I walked through the rooms and found everything turned upside down and that many things had been taken from us .... Dead and wounded men were lying in the house, upstairs and downstairs. Bullets had penetrated the walls of the house in various places.

"On the retreat Sturgis was in the front going at a trot. The final stand was made at my father's house. When the night began my mother, wife, and sisters closed the window shutters, all went into an inner room, and lying flat on the floor, they waited the issue of the conflict. Two Federal soldiers came in the back piazza and surrendered to my mother just as the fight began. The yard was a battleground, the Southern troops were on the south side and the federals on the north side, they made a breastwork of a picket fence on that side. A federal battery was in front of our gate. Rice's battery was just below the bend in the public road, the fight here was nearly as stubborn as the Cross Roads. Capt. Rice told me that the artillery saved the day here. When he came up our cavalry was being repulsed. The defeat was overwhelming and this is doubtless a reason why so little is said in histories about the battle of Tishomingo Creek. It was a signal victory for the Federal force was about three times as great as that of Forrest. There can be no doubt that there was gross mismanagement on the part of Strugis or his officers .... Forrest completely defeated the enemy, capturing all their artillery and their entire wagon train ... the losses incurred in such a rout were necessarily very great. According to the Official Medical History of the war, the losses on the Federal side were 617 killed and wounded and 1,623 missing. The Confederate loss, according to the same authority, was 606 killed and wounded.

"The pursuit was continued beyond Salem. On Monday, the 13th, many soldiers returned from pursuing. Eight hundred prisoners were marched down the road that day. Some officers were among them, and they were nice looking men. (The Negroes) wore the badge, "Remember Fort Pillow," and it is said by some that they carried a black flag and avowed themselves as unwilling to give or receive quarter. This incensed the Southern soldiers.

"Mr. Brice's house was temporarily made a hospital for wounded Confederates. Southern boys lay on pallets there, and some died there. Bethany Church was occupied as a hospital, and many a Federal soldier lay wounded on benches on which worshippers had been wont to sit in days when peace reigned in the land. A bullet passed through the pulpit. The monuments and tombstones to this day show the imprint of minie balls.

"Thirty or more graves containing the bodies of brave Tennessee and Kentuckians, who fell in battle that day, are in Bethany burial. The graves are unmarked; the heroes that lie there are unknown, unhonored and unsung; a man named King of Rice's battery, is buried a few hundred yards below my residence; the little mound which marks his grave can be seen on the roadside. King was from the vicinity of Artesia, Mississippi. The grave of a Tennessean, A.J. Smith, is not far away but the exact spot cannot be pointed out. A nice young man, who was brought wounded on the day of battle into my house and died there that night, was buried under a large post oak in front of my gate. His name was Rice. His friends removed his remains to the family burial ground in Lauderale, County Tennessee in 1865.

"While in carnage and number of the troops engaged, it cannot equal Shiloh, Gettysburg, or Chickamauga, yet it was by no means an insignificant battle. Gen. Chalmers says it was the most brilliant victory of the war on either side and, considering the great disparity of the contending forces, the result was certainly most wonderful...."

Forrest did win a great tactical victory and captured 192 wagons and ambulances, 16 cannons, and 1,500 stand of small arms.

On March 25, 1927, Sally Middleton Franklin wrote a letter to the curator, Mr. D.L. Hewlett, of the Knoxville Confederate Memorial Museum. In the letter, she said that she was giving a homemade knife and "a beautiful silver medal" that her husband wore at reunion meetings, to the museum. The museum closed on February 1, 1936, when Mr. Hewlett died. All the contents of the museum were either sold or the artifacts given back to the relatives. Does anyone know where the medal is? Please contact me I would love to know what happened to it. It would be nice to have all his items reunited.

Adam Rankin Johnson

Inscription reads: "Capt. Paul J. Marrs Compliments Brig. Genl. Adam R. Johnson C.S.A.

In the annals of Civil War history, Adam Rankin Johnson has to stand out as one of the better Civil War cavalry generals. Johnson would not only stand out for his intelligence, wit, and cunning skill, but also for his love of his Southern homeland and family. Johnson's life also touched many people before and after his Civil War career.

Lt. Col. David Logan's Frock Coat-7th Kentucky Cavalry, C.S.A.-The uniform is locally made in Kentucky and made of gray wool, double breasted uniform coat, a variant from the uniform regulations of the Confederate States of America, 1861. It has a 14 double breasted front with edge piping of light blue at front and collar. Gray wool locally manufactured broadcloth faded to a light greenish gray color. All rank and insignia have been removed. Buttons at the front and tails are gilt die stamped brass two piece English manfactured Confederate Staff Officer's buttons marked "extra rich-treble gilt." The sleeves are decorated with triple gilt wire galloons in a pattern consistent with Confederate uniform regulation indicating a field grade officer. Gilt wire sleeve rank insignia is tucked at each seam. The interior of the coat is lined in a dark green polished cotton with a lightly quilted breast. Sleeve lining is white linen. (Blue Grass Historic Trust)

Adam Rankin Johnson was born in Henderson, Kentucky on February 8, 1834. He was the son of Thomas Jefferson Johnson, M.D. and Juliet Spencer Rankin. At an early age, Johnson began to educate himself in reading, history, and biography. He would read tales about romance and adventure that would have a tremendous influence on his later life. At age 12, Johnson worked in a drug store, and at age 16, he gained a position in Burbank's factory in Henderson, and was in charge of 80 people. In 1854, when Johnson was 20, he moved to Texas and settled in Burnett County. He became a scout, surveyor, and mail contractor for the Overland Mail Company. Many times, his surveying and scouting parties would be attacked by the Indians. The Indian attacks taught Johnson: "In

Brig. Gen. Adam R. Johnson

an uncertain light and with the protection of a suitable background, there was little chance of detection or recognition; if the enemy could thus elude me, so also I could deceive them by this and similar devices; and when afterward I had occasion to put this idea in practice, I always acted promptly and confidently, ever holding the conviction that the ruse resorted to whatever it was, would succeed." This outlook would play a major role in how he fought his battles during the Civil War.

When Texas seceded, Johnson returned to his home in Henderson, Kentucky. Two of his brothers had already signed up in the Union army, but he enlisted with Nathan Bedford Forrest as a scout. Johnson's first battle of the Civil War was in Sacramento, Kentucky. On December 27, 1861, Col. Nathan Bedford Forrest's cavalry surprised and engaged 168 men under the command of Maj. Murray of Jackson's regiment, Thomas Crittenden's command. Forrest fought in hand to hand combat and at one point, was surrounded by five men who ordered him to surrender. Forrest killed four of the men, and forced the fifth to surrender. The Federals lost 65 killed and 35 captured. Forrest lost two men and four wounded.

After the battle of Sacramento, Johnson returned to Henderson to see his mother, then he caught up with Forrest in February at Fort Henry just before Fort Henry was taken by Adm. Foote's gun boats. Johnson then moved on with Forrest to help defend Fort Donelson. Johnson helped John Floyd escape by steamboat on the Cumberland River after Fort Donalson fell. When Johnson reached Nashville, the city was in a state of panic because Union General Don Carlos Buell was approaching. Confederate General Albert Sidney Johnson ordered an evacuation of the city, while Johnson waited there for Forrest to catch up. When Forrest arrived he ordered his Texas Rangers to restore order to the city, and then ordered his men to round up every single wagon they could find, and made off with 250,000 pounds of bacon, 600 boxes of army clothing, hundreds of wagon loads of flour and commissary, weapons, and ammunition. He dismantled some of Nashville's foundry machinery for rifling cannons and shipped them and other ordnance equipment to Atlanta. Forrest moved out of the city with this massive wagon train before Don Carlos Buell entered the city.

Gen. Forrest then ordered Robert Martin and Adam R. Johnson to Texas to deliver an important message from Albert Sidney Johnston to Governor Lubbock of Texas. They delivered their message and returned to Forrest at Corinth, Mississippi. The battle of Shiloh was over by the time they arrived. Confederate General Earl Van Dorn, who Johnson knew from his Texas scouting days, ordered Forrest to select two commissioned officers to serve on his staff. Johnson and Robert Martin were selected. Van Dorn was trying to prevent Union General John Pope's advance into Corinth and the result was the Battle of Farmington, a Confederate victory. After the battle, Forrest told Johnson he was now under Confederate Major General John C. Breckinridge's command. Breckinridge sent Johnson with a cipher message to Henderson, Kentucky to be delivered to David Burbank. Johnson delivered the message, and was given several hundred dollars by Burbank, and he promised Breckinridge that 50,000 men would sign up for the Confederate cause. While in Henderson, Johnson decided to recruit his own army. Johnson, Bob Martin, and Frank Owen proceeded to Owensboro and then to Henderson where the three man army boldly attacked the Union provost guard. They suffered no losses. Johnson then heard that a Federal cavalry force of 300 men had

left Louisville and was determined to burn any house that supported the Confederates. Johnson, who now had six men, decided to attack this force. He had heard that the Yankee cavalry was in Madisonville, and on the night of July 5, 1862, Johnson and his men attacked the Federals while they were sleeping. The Federals rode off in haste, without a house being burned. The Yankees fell back to Henderson, and then proceeded to board a steamboat, so that they could reach Louisville in safety. Johnson, who now had 20 men, entered Henderson, and occupied the city, raising a Confederate flag over the courthouse.

On July 18, 1862, Johnson headed for Newburg, Indiana, having heard that there were 100 guns at this location in the care of Col. Bethel. While on the Kentucky side of the river, Johnson decided to build himself some cannons, since he didn't have any with him. He took two wagon wheels with axles, and a stovepipe and a charred log, and fashioned two "cannons," and trained them on the town across the river. Johnson and his men transported themselves to the other side of the Ohio River and entered Newburg, going directly to the hotel in the town. When Johnson walked into the hotel, 80 Union soldiers pointed their guns at him. Johnson ordered the Yankees to surrender, or they would sufffer the consequences from his "troops". The Union soldiers surrendered and stacked their arms. Johnson captured two wagon loads of guns. Col. Bethel's 250 home guards then entered the city. Johnson ordered Bethel to recall his home guard or he would shell

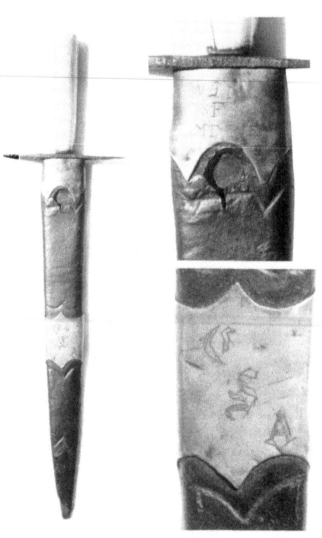

This is a side knife belonging to William Middleton, Company F, 3rd Kentucky Mounted Infantry under Lt. General N. B. Forrest's command, the hero of Brice's Cross Roads. This knife was donated to a Knoxville, TN Veteran's Post at the turn of the century. (BCWM)

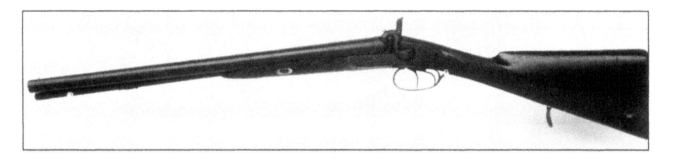

the city with his "cannon." Bethel's house was the largest in the city, and after seeing the "cannon" with his spyglass, Bethel told his home guard to fall back. Johnson then ferried the captured guns across the river to Kentucky. A gunboat soon appeared, and Johnson ordered his men to fire upon it, and seeing Johnson's makeshift cannon, the captain of the gunboat turned back. From this point on Johnson would be called "Stovepipe Johnson."

Johnson soon recruited 300 men, but he needed more weapons, so he made ready to attack Clarksville, Tennessee, where the Federals had supplies. The commander of the Union troops at Clarksville was Col. Mason. Johnson found out where Col. Mason's headquarters were and decided to attack the headquarters by himself. Johnson rushed up the stairs, opened the door, and ordered Col. Mason to surrender, which he immediately did. With their commander captured, the Union soldiers also surrendered. Johnson paroled 370 prisoners, and sent them to Fort Donelson. He captured 500 guns and one million dollars worth of supplies and several thousand wagons. Up to this point, Johnson hadn't lost one single man.

In August 1862, Adam R. Johnson was made a colonel in the 10th Partisan Rangers. Col. Johnson was pleased with his many accomplishments and felt that nothing could stop his men. He prepared to attack Fort Donelson, but on his way there, Johnson was attacked at Madisonville by Capt. Shackelford and his 9th Pennsylvania cavalry. Johnson divided his force and a trap was set for Shackelford, but Shackelford avoided the trap and moved to where Johnson and only seven sick men where positioned. Luckily, this time Johnson had a real cannon and fired a round that struck Shackelford in the foot. Because of a problem with the mules that carried the ammunition, all the honking and braying made it sound like Johnson had more cannons with him so Shackelford decided not to expose his men to further cannon fire and retreated.

In July 1863, Johnson was attached to Confederate General John Hunt Morgan's 2nd Brigade, the 1st Brigade was under Basil Duke. Morgan gave Johnson two brigades and divided his battery. Morgan burned the trestles at Muldraugh Hill, and then encountered Union troops at the Green River Bridge. There were 400 Federals protecting the bridge. Morgan ordered Johnson to charge the Union position, which he did, and lost 50 men during the charge. Morgan then flanked the bridge and moved on to Lebanon. Union troops under Col. Charles Hanson were stationed at Lebanon and on July 5, 1863, Morgan attacked. Col. Charles Hanson and his 350 men surrendered after a seven hour battle. Hanson noted in his report, "Tis considered a good fight on my part." Morgan's brother Thomas, was among those killed at Lebanon. Morgan's raiders then moved on toward Burksville and then to Brandenburg, where they captured two steamboats which they used to cross the Ohio River to Indiana. On July 9, 1863, Morgan fought a small battle at Corydon, Indiana with the home guard, and then trotted off toward Ohio. The Union cavalry was fast closing in and Morgan's men were finally captured at Buffington Island, but Johnson and his men escaped by swimming across the Ohio River as the Federals fired at them from the Ohio side of the river. On July 19, 1863, Johnson and 300 men reached Briar County, Virginia, and headed toward the Virginia capitol.

Upon arriving in Richmond, he was ordered to reorganize Morgan's command. In 60 days, he managed to mount and equip

Top: Cut down for Cavalry use double barrel shotgun used by William Middleton, Company F, 3rd Kentucky Mounted Infantry. (BCWM)

Bottom: Cartes de Visites of William Middleton, Company F, 3rd Kentucky Mounted Infantry was taken at the turn of the century and was bequeathed to his beloved sister. (BCWM)

700 men. Confederate General Simon Bolivar Buckner ordered Johnson to Morristown, East Tennessee and Asheville, North Carolina. Once this assignment was accomplished, he was then ordered by Forrest to Ringgold, Georgia to fight in the Chickamaugua campaign. After Chickamaugua, Johnson was ordered to Athens, Tennessee, and then on May 1864, was ordered back to Richmond, Virginia.

On June 1, 1864, Adam R. Johnson was promoted to brigadier general. He was ordered back to Kentucky after fighting at Cold Harbor and in the Wilderness campaign. By the time he reached Atlanta, he only had 50 men left. He reached Union County, Kentucky in the middle of July. On August 17th, Gen. Hughes and Gen. Hovey and 600 men of the 36th Indiana and 300 of Gen.Willich's Indiana brigade with four 12 pounders in tow, left Evansville, Indiana for Union County, Kentucky to intercept Gen. Johnson's recruits and drive them from the county.

At Mt. Vernon, the Union troops picked up three more cannons and a large force under Warrick and Posey County Home Guards. Johnson had about 3,000 men, and was to concentrate them at Newburg, Indiana, and pick up men and supplies and then was to capture Evansville. Johnson heard that Gen. Hobson was at Grubb's Crossroads, Kentucky, and decided to try and capture Hobson there. At dawn on August 21, 1864, Johnson charged Hobson's men, and managed to capture 50 Union soldiers. He ordered the soldiers to face about and move toward his command which was now approaching them. Johnson's troops saw these Federals with guns in their hands, and opened fire on them. In the process, shooting their own Gen. Johnson in the right eye, the ball coming out of the left temple, after blinding both eyes.

After being wounded, Johnson was captured and imprisoned at Fort Warren, Boston Harbor. He fell while in prison and was severely crippled. He was then exchanged, and sent to Richmond, Virginia. Johnson refused to sign retirement papers and wanted a new command. He received orders, and was transported with his men to Selma, Alabama, then on to Macon, Mississippi. In April 1865, Johnson joined 50 men under Capt. Shanks at Macon. He arrived in time to hear that Lee had surrendered at Appamottox.

Johnson and some of his men returned to Texas, where he

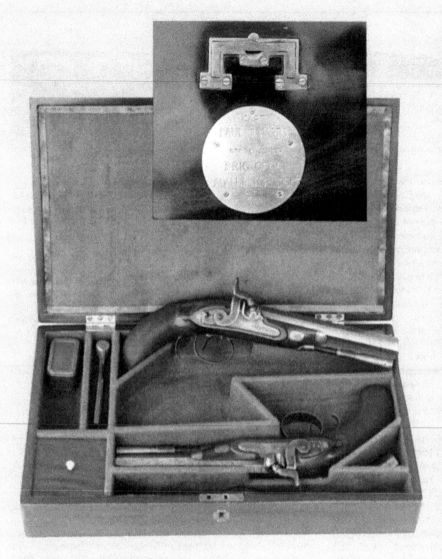

Johnson went on to have a successful career as a business man, and published one of the best books about the 10th Kentucky Partisan Rangers, it's title is The Partisan Rangers of the Confederate States Army and was published in 1904. He died on October 20, 1922, and was buried in Austin, Texas. His monument in Texas reads: "No man in the Southern army, no matter how high his rank, displayed more military skill or intrepidity than Gen. Adam R. Johnson .... He was literally the "Swamp Fox" of Kentucky." Johnson was truly one of the great figures of the Confederate cavalry. His exploits echo great feats of boldness and daring. Johnson must surely be ranked with the great cavalry leaders of the South. [16]

Paul Jones Marrs-Paul Jones Marrs was born in Posey County, Indiana, on February 28; 1838. Marrs was in business before the Civil War and was half owner of the firm of Cromwell and Marrs, a drug retailer. When the Civl War broke out, Marrs sold his interest in the business and enlisted as a private under Col. Adam Rankin Johnson. During his army life, Capt. Marrs was engaged in many skirmishes and several battles. In 1862, he along with others, was captured and sent to prison at Evansville, Indiana; from Evansville he was sent to Camp Morton, Indiana, where he remained for one year. He was then sent to Johnson's Island Prison, and a short time later he was sent to Fortress Monroe. In 1863, Marrs was finally exchanged and returned to his command. During his term of service, Capt. Marrs was promoted to the rank of captain, and was made quartermaster of the command. At the close of the war he returned to Henderson, surrendered himself to Capt. Platter, then in command of the post, and took the oath of allegiance.

On May 11, 1872, Capt. Marrs married Juliet Rankin, granddaughter of Dr. Adam Rankin, one of the earliest pioneer physicians to come to this part of Kentucky. They had three children, William, Juliet, and Mary. After the close of the war, Marrs worked as a clerk for Holloway and Hopkins, and later was with Green Marshall & Company, in the wharfboat business and a commission business that included tobacco sales. In 1882, he invested a telephone enterprise and under his management, the business grew from a small beginning into a corporation of wealth and power. He was one of the organizers for the Great Southern Telegraph and Telephone Company, and from 1882 to 1885 was engaged in establishing the service in Nashville, New Orleans, and other Southern cities. In 1882, he moved to Nashville and remained there until 1885, when he returned to Henderson. In 1885, he was elected Director of the Henderson Cotton Mills.

The dueling pistols were made by T. Monck, Stamford, England.

Presented to Capt. Paul J. Marrs compliments of Brig. Gen. Adam R. Johnson, CSA. (See story on page 159)

first settled in Plano County, but Indian raids forced him to move to Burnett. While there, he opened a land office, built a schoolhouse and employed teachers. He helped build a stretch of railroad so that the marble and granite mined on his ranch could be transported to Austin, where it was used to build the new state capitol building. He founded the town of Marble Falls, Texas in 1887 and for many years it was known locally as "The Blind Man's Town."

Maj. John T. Farris, 5th & 9th Kentucky Cavalry

John Farris was born in 1823, in Bourbon County, Kentucky. John Farris enlisted as a private at Camp Dick Robinson, Eminence, Kentucky on August 6, 1861, and served under Col. Speed Fry. On October 25, 1861, Farris was commissioned as a 1st Lieutenant in the 5th Kentucky Cavalry and served as the regimental quartermaster until February 17, 1862, when he received orders from Brig. Gen. Jeremiah Boyle to report for duty as Boyle's aid.

On April 7, 1862, Lt. Farris participated in the battle of Shiloh. Brig. Gen. Boyle was commanding the 11th Brigade, Army of the Ohio, in Brig. Gen. Thomas Crittenden's 5th Division. At 5 o'clock a.m., on April 7, 1862, the brigade under Boyle attacked the Confederates. This brigade consisted of the 13th and 19th Ohio, the 9th Kentucky, and the 59th Ohio as reserve. During the battle, Boyle's regiments came under heavy fire from rebel artillery. Union guns were then brought forward and silenced the Rebel guns. When this was accomplished, Boyle's brigade began it's advance. Gen. Don Carlos Buell himself rode up and ordered the 9th Kentucky and the 59th Ohio to advance rapidly and drive the enemy back. Col. Grider of the 9th Kentucky lost six killed and 21 wounded during the assault. The 19th Ohio was ordered to the extreme left of the Union line to support Gen. Nelson. The enemy was driven back, and the firing ceased all along the line. The battle was over and the Army of the Ohio, under Buell, had pushed the Confederates out of Shiloh.

Brig. Gen. Boyle had high praise for Lt. Farris. Boyle stated that Farris "deported himself with fearless courage and coolness." As an aide to General Boyle, Farris probably carried messages from Gen. Boyle to his regimental commanders while under fire.

Lt. Farris then marched with the army to Corinth, Mississippi. The Confederates were in the city, behind their earthworks and Union forces were now concentrated around the outskirts of Corinth. The Confederates decided to buy themselves some time by having trains pull into and out of the station, the people cheering as the trains came in, hopefully making the Union troops around Corinth believe that more re-enforcements were arriving. In truth, the trains were taking the Rebels out of Corinth. Finally, in May the Union troops attacked Corinth, only to find the city abandoned.

On August 22, 1862, Farris was commissioned a major in the 9th Kentucky Cavalry for his "gallant service" in the battle of Shiloh.

On December 21, 1862, Confederate General John Hunt Morgan led his Great Christmas Raid into Kentucky. His objective was to break up the Louisville and Nashville Railroad, which was William Rosecrans lifeline for supplies. On December 26, 1862, Brig. Gen. Boyle informed Col. Hoskins of the 12th Kentucky Infantry that Morgan had entered the state of Kentucky with a force of 7,000 to 11,000 men. Morgan actually had only 3,100 men. Col. Hoskins sent out the alarm, and then telegraphed Brig. Gen. Baird, at Danville, Kentucky, for re-enforcements of infantry and artillery. Baird sent a battery of Napoleons and two regiments of infantry. Col. Hoskins chose Lebanon as the most vulnerable town and posted his men two miles from the Louisville and Nashville depot at Lebanon.

On December 27th, Morgan overwhelmed 600 Federal troops in Elizabethtown. On the 28th, Boyle recalled the re-enforcements that he had sent to Col. Hoskins. Cannonading was heard occurring around Elizabethtown, Kentucky. Morgan had burned two huge trestles on the Louisville & Nashville Railroad, near Muldraugh Hill. Gen. Boyle sent re-enforcements again after more requests from Col. Hoskins. Col. Henderson was sent to Lebanon with two regiments of infantry. On the 29th, Col. Hoskins sent out scouts from the 9th Kentucky to

Capt. Paul J. Marrs

find out where Morgan was. The re-enforcements reached Lebanon on that same day.

On December 29th, the 10th Kentucky Infantry under Col. John Harlan overtook some of Morgan's men, from Col. R. S. Cluke's, 2nd Kentucky cavalry. Col. Basil Duke, commander of the 2nd Kentucky, was wounded during a charge. The Confederates withdrew.

On the 30th, the scouts reported that Morgan had been at Fredericksburg. Lt. Porter reported that the cannonading was at the Rolling Fork River Bridge. Col. Hoskins sent out scouts at nightfall on the 30th, and they reported that Morgan was in Springfield, about seven miles from Lebanon. Morgan had split his force and had sent 2,00 men under Col. W. C. P. Breckinridge towards New Haven, Kentucky. Col. Hoskins sent Maj. Farris and Maj.Fidler of the 6th Kentucky Cavalry to reconnoiter

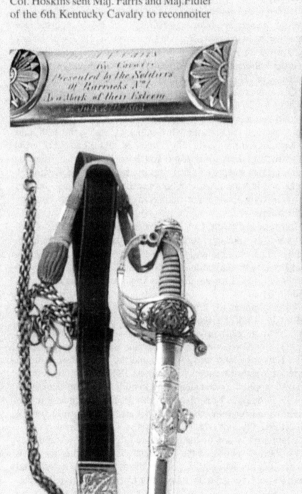

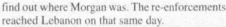

towards Barber's Mill where they were to take the Springfield road and reconnoiter to the rear.

At Barber's Mill, Maj. Fidler and Maj. Farris came across a Confederate picket in the streets of Barber's Mill and captured him. They then advanced towards a battery of artillery and fired a volley, killing two Confederates, then retreated with their Confederate prisoner.

Col. Hoskins then advanced on the Springfield Road, and ordered Col. Henderson and his troops to join him, but Col. Henderson had fallen back to Danville.

On December 31, 1862, Col. Hoskins sent out another reconnoitering party. The scout's reported that Morgan was two miles in their direction. Col. Hoskins ordered Col. Halisy to make another reconnaissance down the Springfield Road. Hailsy found Morgan's camp abandoned and proceeded to Muldraugh's Hill. The citizens there told Col. Hoskins that Morgan was advancing on Springfield. Col. Hoskins sent out the 9th Kentucky, with 300 men under Lt. Col. Boyle.

By 5 p.m., news had reached Col. Hoskins that Halisy was in pursuit of Morgan at Muldraugh Hill. Lt. Col. Boyle reported that Morgan had been in Springfield. On December 31, 1862, Col. Halisy caught up with Morgan and engaged his forces under Capt. Alexander Tribble and Lt. Easting near Raywick, in Marion County, Kentucky. Col. Hailsy was killed in the skirmish.

Col. Hoskins sent out a scouting party under Maj. George Rue, 9th Kentucky Cavalry, towards Rolling Fork. On January 1, 1863, the scouts returned with information that the Rebels had left their camp. Col. Hoskins with the 9th Kentucky Cavalry, the 12th, and 16th Kentucky Infantry, the 7th Tennessee, and a battery of artillery, who together constituted the 34th Brigade, arrived at Muldraugh Hill and pressed on towards Campbellsville, Kentucky. Morgan had left the town five hours earlier, and had also burned the Green River Bridge, preventing any pursuit by Col. Hoskins and his troops.

In a renewed effort, Col. Hoskins sent his whole cavalry force and his artillery to catch Morgan at Columbia, Kentucky, but Morgan had quit Columbia and crossed the Cumberland River. Gen. Speed Fry arrived and called off the pursuit. Col. Hoskins gave a commendation and special thanks to Maj. Farris for his role in the expedition.

On September 13, 1862, Maj. Farris fell off his horse and injured his hip joint. He would never completely recover from his injury. It would constantly flare up and cause him pain. On March 10, 1863, Maj. Farris was sent to command Barracks No. 1 in Louisville, Kentucky, and was to command the State Guard for the District of Western Kentucky. In August 1863, Farris, his hip unimproved, applied for transfer to the Invalid Corps. By then, Maj. Farris had completed his one year term of enlistment and it was decided to muster him out. Farris was given recognition for the "faithful and efficient" service he had given the government.

Maj. Farris is one of the overlooked figures in our country's history. Farris was one of the countless soldiers during the Civil War, who did his duty and carried out his orders to the letter. Even though he was recognized for his valor by being promoted to major, he should be given praise for his courage and undying devotion to his country.(17) (Sword Courtesy of Ralph Handy)

Robert Kerr
6th Kentucky Cavalry

At the age of 23, Robert A. Kerr, from Fayette County, Kentucky, enlisted in the Union cavalry for three years on December 23, 1861, at Camp Irvine, Jefferson County, Kentucky. Kerr was made a 1st Sergeant of Capt. Stephen's Company, 6th Kentucky Cavalry. Kerr was later made a 2nd Lieutenant of Co. A, 6th Kentucky Cavalry to fill a vacancy in that company. Companies A, B, C, D, and E were known as Mundy's (or sometimes spelled Munday's) Battalion. The 6th Kentucky Cavalry was assigned to the division of the Army of the Ohio, commanded by George Morgan.

On December 25, 1862, Maj. James Foley and the 10th Kentucky cavalry left camp for London, Kentucky. Arriving in London, Foley along with Munday's cavalry were then ordered to Williamsburg, in Whitney County, Kentucky where Foley sent out his advance guards to select a camp site, procure forage, and set up camp. The 10th Kentucky along with Munday's cavalry under Buchanan, camped until the next evening. On December 27th, the units moved out at 8 p.m. upon learning that a Rebel force of about 350 men had encamped at Elk Fork in Campbell County, Tennessee, 19 miles from Williamsburg. At 4 a.m., on December 28th, the Federal cavalry encountered the Rebel pickets and Robert Kerr, the commander of the advance guard, captured 16 of the Rebels, who were sleeping at the time. From them Foley learned the location of the Rebel camp, their numbers, and their strength.

Foley now formed his lines and waited for daylight. The fog was very thick, and the visibility was only about 20 paces, but Foley decided to attack anyway. Foley chose 40 men from Mundy's cavalry under Lt. Kerr, and instructed them to approach the camps as near as possible before opening fire. Companies B and M, of the 10th Kentucky Cavalry were sent in support. The order "forward" was given by Foley, and Lt. Kerr and his men approached within a quarter mile of the Rebel camps, when they then opened fire. The Rebels returned fire, but they soon fell back, refusing to stand their ground, and after three unsuccessful attempts to reform their lines the Rebels were routed. Lt. Kerr's men along with the two companies from the 10th Kentucky were elated with their success, and continued to lay down a heavy fire upon the retreating Confederates. Within one hour the Federals had managed to take possession of the Rebel camp.

According to Foley, the Rebels lost 30 killed, 17 wounded, and 51 captured. Foley also mentions that 80 horses and mules were captured along with 200 Enfield rifles and ammunition. Lt. Kerr, and others involved in the action, were praised by Foley for their bravery, "and they deserve alike to share the glory."

In the first days of January, Munday's battalion, being in Gen. Carter's Brigade of Gen. George W. Morgan's command left central Kentucky on an expedition headed for the Cumberland Gap.

By February, the 6th Ky. Cavalry had reached the Cumberland Gap, and on February 14th, Munday's cavalry made an attack on the Rebels at the Gap, inflicting a heavy loss and taking some prisoners. On March 23rd, Gen. Carter's force moved in the direction of Big Creek gap, co-operating with Gen. Morgan's other forces, and the Cumberland Gap was taken on June 16, 1862.

In August 1862, Confederate General Braxton Bragg and Edmund Kirby Smith made their invasion of Kentucky. Union General George Morgan had abandon the Cumberland Gap, and moved across Eastern Kentucky to the Ohio River. On October 12, 1862, Morgan reports that Munday's battalion is still with him, "although they are quite worn down from hard service." Morgan reports that he has the 3rd, 14th, and 22nd Kentucky Infantry, Munday's Battalion, and Neville's battery. Since Munday's battalion was the only organized cavalry in this division, they were responsible for scouting, picketing, conveying dispatches, and making reconnaissance, all of which were difficult and dangerous in the mountainous terrain of the Cumberland Gap.

From the Cumberland Gap, Munday's battalion, along with the infantry, marched towards Ohio. The division was sent towards Richmond, where they fought at both Big Hill and Rogersville, and helped as Metcalf's 7th Kentucky Cavalry and others troops fell back to Lexington, and then to Louisville.

During the Summer of 1862, the other companies of the 6th Kentucky Cavalry were organized in central Kentucky under Col. D. J. Hallisy. In September, Companies F, G, H, I, K, L, and M were consolidated with Mundy's battalion. The 6th Kentucky was commanded by Col. D. J. Hallisy, and Lt. Col. Rueben Mundy. At that time, the 1st Battalion, commanded by Maj. W. H. Fidler, was sent to Leitchfield, Kentucky where they skirmished with the cavalry under Bragg. The 2nd Battalion, under Col. Hallisy, went to Bardstown, Kentucky and encountered Confederate General John

Hunt Morgan's cavalry. The 3rd, under Maj. L. A. Gratz, went to Standford, and was instrumental in capturing prisoners from Bragg's army.

In November, the 1st Battalion was ordered to Louisa to report to Col. Cranor, and on December 9th, Col. Cranor ordered the unit to Mt. Sterling.

In December 1862, the entire regiment was at Lebanon, Kentucky, and in the latter part of the month they engaged Confederate General Morgan's troops. Col. Hoskins, of the 12th Kentucky Infantry reported that Col. Hallisy was pursing Morgan from Springfield, through Lebanon, in the direction of Columbia and Burkesville. On December 31, 1862, at New Market, a fight occurred in which Col. Hallisy was killed.

On January 30, 1863, the 6th Kentucky Cavalry was ordered to join the Army of the Cumberland at Nashville. On February 1, 1863, Louis A. Gratz was made colonel of the 6th. During February, March, April, and May the 6th was stationed at Franklin and Brentwood, Tennessee. In May 1863, Kerr was appointed a 1st Lieutenant in the 6th Kentucky Cavalry, Company A. The duty of the 6th Kentucky Cavalry, while in Franklin and Brentwood, was to protect Rosecrans right flank. In March, Confederate General Nathan Bedford Forrest attacked a small infantry force at Brentwood and captured it. Gen. Granger's headquarters were at Franklin, and he dispatched a cavalry force, including the 6th Kentucky Cavalry, under Gen. Green Clay Smith, to Brentwood. Gen. Smith reports that when he got within three and one-half miles of Brentwood, that he had overtaken the Rebels, and a running fire fight began which continued for a distance of two and one-half miles. Gen. Smith captured all the Rebel wagons and 500 rifles. About six miles from Brentwood he encountered a large force and an engagement took place that lasted an hour and a half. Three charges were made on the 6th Kentucky and 2nd Michigan, and all were repulsed; but Gen. Smith, finding he was outnumbered, was forced to fall back. In his report, Smith says; "I cannot speak too earnestly of the coolness, courage, and daring of Col. L. D. Watkins 6th Kentucky cavalry; attention is also called to the unexceptionable conduct of Maj. W. H. Fidler and Lieut. George Williams, Dan Cheatham and Lieut. Mead, 6th Kentucky."

The 6th Kentucky cavalry was very active in the Spring and Summer of 1863. On March 8th, it aided in driving the enemy beyond Thompson's Station; during the month of April the 6th Kentucky rode from Brentwood to Franklin, where they attacked some Texas troops, capturing the camp with its horses, wagons, and 120 men. Another engagement took place near Franklin on May 1, 1863.

On June 2nd, the regiment moved from Brentwood and on the 4th it was at Triune. At Triune, their orders were to ride quickly to Franklin, where the enemy had appeared. The 6th Kentucky and 2nd Michigan arrived in time to assist the 4th Kentucky and 7th Kentucky Cavalry in repulsing a Confederate attack, and helped to secure a victory for the Federals.

On June 20th, the regiment left Franklin and entered in a series of movements leading up to the Chickamagua campaign.

On July 3rd the regiment reported to Gen. Sheridan at Cowan's Station. On the 5th, Gen. Sheridan sent Col. Watkins in the direction of Stevenson on a reconnaissance. In the official report, Sheridan says of the regiment: "This reconnaissance was very handsomely executed by Col. Watkins, who drove the enemy about three miles, inflicting losses." In Watkins report, he said that during the reconnaissance, Lt. William Murphy and four men were killed, and Lt. Kimbrough and four men were wounded. On July 5th, Watkins proceeded within 20 miles of Bridgeport. Through the months of July and August the Confederate forces were steadily pursued until they crossed the Tennessee River. The cavalry under Rosecrans slowly pushed the Confederates towards Chattanooga. On September 10th, Watkins and his brigade moved on the Summersville Road and charged the pickets, taking the road and capturing 16 prisoners. By September 12th, the brigade had reached Alpine, Georgia.

On September 19th, the 6th Kentucky Cavalry, with Col.

Watkins's other regiments, was desperately engaged in the battle of Chickamauga, at Crawfish Springs. Col. Watkins reported that Maj. Gratz was being repeatedly outflanked and had to slowly fall back. The 6th lost two officers, Lt. Mead was killed and one officer was wounded. The 6th Kentucky also lost 120 men wounded or taken prisoner, and six of them were killed. Chaplin Milton Clarke of the 6th Kentucky was among the wounded.

Col. C. P. Breckinridge

After the capture of Missionary Ridge, the 6th was in Gen. Edward McCook's division, Watkins brigade, which consisted of the 4th, 5th, 6th, and 7th Kentucky. In the first part of January 1864, the regiment re-enlisted as veterans at Rossville, Georgia, and the men were granted 30 days furlough. They returned to Kentucky and after their leave was up, the regiment reformed, and on February 22nd, the regiment was at Lexington, Kentucky.

In March, the regiment moved to Nashville and in April it was at Chattanooga, preparing for Sherman's Atlanta Campaign. The 6th Kentucky Cavalry participated with the Federal cavalry in that campaign, protecting the railroads that supplied Sherman's men. In May, it was at Wauhatchie; in June at LaFayette. It was engaged in a severe fight at Pigeon Mountain, and also at Adairsville and Calhoun.

On June 24th detachments of the 4th, 6th and 7th Kentucky came under attack by Gen. Pillow, with 3,000 men. About 3:00 a.m. the Rebels charged into the town of LaFayette, Georgia, but Col. Watkins was on the alert. The 4th Kentucky took control of the courthouse, and Watkins with the 6th Kentucky, under Maj. Fidler, met the Rebels in the streets where furious fighting occurred. Watkins and the 6th Kentucky fell back to the courthouse and fought off the Rebels. Gen. Pillow demanded a surrender, which was declined, and the fighting was renewed with increased fury. The 4th Kentucky Mounted Infantry, under Col. Croxton, arrived and attacked Gen. Pillow and forced his men to retreat in a panic. Watkins men mounted up and chased Pillow's men for about five miles, capturing a number of prisoners. The 6th lost four men killed and six wounded.

In August, September, and October, the 6th was at Resaca and in the surrounding area, guarding the railroad. In November it was ordered to Louisville, Kentucky to re-equip and was in camp a short time on the Bardstown Road. The advance of Confederate General John Bell Hood into Tennessee caused the 6th Kentucky to move quickly to Nashville, Tennessee. On December 4th, the regiment went into camp at Edgefield until December 12th. On December 23rd, 1864, Lt. Robert Kerr was mustered out of service.

The regiment went on to join the pursuit of John Bell Hood's infantry from Nashville. By January 23rd, the regiment had moved to Waterloo, Alabama. It remained there until February 1865, when it accompanied Wilson's cavalry on the expedition through Alabama and to Macon, Georgia. In June it returned to Nashville and camped at Edgefield. The 6th Kentucky Cavalry was finally mustered out of service on July 14, 1865.(18)

William (Willie) Campbell Preston Breckinridge
9th Kentucky Cavalry, C.S.

William (Willie) Campbell Preston Breckinridge was 27 years and seven months old when he enlisted in the 9th Kentucky Cavalry Battalion, and was made major in early 1862. His battalion

General John Hunt Morgan

Model 1860 Cavalry Officer's sword, manufactured by W.H. Horstmann & Sons, Philadelphia. The sword is engraved with Lt. Robert A. Kerr, 1st Battalion Kentucky Cavalry

consisted of five companies, and was recruited in Central and Northern Kentucky during the occupation of the state by Gen. Braxton Bragg and Edmund Kirby Smith in September and October 1862. After the Battle of Perryville, Bragg and Smith pulled out of Kentucky, and Willie's battalion fell back into Tennessee. Willie's battalion was recruited for and served under the command of Confederate General John Hunt Morgan.

Willie came from one of the most prominent political families in Kentucky. W.C.P. Breckinridge's grandfather had served as United States Senator, was the first cabinet level minister from west of the Appalachians, and had introduced the Kentucky Resolutions of 1798. Willie's father Robert had left a political career for the ministry and reached his church's highest position when he became moderator of the Presbyterian General Assembly. An uncle of Willie's had been a Kentucky Secretary of State, and his cousin John C. Breckinridge held the Offices of Representative, Vice President, Senator, and during the Civil War, Confederate General of the famous Orphans Brigade, and Confederate Secretary of War, all before the age of 45! Another cousin, Clifton Rodes Breckinridge of Arkansas, would serve in Congress.

On December 15, 1862, in Alexandria, Tennessee, Willie's 9th Kentucky Battalion was combined with five companies under Lt. Col. Robert Stoner and the two battalions formed the 9th Kentucky Cavalry Regiment. Willie was made Colonel and Stoner became

his Lt. Colonel. The regiment was assigned to the 2nd Brigade of Gen. John Hunt Morgan's Division of Cavalry. The 9th Kentucky along with the 2nd Kentucky Cavalry under Basil Duke; the 7th Kentucky under Col. Gano; the 8th Kentucky under Col. Cluke; and the 11th Kentucky under Col. Chenault, along with a howitzer battery under Capt. Arnet, left Alexandria, Tennessee on December 22, 1862. Morgan's division totaled to 3,100 men and seven pieces of artillery. Morgan divided the division into two brigades. The first commanded by Col. Duke and the second under the command of Col. Breckinridge. Morgan crossed the Cumberland River, and encamped three miles on the other side at dusk on the 22nd.

On the 23rd, Morgan made an early start and reached Centreville that evening. He had traveled about 30 miles. On December 24th, the division marched to within six miles of Glascow. Morgan encamped his main body of men some six miles from the town, and sent two companies to take possession of it. As they entered town, they encountered the advance guard of a battalion of the 2nd Michigan Cavalry. It was becoming dark so neither side saw the other, at first, but then a skirmish broke out and a private of

Breckinridge's regiment and Capt. W. E. Jones, Company A, 9th Kentucky, were mortally wounded. Lt. Samuel Peyton, of Duke's regiment was seriously wounded and some six or seven of Morgan's men taken prisoner. Morgan's squadron fell back, as the Yankees passed through the town and took the road to Munfordville, Kentucky. Several of the Yankees were killed and wounded and 22 prisoners, including a captain, were captured and paroled.

On December 25th, Morgan passed through Glasgow and took the Bear Wallow Turnpike in the direction of Munfordville. About 10 miles from Green River Morgan's scouts reported that a battalion of cavalry was drawn up in line, awaiting their approach. Morgan quickly moved forward two companies and a section of artillery to meet them, and made ready for a long engagement.

The Yankees didn't wait to receive the charge of the force Morgan had sent forward, but fired a few rounds, took to flight and left the road clear. Morgan then proceeded with his force to the Green River, and succeeded in crossing it with considerable difficulty, since the banks were muddy and steep. Morgan reached Hammondsville with his command at midnight and ordered Col. Breckinridge to send two companies in the direction of Woodsonville with instructions to drive in the Yankee pickets, and he dispatched two companies of Col. Duke's command with similar instructions, in the direction of Munfordville. Morgan's plan was to make the Yankees think that he intended to attack the fortifications at Green River, and by so threatening the Yankees, to divert their attention from the combined attack which he intended to make the next day on the stockades at Bacon Creek and Nolin.

On December 26th, Morgan sent Duke's and Gano's 7th Ken-

Model 1860 cavalry officer's saber, adorned with laurel leaves, acorns, and etched blades. It has shark skin grips, which was denoted by officers. The blade is a German import. (BCWM)

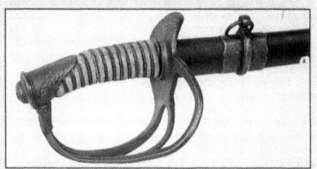

Model 1860 officer's saber manufactured by the Ames Manufacturing Company, Chicopee, Massachusetts. (BCWM)

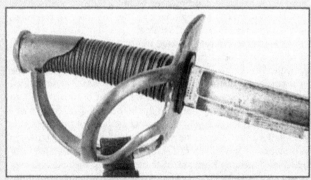

Model 1840 cavalry enlisted men's saber, made by Tiffany & Co. Tiffany only used steel guards and pommels. The sword has the original saber knot which was used to prevent loss of the saber during battle. (BCWM)

tucky Cavalry regiments and a section of artillery from Palmer's battery, under the command of Lt. Col. John Hutcheson of the 2nd Kentucky Cavalry to attack the stockade at Bacon Creek, while he moved on with the main body of men to Upton. A heavy rain had begun to fall during the night, turning the road into a quagmire, and making it very difficult for the artillery and wagon trains to move. It was nearly 11 o'clock before Col. Hutcheson's cannon opened up. On Arriving at Upton, Morgan cut the telegraph wires and his operator "Lighting" Ellsworth was soon in communication with Louisville, Cincinnati, and other points along the railway lines. A message was received that a train loaded with ammunition, small arms, and two pieces of rifled artillery was to arrive soon. Morgan wanted to intercept this train, but unfortunately he missed the opportunity.

It was now 3:00 p.m., when Morgan sent forward the remainder of his force to Nolin, under the command of Col. Duke, holding in reserve Johnson's regiment and the other section of Palmer's battery. Due to the prolonged firing at Bacon Creek, Morgan was fearful that the stockade had been re-enforced from Munfordville and he moved down to Bacon Creek to assist Col. Hutcheson. On

Col. W.C. P. Breckinridge's presentation goblet.

his arrival there, Morgan sent in a flag of truce, and demanded an unconditional surrender of that place, which after some hesitation on the part of Capt. James, commanding officer, was finally agreed to. Ninety three prisoners of the 91st Illinois were taken, including four commissioned officers. The stockade and trestle were burned and Morgan moved on to Nolin. The force at the trestle near Nolin, numbering three officers and 73 privates of the 91st Illinois surrendered to Col. Duke. The stockade and bridge at that point were also burned. While waiting at Upton, Morgan caused large fires to be built along the track for some three miles, in order to warp and destroy the rails.

On December 27th, Morgan learned that seven or eight companies of Yankees were stationed at Elizabethtown and moved his command in that direction. On arriving within sight of the town, a message, written on the back of an envelope was handed to Morgan. The message had been written by H. S. Smith, the commander of the Union forces in Elizabethtown, Kentucky. Smith demanded the unconditional surrender of Morgan and his forces and informed Morgan that he was surrounded. Morgan wrote Smith back and told him that HE was surrounded, and that Smith, not he should surrender. Smith replied that it was his duty as an officer to fight and not to surrender.

Leaving one regiment and a howitzer in reserve to protect the wagon trains, Morgan ordered Col. Duke to deploy his command to the right and Col. Breckinridge to deploy his men to the left of the town and to throw forward skirmishers to discover the position of the Yankees. It soon became apparent to Morgan that Smith's men had taken possession of several brick houses on the outskirts of town, and expected to make a street fight of it. Morgan immediately placed his artillery in position on a hill a little to the left of the road, which completely commanded the town, and sent Capt. C. C. Corbett with one mountain howitzer, to attack the town on the right. After about one hour of vigorous shelling, the town surrendered, and 652 prisoners, including 25 officers, fell into Morgan's hands.

In his report Morgan pointed out that the rapid and accurate fire of Capt. Palmer's battery contributed a great deal to the surrender of the Union forces. Almost every one of his shots had hit the houses occupied by the Yankees. Capt. Corbett was also mentioned by Morgan for his gallantry. Corbett ran one of his howitzers into town while under heavy fire from the houses. Lt. Col. Stoner was also mentioned for charging the town at the head of his men.

On the 28th, Morgan moved his forces from Elizabethtown in the direction of Bardstown to destroy two huge trestles on the Louisville and Nashville Railroad. Each trestle was protected by strong log stockades or blockhouses filled with Yankee infantry. Four miles from Elizabethtown, Morgan ordered Col. Breckinridge to turn his command to the left and to attack the lower stockade near Muldraugh's Hill, while Morgan moved on with Col. Duke's brigade to attack the upper stockade. After two or three hours of shelling both places surrendered and at 7 o'clock that evening Morgan was pleased to find that the objective of his expedition had been attained. The Louisville and Nashville Railroad would now be impassable for at least two months. These two trestles were the largest and finest on the whole road, each of them some 60 feet in height and from 300 to 350 yards in length. Neither of them had ever been destroyed before. Seven hundred prisoners, including 27 officers were captured and a large and valuable amount of medical, quartermaster and commissary stores were destroyed. Morgan encamped at the Rolling Fork River that night.

On December 29th, Morgan sent Col. R. S. Cluke's regiment, and one piece of artillery to attack and burn the bridge over the Rolling Fork; Col. Chenault's regiment and one piece of artillery were to burn the stockade and trestle at Boston and three companies from Col. Breckinridge's regiment and one mountain howitzer were to attack at New Haven. Morgan then set his command in motion and as the rear regiments were crossing the Rolling Fork, a large Union force consisting of cavalry, infantry, and several pieces of artillery, which had followed Morgan from Elizabethtown, came up and began to shell the ford where the troops were crossing. Mor-

gan immediately sent orders to Col. Duke, who was in the rear, to send a courier to Col. Cluke, ordering him to rejoin the command as quickly as possible and to hold the Yankees in check until the entire command had crossed the ford. Col. Duke, assisted by Col. Breckinridge, placed seven companies from different regiments in position and held five in reserve. With this force he repulsed the Yankees advance several times and very nearly succeeded in capturing two pieces of artillery, but Duke, wounded by a shell, fell from his horse. Col. Breckinridge then took command and maintained the position until Col. Cluke's regiment had crossed the river. Morgan then ordered Breckinridge to fall back, this he accomplished in good order and without any further losses.

Meanwhile, Col. Chenault had burned the trestle and stockade at Boston. He rejoined Morgan that night at Bardstown. The force sent to burn the stockade at New Haven was not successful, and didn't rejoin the command until the following night at Springfield.

On the 30th, Morgan left Bardstown, and marched to Springfield, a distance of some 18 miles, where he arrived at nightfall. On Morgan's arrival he learned that the Yankees had withdrawn all their forces from the southern portion of the state, and had concentrated them at Lebanon. Troops from Danville, Burkesville, Campbellsville, and Columbia had been collected there and numbered nearly 8,000 men and several pieces of artillery. Morgan also learned that a force of 10,000 was moving from Glasgow to Burkesville to intercept him. Morgan decided to detour to the right of Lebanon and by a night march, to conceal his movements from the Yankees, out run the column moving from Glasgow to Burkesville and cross the Cumberland before it came within striking distance. Upon arriving in Springfield he sent out two companies on the Lebanon Road, with instructions to drive the Union pickets and to hold the position. This accomplished, they were to build large and extended campfires to fool the Yankees into thinking that Morgan's entire force was in position, and that Morgan was only waiting for daylight to attack. Considerable delay had occurred because Morgan found it difficult to find a guide who was sufficiently well acquainted with the area to lead him over the route he desired, but by 11:00 p.m. the whole column was in motion. The night was dark and stormy and the road rough, so that the morning of December 31st found the command only eight miles from Springfield and 2 miles from Lebanon. By 1 o'clock that afternoon, the top of Muldraugh's Hill was reached and Morgan could clearly see Lebanon and the Yankees skirmishers deployed in the valley below with his telescope. Just as the rear guard of the column reached the foot of the hills, a hand to hand fight broke out between Col. D. J. Hallisy, of the 6th Kentucky Cavalry, commanding brigade, and two other Federal officers on the one side and Capt. Alexander Tribble and Lt. Eastin, of Morgan's command, on the other, in which Col. Hallisy was killed by Lt. Eastin, and his companions captured.

Morgan reached Campbellsville late that evening and found there quite a large amount of commissary stores, this coming just in time, as Morgan's men had eaten little for the past two days.

On January 1, 1863, Morgan started for Columbia, where he arrived at 3 p.m. By a night march from Columbia, Morgan reached Burkesville at daylight the following morning. Morgan halted his command at Burkesville for a few hours to rest and feed, and then crossed the Cumberland without incident. Traveling, then, by easy stages, Morgan and his command reached Smithville, Tennessee on the evening of January 5th.

During Morgan's "Christmas Raid," he managed to destroy the Louisville and Nashville Railroad from Munfordville to Shepherdsville within 18 miles of Louisville, and rendered it impassable for two months. He captured 1,877 prisoners and destroyed over $2,000,000 dollars worth of government property. Morgan lost only two killed, 24 wounded, and 64 missing.

On January 10, 1863, Morgan and his command arrived in Alexandria, Tennessee. Later the command was moved to Liberty, Tennessee. During the Winter and Spring of 1863, the 9th Kentucky Cavalry acted as pickets, scouting and guarding the right of

Bragg's army while it held the line at Tullahoma, Tennessee. On March 19th, Morgan reported to Basil Duke that he had found Col. Breckinridge drawn up in line of battle near Liberty. The Yankees had already attacked Breckinridge's forage wagons, and were massing infantry and cavalry to their front and cavalry in their rear. Morgan hoped to assist Breckinridge's force and capture the Yankees in their front by March 20th. Morgan sent a message to Bragg or Wheeler that the Yankees were not going to fall back, and were massing to the right, not left, of Bragg's army. Morgan was informed that Union soldiers were being transported from Louisville to meet Morgan's command, who were reported to be crossing the Cumberland at Gainsborough. Bragg had been decieved, and the Union forces had concentrated to his right, not his left. When Bragg moved to his right he found two corps of infantry and was forced to fall back to Tullahoma. The Tullahoma campaign was a failure for Bragg, and a victory for Rosecrans, who was able to keep Bragg pinned down in Tennessee.

In June 1863, the 9th Kentucky Cavalry was separated from Gen. Morgan, and did not participate in Morgan's Great Raid. The 9th Kentucky retreated to Chattanooga with the Army of Tennessee, passing through McMinnville and Sequatchie Valley. Col. Breckinridge was driven back to Readyville by the Yankees. The Union force at Readyville consisted of 1,600 men, including one battalion of cavalry and four regiments of infantry led by Gen. Hazen.

From Chattanooga, the regiment was sent to guard the Tennessee River at Decatur, Guntersville, and Tuscumbia, Alabama, guarding these positions until just before the Battle of Chickamauga. The regiment did not play a part in the Battle of Chickamugua, arriving there a few days after the battle.

The 9th Kentucky then served at Lookout Mountain and at Harrison's Landing, Tennessee until the Battle of Missionary Ridge. It took part in this battle, covering the retreat of the army to Dalton, fighting at Ringgold Gap, and then moving to Tunnel Hill, Georgia. The 9th Kentucky spent the winter at Tunnel Hill, picketing and scouting in front of the Army of Tennessee, and then encamped at Dalton, Georgia.

Just before the Battle of Missionary Ridge the Regiment was brigaded with the 1st and 2nd Kentucky Cavalry and Dortch's Battalion. This brigade was known as Grigsby's Cavalry Brigade, later as William's, and later still as Breckinridge's. This brigade was assigned to Gen. Joseph Wheeler's cavalry corps, and served under him until the close of the war. The regiment was on duty at Tunnel Hill, Georgia when Sherman began his Atlanta Campaign on May 7, 1864. On the 8th, the brigade fought and helped defeat Gen. Geary's Division of Hooker's Corps at Dug Gap. On May 9th, the regiment was engaged at Snake Creek Gap, after Resaca, then to Cassville, Cartersville, Altoona, Marietta, Roseville Factory, Peach Tree Creek, and finally the Battle of Atlanta. The regiment was with the troops that captured Gen. Stoneman. Later at Jug Tavern, the regiment, along with Col. Breckinridge, defeated and captured part of Stoneman's force as they made an effort to escape. About May 10, 1864, the 9th Kentucky crossed the Chattahoochie River, marching North with Gen. Joseph Wheeler to destroy Sherman's railroad communications. It marched to Dalton, then to Cleveland, Tennessee, to Maryville, Knoxville, and over the mountains and up the Tennessee Railroad to Bristol, Tennessee, then to Abington, and Saltville, Virginia. It fought in the battle of Saltville, defeating Gen. Burbridge. From there the regiment went through East Tennessee up the French Broad River to Asheville, and then to Charlotte, North Carolina, to Greenville, South Carolina, and Athens, and West Point, Georgia. At West Point, the Regiment met up with Gen. Wheeler and then rode back to Atlanta just in time to confront Sherman on his March to the Sea Campaign, which began on November 16, 1864. The regiment opposed Sherman's march from Atlanta to Savannah, Georgia at Macon, Millidgeville, Louisville and other points. Sherman arrived at Savannah on December 20, 1864. The regiment then opposed Sherman from Savannah to Columbia, South Carolina. It fought Sherman at Columbia on February 17, 1865.

From Columbia to Winnsboro, then to Cheraw, and across the Great Pedee River to Fayettsville, North Carolina, then to the Battle of Bentonville, North Carolina on March 18, 1865. The regiment moved on to Raleigh, North Carolina on April 11, 1865. While in Raleigh, the regiment heard of Robert E. Lee's surrender. Attached to Dibrell's Division of cavalry, the Kentucky Brigade was ordered by Gen. Wheeler to proceed to Greensboro, North Carolina as an escort for President Jefferson Davis and his Cabinet, who had reached that point during their flight from Richmond,

W.M. Mead, 1st Lt. , 6th Ky. Cav.

Virginia. The regiment escorted Mr. Davis and Cabinet to Charlotte, North Carolina on April 18, 1865. At Charlotte it halted a few days pending negotiations between Gen. Johnston and Gen. Sherman. At this time, the regiment was joined by Gen. Duke's Brigade of Gen. Morgan's old division. The regiment left Charlotte, and marched to Petersburg, South Carolina, on the Savannah River, on May 8, 1865. At Abbeville, South Carolina, the last Confederate council of war was held and at this meeting were President Davis, Gen. John C. Breckinridge, Gen. Bragg, and five brigade commanders; Gen. Dibrell, Gen. Furguson, Gen. Vaughn, Gen. Basil Duke, and Col. W.C.P. Breckinridge of the 9th Kentucky Cavalry, who was then commanding the Kentucky Cavalry Brigade. At this council it was decided that the struggle was hopeless and that it would be fatal to make an effort to to reach the Trans-Mississippi Department. Mr. Davis cast the only dissenting vote, but finally accepted the resolution. On May 10, 1865, the 9th Regiment marched to Washington, Georgia and was paroled.

After the war, W.C.P. Breckinridge entered politics as had his father and grandfather, and his famous cousin, John C. Breckinridge. To further his political career he would marry a granddaughter of Henry Clay, the Great Compromiser, and following her death he married a granddaughter of a former Kentucky governor. Breckinridge settled down to family life and was the father of five children. W. C. P. Breckinridge practiced his oratory skills and after a while he became known for his great speeches. He was nicknamed by the papers as "the silver tongued orator from Kentucky." People came from all around to listen to Breckinridge speak on such diverse topics as religion, imperialism, race relations, politics, and morals. To keep his image as a moral person, Breckinridge would not drink, smoke, play cards, or bet. Papers reported Breckinridge as a medium sized man with dark grey eyes and a mellow voice, which was clear, melodious and resonant.

Breckinridge threw his hat in the ring and served five terms as a member of the House of Representatives. Rumors around Washington named Breckinridge as possibly the next speaker of the House, Vice President, or even President.

Life was good for Breckinridge. He had served the Confederacy with distinction, had a good home, and was successful in politics, but an incident occurred in 1893, that would forever change Breckinridge's life. A woman named Madeline Pollard petitioned the court that she be given $50,000 dollars because W.C.P. Breckinridge had promised to marry her but did not.

On April 1, 1884, Pollard filed another petition that stated that at the age of 17, she had been seduced by Breckinridge, who at the time was married and 47 years old and that he later "completed his seduction" of her. She claimed that since that time she not only had been his mistress, but that she had also given birth to two of his children.

Spiller and Burr
Pistol. (BCWM)

In 1893, after Breckinridge's wife had died, Pollard received a promise of marriage from him, but he ended up marrying another woman. Madeline sued for a breach of contract because there was no seduction law in the District of Columbia. Breckinridge decided to contest the lawsuit which would be his downfall. The case was tried and the jury found Breckinridge guilty and ordered him to pay $15,000 dollars. The conviction did damage to W.C.P. Brecinridge's political career. His name had been dragged through the mud by Pollard, and the newspapers couldn't get enough of the moral scandal.

Even with this blot on his political career, Breckinridge opted to run for Congress. In a very tight race Breckinridge lost by only 255 votes out of 19,000 ballots cast. His election drew the attention of the national press, which brought up the scandal and it literally divided families, churches, and neighborhoods. The election brought the moral standards of the society to question and they were discussed in every circle.

Breckinridge would never return to politics, after losing the election. Instead he and his son bought the *Lexington Morning Herald* newspaper. His son, Desha, would serve as the editor of the *Lexington Herald* for many years.

Breckinridge would take pride in watching his children in his later years. His son, Desha as editor, and one of his daughters, Sophonisba, became the first woman in the United States to receive a Ph.D. degree, and was one of the first women to be admitted to the Kentucky bar. She was highly acclaimed as an educator and administrator at the University of Chicago.

On November 17, 1904, Breckinridge fell ill and developed a fever, his lungs filled with fluid, and breathing became difficult. Despite the doctors best efforts William slipped into a coma. On November 19, 1904, at the age of 67, "peacefully like the sinking of the summer sun leaving behind a pathway which no painter's brush can limn, the life spark of Col. W. C. P. Breckinridge went out at the tolling of the midnight bells ... He died at 11:40 o'clock surrounded by his family ... The end came softly as a child would fall asleep within its mother's arms." W. C. P. Breckinridge's life was filled with highs and lows. The Pollard case had caused Breckinridge to be less than admired by some, but to others, especially the old veterans that served under him in the 9th Kentucky Cavalry, he was still admired and revered for his courage, bravery, and devotion. Many people in the community still thought of Breckinridge as a great man. His political career was filled with accolades; he was a Bourbon Democrat. the Bourbon Democrats were ex-Confederates who controlled Kentucky politics after the war and until the turn of the century. He also served five terms in the United States House of Representatives. His children would follow in the footsteps of their father and continue to bring honor to the Breckinridge name. If one thing could be said about W. C. P. Breckinridge it was that he led a unique and interesting life and lived it to it's fullest.

Bluford Watson Adams 2nd Kentucky Cavalry, C.S. 4th Kentucky Cavalry, C.S.

Bluford Watson Adams was one of the many young men who felt that though he was too young to serve, it did not matter to him. Rules were meant to be broken. Bluford Adams felt the stirs of pride, devotion, and patriotism in his heart. Against his parents better wishes, he felt that he must serve his country to the bitter end.

Bluford Watson Adams at the age of sixteen along with his brother and childhood friends, would serve in one of the most legendary cavalry units in the Confederacy; the Second Kentucky Cavalry, and would know one of the greatest Cavalry Generals in the South; Confederate General John Hunt Morgan. His career would span three years and would be involved in some of the most harrowing cavalry chases in history.

Bluford Watson Adams was born on February 3, 1845, and was the son of Presley P. and Polly Stephens Adams. He lived on a farm near Big Bone Springs, Boone County, Kentucky, and was one of five children. He attended the schools in the neighborhood and was a vigorous youth when the Civil War began. Bluford was a strapping young man standing 5' 9" with blue eyes and light hair.

On August 14th, 1862, Confederate General Braxton Bragg and Edmund Kirby Smith invaded Kentucky. Confederate General John Hunt Morgan promised Bragg that if he entered Kentucky, 100,000 recruits would sign up for the Confederacy. While in Kentucky, Confederate John Hunt Morgan put up flyers everywhere he rode asking for volunteers. Bluford, along with his brother, John P. H. Adams, believed the South to be right and cast their lot. Bluford, John, and several other Boone county boys, enlisted in the Confederacy in 1862. John became a member of the Second Kentucky Cavalry, C. S., on September 10, 1862. According to family tradition, Bluford was too young to serve in the cavalry and the recruiting officer sent Bluford home. Against Bluford's parents wishes, he snuck out of the house and joined his brother.

Bluford and John would serve with one of the greatest units in the Confederate service, the Second Kentucky Cavalry, led by Colonel Basil Duke. The Second Kentucky Cavalry was part of Confederate General John Hunt Morgan's command. On October Eighth, 1862, Braxton Bragg fought Union General Don Carlos Buell at Perryville, Kentucky. Although Bragg had won a decisive victory over Buell, Bragg had decided to evacuate Perryville, and reunited with Edmund Kirby Smith at London, Kentucky. Because of the shortage of supplies, burdened with wounded and sick, and vastly outnumbered, Bragg decided to fall back to Tennessee. During Bragg's fall back to Tennessee, the Second Kentucky Cavalry would see action as the rear guard protecting Bragg's supply lines, and later raided Union rail and supply lines in Kentucky before returning to Tennessee.

On December 22nd, 1862, Bragg sent Morgan's command to destroy the railroad supply lines in Kentucky, hoping to slow Union General William Rosecrans advance toward Murfressboro, Tennessee. Morgan left Alexandria, Tennessee. He split his division into two wings; Col. Basil Duke, of the Second Kentucky, commanded one wing of his Division and the newly formed Ninth Kentucky, under Col. W. C. P. Breckinridge, commanded the other. On December 24th, the Second Kentucky saw action at Glasglow, Kentucky. His advance guard fought with four companies of the Second Michigan Cavalry.

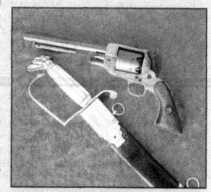

(BCWM)

Spiller and Burr disassembled to show serial number. (BCWM)

Morgan lost three wounded, with Lt. Samuel Peyton, of the Second Kentucky mortally wounded. The Second Michigan lost four killed and wounded and twenty taken prisoners. On December 23rd, Morgan skirmished with the Yankees on the Green River, although no one was hurt. On December 25th, Morgan decided to send part of his command to take the stockade at Bacon Creek, while he rode onto Upton and Nolin. By 4:00 P.M., all the places had surrendered and they burned the stockade and trestles. That night, Morgan camped at Nolin, having taken and paroled two hundred prisoners, with only two slightly wounded in his command.

Morgan moved onto Elizabethtown, Kentucky. Upon arriving near Elizabethtown, a Union soldier approached Morgan, with a message from H. S. Smith, who was commanding the U.S. Forces in Elizabethtown, demanding that Morgan surrender. Morgan refused and shelled the town. Morgan's batteries and the Union skirmishers fought for about forty-five minutes, when Col. Smith decided to surrender. Morgan took and paroled eight companies of Yankees. Morgan's men burned three bridges and the entire track for miles were set on fire.

On December 28th, Morgan and his command split again.

Morgan, along with Col. Duke's command, moved along the trestles, about five miles from Elizabethtown, near Muldraugh Hill. Morgan sent Col. Breckinridge toward one trestle, and was to attack the lower stockade. Morgan demanded the stockade to surrender, the Yankees refused and Morgan opened fire. After about an hour of skirmishing, the stockades surrendered. They burned the stockades, trestles, and a quantity of army stores. They took and paroled about seven prisoners. No one was killed or wounded. Morgan moved onto the Rolling Fork River.

On December 29th, Morgan sent Col. Cluke's regiment with one piece of artillery to attack and burn the bridge over the Rolling Fork; Morgan put Col. Chenault's regiment, the Eleventh Kentucky Cavalry, and one piece of artillery in advance to burn the stockade and trestle at Boston, and three companies of Col. Breckinridge's regiment and one howitzer was to attack New Haven. Morgan was crossing the fork, when the Union troops shelled him from behind. Morgan sent out six or seven companies, which managed to push back the Yankees. After they had pushed the Yankees back, Morgan finished crossing the river, and moved towards Bardstown, Kentucky. A shell wounded Col. Duke, while riding his horse, and they took him to Bardstown, Kentucky for

Bluford Watson Adam's Spiller and Burr pistol, pistol holster, kepi, butternut jacket, spurs and militia sword that belonged to Bluford's father. (BCWM)

medical treatment. Col. Breckinridge took command of Duke's regiment. Col. Chenault managed to burn the stockade at Boston. The force sent to New Haven was not successful.

On the 30th, Morgan left Bardstown, Kentucky and reached Springfield, Kentucky. Morgan heard that there was a large force of 8,000 massing at Lebanon. Morgan wisely decided not to attack them and left Lebanon at night, leaving the Yankees in his rear. Morgan continued to elude his enemy, arriving at Campbellsville. While at Campbellsville, Morgan raided the commissary stores, which came at an opportune time since Morgan was low on food and supplies. On the morning of January Ist, 1863, Morgan and his command arrived at Columbia. He then moved onto Burkesville, and then finally crossed the Cumberland with no major problems.

Morgan's command, including the Second Kentucky Cavalry, managed to destroy the Louisville and Nashville Railroad from Munfordsville to Shepherdsville, within 18 miles of Louisville. Morgan's command managed to capture 1,877 prisoners, including sixty-two commissioned officers, and destroyed two million dollars worth of Government supplies. On the outset, it looked like Morgan was very successful, but Bragg was engaged in the battle at Stone's River. Bragg's army on December 31st, 1862 attacked Union General William Rosecrans army. The resulting three-day battle cost Bragg 1,294 dead, 7,945 wounded, and 1,7027 missing. The Yankee's loss was 1,730 dead, 7,802 wounded and 3,717 missing. Bragg pulled out of Murfressboro, and fell back to Shelbyville, Tennessee. Rosecrans did not pursue Bragg's army. Morgan's men could have been better used at the battle of Murfressboro.

Bluford and his brother's next engagement would be Morgan's raid into Kentucky, Indiana and Ohio. On July 2nd, 1863, Morgan, along with the Second Kentucky Cavalry, crossed into Kentucky. He was hoping to persuade the Copperheads, especially the Knights of the Golden Circle, in Indiana, to overthrow the Union government in the State of Indiana. He was also hoping to strike terror into the hearts of the people in the North. Morgan crossed the Cumberland River near Burkesville, Kentucky. Brig. General Henry Judah, commanding the Third Division, 23rd Corps, had heard of Morgan's plan to invade Kentucky and sent out Brig. General E. H. Hobson, who was leading the 2nd Brigade, General Schakelford, with his brigade, and Brig. General Manson, of his First Brigade, to capture Morgan.

On July 4th, 1863, Morgan's advance had entered Columbia. Col. Orlando Moore, of the 25th Michigan Infantry moved forward and prepared for a fight. Moore engaged Morgan's forces at Tebb's Bend, on the Green River Bridge at 3:30 P.M. Morgan opened with his artillery on Moore's breastworks. Morgan then sent a flag of truce asking for Moore's surrender. Moore refused. Morgan again opened with his artillery. Moore's forces were withdrawn from the opened field into the woods, where Morgan's men advanced and attacked. A three and a half hour battle raged on, when Morgan's men finally fell back with a loss of fifty killed and 200 wounded. Among the killed was Col. Chenault, Major Thomas Brent, Jr., and another Major, and five captains, and six Lieutenants. Moore's forces consisted of only 200 men against Morgan's 2,500. Moore lost only six killed and twenty-three wounded. Morgan asked for a truce to bury the dead and pulled out. Lt. M. A. Hogan of the Eighth Michigan Infantry, held the river near the bridge, and repulsed a cavalry charge.

Morgan decided to move onto Lebanon. Col. Charles Hanson, of the 20th Kentucky Infantry, had heard of Morgan's advance and prepared as best as possible against a force consisting of 2,500 men, and six pieces of artillery. Hanson had no artillery, or cavalry and his force consisted of only 380 men. Hanson's men were soon engaged with Morgan's men, and they drove Morgan's skirmishers back. Lt. Hale came upon Morgan's scouts on the Columbia road and drove them back to Muldraugh's Hill. Capt. Glenn, of Hanson's force encountered Morgan's force on the road leading from the Columbia road to the railroad, and had to fall back. Sergeant Herrill found another of Morgan's force on the road between the Columbia Road and in the direction of Muldraugh Hill. The Union command told that Hanson held his position until reinforcements could arrive. Hanson decided to hold the town. At 6:30 a.m., the next morning, Hanson placed 230 skirmishers in a semicircle, covering the front of Morgan. About fifty more were placed on the Bradfordsville road and to the left of the road, with directions to hold that part of the town until they were overran and had to be forced back by the Confederates. Once they were forced back, they were then to occupy the buildings on Main Street. At 7 o'clock, Morgan opened fire by shelling the camp with three pieces of artillery. Morgan then sent a flag of truce. Morgan demanded Hanson to surrender, Hanson refused. Morgan then advanced on the town, and the shelling renewed with increased intensity, now with four pieces of artillery. The two sides fought for two hours. Being overwhelmed, Hanson's men fell back to the depot building. Capt. Wolcott, with Lt. Hale, Guess, and Young, of the 20th Kentucky, and Lt. Bratton, of the Ninth Kentucky Cavalry, and the men under his command, held the Main street and that portion of the town, firing in the streets and the suburbs. They finally had to fall back to the houses in town.

Twenty-six shots from Morgan's artillery hit the depot, and set the roof on fire. Hanson's men using Enfield and Springfield rifles kept Morgan's men at least a thousand yards away. At 12:00 noon, Rev. T. Clellan, representing the citizens of Lebanon, sent a flag of truce to Hanson with a message from Morgan saying that if Hanson did not surrender, Morgan would shell the town and they would show no quarter. While the flag of truce came to the depot, Morgan's men advanced. Hanson ordered for the firing to continue. Morgan's artillery was moved within 300 yards of the depot. The battle raged until 1:20 p.m.. Hanson was low on ammunition. Morgan's cavalry had exhausted his men, each having fired 125 rounds per man. The guns were so fouled, they became completely useless. Hanson decided to surrender. During the battle in the streets, Hanson' men killed Tom Morgan, John Hunt Morgan's brother. Morgan's men became enraged and wanted to kill Hanson, but Morgan knew Hanson, and he spared Hanson's life. Hanson lost three killed and sixteen wounded.

After paroling Hanson's 350 men, Morgan moved onto Springfield. The main force moved into Bardstown. One brigade of Morgan's moved back toward Columbia, and smaller parties moved onto Frankfort and Lexington. The Union forces, under General Hobson, were now massing in the rear of Morgan. Morgan arrived in Brandenburg, and secured two steamboats to transport his men across to Indiana. Once Morgan had crossed, he burned the Alice Dean, and let the McComb go. It took General Hobson's force twenty four hours to cross the river into Indiana, because it took that long to obtain transports for his men. Once Hobson crossed the river, he resumed the chase.

By that time Morgan had fought a battle at Corydon, Indiana with the local militia. On July 18th, General Shackelford, who was now in command of the Union forces chasing Morgan, reached Chester. On July 19th, Col. Kautz, Col. Sander's, General Shackelford, and Col. Wolford were advancing toward Buffington Island, Ohio. They immediately heard artillery fire on the Ohio river. Then General Shackelford received a message from General Judah. The message told Schakelford to cut off Morgan's retreat. General Shackelford immediately formed his lines; the Ninth Kentucky Cavalry, under Col. Jacob, was put on the extreme right. Shackelford put the 20th Kentucky Cavalry, under Col. Crittenden, on the extreme left; and the First, Third, and the Eighth Kentucky Cavalries were placed in the center; with the 45th Ohio held in reserve. After an hour, the First, Third, and Eighth Kentucky Cavalries were ordered to charge Morgan's men. "With drawn sabers gleaming in the bright sunlight, and a yell that filled the foe with terror, they rushed upon Morgan's men", and Morgan's men fled at the oncoming cavalry. Immediately a flag of truce came from Col. Dick Morgan. General Shackelford told Colonel Morgan that he would allow only unconditional surrender. Col. Morgan, along with W. W. Ward, and D. H. Smith, surrendered. Col. Shackelford captured seven hundred men.

Col. Shackelford moved fifteen miles to Tupper's Plains, up the river. On reaching the Plains, Shackelford received a message reporting that Morgan's forces were posted in some dense woods at the head of a deep ravine, between the forces of Generals Judah, Hobson and Col. Shackelford's. Shackelford ordered that the First Kentucky Cavalry and part of the 12th Kentucky Infantry, to pursue a detachment of Morgan's force. Col. Adams, of the First Kentucky Cavalry captured eighty men and Col. Ham of the 12th captured one hundred men.

In the morning, it was reported to Col. Shackelford that Morgan was four miles from his position and moving in the direction of Eight Mile Island. Col. Shackelford gave chase for fifty-seven miles, and skirmished with Morgan for six miles. Shackelford brought Morgan's force to a stand at 3:00 P.M. on July 20th at Kuger Creek. A fight resulted lasting for an hour. Col. Adams, with the First Kentucky and Capt. Ward, with a company of the Third Kentucky, were ordered to flank Morgan and cut off his escape route. They took the road after a severe skirmish. Morgan fled to an immense bluff for refuge. A flag of truce was flown, and Col. Shackelford asked for Morgan to surrender unconditionally. Col. Duke and his force surrendered. Morgan escaped with six hundred of his men. Col. Shackelford captured between 1,200 and 1,300 men.

Later that evening, on July 20th, Col. Shackelford called for 1,000 volunteers to capture Morgan. Only 500 horses were fit for duty. On the morning of the July 21st, five hundred men chased Morgan. On July 24th, they caught up with Morgan at Washington, Ohio. Capt. Ward, of the Third Kentucky Cavalry, and a detachment of the First Kentucky drove the Rebel pickets, and with a flanking movement drove the unwary Rebel force out of Washington. One mile east of Washington, Morgan made his stand in a dense wood. Col. Shackelford formed his line of battle, and drove Morgan from his position. Morgan fell back two miles, tearing up a bridge and took a position in the woods on a high hill just beyond the bridge. They made the advance on his left flank, while part of the 14th Illinois crossed the stream just above the bridge, and moved up the hill in the face of Morgan's men heavy fire. The 14th Illinois moved up and drove Morgan's men before them. Morgan burned two bridges over Stillwater.

On the 25th, General Shackelford's force met Morgan a mile from Athens, Ohio. Morgan fled to the woods. Shackelford shelled Morgan's forces for thirty minutes. Major Way, of the 9th Michigan Cavalry, had been skirmishing heavily with Morgan and was driving Morgan's forces before him. The main column reached Richmond. General Shackelford received notice that Morgan was moving from Springfield to Hammersville, Ohio. Shackelford immediately sent the column toward Hammersville. On the 26th, they reached Hammersville. General Shackelford was informed that Morgan was at Salineville. Major Way had fought with Morgan and he captured two hundred and thirty additional men. General Shackelford, Major Rue, and Captain Ward went into Salineville. Upon arriving, General Shackelford learned that Morgan, with about four hundred men, were moving towards Smith's Ford. General Shackelford ordered Major Rue to advance on the New Lisbon road. Major Rue informed General Shackelford that he had encountered Morgan's men. General Shackelford advanced as quickly as possible. On his approach, several of Morgan's men began to run. They were told to halt, and when they refused to do so, they were fired upon. Just at that moment, a flag of truce came up. Morgan asked to meet with General Shackelford. Morgan told General Shackelford that he had already surrendered to a militia captain, and he was paroled. General Shackelford captured three hundred and fifty men. General Shackelford wrote to Major General Ambrose Burnside what he should do with Morgan and his forces. Burnside wrote back that Morgan was not to be paroled, and he was to be treated as a common criminal.

Bluford Adams was one of the few men that managed to escape at Buffington Island, but his brother was not so fortunate. The Yankees captured John Adams at Salineville, Ohio on July 26th, 1863. They sent him to Point Lookout Prison in Maryland. They sent Morgan to the Ohio State Penitentiary. On November 27th, 1863, Morgan and six other officers escaped. Morgan would make it back to Tennessee. Morgan made one last raid into Kentucky, and then headed back to Tennessee. His luck would run out on September 3rd, 1864, when Morgan was killed during a surprise attack at Greeneville, Tennessee.

On February 23, 1865, the Yankees paroled John Adams at Camp Lee, near Richmond, Virginia. John decided to rejoin Confederate service, and became a member of the 4th Kentucky Cavalry. Bluford joined his brother and the 4th Kentucky Cavalry. By this time the Confederacy was a lost cause. Sherman was advancing on Columbia and would take it on February 17th. On March 18th, 1865, the 4th Kentucky fought at one of the last great battles of the Civil War, which occurred at Bentonville, North Carolina. The battle was between Confederate General Joseph Johnston forces, and Union General William T. Sherman's forces. By April 11th, 1865, the Kentucky Cavalry units had learned of Lee's surrender to Union General Grant at Appomattox, It was time to evacuate Richmond and what was left of the Confederate Cabinet. At Raleigh, North Carolina, Dibrell's Division of cavalry, of which the Kentucky Brigade was a part of, including the 4th Kentucky Cavalry, was ordered by General Joseph Wheeler to proceed to Greensboro, North Carolina. The Kentucky Brigade was to be an escort for President Jefferson Davis and his Cabinet. Davis and his cabinet had reached that point after retreating from Richmond. They escorted Mr. Davis and Cabinet to Charlotte, N.C. on April 18th, 1865. Here they halted while Joseph Johnston and Sherman negotiated. At this point General Duke's Brigade of General Morgan's old Division joined them. They left Charlotte for Abbeville. It was here that they held the last meeting of the Confederate Cabinet. Secretary of War, General John C. Breckinridge, General Braxton Bragg, and five Brigade commanders; Generals Dibrell, Furguson, Vaughn, General Basil Duke and Col. W. C. P. Breckinridge of the 9th Kentucky Cavalry, then commanding the Kentucky Cavalry Brigade, agreed that to continue the war was useless. Davis objected at first, but then finally accepted. Davis would try to escape on his own. The rest of the command continued to march to Washington, Georgia, and then were paroled on May 10th, 1865. Davis caught up with his family in Georgia, and were only seventy miles from the Florida border, when the Yankees captured him on May 10th, 1865. Bluford Adams surrendered on May 9th, 1865, and took the oath of allegiance on May 10th, 1865, and returned home.

Bluford Adams would marry Fannie Bell Allen on February 9, 1874 and have one child who later died in childhood. Bluford Adams died on February 12th, 1912. They buried him at Big Boone Baptist Church on February 14th, 1912. "Thus closed the life chapter of one of the county's most influential and worthy citizens."

Bluford Watson Adam's Spiller and Burr, .36 caliber pistol was based on the popular Federal manufactured Whitney Revolver, and is a second model type, with the serial number 1059. The Spiller and Burr company manufactured these guns in Atlanta and later Macon, Georgia. During 1863-64, there were a total of 1,532 pistols made by the company.

References:

Jack Rouse, whose great grandmother, Jenney Ossman, was Bluford Adams sister, and without his help this article could have not been written.

Official Records of the War of the Rebellion

O.R. Series I -Volume XXIII/I (S#34) Morgan's raid into Kentucky, Indiana, and Ohio. No 4. report of Lt. Col. Roger Hanson, twentieth Kentucky Infantry, of skirmish at Lebanon, Ky.

O.R. Series I-Volume XXIII/I (S#34) Morgan's raid into Kentucky, Indiana, and Ohio. No. 2 Reports of Brig. Gen. James Shackelford, U.S. Army, commanding First Brigade, Second Division, 23rd Army Corps.

O.R. Series I-Volume XXIII/I (S#34) Morgan's Raid into Kentucky, Indiana, and Ohio. No, 3 Report of Col. Orlando H. Moore, twenty fifth Michigan Infantry (District of Kentucky) of engagement at Green river Brigade, Ky.

O.R. Series I -Volume XX/I (S#29) Morgan's second Kentucky raid. No. 9 Reports of Brig. Gen. John H. Morgan, C. S. Army, commanding expedition.

O.R. Series I-Volume XXIII/I (S#34) Morgan's raid into Kentucky, Indiana, and Ohio. No. 6 Report of Maj. Israel N. Stiles, Sixty-third Indiana Infantry, of skirmish at Shepherdsville, Ky.

O.R. Series I -Volume XXIII/I (S#34) Morgan's raid into Kentucky, Indiana, and Ohio. No 7 report of Brig. Gen. Henry M. Judah, U.S. Army, commanding third Division, Twenty- third Army Corps.

O.R. Series I -Volume XXIII/I (S#34) Morgan's raid into Kentucky, Indiana, and Ohio. No. 1 Reports of Major gen. Ambrose Burnside, U.S. Army, commanding Department of the Ohio, with Return of casualties.

Norman, Matthew, Colonel Burton's Spitler and Burr Revolver, P. 130.

Uniform of Brig. General Edward Henry Hobson-General
Hobson was born on July 11, 1825, in Greensburg, Green County, Kentucky, and was the son of Capt. William Hobson and Lucy (Kirtley) Hobson. His father was an owner of steamboats on Green River and a merchant. Edward attended the local schools of Greensburg and Danville, and entered in business with his father at the age of eighteen. During the Mexican War, Hobson enlisted as a Second Lieutenant of Company A, 2nd Kentucky Infantry. In June 1846, the 2nd Kentucky Infantry left Louisville on board the old steamer "Sultana" and was hurried to Mexico. Soon arriving in Mexico, Hobson's company was selected as escort for the supply train from Seralvo to General Taylor's army, then before the strong works at Monterey. This was a charge of great responsibility. During the battle of Buena Vista, Hobson's company was engaged in fighting along the line as heavy infantry and was four times detached as riflemen to repel the enemy's advances. At one time when detached from the main line, with sixty men Lt. Hobson was attacked by three hundred Mexican infantry. He defeated and pursued them until recalled by Col. McKee for the final charge on the Mexican forces. For his heroism at the Battle of Buena Vista, Hobson was promoted to Ist Lieutenant.

After the Mexican War, Hobson returned home and continued his mercantile business. He became an honorable and upstanding member of the community. He was the Deputy Grand Master of the Masonic order for the state of Kentucky, and became the president of the Board of Trustees in Greensburg, and was always involved in the development of the many industries and enterprises. On October 12, 1847, he married Kate, daughter of Alexander and Elizabeth Adair, and niece of Governor Adair. With political influence, Hobson quickly rose in the banking industry and commerce and became director of the Greensburg Branch Bank of Kentucky in 1853, and president in 1857.

When the Civil War broke out, Hobson was made Colonel of the 2nd Kentucky Infantry and later recruited the 13th Kentucky Union Infantry and became it's Colonel. Hobson also assisted in the forming of the Twenty First and Twenty seventh Infantry regiments. The 13th Kentucky was mustered into service on January 12th, 1862.

In March 1862, at Spring Hill, Tennessee, when drilling his regiment in the presence of General Buell, his horse became unruly and fell backwards on him, fracturing his right leg. Hobson's leg swelled up twice it's size, but on April 6th, Hobson rode twenty miles to Shiloh, and placed his men into line of battle among the cheers of his men. On the second day's heaviest fighting, Hobson's horse was thrown under him and injured by the concussion of a bomb, but was not killed and the General remounted his horse. During the close of the day's battle, Hobson charged and captured a six gun battery and narrowly escaped death, with his clothing riddled by bullet holes. For his heroism at the Battle of Shiloh on April 7th, 1862, Hobson received the rank of Brigadier General, which became official on November 29th, 1862.

During his military career, Hobson was present at the siege of Corinth and contributed largely to the success of the Union army in the siege. At the Battle of Perryville, on October Eighth, 1862, Hobson commanded a special brigade. During Morgan's first raid into Kentucky in December 1862, he drove part of Confederate General John Hunt Morgan's forces out of Munfordsville on December 25th, 1862 and afterwards defeated Morgan's attempt to bum the railroad bridge at Munfordville.

In 1863, Hobson was assigned to command the Southern Central Kentucky Division and was in control of Indiana, Illinois, and Michigan units besides his own. In July 1863, Hobson chased Confederate General John Hunt Morgan for 900 hundred miles and twenty one days. He overtook Morgan at Buffington Island, Ohio on July 19th, 1863. On July 19th, with the help of Union General Benjamin Judah's troops, Hobson captured five cannons, a vast amount of equipment, and five hundred and seventy five men. He was not able to captured Morgan, although Morgan was captured and sent to the Ohio State Penitentiary.

In 1864, Hobson led a brief campaign on the Green River, and conducted a successful campaign against Confederate General Adam Rankin Johnson, completely destroying the Confederate forces along the Cumberland River and breaking up the Confederate control in Southwestern Kentucky. Hobson also led an expedition against Saltville, Virginia, but Morgan, who had escaped the Penitentiary and reformed his command, kept Hobson's men in check. On June 11th, 1864, while approaching Cynthiana, Kentucky, Hobson was captured by Morgan's forces. During this surprise attack, Hobson was injured. Hobson returned to Cincinnati to be exchanged for another Confederate officer. On June 12th, 1864, Union General Steven Burbridge attacked Morgan's forces at Cynthiana and

Gen. Hobson's coat. (Kentucky Military History Museum)

scattered his forces. The union prisoners were freed, and the exchange with Hobson was nullified. Hobson was brought before the War Department for his technical violation of his parole.

After the war, Hobson was appointed by President Grant as collector for the internal revenue department in the fourth district. Hobson also held various offices in the Grand Army of the Republic, being commander of the Department of Kentucky in 1892-93. He was active in the Republican party, serving as vice president of the National Convention in 1880. In Greensburg, he was promoted the construction of the Greensburg to Lebanon railroad, and was president of the Cumberland & Ohio railroad. He was also engaged in lumbering, real estate, and merchandise, until his death in Cleveland, Ohio, in 1901, during the G.A.R. encampment.

Of interesting note is Brig. General Hobson's Union double breasted frock coat, which has eight holes sewn into the uniform. There are four on the left shoulder and four on the right shoulder. The purpose of these holes allowed Hobson to tie on his shoulder boards, more than having them sewed on. (Reference: Biographical Cyclopedia of the Commonwealth of Kentucky, John Gresham, Chicago-Philadelphia, 1896, and Dictionary of American Biography, under the Auspices of the American Council of Learned Societies, Dumas Malone, Charles Scriliner's Sons, New York, 1932.) **Kentucky Military History Museum**

1st Kentucky and National C.S. Flag (BCWM)

1st Kentucky flag made from Ben Hardin Helm's wife's dress. (Kentucky Military History Museum)

1st Kentucky Cavalry - The First Kentucky Cavalry was formed in the summer and autumn of 1861, by Col. Ben Hardin Helm. Helm takes command of all the cavalry companies gathering in Bowling Green, Kentucky. In October 1861, the First Kentucky Cavalry is mustered into Confederate service. After the fall of Forts Henry and Donelson in February of 1862, Confederate General Albert Sidney Johnston orders the evacuation of Bowling Green. The First Kentucky Cavalry guards the rear and left flank, arriving in Nashville. While in Nashville, it guarded the stores. It was ordered to Decatur, Alabama, guarding the bridges of Memphis and Charleston Railroad. Confederate General Nathan Bedford Forrest escapes from Fort Donelson, members of the First Kentucky Cavalry who were assigned to him surrender, others chose to remain with Forrest.

At the Battle of Shiloh, the First Kentucky holds it's position "up the Tennessee". It will guard Johnston's left and rear. On April 17th, 1862, Ben Hardin Helm is made General and leaves the First Kentucky. The command is turned over to Lt. Col. Woodward. In June of 1862, Companies C and D are assigned to Confederate General Nathan Bedford Forrest and participate in his raiding in Middle Tennessee and his attack on Murfressboro. In August of 1862, the prisoners captured at Fort Donelson are exchanged, and the remainder of the First Kentucky join Forrest's command. In September 1862, Confederate General Braxton Bragg begins his Kentucky Campaign. The First Kentucky arrives with Forrest in Munfordsvillle, Kentucky rounding up prisoners, from the Battle of Munfordville. When Bragg arrives at Bardstown, Kentucky, Forrest is sent back to Tennessee to form another command. The First Kentucky Cavalry was assigned to Confederate General Joe Wheeler at the Battle of Perryville (Oct. 7-8, 1862) and the First Kentucky is now commanded by Major Caldwell.

In either October or November, the First Kentucky's one year enlistment is up and the First Kentucky reorganizes. Col. J. Russell Butler is now made commander of the First Kentucky Cavalry, and in January 1863, the First Kentucky is assigned to General Buford. The regiment under Wheeler's command, captures LaVergne, it was engaged at the Battle of Hower's Gap, Chattanooga, McMinnville, Hill's Gap, Missionary Ridge, and covered the retreat of Bragg's army from Tennessee. On December 28th, 1863, it suffered heavy losses at Charleston, Tennessee. On January 1864, the First Kentucky was engaged at Ringgold Gap. On March 1864, it was encamped at Oxford, Alabama. The regiment was constantly engaged opposing Sherman's Atlanta Campaign. The regiment was engaged at Dalton, Dry Gap, New Hope Church, Noonday Creek, Kennesaw Mountain, Pine Mountain, Lost Mountain and Intrenchment Creek. The First Kentucky was in the pursuit and capture of Sherman's raiders in Georgia, and was then ordered to Saltville, Virginia. The regiment then moved on to Ashville, North Carolina, rejoining Wheeler's command. After General Lee's surrender at Appomattox Court House to General Grant in April 1865, the First Kentucky Cavalry was the escort for Confederate President Jefferson Davis, and after his capture, the regiment surrendered and was paroled at Washington, Georgia on May 10th, 1865. General Wheeler said of the First Kentucky: "I am always glad to think and write about the gallant old First Kentucky Cavalry. It was as brave a body of men as any officer had the good fortune to command. If I sent them into action oftener than I should have done, it was because I know they would be equal to any heroic duty which might be imposed upon them." (Reference: The Adjutant General's Report for the State of Kentucky, Confederate.)

CIVIL WAR MEDICINE

A Southern Perspective

The typical dress of the Confederate surgeon varied somewhat from his Yankee counterpart whose surgeon's uniform was very similar to a Union officer's blue-black "chaplins" frock coat. The coat could have a single row of buttons or higher ranking surgeons could wear the double breasted frock coat with two rows of stand Union officer's eagle buttons. The seams on the collar and cuffs were crimson. His rank was worn on his shoulder straps, along with the MS for medical service in gold in the middle of the shoulder strap. His trousers were blue-black, the same as a Union officer. A Union medical steward wore a green arm band with a yellow medical caduceus in the middle. In contrast, a Confederate surgeon's uniform was usually a frock coat, although some surgeons wore a shell jacket or even their civilian frock coats. According to regulations, the frock coat was to be cadet gray and double breasted, with a double row of buttons. The cuffs, collar, and the edging on the coat were black. He could also wear the "Austrian knot" on his sleeves and his rank was worn on his standing collar. His trousers were light blue with black stripes edged in gold down the sides, although variations could exist, and gray or butternut pants could be substituted. Medical officer's wore a green sash like that worn by Union Army medical officer's. His buttons and belt plate were brass, but there was no special emblem for the medical corps used on buttons and belt plates, so the surgeon wore officer's eagle staff buttons, his state buttons, or C.S.A. buttons. His hat was a gray kepi with gold trim and a gold device on the front with MS surrounded by a gold wreath. Head gear varied, and many surgeons on both sides wore slouch hats. The Confederate steward usually wore a red arm band bearing the words "Medical Corps". During battle the surgeon did not wear his frock coat, but wore something similar to a butcher's apron over his clothes. Yankee surgeons, in contrast, wore a white jacket. Confederate surgeons did not wear a Medical Officer's sword, unless they had served previously in the Old Army. Union Medical officer's wore the Medical Officer's sword, although, only as a badge of office. Shoes varied on both sides, but were usually Jefferson boots.

Statistics vary on the number of fatalities during the Civil War. One estimate states that 361,452 Union soldiers lost their lives, and of that number, 110,000 were combat deaths, 26, 872 died in accidents, and 224,580 died of illness. There were 470,000 cases of wounds and injuries North and South, and 600,000 cases of sickness; from diseases such as pneumonia, tuberculosis, scurvy, rheumatism, typhoid fever, scarlet fever, and yellow fever. The Confederate army lost 94,000 men in battle and 164,000 died of disease. As you can see from these numbers, disease killed more men than bullets. Sixty-five percent of all deaths that occurred during the Civil War were caused by disease. Bullet wounds accounted only for 20 percent of all deaths. There were one million cases of disease and wounds reported on both sides. Joseph Jones, the foremost Confederate medical officer, sheds even more light on the plight of the

Surgical kit containing tenaculums and dissection forceps. (BCWM)

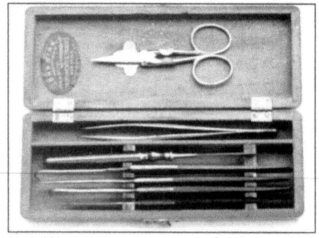

Surgical kit containing scissors, tweezers, scalpels, and tenaculums. (BCWM)

Confederate soldier. He estimated that 600,00 men fought in the Confederate Army and on average, each man fell victim to disease and wounds appropriately six times during the war. Jones estimated that 200,000 soldiers were killed outright or died as a result of illness or wounds. During 1861-65, one million, two hundred and nineteen thousand, two hundred and fifty one (1,219,251) cases of disease were reported to the Confederate surgeon; of these 31,338 died of disease. According to Jones, disease killed 150,000 Confederate soldiers.

When the war broke out there were only 21 medical schools in the South. The most prominent medical school in the country was the University of Pennsylvania and fully one fourth of all physicians in the South were graduates of this school. Other prominent universities were the University of New York, Jefferson Medical College, and the Medical College of South Carolina and the University of Virginia. Augusta, New Orleans, Richmond, Nashville, and Mobile also had medical schools. The University of Lexington and Transylvania University were the only medical schools in Kentucky. The only requirement to enter medical school was that you had enough money to pay for the schooling. To receive a degree as a doctor only required two years of medical school, and the second year was usually a repeat of the first. Prewar medical treatment concentrated primarily on regulating the bowels, the kidneys, and the blood. Medicines were mostly used to help regulate and maintain the proper consistency of bodily fluids and excretions. Surgical procedures were mostly unknown. Most medical schools were not regulated by any requirements of law and many schools espoused outlandish theories and ideas about the practice of medicine. Different schools of thought prevailed among doctors on treating their patients. Some were homeopathic doctors, who believed in small doses of medication, and that no mercury

Tintypes of surgeons wearing standard white surgical coats, which were issued to medical officers. (BCWM)

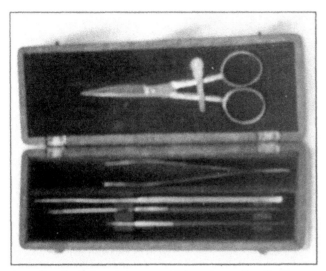
A small medical instrument case containing scissors, dissection forceps, and surgical scalpels. (BCWM)

be used on the patient, allopathic doctors believed in the time tested ways of treating the patient, mostly with the medicines already known at that time, and heavy doses of mercury. Also the Hydrotherapeutic doctor who recommended theraputic baths, and botanic doctors who favored roots and herbs, not to mention many doctors who were nothing but pure and simple quacks.

During the Civil War the Minie ball, or conical bullet, developed by French Captain Claude E. Minie, accounted for 94% of the casualties, and shell and canister accounted for six per cent of the casualties. Even though most Civil War doctors had graduated from a medical school, most of them had never seen a bullet wound and were not qualified to be surgeons. Many were rural doctors who learned their skills by serving an apprenticeship. The rural doctors were only general practitioners, and their surgical skills were very limited, but the Confederate army was desperate for surgeons and hired anyone who had just graduated from medical school or were general practitioners. At the outbreak of the war only 24 medical officers resigned from the U.S. Army to join the Confederacy. These doctors were quickly overwhelmed by the carnage of the battelfield, and needed help. E. A. Craighill, a medical steward of Stonewall Jackson's Brigade, said in 1861, after the Battle of Manassas:

Of course, there were surgeons in our army older than I was, who had much more experience, but none of us up to that time had seen much of gunshot wounds, and we had to unlearn what we had been taught at college, in books, as almost worthless, and only experience was useful in treatment and forming a correct or even an appropriate opinion of results from wounds, particularly, and sometimes from disease...

Books were quickly issued to help the surgeons in the field. Some of these books were A Manual of Military Surgery for the Use of Surgeons in the Confederate Army by John Julian Chisolm in 1861; George MacLeod's, Notes on the Surgery of the Crimea War" edited by Alexander Nicholas Tally in 1862; Edward Warren's, An Epitome of Practical Surgery for Field and Hospital in 1863; and finally A Manual for Military Surgery published by the surgeon general in 1863.

Another problem for these newly inducted surgeons was that they were now required to answer to military rules and regulations. Most of these doctors had never been in the military before and were now required to fill out reports and answer to higher authorities. Many of these doctors were set in their ways, and this presented a problem with discipline in some of the military hospitals.

Doctors also faced the problem of finding qualified nurses. Early in the war, nurses were usually men who were either disabled soldiers, or were soldiers that were assigned to the task. The surgeons soon noticed that men did not make very good nurses. Many

of these men were sick themselves, or could not perform their required duties because of their disabilities. Most of the male nurses also did not have a lot of compassion for their fellow soldiers and had not been taught the basics of cleanliness, and proper hygiene, whereupon doctors soon turned to females nurses. Early in the war the only female nurses were nuns from the Sisters of Charity. The nuns were soon brought to the point of exhaustion, so housewives, mothers, and sisters were filling in with much needed help. Nurses learned to cook, wash the patients' clothing, wash and iron the sheets and make beds. They also wrote letters for the soldiers, and consoled them. Many a patient recovered because a caring nurse watched over them. Nurses very often made sure that the cooks were preparing the meals properly. They also helped in the policing of the hospitals to ensure that they were clean. Nurses were the first to point out what a healthy meal meant to a patient. They recognized the ill effects that coffee, hard bread, salt pork, and beef had on an ill patient, and would very often try to make sure that milk, soup, fruits and vegetables were made available for them. Nurses were often the link between the Lady's Relief Societies and the hospitals. The nurses talked to the local Relief Societies, and asked them for shirts, shoes, socks, food, etc., whatever the hospital needed. If it were not for the female nurses, doctors and their patients would have been much worse off. Nurses provided an invaluable service to the war effort.

The Union government made life for the Confederate surgeon very difficult. Surgical instruments and medications were deemed contraband. Because of the Union blockade, the South acquired its medications by three means; capture enemy medical stores, run the blockade, or manufacture medicines from ingredients on hand.

Wooden device containing sharpening stone, with "49th Ill. Hospital" engraved into the wood. This item was used to sharpen the blades of the surgical instruments. (BCWM)

Field Medicine Chest containing glass medicine vials. The two books on either side are the "Medical and Surgical History of the War of the Rebellion" parts two and three. (BCWM)

Medicines acquired through capture became more infrequent and could not be relied upon. Buying medications from blockade runners became too expensive, so the running of drugs from the North to the South by land took place. Drugs were sent from Paducah, Kentucky or Cairo, Illinois down the Mississippi River to Tennessee or Arkansas. Women and children smuggled drugs into the South in many inventive ways. Secreted beneath hoop skirts, inside shirts and dolls, and in luggage. But this was also unreliable and could not meet the demands of the doctors, so the South began to rely upon its own resources. Surgeons had to make do with what they had and many times they resorted to home remedies. The Confederate government finally set up pharmaceutical labs in the South to manufacture their own medications. Labs were set up in Macon, Augusta, Milledge-ville, and Atlanta, Georgia; Columbia and Charleston, South Carolina; Charlotte and Lincolnton, North Carolina; Montgomery and Mobile, Alabama; Knoxville, Tennessee; Arkadelphia, Arkansas and Tyler, Texas. The labs were under the direction of purveyors, who were surgeons and assistant surgeons under the authority of the surgeon general, and who collected and acquired the needed herbs, roots and supplies. Druggists and chemists were employed to prepare the medicines. Joseph LeConte was the best medicine maker in the Confederacy and one of the most able druggists was Charles Theodore Mohr of Mobile, Alabama. The laboratory in Columbia, South Carolina made alcohol, silver nitrate, sulfuric ether, nitric ether, and podophyllin resin. When laboratories couldn't handle the massive orders for medications, the surgeon general made a plea to all regions to collect native

Standard white surgical coat. Blood stains are across the uniform and sleeves. In background are wooden crutches. Since their were no antisecptic means during the Civil War, surgeons would wash up before the surgery but had little concern for the cleanliness during the operations, including their clothes, instruments, tables, etc. (BCWM)

Standard Model 1840 Medical Officer sword. The "M.S." in the guard denoted Medical Service, was made of silver, which was applied to the guard. Of interesting note is that the Medical Officers sword's style didn't change for 60 years. (BCWM)

Set of mortars and pestals. The mortar on the left is copper, the one on the right is made of iron. (BCWM)

Portable measuring scales. Glass medical vials are balancing on the scales. This item was used to measure the correct amounts of medication to be used. (BCWM)

Traveling medicine kit with glass vials. Displayed above the green kit are ivory measuring intruments. (BCWM)

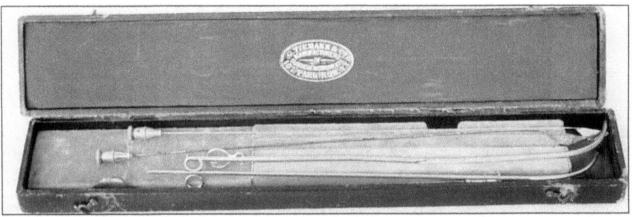

Early catheter made of steel, made by G. Tiemann & Co., Row, New York. (BCWM)

This medical kit contains a syringe from the Civil War made by Whitall & Tatum, Philadelphia. (BCWM)

Cobalt blue medical flask with back to back "P" in a circle. (BCWM)

plants so that they could be used in the manufacture of medicines. It was found that the native remedies were not as effective as prepared drugs, but they were used just the same.

Doctors used alcohol as a major stimulant during the Civil War, and prices increased rapidly. The surgeon general found most of the purchased alcohol to be of inferior quality, and ordered alcohol distilleries set up in Salisbury, North Carolina; Columbia, South Carolina; Macon, Georgia and Montgomery, Alabama. Barley, wheat, rye and corn were all employed in the making of alcohol.

Quinine, morphine, and chloroform were in extremely short supply. In 1863, Quinine sold for $400 to $600 an ounce! Medical instruments were also very difficult for the South to obtain. She just did not have the factories nor the expertise to make delicate surgical instruments. Many times doctors had to make do with carpenters saws, forks, knitting needles, penknives, a strip of bark, and fence rails, taking the places of surgical saws, surgical hooks, tenaculum, scalpels, tourniquets, and splints. Often supplies already on hand could not be sent to the front because of a lack of boxes and bottles in which to ship them. Other times a shortage would occur when one state had fewer supplies than another state but would be unaware of the others abundance and the much needed supplies would never be requisitioned. Another problem in maintaining a store of medical supplies was that the army was very often on the move, and the supply trains could not keep up.

Diseases were a major problem for the surgeon and often he knew neither the cause nor the cure for his ailing patients. As the war progressed, many Confederate surgeons saw that insufficient food, exposure to the elements, fatigue, salt and fat fried food, poor shelter, lack of clothing, and infected tents and camps were a major cause of sickness and disease. Food rations became shorter and shorter as the war went on and many times the food delivered to the troops was inedible. Beef was either rancid or had worms in it. If bread was purchased it was either moldy or had infestations of bugs in it. Baked bread was another problem. Many times it was made with whatever was lying around that resembled flour. The Confederates main bread source was "coosh," which was raw corn meal mixed with bacon grease and water and cooked in a frying pan. Scurvy became a major problem because of the lack of proper food, and poorly prepared food brought about one of the worst ailments a soldier could get, dysentery. Food was almost always cooked or fried in grease and the cook was anyone that could boil water. Men went days without eating any food, and when three days rations were drawn, the soldiers would eat all three days rations in one day and go hungry for the next two. As the war dragged on, Southern soldiers went without shoes or clothing and were exposed to the elements and this would bring on bouts of pneumonia, rheumatism and frostbite.

One major reason for the increase in disease was because doctors let almost anyone enlist in the army, regardless of his health, and as more soldiers were needed to fight in the field, regulations became lax. Doctors let more and more men into the army who were already sick or diseased. Men from rural areas were also a problem for the doctors because they had never developed an immunity to smallpox, measles, or chickenpox and once these diseases became established in the camp, they would practically put the entire camp on the sick list. Sometimes entire regiments would be infected. Surgeon E. A. Craighill, wrote on March 4, 1862, in Gordonsville, Virginia,

"There were a great many sick and very sick, particularly among the green men who had experienced none of the hardships of camp life ... This was particularly the case with Lawton's brigade of Georgians, said to be 5,000 strong ... They camped in a

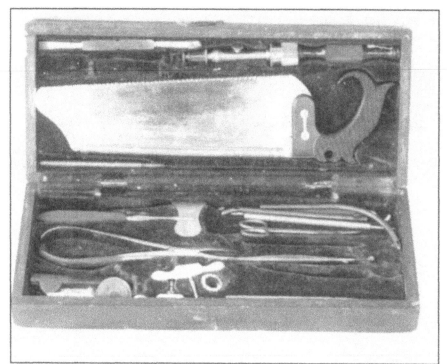

Large 1840-50's period surgical kit marked "Hernstein." Earlier kits contained ivory handled instruments, and usually contained a fleam. Kit also contains a chain saw, along with other instruments. (BCWM)

Amputees knife and fork combination. These utensils were designed to be used by a one armed veteran. (BCWM)

This crudely made artificial leg belonged to a Confederate Veteran that lived in Bowling Green, Kentucky. The state of Mississippi spent over forty percent of its budget on artificial limbs in 1865. (BCWM)

field nearby, and very soon after they arrived measles broke out among them, which few had ever had, and to add to their discomfort, a steady cold rain set in, which lasted for days. We had no comforts or hospital accommodations for the poor fellows, not even tents, and their suffering was intense. The usual sequel of measles from exposure set in, and many of them were down with Pneumonia and Diarrhea. The mortality was frightful. I believe it is no exaggeration to say that out of the 5,000 at least 1,500 were sick, and the number who died was appalling. These were no quarters to take the sick to, no hospitals had then been built, and I have many times seen these suffering ill men lying out-of-doors in the rain with Pneumonia. How many of them died the good Lord only knows, I do not."

Even though the old army knew the proper procedures for personal bathing, and regular airing of tents and bedding; the careful placement of latrines and garbage pits, with daily application of lime and earth, and for purifing water, the volunteer army totally ignored these procedures because of the ignorance and inexperience of the green officers and men. Men from rural areas also encouraged disease by not bathing and they would relieve themselves anywhere. Dysentery, pneumonia and typhoid fever, accounted for one fourth of all non combatant deaths in the Confederacy, and would run rampant in many camps because latrines were dug too near the camp water source. Trash, fruit scraps, animal carcasses, and feces were left lying around the camp and brought in hoards of rats, mosquitos, flies, lice, chiggers, and roaches. The bite of the anopheles mosquito caused malaria, and one of every four men who fell ill suffered from this disease. The Confederate States Medical and Surgical Journal, 1864, Vol. 1 No. 2, stated:

"Article 1, Report on the Yellow Fever epidemic at Wilmington, North Carolina, in the Autumn of 1862, by William T. Wragg, surgeon, P.A.C.S. {Surgeon Wragg premises his report with a sketch of the topography of Wilmington. A sand soil rests upon a sub layer filled with water, so that slight depressions result in the formation of ponds which stagnate under the vertical rays of a tropical sun. These ponds were increased in size and number by the breastworks thrown up for the defense of the city, while the artificial drainage heretofore in use had, owing to the extingency of the times, been almost entirely neglected.

The hygienic condition of the city is described as being terrible in the extreme. The streets and yards were filled with heaps of filth and ordure, rotting in the sun. Disagreeable odors filled the air, requiring tar fires, whilst a dark canopy of smoke overhung the devoted spot. When we add to this the fact that many of the population were in want of the necessities and comforts of life, being in the midst of this mass of decaying matter, we will not be surprised to hear that the physicians of the place stated that the season was unusually sickly, and that fevers of a malarial type, often terminating in jaundice, were becoming daily more prevalent.-editor (James Brown McCaw)}

The newly developed Minie ball caused massive destruction of the human body. The soft lead projectiles would smash bone and ligaments. Amputations were the only way a surgeon could save a life. Doctors very often received patients with multiple wounds. Patrick Cleburne, who was killed at the battle of Franklin, received 49 bullet wounds. When a surgeon arrived on the scene at the field hospital, he often used a door and two barrels for an amputation table. The surgeon applied a tourniquet to the area to be amputated, and the patient was given chloroform if it was available. The surgeon then used his finger to probe for the bullet. If the bullet was deep, he would use a longer probe. Once the bullet was found, the surgeon would pry it out with his bullet extractor. If damage to the area was too massive, the surgeon performed an amputation. However, most amputations were performed to prevent septicemia and gangreen. The surgeon would cut at an angle forming a point,and the skin would be pulled back to expose the bone, the surgeon would then saw off the limb. He would then put a ligature on the arteries to prevent bleeding. The ligature was applied by looping thread around the ruptured artery leaving the end of the thread dangling from the wound or incision. Every day the surgeon would tug at the thread until, the loop having rotted, the strand came away in his hand. The only problem with this procedure was that if the artery wall had any infection or if the clot had not formed, the tugging would open the artery and the patient would bleed to death, which occurred in two out of three cases in which the artery opened up.

Surgeons had to act quickly to stave off infection and blood loss, so most amputations were done within 24 hours. Surgeon David Smith (Union Army), in January 1862, after the Battle of Mill Springs, Kentucky, wrote:

"... the dreadful roads over which all of the wounded had been brought had induced profuse suppuration. All the food that could be procured was beef, pork, and hard bread. Shortly after my arrival I saw one man die from the irritation produced by fragments of the upper jaw; which although split in every direction by passage of a Minie ball, had been left without excision. The same state of things existed also in the case of a fractured lower jaw, and was followed by the same result. Two cases of gunshot wounds of knee joint, in which amputation had not been performed, also came to a rapidly fatal termination. In four cases of gunshot fracture of the humerus, reported to me as doing well, I found such complete comminution that in two cases I excised large portions of the shaft and in the remaining two, the head of the bone ..."

Blood transfusions were unknown to most surgeons, and every drop of blood shed by the patient would put him one step closer to death. Abdomen, and head wounds were 90% fatal. If the small intestine was involved, death was inevitable. The mortality rate for chest wounds was 60%. Surgeons just did not have the knowledge to repair such massive wounds to vital areas, or to prevent internal bleeding.

Since there was no concept of sterilization of instruments or the use of antiseptics to combat infection, soldiers very often came down with tetanus, blood poisoning, and gangrene. Surgeons very often went without washing their hands or instruments. Pyaemea, or blood poisoning, comprised 43% of all deaths from primary amputations, and was usually 97% fatal once the patient acquired this disease. Infections were the chief cause of mortality following surgery and also for untreated wounds.

Surgeons thought that laudible pus was a good sign of healing and usually encouraged it. Doctors often used water dressings, which usually encouraged gangrene and infections. S. H. Melcher, assistant surgeon in the 5th Missouri Volunteers at Wilson Creek, reported in 1861:

"The wounded were sent to the rear in wagons as the fight progressed. The attendance they re-

Wooden mortar and pestle. Used by surgeons to make medications for patients. If they were lucky, surgeons had a pharmacist who could make the medications for the soldiers. If not, the surgeon would have to make them himself. (BCWM)

Set of different fleams. Prior to and during the Civil War, surgeons would cut open an artery and bleed a patient. They thought that a patient may have "bad blood" and it needed to be relieved. This practice was done away with after the Civil War. (BCWM)

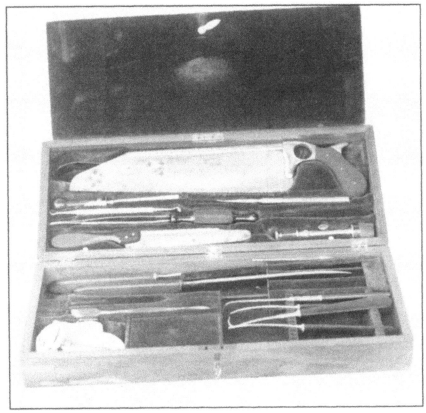

Intact large surgical kit marked "A. Fischer," made in Louisville, Kentucky. It has a blue lined interior with amputation saw, tourniquet, amputation knives, tenaculums, and trephine. (BCWM)

Model 1840 Medical Staff Officer's Presentation Sword belonging to Surgeon General C. C. Huff. Manufactured by Horstmann & Sons, Philadelphia. (BCWM)

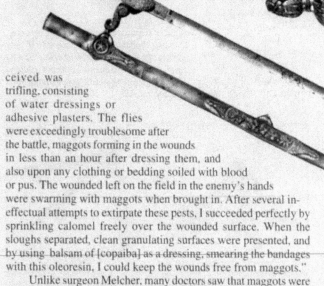

ceived was trifling, consisting of water dressings or adhesive plasters. The flies were exceedingly troublesome after the battle, maggots forming in the wounds in less than an hour after dressing them, and also upon any clothing or bedding soiled with blood or pus. The wounded left on the field in the enemy's hands were swarming with maggots when brought in. After several ineffectual attempts to extirpate these pests, I succeeded perfectly by sprinkling calomel freely over the wounded surface. When the sloughs separated, clean granulating surfaces were presented, and by using balsam of [copaiba] as a dressing, smearing the bandages with this oleoresin, I could keep the wounds free from maggots."

Unlike surgeon Melcher, many doctors saw that maggots were actually beneficial, since maggots only destroy the dead flesh and will not touch the healthy flesh.

Surgeons did not have any idea how to administer medication properly, and they always ran the risk of under medicating or over medicating their patients. Surgeons were also not aware of the addictive effects of some medications, like opium and morphine. After surgery, many patients suffered withdrawal symptoms, and after the war thousands were lifetime drug addicts. Alcoholism was also another major problem. Boredom and/or the proclivity for surgeons to use the numbing effects of alcohol upon their patients often led to soldiers suffering from D.T.s. Surgeons were not immune to the gore and boredom they faced every day and they themselves succumbed to the effects of drug addiction and alcoholism.

This was a day and age when there was no x-ray, no antibiotics, vitamins, concentrates, plasma, or vaccines to prevent typhoid and tetanus. We were a nation at war, and America was still a budding young country. Surgeons did try to improve their conditions, though. The Confederacy had one of the most important medical publications, the Confederate States Medical and Surgical Journal. This publication helped spread new ideas and many new innovations arose from this magazine. Confederate doctors came up with the development of an effective replacement for litmus paper in acidity/alkaline determinations; a detailed thesis "On the Microscopic Anatomy, Physiology, and Pathology of the Human Liver," and geometrical ballistics of Minie bullets relating to gunshot injuries. Surgical articles considered such topics as skull wounds, and the re-establishment of sound mental function, advances in bone pinning techniques, removal of cancerous tumors, and cosmetic surgery after facial wounds. Extracted from foreign journals, the Confederate Journal published articles on the removal of catarrhs by suction, treatment of glaucoma, utilization of blood transfusions, hermetical sealing of gunshot wounds and the use of carbolic acid as an antiseptic. They formed societies and they had quiz classes. By the end of the war, the Confederacy had 150 general hospitals, 49 were in Richmond, Virginia alone! Chimborazo, was the largest with 150 wards, and held 8,000 patients. It had a bakery that turned

out 10,000 loaves of bread a day, and a brewery that turned out 400 kegs a day, five ice houses, a soap factory, cultivated fields, and large herds of livestock. Considering the South was very short of supplies, the Confederacy still managed to have some of the best hospitals. The Confederate medical service must be commended for it's contribution to the field hospital and its mobile surgical units, which would become so important during the World Wars.

Separate wards were set up for smallpox. Good nursing was recognized as an important factor in the recovery of the patient. Well ventilated, clean hospitals became an important requirement and a good diet was recognized as beneficial to the well being of the patient. Surgeons also improved their skills with anesthesia, and antiseptics. The re-using of bandages was halted and fleams were completely done away with.

Many of the Confederate surgeons also helped in advancing dentistry as a profession. Some Confederate surgeons also went on to become outstanding members of the medical field. Dr. David Yandell became the professor of clinical surgery at the University of Louisville after the war, and later collaborated with Dr. Theophilus Parvin to establish the American Practitioner magazine, in 1870. In 1871, Dr. Yandell was elected president of the American Medical Association. Surgeon Gen. Thomas Moore formed the first American military medical society. He introduced the pavilion hospital, forerunner of the modern hospital with independent wards. During the war, Moore sent hospital stewards to attend lectures at the Virginia Medical College in Richmond. After the war, he helped bring education to the forefront by setting up School Boards.

Joseph Jones, who wrote articles for the Confederate Journal, studied gangrene, typhoid fever, and other diseases. Because of his research, Jones was the first to describe the microscopic bacterium that cause typhoid fever. Jones collected information on all aspects of the Confederate medical effort, and his work helps historians of today gain a better understanding of the massive undertaking the Confederate medical service struggled with during the war. Jones also stumbled across aseptic(sterile) surgical techniques.

The Confederacy also was instrumental in establishing private soldiers aid societies and hospital relief societies that would later lead to the founding of the International Red Cross. The Confederate army was also the first to treat surgeons as noncombatants. During the Battle of First Manassas in 1861, Thomas "Stonewall" Jackson came across Union surgeons working in their hospitals, and rather than take them prisoner, Jackson let them go. In 1865, at the Geneva Convention, the International Red Cross passed rules for the conduct of nations during hostilities and following the practice of the Confederacy, medical officers were to be treated as neutrals during armed conflict.

By the end of the war there were 3,000 military medical surgeons in the Confederacy. The ratio of surgeon to patient was one to 300, but the Confederate surgeon must be praised for his ingenuity, his courage, his tenacity against overwhelming odds, and his ability to deal with the horrors brought on by war. The Confederate surgeons greatest accomplishment was setting up one of the largest and best hospitals in the world at that time; Chimborazo. They also founded medical societies, established the Confederate Journal, and erected many successful laboratories.

Surgeon General C.C. Huff

The duties of the surgeon general were varied and covered many different areas. His first duty was to oversee the vast medical service. He was charged specifically "with the administrative details of the medical department, the government of hospitals, the regulation of the duties of surgeons and assistant surgeons, and the appointment of acting medical officers, when needed, for local or detached service." He was also responsible for the issuance of directives "relating to the professional duties of his officers."

The first assistant surgeon general of the Confederate Medical Service was David Leon. The Confederate surgeon general was Samuel Preston Moore, who became surgeon general in July 1861 and served until 1865. The first surgeon general in the Union Army was William Hammond, who served from 1861-64.

Interesting Fact: The rank of surgeon general was equivalent to Brigadier General in the Regular Army. When the war broke in 1861, the Medical Corps of the United States Army consisted of one surgeon general and only 30 surgeons and 83 assistant surgeons. Three surgeons and 21 assistant surgeons resigned and went with the Confederacy. By the end of the Civil War there were 3,000 surgeons in the Confederate Medical Service alone!

Surgeon Hugh Mulholland's Medical Officer's sword-Hugh Mulholland enlisted with the Union 5th Kentucky Cavalry on February 1st, 1862 for three years of service at Gallatin, Tennessee. The 5th Kentucky Cavalry was actively engaged on military duty several months before it was officially mustered into service. All through December 1861, and January of 1862, Col. Haggard's 5th Kentucky Cavalry was scouting the country south of Columbia. In February after the Confederates fell back from Bowling Green, the 5th Kentucky Cavalry went to Gallatin, Tennessee. It was there mustered into the United States service at Camp Sandige March 31st, 1862. The unit participated in the engagement with Confederate General John Hunt Morgan at Gallatin, but were defeated. The 5th participated in the march with Buell's army in the pursuit of Confederate General's Braxton Bragg's army. The 5th then was in service at Nashville, Tennessee from December 1862 till the spring of 1863. Mulholland was a surgeon at Hospital No. 2 in Nashville, Tennessee. He resigned on April 11th, 1863. Hugh Mulholland was recognized as a "faithful and excellent officer." The 5th Kentucky Cavalry Regiment would go on to fight at the Battles of Chickamagua, at Crawfish Springs, in December 10th, 1863, it went on an expedition against General Forrest across the Tennessee River, it participated in the Atlanta campaign fighting at the Battle of Jonesboro. After Sherman ended his Atlanta Campaign, he marched onto Savannah. The 5th then followed Sherman into the Carolinas, and fought in the battle of Bentonville. The unit was mustered out on May 3rd, 1865 in Louisville, Kentucky. [Reference: Union Regiments of Kentucky, Union Soldiers and Sailors Monument Association] (Kentucky Military History Museum.)

Surgeon Hugh Mulholland's Medical Officer's sword. (Kentucky Military Museum)

MILITARY BANDS

Confederate and United States Army regulations stated that each regiment would be provided with a military band at its commanders request. This regulation, retained from antebellum army organization, did not anticipate forces made up of thousands of volunteer regiments and subsequently, thousands of bands. Hundreds of company and regimental bands and thousands of bandsmen signed up for service in the Union armies. By the end of 1861 the government had to limit the number of bands to free more men to fight. In December 1861, the Union War Department suggested eliminating military bands to realize a savings of five million dollars. Instead, Federal musicians were reorganized on July 1862. Volunteer members of regimental bands were ordered back to the fighting ranks or offered the opportunity to join consolidated brigade-band organizations. It is believed that at least 500 bands and 9,000 bandsmen served in the Union army.

Confederate army bands, less numerous at the outset of the war, were never reduced by order. Southern manpower shortages dictated that more men serve in the ranks than in bands. Regulations for both armies stated that musicians should be trained as infantry, organized as a squad, and led by a chief musician, who was usually a noncommissioned officer. In crisis they could be pressed into combat service, but during most battles, large numbers of band members were detailed to duty as stretcher bearers, messengers, or hospital stewards.

Regulations called for 24 musicians in infantry and artillery brigade bands and 16 in cavalry bands. In Federal service, each month members of a 16-man mounted band or a 24-man infantry band earned from $45, for the leader, to $17 for junior members. Individual musicians and drummers and buglers who were not band members, earned $12 each month. Confederate principal musicians earned $21 a month, cavalry musicians $13 a month, and infantry and artillery musicians each received $12 a month.

Federal base drum with leather covered wooden beaters. This drum was usually only found in regimental bands. This instrument was used to time the footsteps of the troops. (BCWM)

In both armies these bandsmen were often recruited from existing civilian organizations. Sometimes entire civilian bands enlisted as a group. The Mountain Saxhorn Band from Staunton, Virginia, organized in 1855, became the 5th Virginia Regiment Band, known later as the Stonewall Brigade Band. Civilian band leaders with outstanding reputations were often recruited by specific volunteer bands seeking to enhance their reputations.

The band instruments used were cornets, saxhorns, alto horns, tenor horns, baritones, flat bases, side drums, base drums and cymbals. Occasionally, such woodwind instruments as clarinets and piccolos were used. Also used was the rotary-valve horn called a saxhorn, invented by Adolpe Sax. The saxhorn was a brass instrument with the bell facing to the rear, over the player's shoulder. This allowed the band to be placed at the head of the marching column, and enabled the troops in the rear of the column to hear the music better. Rarely seen in the 20th century, they gave military bands a unique sound.

The Civil War was the last major conflict in which bands played on the field of combat. At Dinwiddie Courthouse, Gen. Philip Sheridan ordered his bands to the firing line, to loudly play their best tunes, and to "never mind if a bullet goes through a trombone or even a trombonist now and then." Gen. Horace Porter saw one of Sheridan's bands under heavy fire, "playing Nellie Bly as cheerfully as if it were furnishing music for a country picnic." Sherman hoped that the morale of the men would be uplifted by the upbeat music of the bands.

Music was not only used to lift the morale of the men, but it was used in recruitment drives. The martial strains of military bands coupled with patriotic appeals and waving flags spurred thousands of young men to volunteer for military service. One young recruit called the band of the 8th New York, "the gayest band I have ever seen. Their music fairly made me take the double shuffle right on the parade ground."

Music also helped the time go by, and at night the soldiers would sit around the campfire and sing the popular songs of the day. Very often bands on either side would have competitions, and recitals at night for the officers of the camp.

But music could also have a detrimental effect on the men. For example, morale was so low sometimes that the regimental bands were forbidden to play the songs "Home Sweet Home" and "Auld Lang Syne" for fear that the woeful songs would cause spirits to plummet even deeper, and the men would attempt to go home and see their families without authorization.

The Civil War produced several notable band organizations. Musicians from the 7th New York regiment, organized as militia before the war, had outstanding reputations, as did the members of the United States Marine Band, then as now composed solely of United States Marine Corps regulars. Among Confederate bands, the North Carolina Regimental Band from Salem, North Carolina was made up of members of a Moravian musical group. Its history and sheet music were preserved by its descendant organization, the Salem Band, and provides one of the best written records of band music and service in regimental bands during that time.

Bugle and Drum Calls

Life in Civil War camps included many common experiences for the almost 3,000,000 soldiers who served in the Union and Confederate armies. Their daily activities, from reveille in the morning until taps was played at night were signaled and regulated by bugle and drum calls. The calls used by the two sides were practically identical.

The drum call was an effective and simple means of communication for directing vast numbers of men on the battlefield and for regulating the camp life of the soldier. The drum was beginning to lose it's effectivesness as a signaling device during the Civil War because of the deafening roar of modern weapons that were appearing on the battlefield. No longer could the drum drown out the sounds of battle and the bugle was beginning to replace the drum in battle and in camp.

The first of the 19 bugle calls a soldier heard each day was called the "Assembly of Bugler" and sounded at 5:00 a.m. in the summer and 6:00 a.m. in the winter. The sound of "Reveille" told the men to crawl out of their blankets and prepare for the day and was followed by "Assembly", signaling them to form ranks for the first of three roll calls held throughout the day. "Stable Call" sent men to tend to their horses; after the animals were cared for, the soldiers heard "Breakfast Call" which was immediately followed by the aroma of coffee boiling on dozens of campfires. After breakfast, "Sick Call" summoned those with ailments to report to the camp doctor, "Water Call" sent details to fetch water for men and horses, and "Fatigue Call' directed men to clean up the camp. Assignments for guard duty followed the 9:00 a.m. call of "Guard Mount."

"Drill Call," "Recall," "Dinner Call," Assembly for Regimental Drill," "Assembly for Dress Parade," another "Stable Call" and "Water Call" regimented the rest of the soldier's day until it was time to return to his tent and prepare the evening meal, which was signaled by the "Supper Call." After another "Roll Call," the soldiers were free to tend to their own needs until the 10:00 p.m. "Taps" sent them to bed with all lights out.

During battle there were more than 25 bugle calls that regulated the different activities of the cavalry and artillery. The bugle call to horse became an important cavalry signal, and fit perfectly with the new rapid tactics of the cavalry under leaders like J.E.B. Stuart, and Nathan Bedford Forrest. Bugle signals on the battlefield included "Charge," "March," "Rally," "Retreat," "Cease Firing," and "Quick March."

76th Ohio Regimental Drum-By looking through the percussion hole on the drum, the drummer boy wrote in pencil all the engagements that the 76th Ohio participated in. Captain Charles R. Woods, of the 9th United States Infantry, was authorized to raise a regiment for three years service. He formed the 76th Ohio Volunteer Infantry at Newark, Ohio on February 9th, 1862. The regiment left Newark, Ohio, to Paducah, Kentucky, and then onto Fort Donelson. The regiment participated in the Battle of Fort Donelson. On March 6th, the Regiment moved to the Tennessee River, and then up to Crump's Landing, where it remained until March 31st, when it marched to Adamsville, and took position in General Lew Wallace's Division, in the right wing of General Grant's army. The division made a forced march to Pittsburg Landing on April 6th, 1862, and was in line of battle by dark, and during the engagement was constantly exposed to the Rebel's fire. In late April, the regiment moved to Corinth, charging the Rebels, driving them from their position, and destroying their camp equipage. It formed part of the grand reserve during the advance on Corinth, and after the evacuation, moved to Memphis, arriving on June 17th, 1862, having marched 130 miles with wagon supplies. By July 27th, the regiment was encamped near Helena, Arkansas.

On August 16th, the Regiment formed part of an expedition of observation, moved down the Mississippi, landed at Milliken's Bend on the 18th, surprised the 31st Louisiana Regiment, and captured all its camp and garrison equipment. The fleet of gunboats carrying the Division, proceeded up the Yazoo River, and captured Haines Bluff and captured 4 siege guns. The expedition returned to Helena on the 27th.

On December 21st, the 76th Ohio formed part of General Sherman's expedition for Vicksburg. The fleet carrying the expedition landed at Johnson's Landing, on the Yazoo, on the 26th, and the division, then commanded by General Steele, disembarked, and Hovey's Brigade, which the 76th was apart of, made a feint on Haines Bluff, and then took position on the extreme left of the army. On the 29th, the division moved to the main army at Chickasaw Bayou; and during the battle, the regiment was held in reserve.

Sherman abandoned the assault on Vicksburg and proceeded up the Mississippi, landing at Arkansas Post on January 10th, 1863. The 76th Ohio charged the Rebels earthworks, and held their posi-

Upright horns with berlinger piston valves, and doved tail construction. These saxhorns were picked up along Bragg's retreat from Perryville. (BCWM)

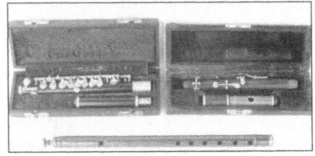

Grouping of different types of flutes. The instrument on the bottom is a standard fife from the Civil War, the two cased instruments are piccolo style fifes. (BCWM)

tion in the rifle pits for three hours until the Rebels surrendered. On the 23rd, the troops landed at Young's Point, La. During the next month the regiment worked on the canal then in progress across the neck of land opposite Vicksburg. On April 2nd, the 76th proceeded to Greenville, Mississippi, and marched down Deer Creek after Rebel forces under Col. Ferguson, and routed them. The command returned destroying a million dollars worth of corn and mules.

On the 24th, the Regiment returned to Young's Point and on the 26th moved to Milliken's Bend, and prepared to march with the main army southward. On May 2nd, the 15th Corps started for Hard Times Landing, where it arrived on the 6th, and crossed the Grand Gulf at Jackson, Mississippi, the 76th charged the works on the Rebel's left. the works were evacuated and the city surrendered. On the 16th, the Regiment marched for Vicksburg, and took position in the lines around Vicksburg. After the surrender of Vicksburg, the Regiment marched in pursuit of Joe Johnston's army, and arrived at Jackson on July 10th. During the months of October and November, the regiment marched and skirmished in northern Alabama and Tennessee, arriving in Chattanooga in time to join General Hooker in his assault on Lookout Mountain. the regiment was also engaged at Missionary Ridge, and on the 27th assaulted Ringgold Gap, Georgia. The Regiment re-enlisted on January 4th, 1864, and would participate in Sherman's Atlanta Campaign on May 1st to September. It fought at the Battle of Resaca (May 14-15). It would advance on Dallas, Ga. on May 18-25. It also fought in the Battles of Pumpkin vine Creek, New Hope Church, and Allatoona Hills (May 25- June 5). It did operations at Marietta and against Kennesaw Mountain (June 10-July 2). It assaulted Kennesaw Mountain on June 27th. It participated in the Battle of Atlanta on July 22nd. It participated in the siege of Atlanta (July 22-August 25). It participated in the Battle of Ezra Church on July 28th. It did a flanking movement against Jonesboro on August 25-30 and fought

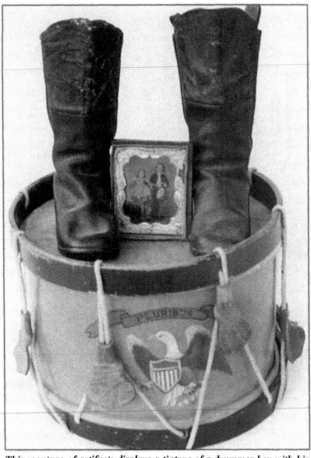

This montage of artifacts displays a tintype of a drummer boy with his sister, his boots, and his miniature Federal style "eagle" drum. Children as young as ten years of age became drummer boys and faced the dangers of battle on both sides during the war. (BCWM)

Cut down Federal snare drum pictured with an imported cavalry bugle. Drums served the utilitarian purpose and many were retrofitted after the war to current regulatory specifications. (BCWM)

Large single turn brass infantry bugle. The bugle was used to call out over 19 different calls that regulated the infantry man's life from when he got up in the morning until he laid down to sleep. Horns of this period normally used the dove tailed "seaming" construction. This bugle was found after the Confederates retreated from Perryville in October 1862 and on the bell has a Confederate battle flag etched into it. The blue bugle cord denotes infantry use. (BCWM)

Fact: Union Gen. Daniel Butterfield wrote Taps in July 1862 at Harrison's Landing, Va.

This picture depicts a relic pre-war Kentucky Military Institute coat and rare over the shoulder leather drumstick holders, with it's original drumsticks in place. (BCWM)

76th Ohio's Regimental Drum. (BCWM)

This is a miniature drummer boy style snare drum, with U.S. eagle motifs and slogan saying with "Malice towards None and Charity for all", with miniature style drum sticks. The drum is made by Wurlitzer of Cincinnatti, Ohio, who made many drums and muscial instruments for the Western armies of the North during the Civil War. (BCWM)

the Battle of Jonesboro on August 3 1 -September 1). It fought Confederate General John Bell Hood's army through North Georgia and North Alabama (September 29-November 3) It participated in Sherman's march to the Sea campaign, the siege of Savannah, and also participated in the Campaign of the Carolinas. It participated in the Battle of Bentonville, North Carolina on March 19-21st. It occupied Goldsboro on March 24th. It advanced on Raleigh on April 10th. It occupied Raleigh on April 14th. It was at the Bennett's House on April 26th, and was present at the surrender of Joe Johnston's army. It marched to Washington, D. C., and was in the Grand Review on May 24th, 1865. It then moved to Louisville, Kentucky and was mustered out on July 15th, 1865. the Regiment lost 9 officers, and 82 enlisted men killed and mortally wounded and 5 officers and 265 enlisted men by disease. Total 361. Resources: Dyer's Compendium Report of the Ohio Vicksburg Battlefield Commission by W.P. Gault, Sergt. Co. F, 78th O.V.1.

An eagle Federal snare drum with drum sticks. The leather tugs were used to tighten the calf hide drum heads to give it the sharp tone. (BCWM)

This is a late war production Federal snare drum, of which over 30,000 of this type were purchased by the U.S. government during the war. This drum features the star sunburst emblem, which has been inlaid into the drums shell. Drum sticks feature the silver head caps. BCWM

The drum pictured is a Mexican War vintage drum used by the 38th Indiana Infantry, and saw action in all the campaigns of the Western theater. (BCWM)

Navy

"The Great Age of the Ironclads"

Naval Officer's Rank
Union

The lowest ranking officer grade in the Union Navy was the Ensign, followed by Master, Lieutenant, Lieutenant Commander, Commander, Captain, Commodore, and finally Rear Admiral.

Confederacy

In the Confederacy, Passed Midshipman was the lowest ranking officer, then Master, Lieutenant, Commander, Captain, and finally Flag Officer.

The Confederates wore their rank on their sleeves and collar, while the Union navy wore their rank on their epauletts, shoulder straps and on their sleeves. Each rank had a different design, unique to that rank only. The Union navy officers had a star on the front of their hat, while the Confederates wore their same rank insignia on their collar and hat.

The Confederate iron-clad "Tennessee." From a war-time sketch.

The Confederate iron-clad "Louisiana" on the way to Fort St. Philip.

The Confederate Ram "Arkansas," alongside the Union gun-boat "Carondelet."

Carte De Viste of river boats tied up at the wharf in Louisville, Kentucky, in 1861. (BCWM)

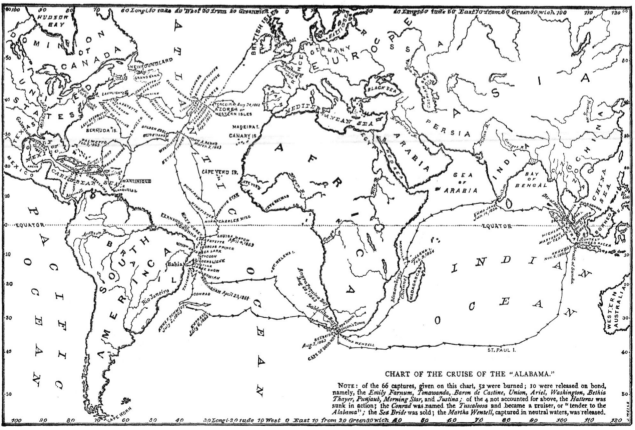

CHART OF THE CRUISE OF THE "ALABAMA."

NOTE: of the 66 captures, given on this chart, 52 were burned; 10 were released on bond, namely, the *Emily Farnum, Tonawanda, Baron de Castine, Union, Ariel, Washington, Bethia Thayer, Punjaub, Morning Star,* and *Justina*; of the 4 not accounted for above, the *Hatteras* was sunk in action; the *Conrad* was named the *Tuscaloosa* and became a cruiser, or "tender to the *Alabama*"; the *Sea Bride* was sold; the *Martha Wentell*, captured in neutral waters, was released.

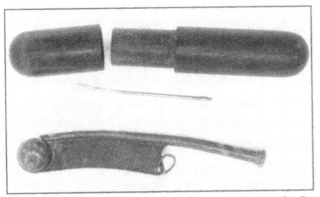

Metal bousun mate's whistle, used to pipe "Officer's Aboard." Also displayed is a seaman's sail sewing needle in a wooden carrying case. (BCWM)

Tin type of 1st Gunner's Mate, who was on the USS Hartford, William Adams and his mother Matilda. (BCWM)

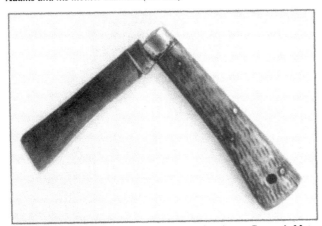

Personnel folding knife in the naval style, belonging to Gunner's Mate Adams, with standard square tipped blade, bone handle and hole in handle for tying a lanyard. (BCWM)

Pook's Turtles was the nickname given to seven iron clad Union gunboats designed by Samuel M. Pook to operate on the Mississippi River and its tributaries. On August 7, 1861, the War Department contracted with James Eads to construct the vessels and have them ready for their crews in 65 days. Eads employed Thomas Merritt as engine designer. Within two weeks, more than 4,000 people in seven states were employed in the construction of the boats, cutting trees for lumber, building 21 steam engines and 35 boilers, and rolling the iron armor. Four were built at Carondelet, near St. Louis, Missouri, and three in Mound City, Illinois. The workers worked night and day and on October 12, 1861, the first of the gunboats, the St. Louis, was launched. By January 15, 1862, all seven were accepted by the War Department.

The gunboats, which cost $100,000 each, were called "city class" because they were named after cities on western rivers. Be-

sides the St. Louis, there were the Carondelet, Cincinnati, Louisville, Mound City, Cairo, and Pittsburgh. Each round nosed, flat-bottomed vessel weighed 512 tons, was 175 feet long and 51.5 feet wide and drew only six feet of water. Plated with two and one-half inch thick iron, the gunboats had flat sides, with front and rear casemates sloping at a 25 degree angle, and carried 13 heavy guns each, both rifled and smoothbore. Propelled by a stern paddle wheel that was completely covered by the rear casemate, the coal powered Pook Turtles proved to be underpowered and cumbersome-but also very deadly.

The Turtles were manned by sailors of the regular navy, volunteers, detailed army personnel and contracted civilians.

These ironclad gunboats rapidly became the backbone of the Union river fleet. In early 1862, they were instrumental in the capture of Fort Henry on the Tennessee River, Fort Donelson on the Cumberland River, and Island No. 10 on the Mississippi River. Pook's Turtles also participated in the successful campaigns against Fort Pillow and Memphis. On December 11, 1862, the Cairo was sunk by Confederate torpedoes (mines) in the Yazoo River while participating in operations against Vicksburg. The next year, nine days after Vicksburg surrendered, the St. Louis was also sunk in the Yazoo River by torpedos. The Carondelet, the most famous of the Turtles, engaged in more battles and saw more action than any other ship in the western flotilla. After the war, her plating was removed and she was sold.

The cased naval sexton was an optical instrument used for the measurement of the angular distance between any two objects. It's chief use was to establish one's position on the planet. (BCWM)

The Confederate Gunboat Program

The Confederacy faced many problems in their iron clad program. In 1861, the Confederate Navy saw no need for building ironclads, especially for use in the West. They put more emphasis on warships. They had little foresight reguarding the importance of ironclads in the upcoming battles for control of the Mississippi River. The Union Navy had

Explosion of the Confederate Ram, "Louisiana."

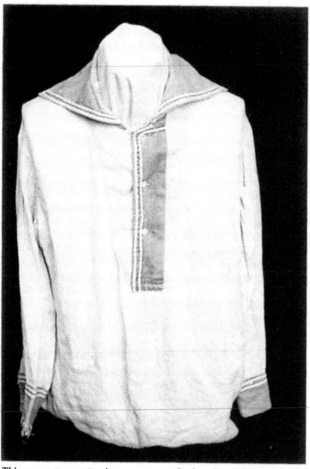

This rare summer cotton jumper was worn by the enlisted men. The jumper is white in color and had blue trim on the collar and sleeves. On the back of the collar are two stars, one on each side. The buttons are made of milk glass. (BCWM)

This ensigns naval coat was made according to the regulations of 1864. It has the single gold braid and single star on the sleeve. The double breasted coat has 18 imported buttons from the Joseph Starkey's company. (BCWM)

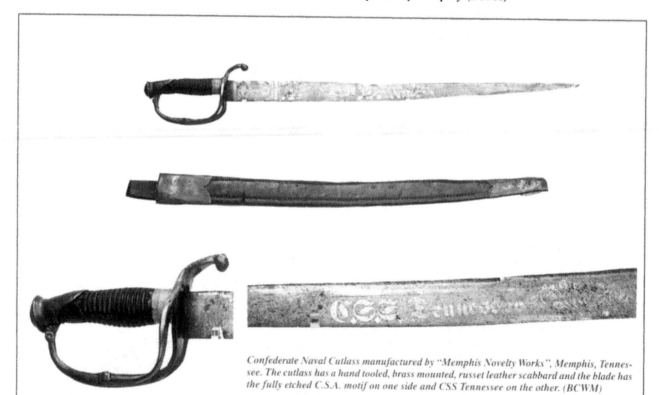

Confederate Naval Cutlass manufactured by "Memphis Novelty Works", Memphis, Tennessee. The cutlass has a hand tooled, brass mounted, russet leather scabbard and the blade has the fully etched C.S.A. motif on one side and CSS Tennessee on the other. (BCWM)

Rare Confederate Naval sideknife. Wooden scabbard wrapped with oil cloth. The blade is 16 inches long and overall length is 22 inches. It has a hand forged, double edged blade. The knife was more than likely made in North Carolina. (BCWM)

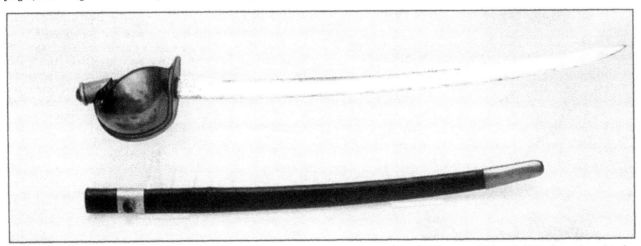

U. S. Naval Cutlass, Model 1860 with scabbard. This sword was made by the Ames Manufacturing Company, Chicopee, Mass. It was issued to the enlisted men and was stored in the ships magazine, and was only brought out when the ship was being attacked or the ship was preparing for battle. This sword stayed in service for 75 years. (BCWM)

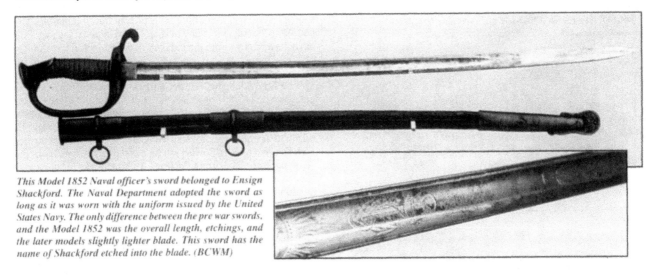

This Model 1852 Naval officer's sword belonged to Ensign Shackford. The Naval Department adopted the sword as long as it was worn with the uniform issued by the United States Navy. The only difference between the pre war swords, and the Model 1852 was the overall length, etchings, and the later models slightly lighter blade. This sword has the name of Shackford etched into the blade. (BCWM)

started building ironclads right after the war began and had assembled Pook's turtles in time for the important battles of Fort Henry and Ft. Donelson. Finally on October 1, 1861 an army commander started the Confederate ironclad program. Gen.Leonidas Polk purchased the river steamer Eastport for $12,000 dollars. By February he had purchased four more vessels to turn into ironclads. In the port of New Orleans, the Louisiana, the Mississippi and the Manassas were built. The Arkansas was built in Memphis.

By 1862, Mallory and a few progressive naval officers and congressmen believed that armored vessels could offset Union naval superiority, especially after the successes of the Arkansas and Virginia. In 1862, the South believed that ironclads could break the Union blockades and special fund raising organizations were formed, especially by the Confederate women. The floating battery, Georgia, was built entirely by funds from the state of Georgia, women's organizations, business men and the government of Savannah. Unfortunately the people were not aware that Mallory did not want to build iron clads to beat back the Union blockaders, but only wanted to defend the harbors with them.

This Naval Shrapnel Fuse Box is made of heavy pine construction, and is marked with "Shrapnel Fuse Box" and dated 1864. (BCWM)

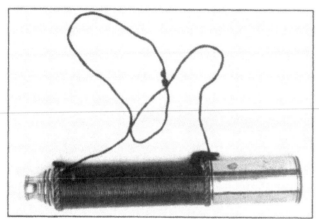

Brass constructed, five draw naval telescope, manufactured in London in 1860. Overall length is four feet when extended. (BCWM)

The Confederate cruiser "Alabama."

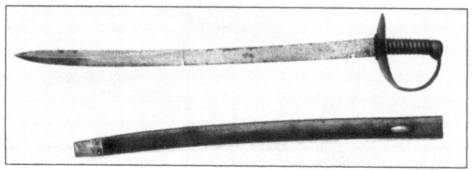

Model 1858 British Naval Cutlass with brass mounted leather scabbard. A favorite among the enlisted men in the Confederate Navy. This cutlass was imported during the blockade early in the war, through Charleston, South Carolina. (BCWM)

By 1863 funds had become non-existent, and criticism had fallen on the Confederate iron clad program. The cities of New Orleans, Memphis, and Norfolk had all fallen to the Union forces. The loss of all but five ironclads built in 1861 was a devastating blow to the Confederacy.

The South's attempts to build ironclads had become increasingly more difficult by 1863. Due to the blockades, ironclads now had to be built on inland sites, and once the ships were built, transportation to get them out into open water was next to impossible to procure. Railroads were inefficient and inadequate, and manpower was a problem, as most of the skilled men were fighting in the army. Materials were a problem in the West. Wood was plentiful, but iron was next to impossible to obtain. There were only two rolling mills that could produce two inch thick iron for armor, and they were in Richmond and Atlanta. T-rails from the railroad had to be used as a substitute.

The last hope of the Confederate iron clad program was the Atlanta. She was completed on January 5, 1863, and was built from an English ship called the Fingal. The Atlanta was the most able ironclad the South had. She was 204 feet long and 41 feet wide, and she had four guns, a spar torpedo and a ram. She sailed down the Savannah River and was soon engaged by a Union monitor. The Weehawken heavily damaged the Atlanta and on June 16, 1863, Commander Webb surrendered the Atlanta. It was a great shock to the Confederacy. The Atlanta was the last serious threat to Union control of the Mississippi River. There was no longer a Confederate Navy in the West.

In 1864, Savannah, Georgia was invaded by Sherman's army on its March to the Sea Campaign. At Savannah, the Confederates burned the Milledgeville, sank the Georgia and the Isondiga was set afire. The Resolute and the Savannah were destroyed. The last remaining ironclad, the Missouri, was launched on April 14, 1863. She was immediately stranded in Shreveport, Louisiana when Grant took Vicksburg. She held out until June 3, 1865, when Commander Carter surrendered his ironclad to the Union forces.

For the most part the Confederate Navy never realized the importance of ironclads. But not all blame can be put on the Naval officers. They were facing a Union Army that had vast resources. They had the rolling mills to pour out iron plating. They had skilled labor, and plenty to spare. The Confederacy just didn't have the manpower nor the industry to maintain a successful ironclad program.

CSS *Tennessee*-Adm. Franklin Buchanan had four ships at Mobile Bay, Alabama, but the only one of significance was the great ironclad CSS. *Tennessee*, the pride of the Confederate squadron. She was 209 feet long, with a beam of 48 feet, and a 14 foot draft, and was the largest ironclad built by the Confederacy. The ship was framed with 13 inch yellow pine timbers and covered with five and one-half inches of pine, and then four inches of oak. With six inches of armor forward, two inches of armor on the deck, and a battery of six powerful guns, the warship was one of the South's best.

Outside Mobile Bay, United States Rear Admiral David Farragut had 18 warships, four of these were tough, deadly monitors, and ready to brave the forts and the fleet at Mobile. The Federal fleet rode in on the flood tide on the morning of August 5, 1864. Fort Morgan opened for the defense, and Buchanan moved the CSS *Tennessee* behind a line of water mines or torpedoes. Farragut's lead monitor, the USS *Tecumseh*, turned directly for the CSS *Tennessee*, struck a mine, and sank within two minutes. Farragut's flagship, the USS *Hartford*, then took the lead and brought his fleet safely through the minefield.

Buchanan attacked the Yankee fleet but the quicker Union vessels evaded the *Tennessee's* efforts to ram them, but her guns damaged six of Farragut's ships. Union shot bounced off the big ironclad's armor as the CSS *Tennessee* traded broadsides with the Federal's until midmorning, then retired to the safety of Fort Morgan.

As Farragut brought his ships to anchor and called his crews to breakfast, Buchanan had decided to risk all in another attack. Again the CSS *Tennessee* came on, and the Federals rushed to meet her. One ship rammed the Confederate vessel, then the entire fleet closed in, ringing the CSS *Tennessee* with fire. For a mile around, Union ships rammed and fired, while the CSS *Tennessee* replied with every gun, but the Unions superior numbers soon began to tell. The monitor USS *Chickasaw's* giant solid shot opened a hole in the Rebel ironclad's side, the storm of fire riddled its smokestack, and its engines lost power. Then its steering chains were shot away and the warship was out of control. Shot and shell ricocheted through open gunports, wounding Buchanan, killing others. With the ironclad dead in the water, and its armor giving away, the Confederates surrendered. Farragut, the conqueror of New Orleans, had beaten the mighty CSS *Tennessee*.

CSS *Alabama*

Shortly after the start of the Civil War, Confederate commerce raiders began roaming the seas to prey on Union merchant ships. The most famous of these raiders was the CSS *Alabama*, built for the Confederate government by the Laird shipyards in Birkenhead, England and commissioned off the Azores on August 24, 1862. She was 230 feet long with a beam of 32 feet, was powdered by two 300 horsepower engines that operated her double wheel and also had a full compliment of sails. Under full power she could travel at a speed of 13 knots, and was designed to outrun and overtake unarmed merchant vessels. Her armament included a 110 pounder rifled gun, an 8 inch solid-shot gun, and six 32 pounders. The *Alabama* had a crew of 120 men and 24 officers, and was commanded by Raphel Semmes.

The *Alabama* began her career by decimating the Yankee whaling fleet in the Azores, destroying 10 ships in two weeks. Next she sailed for Newfoundland, and the coast of New England, where she captured 11 more ships. Most of the captured ships were burned after the crew and any needed provisions had been removed. Adm. Semmes would usually take his time after he had captured a Yankee ship, waiting for nightfall before he would set her ablaze. He knew that any other United States ships that were in the area would rush in to help the blazing vessel and he would then capture and burn that ship also. The *Alabama* hunted down the East Coast of the United States and into the Caribbean Ocean, and then, in January 1863, she sailed the Gulf of Mexico toward Galveston, Texas, where she attacked and sank a blockading Union warship, the USS *Hatteras*. To prevent capture by pursuing Union warships, the *Alabama* sailed down the coast of South America and, after burning a few more Yankee ships, crossed the Atlantic to the Cape of Good Hope. Sailing across the Indian Ocean to Singapore, the *Alabama* paralyzed Union trade in that area to such an extent that United States ships would not leave port. The *Alabama* sailed to India then down the east coast of Africa, and back across the Atlantic to South America.

By now the ship was badly in need of repair and Semmes sailed to France for a thorough overhaul, arriving at the port of Cherbourg on June 11, 1864. During the 22 months since her commissioning, the Alabama had traveled 75,000 miles and captured 66 Union merchant ships worth more than six and one-half million dollars.

The *Alabama* was anchored in the harbour at Cherbourg, France when the USS *Kearsarge* took up a position just outside the harbor, issuing a challenge to the CSS *Alabama*. Al-

Left: Rare Revenue Cutter's shoulder straps. Right:Rare Carte De Viste of a Lieutenant in the Revenue Cutter Service. (BCWM)

though the *Alabama* was in very poor condition, Semmes accepted the challenge and prepared his crew for battle. Semmes sent the following message to John Winslow, commander of the *Kearsarge*: "... My intention is to fight the *Kearsarge* as soon as I can make the necessary arrangements. I beg she will not depart before I am ready to go out."

Sunday morning, June 19th, 1864, the *Alabama* steamed out of the harbor escorted by a French warship whose job was to insure that the two ships did not do battle inside France's three mile limit. Winslow turned the *Kearsarge* and steamed seaward, with the *Alabama* following, another three or four miles past the limit to be sure neither ship could break off the fight and escape to neutral waters. Then he turned and came straight toward the *Alabama*. The two ships began circling clockwise in ever-decreasing circles, raking each other with broadsides from their

Admiral David Farragut

Rear Admiral Raphael Semmes, C.S.N., Captain of the "Alabama."

starboard guns. *The Kearsarge's* 11 inch pivot guns wreaked havoc on the *Alabama*, whose decks were soon covered with dead and wounded men. The *Alabama's* guns were smaller than her foe's, and her ammunition had become defective during her 22 month voyage; consequently, little damage was caused to the *Kearsarge*. By the seventh circle the *Alabama* was hurt badly; water poured into her hold from holes punched in her hull, and she listed to starboard. Semmes struck his colors and at 12:24 p.m., after 90 minutes of battle, the *Alabama* disappeared beneath the waves. The *Kearsarge* had three casualties. Half of the *Alabama's* 43 casualties were killed or drowned.

Semmes, 14 officers, and 24 crewmen were saved from Union prisons by the *Deerhound*, an English yacht that had sailed out to watch the battle. The owner of the yacht plucked Semmes and his mostly English crew from the water and delivered them safely to England.

1851 Colt Navy Revolver-.36 caliber-This weapon saw extensive service on the battlefield. Many cavalrymen, citing the Navy's greater handiness, chose it over the larger-caliber Army revolver. Colt produced more than 200,000 of the Navy six shooters from 1851 until 1861.

1850 Naval officer sword with scabbard-W. Shackford acting ensign Sept. 1, 1864; honorably discharged June 18, 1865. He served aboard the USS *Maumee*. The *Maumee* was one of eight

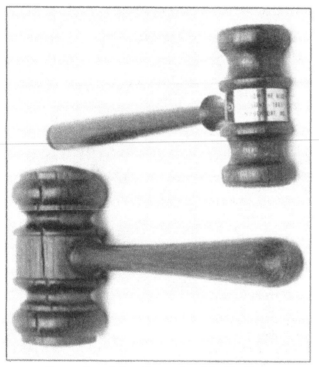

Two gavels made from the remains of the Alice Dean.

Enlisted men's leather belt with buckle marked "U.S.S. Merrimack". (BCWM)

vessels in the "Nipsic" class of gunboats, designed for fast inshore cruising. The *Maumee* was a wooden hulled, two masted topsail, schooner rigged, crew steamer measuring 190 feet in length, 29 feet in beam, and 12 foot depth of hold, and with a loaded draft of eight foot six inch forward and 11'3"aft. The vessel was laid down at the New York Navy Yard in 1862, and launched on July 2, 1863, at a cost of $258,408.93. Propelled by a single screw propeller, the *Maumee* was capable of a maximum speed of 11.5 knots but her normal speed was seven knots. A artillery crew of 154 men served her guns, which were a 100 pounder Parrott rifled cannon, a 30 pound Parrott rifle, four 24 pound howitzers, and one 12 pound rifled cannon. The *Maumee* was commissioned at New York on September 29, 1864, and assigned to the North Atlantic Blockading Squadron. On November 17, 1864, two 32 pounder 57 cwt. cannons were added. The *Maumee* participated in the unsuccessful attack on Fort Fisher off Wilmington, North Carolina on December 24-25, 1864, and in the second attack on Fort Fisher on January 13-15, 1865. On January 25, 1865 her armament was altered to one 100 pounder and two 30 pound Parrott rifles. On February 20-21, 1865, the *Maumee* bombarded the Confederate Forts Strong and Lee on the Cape Fear River near Wilmington, North Carolina. On February 25, 1865, the *Maumee* was in action on the James River, in Virginia. On June 15, 1865, the *Maumee's* armament consisted of one 11' Dalhgren smoothbore, two 32 pounder, one 32 pounder Parrott rifle, and four 24 pound howitzers. The *Maumee* was decommissioned at Philadelphia on June 17, 1865. On December 15, 1869, the *Maumee* was sold to Mr. Landstein, of Hong Kong, China for $3,726.87 (Reference: Special thanks must be given to Bob Birmingham for the information on the *Maumee*.)

1860 Cutlass with scabbard-Worn by enlisted sailors, the cutlass was adopted around 1860 and had a slightly curved blade. The large guard was designed to protect the hand and fingers during close shipboard combat. Most of the time, the swords were locked up in the arms locker, and were only brought out when there was imminent danger of being boarded.

Two wooden gavels made from the *Alice Dean*- In 1863, on John Hunt Morgan's raid through Kentucky, Indiana, and Ohio, Morgan needed to transport his men across the Ohio river to Indiana. The Federal Cavalry was hot on his tail and he needed to transport his men quickly. Capt. Thomas Henry Hines, who was commander of the 9th Kentucky Cavalry and also a spy, had captured the *Alice Dean*, a transport ship, earlier in the day at Brandenburg, Kentucky. Morgan's advance scouts met Hines later that day and helped to capture the McComb, a mail carrier. The following day, Morgan arrived at Brandenburg with his 2,000 men. A sharp skirmish broke out with Indiana militia, and a small wooden gunboat that mounted only one gun, a 12 pound howitzer. Morgan's Parrot Rifles quickly brushed aside the militia and the boat.

As the last of Morgan's men crossed the Ohio River the Federal soldiers began to arrive on the bank of the Kentucky side of the river just in time to watch as Morgan burned the *Alice Dean*. The commander of the McComb was a friend of Basil Duke, Morgan's second in command, so the ship was let go as long as it didn't transport the Federal troops across the river. The flames of the *Alice Dean* could be seen for miles and illuminated the night sky.

In the 1960's the Ohio River was at a very low point and the *Alice Dean* could still be seen sticking out of the water. Pieces of the ship were broken off and made into gavels. The anchor of the *Alice Dean* sits in the Battlefield Park at Corydon. After Morgan crossed the Ohio River, he rode into Corydon, Indiana and fought a battle with the militia and the Home Guard. Morgan lost about nine men. The Battle of Corydon and the Battle of Gettysburg, Pennsylvania are the only two battles recognized by the Federal government as being fought on Northern soil.

PRISONS

Even before the first shots were fired on Fort Sumter, the North had begun to arrest and imprison certain politicians and Southern sympathizers. When hostilities finally erupted, forts were turned into makeshift prisons while new prisons were being built. Neither side could foresee just how many soldiers were going to be admitted to these new prisons and as the war dragged on, the

Libby Prison

Castle Pickney

Andersonville

Prison art depicting a linked chain made of wood made by a Confederate inmate at Johnson Island Prison. (BCWM)

South found that it did not have the resources to house all the captured soldiers that were pouring in. An exchange system was set up to help relieve the massive overcrowding, but by mid war, the exchange system was done away with. The South's inability to handle the massive influx of Union prisoners soon resulted in the Northern captives being exposed to starvation and disease due to a lack of shelter and proper food. When the North found out about the poor conditions in Southern prisons, in retaliation, the rations given to the captured Confederates were drastically cut, exposing them to disease, and starvation also. When the war finally ended, hard feelings would be held by ex-prisoners on both sides regarding the treatment they had received in prison. Capt. Henry Wirz, the commander of Andersonville prison, would pay the ultimate price for his maltreatment of Union prisoners, being tried and hanged after the war. Some prisoners had it better than others, but for the most part, the prison system failed to provide the minimal needs of its captives. There were at least a hundred military prisons throughout the country and during the course of the war 56,000 men died in, and one out of every seven non-battle deaths occurred in prisoner-of-war camps.

Some of the better known prisons were:

Castle Thunder-There were two Castle Thunders, one in Richmond and one in Petersburg, Virginia, both were originally tobacco warehouses. Castle Thunder in Richmond was used to house political prisoners, spies and criminals, who were all treated harshly by the guards. The commandant of Castle Thunder in Richmond was Capt. George Alexander. Castle Thunder in Petersburg was so named by Union prisoners during the last siege of the city, when the sound of artillery fire was "Thunderous."

Libby Prison-The Libby & Son Ship Chandlers & Grocers warehouse near Richmond was turned into a prison for captured Union officers. Conditions were second only to Andersonville. The 150 by 100 foot, three story prison held 1,200 men in eight crowded rooms. Union Colonel Thomas Rose of the 77th Pennsylvania decided to try and tunnel out of the prison and on February 9th, 109 men escaped but only 59 men made it back to Union lines. Col. Rose and 48 others were recaptured and two men drowned during the escape attempt.

Belle Isle- Located in Richmond Virginia on the James River. It became a prison after the Battle of First Bull Run when Union non commissioned officers and enlisted men were confined there. By the end of 1863, it held over 7,000 prisoners. During one period there were 10,000 men on Belle Isle. There were no barracks and only tents were provided to shelter the prisoners.

Castle Pinckney-Castle Pinckney was a small masonry fortification built in 1790 in the harbor at Charleston, South Carolina. It became one of the first prisoner-of-war camps and one of the few that was not a death camp. It was garrisoned by the Charleston Zouave Cadets. The prisoners were clean and sanitary conditions were maintained throughout the prison, and for the most part it was a fairly peaceful place.

Old Capitol Prison-After the United States Capitol was burned in the War of 1812, a brick building was built on 1st Street in Washington, DC to serve as the temporary capitol. When the new capitol was completed the government moved back in and the Old Capitol on 1st Street was made into a boarding house. By the time of the Civil War, the Old Capitol had been empty for years and was in poor shape. Originally the government made it into a political prison, but as the war dragged on it housed Confederate generals, Northern political prisoners, blockade runners and spies. Henry Wirz and the Lincoln assassination conspirators were hanged on the gallows in the yard of the Old Capitol prison.

Fort McHenry-Located in Baltimore, Maryland. It originally housed Southern sympathizers, but these prisoners were later transferred to Fort Warren in the Boston Harbor. The prison also held 110 Confederate surgeons and 10 chaplains. It was one of the better prisons and the prisoners were allowed to buy items from the local sutlers.

Camp Douglas-Located in Chicago, Illinois. It had five dozen, 90 foot long barracks, each designed to hold 200 prisoners. Treatment of the prisoners was good at first, but as soon as more prisoners arrived, conditions worsened. Rations were cut to one third of their bread, and two thirds of their meat and all vegatables were done away with. Blankets and clothes were not given to prisoners. Drainage was poor because of the flat, low ground that the prison was built on and disease soon took its toll. Soldiers died of scurvy, exposure, and smallpox. In the month of February 1863, 387 prisoners died from disease. Col. Hoffmann, the Union Commissary General of Prisoners, reported the poor conditions at Camp Douglas to Secretary of War, Edwin Stanton and Col. B. J. Sweet, the commander of Camp Douglas, was ordered to make improvements. By June 1864, all improvements had been made. There were 5, 277 prisoners in that month, and by the wars' end, 11,702 prisoners were being housed at Camp Douglas.

Castle Thunder

Camp Morton-Located in Indianapolis, Indiana. In 1861, the 35 acre Indiana State Fair Grounds became Camp Morton. Over 3,000 prisoners-of-war were sent there, most of them from the battle of Fort Donelson. Governor Oliver Morton was the administrator. Following a prisoner exchange in August 1862, Camp Morton reverted back to a troop facility until early 1863, when it was made a prison again, and placed under army administration, and was commanded by Col. Hoffman. Thirty five prisoners tried to escape, but were recaptured. Col. Hoffman tried to cut costs by reducing the rations given to the prisoners but they soon became disgruntled and Hoffman had to bring in more guards. Because of the lack of rations, scurvy became rampant and 1,763 prisoners died. About 3,500 prisoners were confined here during the war.

Camp Chase-Located in Columbus, Ohio. In November 1861, it was used as a training camp for Union soldiers. Later, it housed political and military prisoners from Kentucky and Western Virginia. Soon, enlisted men, along with a few of their black servants, were flowing from the West and Camp Chase became a tourist attraction. Later the camp was controlled by the Federal government and conditions radically changed. Rules were tightened, visitors prohibited, and mail was censored. As the war dragged on, conditions worsened. Facilities intended for only 3,000 to 4,000 soon held over 7,000 prisoners. Near the end of the war the prison abuses were addressed, and the Union parole guards were sent off to the Indian Wars, sewer modifications were made, and barracks and facilities were improved, but even with the improvements, the unhealthy conditions were never solved. About 10,000 men were held at Camp Chase during the war.

Rock Island Prison-Located on the Mississippi River between the cities of Rock Island, Illinois, and Davenport, Iowa. The three mile long island was prone to poor drainage and was a virtual swamp. In August 1864 construction began on 84 barracks, each 82 feet long, 22 feet wide, and 12 feet high, lined up in six rows of 14

Old Capitol Prison

barracks each, and all enclosed by a high fence. A cookhouse was at the end of each barrack. All the barracks were poorly ventilated and inadequately heated, with only two stoves per barrack. Water was scarce and sometimes non-existent. In December 1863, 5,000 prisoners were sent to Rock Island. Rations were cut to save money to build a hospital. Rock Island had a smallpox epidemic which killed 636 prisoners. During the war the prison population fluctuated between 5,000 and 8,000. The prison was closed in July 1865.

Point Lookout Prison-Located in Point Lookout, Maryland, it was the largest Union prison camp. Established on August 1, 1863, it was made up of two enclosures of flat sand, one of about 30 acres and the other about 10 acres, each surrounded by a fence 15 feet high. No barracks were built within the prison enclosure and all the prisoners lived in tents. Black troops formed a large part of the guard. Food was scarce and some prisoners froze to death for want of blankets.

Fort Delaware-Located on Pea Patch Island on the Delaware River, and built by Maj. Gen. George McClellan. It originally housed political and naval prisoners, but later it accepted Confederate soldiers, and it was the prison above all others that the captives dreaded. Brig. Gen. Albin Schoepf was the commandant of the prison and his nickname was "General Terror." In 1861, 2,000 Confederates arrived. In 1863, new barracks were built but they sank in the mud, and some almost fell over. By September 1863, 331 of the 7,000 prisoners had died. Smallpox and scurvy were a major factor in the deaths at Fort Deleware. Over 8,000 men were held there during the war.

Fort Warren-Located on George's Island, Boston Harbor. It was a fort with pentagonal walls and gun emplacements and was originally a training camp for state volunteers and garrisoned the 14th Massachusetts Infantry. It held a few smugglers and political prisoners from Maryland and the border States. In August 1861, Confederate prisoners arrived from Governors Island in New York City. Within two years, Fort Warren had become the elite Northern prison. Food was sufficient, entertainment and exercise yards were provided, and discipline was maintained. Famous Confederate General Basil Duke and General Adam Rankin Johnson arrived in 1863. Only 12 deaths were recorded at Fort Warren during the entire war.

Ohio State Penitentiary-Located in Columbus, Ohio. The three story stone structure was used to house hardened convicts until July 30, 1863, when Confederate prisoners were confined there. Confederate General John Hunt Morgan and 30 of his officers were sent to this penitentiary. On November 27, 1863, Morgan and six of his officers escaped. On March 18, 1864, all remaining Confederate prisoners were sent to Fort Delaware.

Andersonville-Located in Sumnter County, Georgia, and nicknamed "Hell on Earth." In February 1864, 16.5 acres of open land was enclosed by a 25 foot tall wooden stockade fence. In June it was expanded to 26 acres. The prison, which was only designed to hold 10,000 men eventually held 26,000. There was no medical care, no housing, and no clothing. Because of the drainage problem, fresh water became almost non-existent. Since the South was lacking food itself, the prisoners also suffered. Scurvy, smallpox, and disease overran the camp. Of the 45,000 men that would be held at Andersonville, 13,000 would die.

Camp Ford-Located in Tyler, Texas, it was the largest Confederate military prison in Texas. It was established in August 1863, and the prison population fluctuated from 100 to 4,900. Most of the prisoners came from the ill fated Red River Campaign in July

1864. Both officers and enlisted men were held here in an open stockade. No shelters had been provided, but the prisoners built a variety of enclosures. Shelter was adequate compared to other camps. It had a good water supply and there seemed to be an ample supply of fresh beef, cornmeal, some bacon and baked beans. In 1864, farmers were permitted to sell their produce to the prisoners. Sulter stores were opened and were managed by the 42nd Massachusetts. Prisoners manufactured over 40 items to be sold to the town. There were three known escapes planned, but only one was successful. In late 1864, 50 men escaped but were later recaptured. Between 232 and 286 soldiers died there. The camp was closed on May 17, 1865.

Elmira Prison-Located in Elmira, New York, and nicknamed "Hellmira." Of the 12,123 prisoners that were held at Elmira, 25% of them would never see home again. The death rate was double the rate of other Union prison camps and only two percent less than Andersonville. The horrible conditions, starvation and disease were deliberate. Col. William Hoffman built the 40 acre prison around a Union army training camp. Thirty five barracks were made to house 5,000 men, but by the end of August 10,000 men were being held there. On August 18, 1864, in retaliation for the conditions in Southern prison camps, Col. Hoffman reduced rations to bread and water. With no fresh meat or vegetables, the soldiers suffered from scurvy, then smallpox, and other diseases, as their immune systems weakened. There were 1,870 cases of scurvy by September 11th. When families sent clothes and blankets to the captive Southern soldiers, Col. Hoffman only allowed clothes and blankets made from grey material, all others items were burned. By the end of the war, 2,963 prisoners had died there. The chief surgeon at Elmira claimed that he killed more Rebels than any other Union soldier.

Chalice given to Charles Hill
Adjutant General of the Ohio Militia
Colonel-Civil War
Col. Hill was the last commander of Johnson Island Prison.
On October 7, 1861, Lt. Col. Hoffman, Commissary General of prisoners, selected Johnson Island as the site for a prisoner of war camp in the North. Also in 1861, the Secretary of War directed Ohio Governor William Dennison to organize a volunteer military unit to serve as a guard detail on Johnson Island. In 1864, this guard detail was expanded to regimental size and designated the 128th Ohio Volunteer Infantry. Their commander was Col. Charles Hill.

Johnson Island was located in Ohio in Sandusky Bay on Lake Erie. It was one mile off shore and two and one-half miles from Sandusky. Col. Hoffman was to take charge of the prison and the first Commandant was W.S. Pierson, who was commissioned as major and commanded the battalion of prison guards. Pierson was a businessman from Sandusky and had no military training whatsoever. He was later succeeded by Col. Charles W. Hill. The 300 acre island was about a mile and a half long and one quarter to one third of a mile wide and covered with trees. In a 40 acre waterfront clearing, quarters were built for 100 guards and an estimated 1,000 prisoners. The prisoners quarters were army type barracks, two stories high, each 125 feet by 24 feet, with nine foot walls; each barrack was divided into three rooms and designed to house 180 men. A washhouse, a hospital, and two mess halls were added. Johnson Island was one of the few prisons where the prisoners did not have to do their own cooking. A prison fence enclosed about 17 acres, and was topped by a walkway and guard posts, which encircled the buildings. A blockhouse with a howitzer and a guard boat completed the installation.

There were about 3,000 prisoners at Johnson Island at wars' end, with more than 6,000 being admitted during the course of the war, and on average the prison housed 2,550 prisoners. Initially, Confederates of every rank were sent to this prison, but

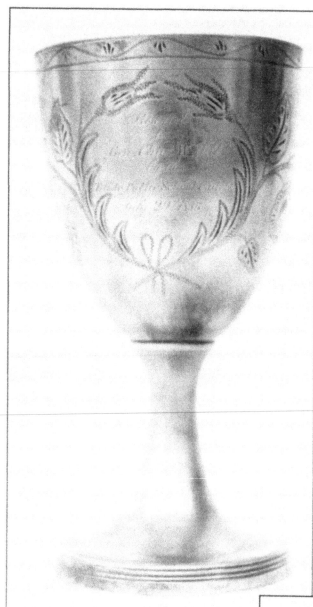

Bibliography

Street, James, Jr. & The Editors of Time Life, **The Road to Shiloh: Early Battles in the West,** Time Life Series, Alexandria, Virginia, 1985.

Korn, Jerry & The Editors of Time Life, **War on the Misisssippi: Grant's Vicksburg Campaign,** Time Life, Inc., Alexandria, Virginia, 1985.

Street, James, Jr. & The Editors of Time Life, **The Struggle for Tennessee: Tupelo to Stone's River,** Time Life, Inc., Alexandria, Virginia, 1985.

Korn, Jerry & The Editors of Time Life, **The Fight for Chattanooga: Chickamagua to Missionary Ridge,** Time Life, Inc., Alexandia, Virgnina, 1985.

Bailey, Ronald & The Editors of Time Life, **Battles for Atlanta: Sherman Moves East,** Time Life Books, Inc. Alexandria, Virginia, 1985.

Ripley, Warren, **Artillery and Ammunition of the Civil War,** The Battery Press, Charleston, South Carolina, 1984.

Faust, Patricia, **Historical Times Illustrated Encyclopedia of the Civil War,** Harper Perennial, New York, New York, 1991

Davis, William, **Fighting Men of the Civil War,** Smithmark Publishers, Inc., New York, New York, 1991.

Davis, William, **Battlefields of the Civil War,** Smithmark Publishers, Inc. New York, New York, 1991.

Davis, William, **Commanders of the Civil War,** Smithmark Publishers, New York, New York, 1991.

Sifakis, Stewart, **Who was Who in the Confederacy,** Facts on File, Inc., New York, New York, 1988.

Sifakis, Stewart, **Who was Who in the Union,** Facts on File, Inc., New York, New York, 1988.

Dammann, Gordon, **Pictorial Encyclopedia of Civil War Medical Instruments and Equipment,** Volumes 1 & 2, Pictorial Histories Publishing Company, Missoula, Montana, 1996.

Foster, Stephen, **Civil War Cards,** Columbus, Ohio, Newfield Publications, Inc., 1996.

Wiley, Bell & Davis, William, **The Civil War Times Illustrated Pictorial History of the Civil War,** Black Dog & Leventhal Publishers, New York, New York, 1994.

Reid, Richard, **The River Ran Red: The Battle of Stone's River,** Commerical Printing Company, Owensboro, Kentucky, 1986.

Hafendorfer, Kenneth, **Perryville: Battle for Kentucky,** K. H. Press, Louisville, Kentucky. 1991

after June of 1862, only Confederate Officers were imprisoned there. More than 280 general staff and field officers and 2,274 company officers were held at Johnson Island. Col. Basil Duke, Maj. Gen. Isaac Trimble, Brig. Gen. John Marmaduke, and Brig. Gen. James Archer were imprisoned here. By wars end, 206 prisoners had died at Johnson Island. The prison closed on September 5, 1865.

Some of the other prisoner of war camps were Gratiot Street Prison in St. Louis, the Illinois State Prison at Alton, Camp Butler in Springfield, Illinois, Camp Randall in Madison, Wisconsin, Camp Parole in Annapolis, Maryland, The Pennsylvania State Penitentiary, Hart's Island in New York, Millen, Georgia, Morris Island in Charleston, South Carolina, Columbia, South Carolina, Florence, South Carolina, Salisbury, North Carolina, and many others throughout the North and South.

McDonough, James, **War In Kentucky: From Shiloh to Perryville,** University of Tennessee Press, Knoxville, Tennessee, 1994.

Harrison, Lowell, **The Civil War in Kentucky,** The University Press of Kentucky, Lexington, Kentucky, 1975.

Cunningham, H.H., **Doctors in Grey: The Confederate Medical Service,** Louisiana State University Press, Baton Rouge, Louisiana, 1958, 1993.

Woodhead, Henry & The Editors of Time Life, **Echoes of Glory: Illustrated Atlas of the Civil War,** Time Life, Inc., Alexandria, Virginia, 1996.

Woodhead, Henry, & the Editors of Time Life, **Echoes of Glory: Arms and Equipment of the Union,** Time Life, Inc., Alexandria, Virginia, 1996.

Woodhead, Henry & The Editors of Time Life, **Echoes of Glory: Arms and Equipment of the Confederacy,** Time Life Inc., Alexandria, Virginia, 1996.

The 1864 Campaign: The Re-enactment of the Battles of Spring Hill, Franklin, and Nashville. Hatcher Commincations, Mt. Pleasant, Tennessee, 1995.

Drury, Ian & Gibbons, Tony, **The Civil War Military Machine: Weapons & Tactics of the Union and Confederate Armed Forces,** Smithmark Publishers Inc, New York, New York, 1993.

Still, William, Jr., **Iron Afloat: The Story of the Confederate Ironclads,** University of South Carolina Press, 1985, 1991.

Chisolm, Julian, J., **A Manual of Military Surgery for the Use of Surgeons in the Confederate States Army; with explanatory Plates of all Operations,** Evans & Cogswell, Columbia, South Carolina, 1864, reprint, Morningside Press, Dayton, Ohio, 1992.

Gunn, John, **Gunn's Domestic Medicine: A Facsimile of the First Edition,** University of Tennessee Press, Knoxville, Tennessee, 1986

The Field Manual for The Use of the Officers on Ordnance Duty, Prepared by the Ordnance Bureau, Richmond, Virginina, 1862, re-print, Dean Thomas, Gettysburg, Pennsylvania, 1984.

Kernek, Clyde, **Field Surgeon at Gettysburg: A Memorial Account of the Medical Unit of The Thirty-Second Massachusetts Regiment,** Guild Press of Indiana, Inc., Indianpolis, Indiana, 1993.

Robertson, James & The Editors of Time Life, **Tenting Tonight: The Soldiers Life,** Time Life, Inc., Alexandria, Virginia, 1985.

Conway, Fred, **Corydon: The Forgotten Battle of the Civil War,** FBH Publishers, New Albany, Indiana, 1991.

Denney, Robert, **Civil War Medicine: Care and Comfort of the Wounded.**

MacDonald, John, **Great Battles of the Civil War,** Macmillan Publishing Company, New York, New York, 1988.

McDonough, James, **Stone's River-Bloody Winter in Tennessee,** The University of Tennessee Press, Knoxville, 1980.

Compiled Service Records of Volunteer Union Soldiers for the State of Kentucky.

Straubing, Harold, **In Hospital and Camp,** Stackpole Books, Harrisburg, Pennsylvania, 1993.

Cozzens, Peter, **The Battle of Chickamauga: This Terrible Sound,** University of Illinois Press, 1992.

Report of the Adjutant General of the State of Kentucky. Vol II. Frankfort, Kentucky 1867.

Dyer, Fred, **A Compendium of the War of the Rebellion,** Volumes I & III, New York, London, Thomas Yoseloff.

Speed, Thomas, The Regimental Histories and Sketch of Military Campaigns: **Union Regiments in Kentucky,** Published under the Auspices of the Union Soldiers & Sailors Monument Association, Lousiville, Kentucky Courier-Journal Job Printing Co., 1897.

War of the Rebellion-A Compilation of the Official Records of the Union and Confederate Armies, Washington Government Printing Office, 1884.

Stone, Henry, **Morgan's Men: A Narrative of Personal Experiences,** Free Public Library, 1919.

Moore, Frank, **The Rebellion Record: A Diary of American Events,** 7th Volume, New York, D. Van Nostrand Publisher, 1864.

McClellan, George, **McClellan's Own Story: The War for The Union,** New York, Charles Webster & Co., 1887.

Schumucher, Samuel. **The History of the Civil War in the U.S.: It's Cause, Origin, Progress, & Conclusion, From the Essex Collection,** Gen. Frederick Lander's.

Newman, Fred, **Paducahans in History,** from the Paducah Historical Society.

Casey, Powell, **Casey's Encyclopedia of Forts, Posts, named Camps, and other Military Installations in Lousiana, 1700-1981.**

Crute, Joseph, Jr., **Units of the Confederate States Army, Olde Soldier Books, Inc.,** Gaithersburg, Maryland.

Smithland, William, **Camp Fires of Georgia Troops, 1861-65,** Kenesaw Mountain Press.

Coggins, Jack, **Arms and Equipment of the Civil War,** Doubleday & Co., Garden City, New York, 1962.

Fladerman, Norm, **Fladerman's Guide to Antique American Firearms,** 6th Edition.

Johnson, Adam, **The Partisan Rangers of the Confederate States Army: Memoirs of General Adam R. Johnson,** State House Press, Austin, Texas, 1995, originally published in 1904.

Personal Memoirs of U. S. Grant, **Selected Letters, 1839-1865, The Library of America,** Literary Classics of the United States, Inc., New York, 1990.

William Tecumseh Sherman: Memoirs of General W. T. Sherman, The Library of America, Literary Classics of the United States, Inc., New York, 1990.

Arnold, James, **Classic Battles: Chickamagua: The River of Death,** Reed International Books, Ltd. 1997.

Hankinson, Alan, **Classic Battles: Vicksburg: Grant Clears the Mississippi,** Reed International Books, Ltd., 1997.

Martin, David, **Great Campaigns; The Shiloh Campaign,** Combined Books, Ind., Conshohocken, Pennsylvania, 1996.

Thompson, Ed Porter, **The History of the Orph**an Brigade, Louisville, Kentucky, 1898.

Articles:

Suhr, Robert, **Charge of the Orphan Brigade,** Americas Civil War Illustrated, January 1996.

Ronan, James II, **Catching "Regular Hell" At Shiloh,** America's Civil War, May 1996.

Cheeks, Robert, **Little Phil's Fighting Retreat,** America's Civil War, January 1997.

Frazier, Donald, **Texas General Hiram Granbury led one of the finest brigades in the Confederate Army,** America's Civil War Illustrated, January 1997.

Powles, James, **The Ironclad that Never Was,** Civil War Times, Illustrated, December 1996.

Stier, William, **Morgan's Last Battle,** Civil War Times Illustrated, December 1996.

Rogge, Robert, **Wrecking on the Railroad,** America's Civil War, September 1995.

Noblitt, Phil, **A Flank Unturned at Chickamagua,** America's Civil War, November 1996.

Ross, Charles, **SSh! Battle in Progress,** Civil War Times Illustrated, December 1996.

Bradley, Mark, **Bentonville: We Would have Charged Old Nick Himself: Hardee's Repulse of Mower at Bentonville,** Confederate Veteran, Volume 4, 1995.

Death of Charles Hanson, Kentucky Yeoman, November 16, 1875.

Cheeks, Robert, **Failure on the Heights,** America's Civil War, November 1992.

Phillips, Gill, **Johnson's Island,** North South Trader, July-August, 1977, p. 20-24.

Military Images, Vol. XII, Number 3, Nov.-Dec. 1990, Gunners, p. 22.

References

Chapter 1: Dark Clouds Gather
1. Stephen Foster, Slave Trade, Atlas Editions
2. 1860 Census Records for the U.S.
3. Patricia Faust, Historical Times Encyclopedia of the Civil War, p. 502
4. Stephen Foster, The Missouri Compromise, Atlas Editions.
5. Patricia Faust, Historical Times Illustrated Encyclopedia of the Civil War, p. 156
6. Ibid. p. 408
7. Stephen Foster, Bleeding Kansas, Atlas Editions
8. Patricia Faust, Historical Times Encyclopedia of the Civil War, p. 66-67
9. Stephen Foster, Harper's Ferry, Atlas Editions
10. Patricia Faust, Historical Times Illustrated Encyclopedia of the Civil War, p.. 82-83
11. Ibid. p.439
12. Ibid. p. 238
13. Ibid. p. 703, 208
14. Stephen Foster, South Carolina Secedes, Atlas Editions

Chapter 2: The War Begins
1. Stephen Foster, Fort Sumter; The War Begins, Atlas Editions
2. Civil War Sites Advisory Commission Report: Battle Summaries: Fort Sumter
3. Ibid. Manassas I
4. Stephen Foster, 1st Battle of Bull Run, Atlas Editions
5. Patricia Faust, Historical Times Encyclopedia of the Civil War, p. 91-92.
6. George B. McClellan, McClellan's Own Story: The War for the Union, 1887, New York, Charles Webster & Co. P. 60-61, 80-81, 186-187, 190-191, 316-317.
7. Historical Collection of the Essex Institute, Vol. XL, Oct.. 1904, No. 4, A Sketch of Gen. Frederick W. Lander, p. 313-320
8. Salem Gazette, March 11, 1862, Burial of Gen. Lander
9. Samuel Schmucher, The History of the Civil War in the United States: It's Cause, Origin, Progress, and Conclusion, p. 193-195.
10. War of the Rebellion-Series I, Vol. V, 1818, p.48-49, 66, 405, 407, 623, 631, 647, 673, 678.
11. War of the Rebellion-Series I, Vol. LI, in two parts, Part I, 1897, P. 472, 475, 520-529, 531, 533-534, 535-537, 539, 541, 543, 544-546.

Chapter 3: Early Missouri
1. Civil War Sites Advisory Commission Report: Wilson's Creek
2. The Editors of Time Life, Early Battles of the West: The Road To Shiloh, PPgs. 8-21, 24-30.
3. Patricia Faust, Historical Times Illustrated Encyclopedia of the Civil War, p. 435-436
4. The Editors of Time Life, Early Battles of the West: The Road to Shiloh, p. 32-33
5. Patricia Faust, Historical Times Illustrated Encyclopedia of the Civil War, p. 54
6. Stephen Foster, Battle of Belmont, Atlas Editions
7. The Editors of Time Life, Early Battles of the West: The Road To Shiloh, p. 42, 44-46.

Chapter 4. Early Kentucky
1. Civil War Sites Advisory Commission: Middle Creek
2. Patricia Faust, Historical Times Illustrated Encyclopedia of the Civil War, p. 491
3. The Editors of Time Life, Early Battles of the West: The Road to Shiloh, P. 44-46
4. Civil War Sites Advisory Commission: Mill Springs
5. Patricia Faust, Historical Times Illustrated Encyclopedia of the Civil War, p. 495.

Chapter 5: The Battles of Fort Henry and Fort Donelson
1. Civil War Sites Advisory Commission Reports: Fort Henry & Fort Donelson
2. The Editors of Time Life, Early Battles of the West: The Road to Shiloh, p. 48-49, 52-57, 78-88, 90-101.
3. Stephen Foster, Battle of Fort Henry, Battle of Fort Donelson, Atlas Editions
4. Stewart Sifakis, Who Was Who in the Confederacy, p. 281
5. Patricia Faust, Historical Times Illustrated Encyclopedia of the Civil War, p. 756
6. Military Images, p.22
7. Fred Newman, Paducahans in History, 1922, P. 35-49.
8. War of the Rebellion, Vol. I, XII, p. 197, 423, 479.

9. Stewart Sifakis, Who Was Who in the Confederacy, p.279.
10. Fred Newman, Paducahans in History, 1922, p. 55-71.

Chapter 6: Shiloh
1. The Editors of Time Life, Early Battles of the West: The Road To Shiloh, p. 104-126, 128-129, 136-152, 154-157.
2. Stephen Foster, Shiloh, Atlas Editions
3. Patricia Faust, Historical Times Illustrated Encyclopedia of the Civil War, p. 684-685.
4. Civil War Sites Advisory Commission: Shiloh
5. Great Campaigns: The Shiloh Campaign, David Martin, Combined Books, Inc., Pennsylvania, 1996.

Chapter 7: Corinth, Mississippi
1. Patricia Faust, Historical Times Illustrated Encyclopedia of the Civil War, p. 166-167.
2. The Editors of Time Life: War On The Mississippi: Grant's Vicksburg Campaign, p. 84-91.
3. Civil War Sites Advisory Commission: Corinth
4. Stephen Foster: Corinth, Atlas Editions
5. War of the Rebellion, Chapter. XXXVIII, p. 120-122.
6. War of the Rebellion, Chapter. XXVII, p. 409-411
7. Powell Casey, Casey's Encyclopedia of Forts, Posts, named Camps, and other Military Installations in Louisiana, 1700-1981, P. 111-113.
8. National Archives

Chapter 8: Perryville
1. James McDonough, War in Kentucky
2. Kenneth Hafendorfer, Battle of Perryville
3. Civil War Sites Advisory Commission: Perryville
4. Stephen Foster, Perryville, Atlas editions
5. Stewart Sifakis, Who Was Who In the Confederacy, Vol. II, p. 121.
6. Patricia Faust, Historical Times Illustrated Encyclopedia of the Civil War, p. 346

Chapter 9: Stone's River
1. Patricia Faust, Historical Times Encyclopedia of the Civil War, P. 722-723
2. Time Life Series: The Struggle for Tennessee: Tupelo to Stone's River, p. 112-124, p. 126-133, p.142-145, p.148-161.
3. "Charge of the Orphan Brigade", Suhr, Robert, America's Civil War Illustrated
4. Davis, William, Battlefields of the Civil War
5. Reid, Richard, Stone's River Ran Red
5. The Editors of Time Life, Illustrated Atlas of the Civil War, p. 210
6. McDonough, James Lee, Stone's River-Bloody Winter in Tennessee
7. Compiled Service Records of Volunteer Union Soldiers for the State of Kentucky Roll #169 (William Woodruff)
8. War of the Rebellion Records

Chapter 10: Vicksburg
1. Patricia Faust, Historical Times Illustrated Encyclopedia of the Civil War, p. 781-784.
2. The Editors of Time Life, War on the Mississippi: Grant's Vicksburg Campaign, p. 100-105, 108-116, 118-134, 153, 156-159.
3. Civil War Sites Advisory Commission: Vicksburg
4. Classic Battles: Vicksburg 1863, Alan Hankinson, Reed International Books, London, 1997.

Chapter 11: Chickamauga
1. The Editors of Time Life, The Fight for Chattanooga: Chickamagua to Missionary Ridge
2. Patricia Faust, Historical Times Illustrated Encyclopedia of the Civil War, p. 136-138
3. Stephen Foster, Chickamagua
4. Civil War Sites Advisory Commission: Chickamagua
5. Peter Cozzens, The Battle of Chickamagua: This Terrible Sound.
6. Classic Battles: Chickamauga 1863: The River of Death, James Arnold, Reed International Books, Ltd. , London, 1997

Chapter 12: Lookout Mountain
1. Patricia Faust, Historical Times Illustrated Encyclopedia of the Civil War, p. 445-447
2. The Editors of Time Life, The Fight for Chattanooga: Chickamagua to Missionary Ridge.
3. Battle of Lookout Mountain, Steven Foster, Atlas Editions

Chapter 13: Missionary Ridge
1. Patricia Faust, Historical Times Illustrated Encyclopedia of the Civil War, p.498-499.
2. The Editors of Time Life, The Fight for Chattanooga: Chickamagua to Missionary Ridge.
3. War of the Rebellion, Chapter. XLIII, p. 384-389, Chapter. XLVIII p. 606-610, Chapter. XXXIV p. 751-752, Chapter. LVIII p. 873, Chapter. XXIV p. 303-305, Chapter. LII p. 471-472.
4. Robert Cheeks, Failure on the Heights, America's Civil War, Nov. 1992. P.42.

Chapter 14: Georgia Campaign
1. Ronald Bailey, Sherman Moves East: The Battles for Atlanta,
2. Patricia Faust, Historical Times Illustrated Encyclopedia of the Civil War, p. 413
3. Stephen Foster, Battle of Peachtree Creek, Atlas Editions

Chapter 15: Atlanta Campaign
1. Ronald Bailey, Sherman Moves East: The Atlanta Campaign,
2. Patricia Faust, Historical Times Illustrated Encyclopedia of the Civil War, p. 404, 250
3. Stephen Foster, Battle of Jonesboro, Atlas Editions
4. Stewart Sifikas, Who Was Who In The Confederacy, p. 295
5. Patricia Faust, Historical Times Illustrated Encyclopedia of the Civil War, p. 798-799.

Chapter 16: Battles of Franklin & Nashville
1. Patricia Faust, Historical Times Illustrated Encyclopedia of the Civil War, p. 285
2. The Editors of Time Life, The Battles for Atlanta: Sherman Moves East, p. 110-105, 112-118, 120-126, 128-130, 132-139, 142-150, 155-156, 158-159.
3. Civil War Sites Advisory Commission: Franklin & Nashville, Spring Hill, Columbia.
4. The Battle of Franklin and Nashville, Steven Foster, Atlas Editions

Chapter 17: Sherman's March to The Sea
1. Patricia Faust, Historical Times Illustrated Encyclopedia of the Civil War, p. 474-475.
2. Civil War Sites Advisory Commission: Fort McAllister
3. The Editors of Time Life, Sherman's March: Atlanta to the Sea, ppgs. 14-29, 32-35, 44-50, 52-54, 56, 58-63, 70-73, 82-85, 155-156, 158-159.
4. Stephen Foster, Sherman's March, Atlas Editions

Chapter 18: Sherman's Last Battle: The Battle of Bentonville
1. Civil War Sites Advisory Commission: Bentonville
2. Mark Bradley, Bentonville: We Would Have Charged Old Nick Himself: Hardee's Repulse of Mower at Bentonville, Confederate Veteran, Vol. 4, 1995.

Brother Vs. Brother
1. Stephen Foster, Brother Vs. Brother

Orphan Brigade
1. Stephen Foster, The Orphan Brigade
2. Ed Porter Thompson: The History of the Orphan Brigade.

Lincoln & Davis
1. Patricia Faust, Historical Times Illustrated Encyclopedia of the Civil War, P. 208, 439.

Zouave Uniforms
1. Stephen Foster, Zouave Uniforms: The French Connection
2. William Davis, Battlefields of the Civil War, p. 179
3. Patricia Faust, Historical Times Illustrated Encyclopedia of the Civil War, p. 240

Militia Items
1. Ian Drury & Tony Gibbons, The Civil War Military Machine, p. 53

Artillery
1. Tony Gibbons & Ian Drury, The Civil War Military Machine,
2. Foster, Stephen, Canister
Warren Ripley, Artillery and Ammuntion of the Civil War.
Patricia Faust, Historical Times Illustrated Encyclopedia of the Civil War, p. 321

3. Ian Drury and Tony Gibbons,The Civil War Military Machine, 1993
4. Ripley, Warren, Artillery and Ammunition of the Civil War
Gibbons, Tony, & Drury, Ian, The Civil War Military Machine
5. Ripley, Warren, Artillery and Ammunition of the Civil War
6. Foster, Stephen, Washington Artillery-No Finer Organization
7. Warren Ripley, Artillery and Ammunition of the Civil War,
8. Tony Gibbons & Ian Drury, The Civil War Military Machine.
9. Department of the Army, Savannah Military Companies; Linage and Honors: Headquarters and Headquarters Battery 118th Artillery Group.
The Savannah Morning News, "Chatham Artillery Traces It's Linage Back to Revolution, Jan. 15th, 1950.
The Daily Georgian, January 9, 1847.
Georgia Historical Society, Special thanks to Jessica Burke
Georgia State Archives: Special Thanks to Andy Phydas
Joseph Crute, Jr., Units of the Confederate States Army, Olde Soldier Books, Inc., Gaithersburg, Maryland.
William Smedlund, Camp Fires of Georgia's Troops, 1861-65, Kenesaw Mountain Press.

Some Illustrations from Arms and Equipment of the Civil War, Coggins, Jack, Doubleday & Company, Garden City, New York, 1962

Infantry
1. Foster, Stephen, Civil War Cards: Bayonet, Davis, William, Fighting Men of the Civil War, p. 47, 230-231
2. Foster, Stephen, Loading a Muzzle Loader
Patricia Faust, Historical Times Illustrated Encyclopedia of the Civil War, pps. 338, 118.
3. Fladerman, Norm, Fladerman's Guide to Antique American Firearms, 6th Edition, Davis, William, Fighting Men of The Civil War, p. 58 Time Life, Inc., Arms & Equipment of the Union Civil War, p. 28-43. William Davis, Fighting Men of the Civil War, p. 38-42.
4. Patricia Faust, Historical Times Illustrated Encyclopedia of the Civil War, p. 710. Echoes of Glory: Arms & Equipment of the Civil War, P. 41
5. The 1864 Tennessee Campaign: The Re-enactment of Spring Hill, Franklin, and Nashville, Tennessee. The Organization of Civil War Armies by Bob Duncan., Hatcher Commincations, Mt. Pleasant, Tennessee, 1995.
Civil War Board, America Online, How Armies were Organized.
6. Foster, Stephen, Union Generals' Uniforms
Foster, Stephen, Confederate General's Uniforms
7. Patricia Faust, Historical Times Encyclopedia of the Civil War, p. 352.
8. Indiana State Archives
9. Speed, Thomas, Union Regiments in Kentucky, 436-442.
10. Report of the Adjutant General of the State of Kentucky, Vol. II, Frankfort, Kentucky, 1867, Frankfort Yeoman Press, p. 383. Speed, Thomas, Capt., A Compendium of the War of the Rebellion, Vol. III, P. 1206 Vol. I, p. 148, New York, London, Thomas Yoseloft, Dyer, Fred, The Regimental Histories and Sketch of Military Campaigns, Union Regiments of Kentucky, published under the auspices of the Union Soldiers and Sailors Monument Association. Courier-Journal Job Printing Co, 1897. P. 480- 483.
War of the Rebellion, 1884, P. 326. Series I Vol. I Part I Report, Chapter. XXII p. 352-353, 348-349, 844-45, 693-694, 695, 696, 697, 698, 682-683, Chapter XXI p. 848-850.
War of the Rebellion, Series I Vol. XXIII, Part I Reports Chapter. XXVIII p. 1152-53
War of the Rebellion, Series I Vol. XXIII Part I Reports, Chapter. XXXV, P. 647-651.
War of the Rebellion, Series II, Vol. VIII p. 154-55, p. 184-187.
War of the Rebellion, Chapter LI P. 564
Kentucky Yeoman, Frankfort, Kentucky, November 16, 1875, Death of Charles Hanson.
Stone, Henry, Morgan's Men: A Personal Narrative of Experiences, Free Public Library, April 8, 1919. P. 10-13.
The Rebellion Record: A Diary of American Events Edited by Frank Moore, 7th Volume New York, D. Van Nostrand, Publisher 1864, P. 25, 258-259. 358-359.
11. War of the Rebellion, Vol. I, Chapt. XXVIII, ppgs.1152-1153.
War of the Rebellion, Vol. I, Chapt. XIV, ppgs. 272-274.
War of the Rebellion, Vol. I, Chapt. XXXII, ppgs. 535-536.
War of the Rebellion, Vol. I, Chapt. LXIII, ppgs. 420-421, 465, 468
War of the Rebellion, Vol. I, Chapt. XXII, ppgs. 350-351, 692-693.
War of the Rebellion, Vol. I, Chapt. XLIV, ppgs. 387, 474-475, 423-431.
Compiled Service Records of Volunteer Union Soldiers for the State of Kentucky, Lt. Col. David Enyart.
Thomas, Speed, The Regimental Histories and Sketch of Military Campaigns, Union Regiments in Kentucky, published under the auspices of the

Union Soldiers and Sailors Monument Assocation, Courier-Journal Publsihing Company, 1897. ppgs.274-277.

12. (Col. Fenton) Special thanks to Michigan Department of State
Fox's regimental Losses, Chapt. X-Eighth Michigan Infantry
Official Records of the War of the Rebellion Series 1-Vol. VI, Chapt. XV (S#6) No. 3
Official Records of the War of the Rebellion Series 1—Vol. XIV (S#20) No. 5
Official Records of the War of the Rebellion Series 1-Vol. XIV (S#20) No. 9

Cavalry

1. Davis, William, Fighting Men of the Civil War, Join the Cavalry, p. 67-93.
2. Patricia Faust, Historical Times Illustrated Encyclopedia of the Civil War. P. 510
3. Patricia Faust, Historical Times Illustrated Encyclopedia of the Civil War, P. 229.
5. Patricia Faust, Historical Times Illustrated Encyclopedia of the Civil War, p. 269-70
6. Encyclopedia of the Civil War: Echoes of Glory: Arms & Equipment of the Union
7. Encyclopedia of the Civil War/Arms and Equipment of the Union
Gibbons, Tony & Drury, Ian, The Civil War Military Machine, p. 62
8. Echoes of Glory: Arms and Equipment of the Union
Historical Times Illustrated Encyclopedia of the Civil War.
9. Echoes of Glory: Arms & Equipment of the Union
Gibbons, Tony & Drury, Ian, The Civil War Military Machine, p. 58
10. Historical Times Illustrated Encyclopedia of the Civil War, p. 623
11. Historical Times Illusrtated Encyclopedia of the Civil War p. 714.
12. Historical Times Illustrated Encyclopedia of the Civil War P. 152.
13. The Civil War Machine by Ian Drury & Tony Gibbons p. 47
14. Echoes of Glory: Arms and Ammunition of the Union
The Civil War Military Machine, p.49
15. The Civil War Machine by Ian Drury and Tony Gibbons, P. 49
16a. Time Life, Inc., Echoes of Glory: Arms and Equipment of the Confederacy.
Tony Gibbons and Ian Drury, The Civil War Military Machine.
16b. Stephen Stifikas, Who Was Who in the Confederacy, p. 148
Patricia Faust, Historical Times Illustrated Encyclopedia of the Civil War, p. 395
Johnson, Adam, The Partisan Rangers of the Confederate States Army: Memoirs of General Adam R. Johnson, State House Press, Austin, Texas, 1995, originally published in 1904. Compiled Service Records for Union Soldiers for the State of Kentucky
War of the Rebellion: Engagements in Kentucky, Virginia, Tennessee, Shiloh.
History of Henderson County, Kentucky.
17. Dyer, Fred, The Regimental Histories and Sketch of Military Campaigns, Union Regiments in Kentucky, published under the auspices of the Union Soldiers and Sailors Monument Association, Courier-Journal Publishing Co., 1897, ppgs. 169-174.
War of the Rebellion, Vol. I, Chapt. XXXII, ppgs. 162-163.

18. Compiled Service Records of Volunteer Union Soldiers for the State of Kentucky, (Robert Kerr).
19. Adjutant General's Report for the State of Kentucky, Confederate. ppgs. 2-5
A History of Morgan's Cavalry, Basil Duke, Indiana University Press.
The Historian. Gilded Age. 228-243
Lexington Herald, Nov. 19th, 1904. The Death of W. C. P. Breckinridge.
War of the Rebellion Records

Medical Corps

1. Cunningham, H. H., Doctor's In Grey
2. Mary Elizabeth Massey, Erzatz in the Confederacy
3. Denney, Robert, Civil War Medicine: Care and Comfort of the Wounded
4. The Confederate States Medical and Surgical Journal
5. Davis, William, The Fighting Men of the Civil War
6. Robertson, James Jr. and the Editors or Time Life, Tenting Tonight: "The Soldier's Life"
7. Stewart Brooks, Civil War Medicine
8. Chilsom, John, A Manual of Military Surgery, 1863
9. Kernek, Clyde, M.D., Field Surgeon at Gettysburg: A Memorial Account of the Medical Unit of the Thirty Second Massachusetts Regiment
10. Gunn, John, Domestic Medicine, 1830 re-published 1996
11. Dammann, Gordon, Dr., Pictorial Encyclopedia of Civil War Medical Instruments and Equipment, Vol. 1 & II.

Military Bands

1. Faust, Patricia, Historical Times Illustrated Encyclopedia of the Civil War. P. 494
2. Foster, Stephen, Union Bands, Atlas Editions
3. Foster, Stephen, Bugle Calls, Atlas editions
4. Foster, Stephen, Confederate Bands

Navy

1. William Davis, Commanders of the Civil War, p. 144-145.
2. Foster, Stephen, Pook's Turtles and Historical times Illustrated Encyclopedia of the Civil War, Patricia Faust, Pook's Turtles. P. 593.
3. William N. Still, Jr., Iron Afloat: The Story of the Confederate Ironclads
4. Foster, Stephen, Atlas Editions: Civil War Cards: C.S.S. Alabama
5. Foster, Stephen, Atlas Editions: Civil War Cards: Sinking of the C.S.S. Alabama
6. Faust, Patricia, Historical Times Illustrated Encyclopedia of the Civil War, p. 3-4.

Prisons

1. Stephen Foster, Castle Pinckney, Old Capitol Prison, Ohio State Penitentary, Libby Prison, Belle Isle Prison, Fort McHenry, Camp Douglas, Andersonville, Elmira Prison, Atlas Editions.
2. Patricia Faust, Historical Times Illustrated Encyclopedia of the Civil War, p. 16-17, 109-110, 119-120, 241, 272, 280, 389-399, 543, 588, 639.
3. Patricia Faust, Historical Times Illustrated Encyclopedia of the Civil War, P. 398-99.
4. Gill Phillips, Johnson's Island, North South Trader, July-August 1977. p. 20-24.
Stephen Foster, Johnson Island Prison, Atlas Editions.

About the Author

Bryan Bush was born in 1966 in Louisville, Kentucky and has been a native of that city ever since. He graduated with honors from Murray State University with a degree in History and Psychology. Bryan has always had a passion for history, especially the Civil War. Bryan has been a member of many different Civil War historical preservation societies, has consulted for movie companies, coordinated with other museums on displays of various museum articles and artifacts, has written for magazines, such as Kentucky Civil War Magazine, and worked for many different historical sites, and has always fought hard to maintain and preserve Civil War history in the Western Theater.

Bryan has been a Civil War re-enactor for four years, portraying a Confederate Artillerist, and later a Lt. Colonel in the Confederate Medical Corps. He has also been a member of the Sons of Confederate Veterans since 1994. For the last year, Bryan has been the assistant curator of the Old Bardstown Civil War Museum and Village: The Battles of the Western Theater Museum in Bardstown, Kentucky.

204

(From the original back cover flap)

The Civil War Museum
in
Bardstown, Kentucky

The Civil War Museum of Bardstown, Kentucky features the "War of the West."It was opened in 1988 in the old water works building in Bardstown and between 1988-1992 has served over 250,000 visitors.

Between 1992 and 1996 the museum was totally renovated and was incorporated into the Kentucky State Parks system. It officially re-opened on June 28, 1996 to the pleasure of Civil War buffs from around the world. The Civil War Museum is now in the process of opening a 1800s village adjacent to the Civil War Museum featuring several original log cabins to depict life during these times.

It was our pleasure to be included in this great undertaking and to be a part of the ***"The Civil War Battles of the Western Theatre"*** book, published by Turner Publishing and written by Mr. Bryan Bush.

Printed in the USA
CPSIA information can be obtained
at www.ICGtesting.com
JSHW051349220424
61664JS00017B/745